BIG BOOK OF MPLS (MULTIPROTOCOL LABEL SWITCHING) RFCS

D1709409

BIG BOOK OF MPLS (MULTIPROTOCOL LABEL SWITCHING) RFCs

Compiled by Pete Loshin

Morgan Kaufmann

An Imprint of ACADEMIC PRESS
A HARCOURT SCIENCE AND TECHNOLOGY COMPANY
San Diego   San Francisco   New York   Boston
London   Sydney   Tokyo

ACADEMIC PRESS

A Harcourt Science and Technology Company

525 B Street, Suite 1900, San Diego, CA 92101-4495 USA

http://www.academicpress.com

Academic Press

Harcourt Place, 32 Jamestown Rd., London NW1 7BY, UK

Morgan Kaufmann

A Harcourt Science and Technology Company

340 Pine Street, Sixth Floor, San Francisco, CA 94104-3205

http://www.mkp.com

Library of Congress Catalog Number: 00-111078

International Standard Book Number: 0-12-455853-4

Printed in the United States of America

00 01 02 03 IP 9 8 7 6 5 4 3 2 1

Dedication

This book is dedicated to the members of the Internet Engineering Task Force.

Table of Contents

Preface

The vast majority of this book is available online, free for the downloading. If you know what you're looking for, you can download very easily all the RFCs in this book, along with any RFCs that have been released since this book was published. You can even go to my web site, www.Internet-Standard.com, and download them from there.

That's what I had always done when I needed to look something up about an Internet standard or specification or protocol. I found myself downloading many of the same RFCs, over and over. And depending on what project I might be working on, I'd even print out some of those RFCs, for easy reference or for taking notes.

This is when I realized that there must be other networking professionals who had the same problem—and when I started asking them about it, my suspicions were confirmed.

The full copyright statement now included at the end of all RFCs specifies (among other things) that:

> *This document and translations of it may be copied and furnished to others, and derivative works that comment on or otherwise explain it or assist in its implementation may be prepared, copied, published and distributed, in whole or in part, without restriction of any kind, provided that the above copyright notice and this paragraph are included on all such copies and derivative works....*

The goal is to distribute RFCs as widely as possible, and the IETF puts only the most minimal restrictions on those who wish to redistribute them. After all, the more aware people (and vendors) are of the specifications, the more likely they are to build implementations that conform to them—or to do experiments to see if there is some better solution.

So, why buy this book? If you are looking for answers about Internet specifications for Multiprotocol Label Switching, you can do what I've already done:

- Search out relevant, and current, RFCs on MPLS. I usually start with the RFC archives maintained by the RFC Editor's search page at www.rfc-editor.org/rfcsearch.html, but there are several others that I use. Not to mention searches of offline literature and just plain asking around.
- Read through all of them, and then decide on which ones to print out. And then print them out. I've estimated the cost, in paper, toner, and electricity, of printing out 500 pages of RFCs yourself at about $10–$15. With a high-capacity, high-speed, highly reliable printer, you could print them all out in a few minutes. Otherwise, it might take half an hour or more to print them all out.
- Write summaries of each RFC, so you can quickly find what you're looking for just by skimming the summaries instead of reading through each one.
- Get the whole thing indexed, so you can find any term you need, across all the RFCs.

Or you can just go ahead and buy the book. You'll find just about all the background information you need about MPLS, as well as all the current RFCs published on MPLS. Which means you'll have as good an introduction to MPLS as possible, using first-hand sources.

The RFCs included in this book were selected so as to provide the most complete reference of the topic in a reasonably sized book. Historic or marginally relevant RFCs have been left out, but everything else you need (and nothing else) has been included. If you need to know more than is in this book, you'll probably have to get in touch with the people who wrote the RFCs.

You should also realize that this is not the last word on MPLS: new RFCs will be coming out, and older ones (such as those reproduced here) are being obsoleted quite frequently. Think of this as Volume 1 of the Big Book of MPLS RFCs—we may need to publish Volume 2 in just a few years.

Finally, one of the best things about having it all in a book is that you can read the MPLS RFCs without your computer, without Internet access, even without any electricity (as long as the sun is out). And you can read it on the plane, even during takeoff and landing, and no one will ask you to turn it off.

For more information about RFCs and the Internet standards process in general, as well as updated information about MPLS specifications, see my web site:

www.Internet-Standard.com

If you have any comments, complaints, or suggestions about this or any book in the Big Book of RFC series, please contact me at:

loshin@Internet-Standard.com

Hearing from readers, whatever they have to say, is always one of the highlights of my day.

Introduction

At one time, ATM was viewed as an IP-killer: you could build huge, switched networks that passed data across organizational boundaries, and if you can do that you don't need to use the Internet Protocol (IP) anymore. It didn't work out that way, though, as IP continues to provide seamless interoperability across and between virtually any network medium and any computer.

ATM switches data, whereas IP routes data. Switching is faster, since it doesn't have to make any decisions and can be implemented in hardware; routing is not as fast because it is often implemented in software (though that is changing) and because decisions need to be made for every packet, requiring some processing of packet headers.

But the speed of switching is not the primary consideration when weighing switching against routing: routing algorithms can be burned into hardware just as easily as switching algorithms, and IP switches can move data quite rapidly.

However, the use of switching, particularly MPLS, means that the processes of routing and forwarding can be separated. IP routing is very much tied to forwarding, and that tends to make any advances in routing expensive to implement.

The forwarding mechanism consists of the set of rules the router uses to decide on which port to send an outgoing packet. The routing mechanism, on the other hand, consists of those rules that feed information into the forwarding mechanism. In simple terms, the forwarding mechanism defines how the router uses its routing tables, whereas the routing mechanism is what builds those tables.

A change in forwarding mechanisms means that every router must be upgraded to support the new mechanism. Traditional IP routing and forwarding relied heavily on the use of network classes: a Class A network could be uniquely identified by the first eight bits of its address, a Class B network by the first 16 bits of its address, and a Class C network by the first 24 bits of its address. Routers would check the destination address, determine whether it was a Class A, B, or C, and then compare the relevant bits with entries in its routing table to determine where to send a packet.

With the advent of Classless Interdomain Routing (CIDR), routers had to use another simple, but still quite different, mechanism to figure out where to forward packets. With CIDR, a network can be identified by any number of bits, not just 8, 16, or 24. Addresses are represented as a set of [dotted-quad network address] and [/number of bits representing the network prefix]. Routers now have to locate the appropriate network address based on these two values, not network classes. This improvement in routing scalability also meant that the dominant forwarding mechanism had to change as well.

One of the key benefits to MPLS is that it separates forwarding from routing, and thus permits changes to the routing mechanism without the overhead costs of updating the forwarding mechanism at the same time.

One of the key challenges of implementing MPLS is that it is necessary to meld networking models (ATM and TCP/IP) that do not map nicely onto each other. There must be mechanisms for carrying IP packets across ATM networks; there must be mechanisms for transporting switching information across various types of networks; there must be mechanisms for determining the appropriate route through or across ATM networks.

What's in This Book (And What's Not)

MPLS is still a work in progress as of the end of 2000; there are numerous Internet-Drafts still working their way through the process of becoming RFCs, and, in many cases, getting on the Standards track. In fact, there are a number of Internet-Drafts that have been approved for publication as RFCs but that are being held for a number of reasons—see the section at the end of this introduction for details.

This book, like others in this series covering subject areas that are still in development, should be considered Volume 1 of the Big Book of MPLS RFCs rather than a definitive and complete stand-alone reference.

Some of the earlier RFCs included in this book describe early proprietary approaches to label switching, sometimes called IP switching, tag switching, or any number of other names. Toshiba published the first accounts of a label-switching precursor (RFCs 2098 and 2129), followed by Cisco (RFC 2105). These documents are included here because they help trace the development and justification for much of the work done on MPLS.

This book contains a considerable number of RFCs that provide no direct discussion of MPLS but rather serve as important foundational or background material. For example, documents on Integrated Services (INTSERV, RFC 1633) and Differentiated Services (DIFFSERV, RFC 2475 and others) are both included here because MPLS is seen as an important enabling technology for doing traffic engineering and Quality of Service functions that are provided in both INTSERV and DIFFSERV.

Likewise, documents describing the use of IP over ATM, including RFCs 2225 and 2684, are included because MPLS helps facilitate the use of IP over ATM.

Also included are RFCs on the Next Hop Resolution Protocol (NHRP, RFCs 2332 and 2333) and per hop behaviors (PHBs, RFC 2836) because these provide fundamental services necessary to the deployment of MPLS.

Internet-Drafts Not in This Book

Normally, Internet-Drafts (I-Ds) are to be considered ephemeral documents, not to be referenced because they are intended to expire after six months unless commented upon and updated. However, since all RFCs start out as I-Ds, the final, approved version of the I-D eventually will be archived as an RFC.

The I-D may not be published as an RFC until all internal references to other I-Ds can be fully resolved—without referring to "works in progress" as I-Ds are usually referenced.

This presents a serious problem: the fundamental MPLS RFC, "Multiprotocol Label Switching Architecture," may not be published until as many as eight other I-Ds are completed and published as RFCs. These I-Ds cover topics such as MPLS label encapsulation, MPLS over Frame Relay, and the MPLS framework document.

The result is that even though the "Multiprotocol Label Switching Architecture" I-D has been approved for publication as an RFC (meaning that all the information in it is considered "complete"), it is being held back until all those other I-Ds are complete as well.

In keeping with IETF policy of not referencing or reproducing I-Ds, this document and others that have been approved for publication but have not yet been released by the RFC Editor are not included in this volume (though they will certainly be included in any revisions to this book).

This section lists the I-Ds that have been approved but are being held for some reason. The following table lists the document titles as well as URLs where they can be found (if they are not available as I-Ds, they have most likely been released and should be accessible in any RFC archive). Ideally, you should review "Multiprotocol Label Switching Architecture" while using this book.

Title	Status	URL
Multiprotocol Label Switching Architecture	Standards Track	http://www.ietf.org/ internet-drafts/ draft-ietf-mpls-arch-07.txt
MPLS Label Stack Encoding	Standards Track	draft-ietf-mpls-label-encaps-08.txt
The Assignment of the Information Field and Protocol Identifier in the Q.2941 Generic Identifier and Q.2957 User-to-user Signaling for the Internet Protocol	Standards Track	draft-ietf-mpls-git-uus-04.txt
MPLS using LDP and ATM VC Switching	Standards Track	draft-ietf-mpls-atm-04.txt
Use of Label Switching on Frame Relay Networks Specification	Standards Track	draft-ietf-mpls-fr-06.txt
LDP Specification	Standards Track	draft-ietf-mpls-ldp-11.txt
VCID Notification over ATM link for LDP	Standards Track	draft-ietf-mpls-vcid-atm-05.txt
LDP Applicability	Informational	draft-ietf-mpls-ldp-applic-02.txt

The RFCs

As of September 2000, the following documents comprise the full selection of MPLS-related RFCs. Included in this volume are five Internet-Drafts (I-Ds) that have been approved by the IESG. I-Ds are normally not considered to be archival documents and the IETF frowns on any references to I-Ds because they expire six months after they are published. However, these documents have received approval from the IESG to be published as RFCs, but they have not yet been assigned RFC numbers.

They also are being held from publication until some of the documents they refer to are published as RFCs. Rather than leave them out of this volume, they are included here so as to provide you with a complete (if perhaps slightly premature) view of MPLS. The alternative would be to publish a less comprehensive volume that would be more "correct" in terms of IETF practice but would be far less useful.

RFC 1633: Integrated Services in the Internet Architecture: an Overview
This is an informational document published in June of 1994. The authors open by suggesting that the lack of a real-time Quality of Service (QoS) mechanism, as well as the lack of mechanism for Internet traffic management, are holding back deployment of voice/video-based applications. As a solution, they propose a service model called "integrated services" (int-serv) under which classical best-effort service as well as real-time service and controlled link sharing are included.

RFC 1633 describes a proposed architecture for such a service model, as well as the core services to be provided within the model. MPLS support for int-serv comes about in the form of MPLS support (and mirroring) of IP QoS features; MPLS also supports Differentiated Services (see RFCs 2430 and 2475), for the same reasons.

RFC 2098: Toshiba's Router Architecture Extensions for ATM: Overview
This informational RFC outlines one of the first implementations of an MPLS-like architecutre. Toshiba implemented an architecture under which "IP datagrams are transferred along hop-by-hop path via routers, but datagram assembly/disassembly and IP header processing are not necessarily carried out at individual routers in the proposed architecture."

Toshiba's new product, dubbed a "Cell Switch Router," was able to switch ATM cells as well as conventionally forward IP datagrams. Benefits of the proposed architecture included the ability to "provide applications with high-throughput and low-latency ATM pipes while retaining current router-based internetworking concept" as well as giving applications "specific QoS/bandwidth by cooperating with internetworking level resource reservation protocols such as RSVP."

RFC 2105: Cisco Systems' Tag Switching Architecture Overview
This is also an informational RFC, submitted by a team from Cisco Systems, Inc., that documents Cisco's approach to network layer packet forwarding, which they called "tag switching." Tag switching did forwarding through the use of "label-swapping techniques" while retaining existing network layer (that is, IP) routing performed control functions. The document describes how mechanisms for binding and distributing tags for control purposes is accomplished.

Also included in this document are descriptions of example tag switching applications and deployment scenarios.

RFC 2129: Toshiba's Flow Attribute Notification Protocol (FANP) Specification
This is another informational RFC documenting Toshiba's Flow Attribute Notification Protocol (FANP), which was intended to provide a mechanism for managing cut-through packet forwarding functions among neighboring nodes. Cut-through forwarding allows routers to skip conventional IP packet processing for inbound packets. Instead, FANP provides network mapping information between a data connection and the flow of packets to the neighbor nodes. FANP was originally designed to be used by Toshiba's Cell Switch Routers (see RFC 2098).

RFC 2225: Classical IP and ARP over ATM
This is a proposed standard RFC that describes the mechanisms by which IP and the Address Resolution Protocol (ARP) are carried over ATM. Since ATM acts like a point-to-point protocol, ARP, which depends on broadcasts, must be imple-

mented more carefully over it. This document obsoletes precursor RFCs 1626 and 1577, on the same topic.

RFC 2332: NBMA Next Hop Resolution Protocol (NHRP)

ATM networks are NBMA: Non-Broadcast, Multi-Access. As described in RFC 2225 and elsewhere (including RFC 1735, "NBMA Address Resolution Protocol (NARP)"), NBMA networks present a problem for transit IP packets. When an IP packet is received by a router that is connected to an NBMA network, the router must somehow determine the next hop for the packet. If the destination of the packet is on the same NBMA network, then the next hop will be the destination node. But if the destination is outside the NBMA, the router must determine the appropriate egress router to which to forward the packet.

Determining the next hop is not a trivial task. The node (host or router) requiring the next hop needs not only the IP address of the next hop but also the NBMA network address.

This proposed standard RFC defines a mechanism based on Next Hop Servers (NHSs) that are queried by nodes seeking next hop information.

RFC 2333: NHRP Protocol Applicability Statement

This RFC, like RFC 2332, is a proposed standard that discusses how the Next Hop Resolution Protocol (NHRP) can be applied to routing IP packets across NBMA networks including ATM.

RFC 2430: A Provider Architecture for Differentiated Services and Traffic Engineering (PASTE)

This is another informational RFC that presents an architecture for Internet service providers (ISPs) to offer differentiated services (see RFC 2475) and to do traffic engineering by using MPLS. MPLS supports aggregated packet flows (flows of packets that have the same forwarding state and the same resource reservation along a sequence of routers), making such an application possible.

RFC 2474: Definition of the Differentiated Services Field (DS Field) in the IPv4 and IPv6 Headers

This proposed standard RFC defines the Differentiated Services (DS) field for carrying Differentiated Services information in IPv4 and IPv6 packet headers. The field itself replaces the IPv4 Type of Service (TOS) octet and the IPv6 Traffic Class octet.

As with other RFCs related to Differentiated Services (for example, RFCs 2475 and 2836), this RFC is included because it describes an important aspect of Differentiated Services that MPLS must use or be able to interoperate with.

RFC 2475: An Architecture for Differentiated Services

The Integrated Services approach to supporting Quality of Service (QoS) is to allow sources and receivers to set up packet classifications and to share forwarding state along the paths between nodes; where that information is unavailable, individual nodes handle traffic management independently. The Differentiated Services approach is to aggregate traffic classification state at the network boundaries rather than allow individual nodes to unilaterally decide how to handle packets.

RFC 2475 is an informational RFC that provides a blueprint for Differentiated Services, and should be read in parallel to RFC 1633 on Integrated Services.

RFC 2481: A Proposal to add Explicit Congestion Notification (ECN) to IP

This is an experimental RFC that details a proposal for adding a mechanism that permits routers to explicitly report congestion, rather than the traditional mechanism (letting packets fall on the floor and have the higher layer protocols, such as the Transmission Control Protocol (TCP) or even application layer protocols, handle flow control issues).

With ECN, routers could explicitly notify senders at the IP layer that they are experiencing congestion and thus allow the senders either to seek other routers or to take other action.

ECN is relevant to MPLS because it is poised to become an important Quality of Service (QoS) mechanism that MPLS would have to support (in the same way MPLS supports Differentiated Services and Integrated Services models) in order to fulfill its potential for improving routing performance across the Internet.

RFC 2547: BGP/MPLS VPNs

This informational RFC explains how a service provider could use Border Gateway Protocol (BGP) and MPLS to implement virtual private networks (VPNs) for customers. BGP functions as the backbone routing mechanism and MPLS serves as the mechanism by which packets are forwarded within the VPN.

This document provides a good description of a practical business application of MPLS.

RFC 2684: Multiprotocol Encapsulation over ATM Adaptation Layer 5

This standards track RFC describes two methods for encapsulating network interconnect traffic (that is, IP or any other network layer protocol) over ATM. According to the RFC's abstract, "The first method allows multiplexing of multiple protocols over a single ATM virtual connection whereas the second method assumes that each protocol is carried over a separate ATM virtual connection."

Though the document does not specifically refer to MPLS, it is another foundational document (like RFC 2225) describing how IP can be encapsulated over ATM.

RFC 2702: Requirements for Traffic Engineering Over MPLS

Also an informational RFC, this document describes what is required to make it possible to do traffic engineering over MPLS. According to the abstract: "It identifies the functional capabilities required to implement policies that facilitate efficient and reliable network operations in an MPLS domain. These capabilities can be used to optimize the utilization of network resources and to enhance traffic oriented performance characteristics."

RFC 2764: A Framework for IP Based Virtual Private Networks

This informational RFC presents a framework within which Virtual Private Networks (VPNs) can be deployed across IP backbones. It has relevance to MPLS because MPLS is such an important component of many approaches to building VPNs (see RFCs 2547 and 2917). This RFC describes different types of VPNs and suggests how specific mechanisms could be used to build such VPNs in existing or proposed situations.

This RFC is offered to provide "a framework for related protocol development in order to develop the full set of specifications required for widespread deployment of interoperable VPN solutions."

RFC 2836: Per Hop Behavior Identification Codes

Introduced in RFCs 2474 and 2475 on Differentiated Services, the concept of Per Hop Behaviors (PHBs) is used to describe the way in which network traffic belonging to a "behavior aggregate" is treated at a particular node. A behavior aggregate is the set of packets crossing a particular link that is treated the same way for the purpose of Differentiated Services.

This proposed standard RFC describes a binary encoding that uniquely identifies PHBs (and in some cases, sets of PHBs) in protocol messages. This comes in handy when nodes need to negotiate bandwidth management or path selection, particularly in cases where the negotiations cross management domains. For example, bandwidth brokers would be able to use PHB identification codes.

Another important instance where PHB identification codes are helpful is in MPLS support for Differentiated Services, because they can be used to map the Differentiated Services behavior aggregate membership onto appropriate labels for proper treatment within the MPLS domain.

RFC 2917: A Core MPLS IP VPN Architecture

This is another informational RFC describing one approach used to build Virtual Private Network (VPN) services to be offered a server provider's MPLS backbone by using MPLS on the backbone for premium services in addition to traditional best-effort services.

Network Working Group   R. Braden
Request for Comments: 1633   ISI
Category: Informational   D. Clark
                                                             MIT
                                                      S. Shenker
                                                     Xerox PARC
                                                      June 1994

        Integrated Services in the Internet Architecture: an Overview

Status of this Memo

    This memo provides information for the Internet community. This memo
    does not specify an Internet standard of any kind. Distribution of
    this memo is unlimited.

Abstract

    This memo discusses a proposed extension to the Internet architecture
    and protocols to provide integrated services, i.e., to support real-
    time as well as the current non-real-time service of IP. This
    extension is necessary to meet the growing need for real-time service
    for a variety of new applications, including teleconferencing, remote
    seminars, telescience, and distributed simulation.

    This memo represents the direct product of recent work by Dave Clark,
    Scott Shenker, Lixia Zhang, Deborah Estrin, Sugih Jamin, John
    Wroclawski, Shai Herzog, and Bob Braden, and indirectly draws upon
    the work of many others.

Table of Contents

Braden, Clark & Shenker   [Page 1]

1. Introduction

     The multicasts of IETF meetings across the Internet have formed a
     large-scale experiment in sending digitized voice and video through a
     packet-switched infrastructure. These highly-visible experiments
     have depended upon three enabling technologies. (1) Many modern
     workstations now come equipped with built-in multimedia hardware,
     including audio codecs and video frame-grabbers, and the necessary
     video gear is now inexpensive. (2) IP multicasting, which is not yet
     generally available in commercial routers, is being provided by the
     MBONE, a temporary "multicast backbone". (3) Highly-sophisticated
     digital audio and video applications have been developed.

     These experiments also showed that an important technical element is
     still missing: real-time applications often do not work well across
     the Internet because of variable queueing delays and congestion
     losses. The Internet, as originally conceived, offers only a very
     simple quality of service (QoS), point-to-point best-effort data
     delivery. Before real-time applications such as remote video,
     multimedia conferencing, visualization, and virtual reality can be
     broadly used, the Internet infrastructure must be modified to support
     real-time QoS, which provides some control over end-to-end packet
     delays. This extension must be designed from the beginning for
     multicasting; simply generalizing from the unicast (point-to-point)
     case does not work.

     Real-time QoS is not the only issue for a next generation of traffic
     management in the Internet. Network operators are requesting the
     ability to control the sharing of bandwidth on a particular link
     among different traffic classes. They want to be able to divide
     traffic into a few administrative classes and assign to each a
     minimum percentage of the link bandwidth under conditions of
     overload, while allowing "unused" bandwidth to be available at other
     times. These classes may represent different user groups or
     different protocol families, for example. Such a management facility
     is commonly called controlled link-sharing. We use the term
     integrated services (IS) for an Internet service model that includes
     best-effort service, real-time service, and controlled link sharing.

     The requirements and mechanisms for integrated services have been the
     subjects of much discussion and research over the past several years

(the literature is much too large to list even a representative
sample here; see the references in [CSZ92, Floyd92, Jacobson91,
JSCZ93, Partridge92, SCZ93, RSVP93a] for a partial list). This work
has led to the unified approach to integrated services support that
is described in this memo. We believe that it is now time to begin
the engineering that must precede deployment of integrated services
in the Internet.

Section 2 of this memo introduces the elements of an IS extension of
the Internet. Section 3 discusses real-time service models [SCZ93a,
SCZ93b]. Section 4 discusses traffic control, the forwarding
algorithms to be used in routers [CSZ92]. Section 5 discusses the
design of RSVP, a resource setup protocol compatible with the
assumptions of our IS model [RSVP93a, RSVP93b].

2. Elements of the Architecture

   The fundamental service model of the Internet, as embodied in the
   best-effort delivery service of IP, has been unchanged since the
   beginning of the Internet research project 20 years ago [CerfKahn74].
   We are now proposing to alter that model to encompass integrated
   service. From an academic viewpoint, changing the service model of
   the Internet is a major undertaking; however, its impact is mitigated
   by the fact that we wish only to extend the original architecture.
   The new components and mechanisms to be added will supplement but not
   replace the basic IP service.

   Abstractly, the proposed architectural extension is comprised of two
   elements: (1) an extended service model, which we call the IS model,
   and (2) a reference implementation framework, which gives us a set of
   vocabulary and a generic program organization to realize the IS
   model. It is important to separate the service model, which defines
   the externally visible behavior, from the discussion of the
   implementation, which may (and should) change during the life of the
   service model. However, the two are related; to make the service
   model credible, it is useful to provide an example of how it might be
   realized.

   2.1 Integrated Services Model

      The IS model we are proposing includes two sorts of service
      targeted towards real-time traffic: guaranteed and predictive
      service. It integrates these services with controlled link-
      sharing, and it is designed to work well with multicast as well as
      unicast. Deferring a summary of the IS model to Section 3, we
      first discuss some key assumptions behind the model.

The first assumption is that resources (e.g., bandwidth) must be explicitly managed in order to meet application requirements. This implies that "resource reservation" and "admission control" are key building blocks of the service. An alternative approach, which we reject, is to attempt to support real-time traffic without any explicit changes to the Internet service model.

The essence of real-time service is the requirement for some service guarantees, and we argue that guarantees cannot be achieved without reservations. The term "guarantee" here is to be broadly interpreted; they may be absolute or statistical, strict or approximate. However, the user must be able to get a service whose quality is sufficiently predictable that the application can operate in an acceptable way over a duration of time determined by the user. Again, "sufficiently" and "acceptable" are vague terms. In general, stricter guarantees have a higher cost in resources that are made unavailable for sharing with others.

The following arguments have been raised against resource guarantees in the Internet.

o   "Bandwidth will be infinite."

        The incredibly large carrying capacity of an optical fiber
        leads some to conclude that in the future bandwidth will be
        so abundant, ubiquitous, and cheap that there will be no
        communication delays other than the speed of light, and
        therefore there will be no need to reserve resources.
        However, we believe that this will be impossible in the short
        term and unlikely in the medium term. While raw bandwidth
        may seem inexpensive, bandwidth provided as a network service
        is not likely to become so cheap that wasting it will be the
        most cost-effective design principle. Even if low-cost
        bandwidth does eventually become commonly available, we do
        not accept that it will be available "everywhere" in the
        Internet. Unless we provide for the possibility of dealing
        with congested links, then real-time services will simply be
        precluded in those cases. We find that restriction
        unacceptable.

o   "Simple priority is sufficient."

        It is true that simply giving higher priority to real-time
        traffic would lead to adequate real-time service at some
        times and under some conditions. But priority is an
        implementation mechanism, not a service model. If we define
        the service by means of a specific mechanism, we may not get
        the exact features we want. In the case of simple priority,

the issue is that as soon as there are too many real-time streams competing for the higher priority, every stream is degraded. Restricting our service to this single failure mode is unacceptable. In some cases, users will demand that some streams succeed while some new requests receive a "busy signal".

o   "Applications can adapt."

The development of adaptive real-time applications, such as Jacobson's audio program VAT, does not eliminate the need to bound packet delivery time. Human requirements for interaction and intelligibility limit the possible range of adaptation to network delays. We have seen in real experiments that, while VAT can adapt to network delays of many seconds, the users find that interaction is impossible in these cases.

We conclude that there is an inescapable requirement for routers to be able to reserve resources, in order to provide special QoS for specific user packet streams, or "flows". This in turn requires flow-specific state in the routers, which represents an important and fundamental change to the Internet model. The Internet architecture was been founded on the concept that all flow-related state should be in the end systems [Clark88]. Designing the TCP/IP protocol suite on this concept led to a robustness that is one of the keys to its success. In section 5 we discuss how the flow state added to the routers for resource reservation can be made "soft", to preserve the robustness of the Internet protocol suite.

There is a real-world side effect of resource reservation in routers. Since it implies that some users are getting privileged service, resource reservation will need enforcement of policy and administrative controls. This in turn will lead to two kinds of authentication requirements: authentication of users who make reservation requests, and authentication of packets that use the reserved resources. However, these issues are not unique to "IS"; other aspects of the evolution of the Internet, including commercialization and commercial security, are leading to the same requirements. We do not discuss the issues of policy or security further in this memo, but they will require attention.

We make another fundamental assumption, that it is desirable to use the Internet as a common infrastructure to support both non-real-time and real-time communication. One could alternatively build an entirely new, parallel infrastructure for real-time services, leaving the Internet unchanged. We reject this

approach, as it would lose the significant advantages of
statistical sharing between real-time and non-real-time traffic,
and it would be much more complex to build and administer than a
common infrastructure.

In addition to this assumption of common infrastructure, we adopt
a unified protocol stack model, employing a single internet-layer
protocol for both real-time and non-real-time service. Thus, we
propose to use the existing internet-layer protocol (e.g., IP or
CLNP) for real-time data. Another approach would be to add a new
real-time protocol in the internet layer [ST2-90]. Our unified
stack approach provides economy of mechanism, and it allows us to
fold controlled link-sharing in easily. It also handles the
problem of partial coverage, i.e., allowing interoperation between
IS-capable Internet systems and systems that have not been
extended, without the complexity of tunneling.

We take the view that there should be a single service model for
the Internet. If there were different service models in different
parts of the Internet, it is very difficult to see how any end-
to-end service quality statements could be made. However, a
single service model does not necessarily imply a single
implementation for packet scheduling or admission control.
Although specific packet scheduling and admission control
mechanisms that satisfy our service model have been developed, it
is quite possible that other mechanisms will also satisfy the
service model. The reference implementation framework, introduced
below, is intended to allow discussion of implementation issues
without mandating a single design.

Based upon these considerations, we believe that an IS extension
that includes additional flow state in routers and an explicit
setup mechanism is necessary to provide the needed service. A
partial solution short of this point would not be a wise
investment. We believe that the extensions we propose preserve
the essential robustness and efficiency of the Internet
architecture, and they allow efficient management of the network
resources; these will be important goals even if bandwidth becomes
very inexpensive.

2.2 Reference Implementation Framework

We propose a reference implementation framework to realize the IS
model. This framework includes four components: the packet
scheduler, the admission control routine, the classifier, and the
reservation setup protocol. These are discussed briefly below and
more fully in Sections 4 and 5.

In the ensuing discussion, we define the "flow" abstraction as a distinguishable stream of related datagrams that results from a single user activity and requires the same QoS. For example, a flow might consist of one transport connection or one video stream between a given host pair. It is the finest granularity of packet stream distinguishable by the IS. We define a flow to be simplex, i.e., to have a single source but N destinations. Thus, an N-way teleconference will generally require N flows, one originating at each site.

In today's Internet, IP forwarding is completely egalitarian; all packets receive the same quality of service, and packets are typically forwarded using a strict FIFO queueing discipline. For integrated services, a router must implement an appropriate QoS for each flow, in accordance with the service model. The router function that creates different qualities of service is called "traffic control". Traffic control in turn is implemented by three components: the packet scheduler, the classifier, and admission control.

o   Packet Scheduler

     The packet scheduler manages the forwarding of different
     packet streams using a set of queues and perhaps other
     mechanisms like timers. The packet scheduler must be
     implemented at the point where packets are queued; this is
     the output driver level of a typical operating system, and
     corresponds to the link layer protocol. The details of the
     scheduling algorithm may be specific to the particular output
     medium. For example, the output driver will need to invoke
     the appropriate link-layer controls when interfacing to a
     network technology that has an internal bandwidth allocation
     mechanism.

     An experimental packet scheduler has been built that
     implements the IS model described in Section 3 and [SCZ93];
     this is known as the CSZ scheduler and is discussed further
     in Section 4. We note that the CSZ scheme is not mandatory
     to accomplish our service model; indeed for parts of the
     network that are known always to be underloaded, FIFO will
     deliver satisfactory service.

     There is another component that could be considered part of
     the packet scheduler or separate: the estimator [Jacobson91].
     This algorithm is used to measure properties of the outgoing
     traffic stream, to develop statistics that control packet
     scheduling and admission control. This memo will consider
     the estimator to be a part of the packet scheduler.

o   Classifier

     For the purpose of traffic control (and accounting), each
     incoming packet must be mapped into some class; all packets
     in the same class get the same treatment from the packet
     scheduler. This mapping is performed by the classifier.
     Choice of a class may be based upon the contents of the
     existing packet header(s) and/or some additional
     classification number added to each packet.

     A class might correspond to a broad category of flows, e.g.,
     all video flows or all flows attributable to a particular
     organization. On the other hand, a class might hold only a
     single flow. A class is an abstraction that may be local to
     a particular router; the same packet may be classified
     differently by different routers along the path. For
     example, backbone routers may choose to map many flows into a
     few aggregated classes, while routers nearer the periphery,
     where there is much less aggregation, may use a separate
     class for each flow.

o   Admission Control

     Admission control implements the decision algorithm that a
     router or host uses to determine whether a new flow can be
     granted the requested QoS without impacting earlier
     guarantees. Admission control is invoked at each node to
     make a local accept/reject decision, at the time a host
     requests a real-time service along some path through the
     Internet. The admission control algorithm must be consistent
     with the service model, and it is logically part of traffic
     control. Although there are still open research issues in
     admission control, a first cut exists [JCSZ92].

     Admission control is sometimes confused with policing or
     enforcement, which is a packet-by-packet function at the
     "edge" of the network to ensure that a host does not violate
     its promised traffic characteristics. We consider policing
     to be one of the functions of the packet scheduler.

     In addition to ensuring that QoS guarantees are met,
     admission control will be concerned with enforcing
     administrative policies on resource reservations. Some
     policies will demand authentication of those requesting
     reservations. Finally, admission control will play an

important role in accounting and administrative reporting.

The fourth and final component of our implementation framework is
a reservation setup protocol, which is necessary to create and
maintain flow-specific state in the endpoint hosts and in routers
along the path of a flow. Section discusses a reservation setup
protocol called RSVP (for "ReSerVation Protocol") [RSVP93a,
RSVP93b]. It may not be possible to insist that there be only one
reservation protocol in the Internet, but we will argue that
multiple choices for reservation protocols will cause confusion.
We believe that multiple protocols should exist only if they
support different modes of reservation.

The setup requirements for the link-sharing portion of the service
model are far less clear than those for resource reservations.
While we expect that much of this can be done through network
management interfaces, and thus need not be part of the overall
architecture, we may also need RSVP to play a role in providing
the required state.

In order to state its resource requirements, an application must
specify the desired QoS using a list of parameters that is called
a "flowspec" [Partridge92]. The flowspec is carried by the
reservation setup protocol, passed to admission control for to
test for acceptability, and ultimately used to parametrize the
packet scheduling mechanism.

Figure shows how these components might fit into an IP router
that has been extended to provide integrated services. The router
has two broad functional divisions: the forwarding path below the
double horizontal line, and the background code above the line.

The forwarding path of the router is executed for every packet and
must therefore be highly optimized. Indeed, in most commercial
routers, its implementation involves a hardware assist. The
forwarding path is divided into three sections: input driver,
internet forwarder, and output driver. The internet forwarder
interprets the internetworking protocol header appropriate to the
protocol suite, e.g., the IP header for TCP/IP, or the CLNP header
for OSI. For each packet, an internet forwarder executes a
suite-dependent classifier and then passes the packet and its
class to the appropriate output driver. A classifier must be both
general and efficient. For efficiency, a common mechanism should
be used for both resource classification and route lookup.

The output driver implements the packet scheduler. (Layerists
will observe that the output driver now has two distinct sections:
the packet scheduler that is largely independent of the detailed

mechanics of the interface, and the actual I/O driver that is only
concerned with the grittiness of the hardware. The estimator
lives somewhere in between. We only note this fact, without
suggesting that it be elevated to a principle.).

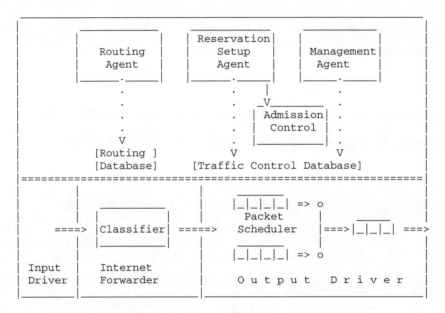

Figure 1: Implementation Reference Model for Routers

The background code is simply loaded into router memory and
executed by a general-purpose CPU. These background routines
create data structures that control the forwarding path. The
routing agent implements a particular routing protocol and builds
a routing database. The reservation setup agent implements the
protocol used to set up resource reservations; see Section . If
admission control gives the "OK" for a new request, the
appropriate changes are made to the classifier and packet
scheduler database to implement the desired QoS. Finally, every
router supports an agent for network management. This agent must
be able to modify the classifier and packet scheduler databases to
set up controlled link-sharing and to set admission control
policies.

The implementation framework for a host is generally similar to that for a router, with the addition of applications. Rather than being forwarded, host data originates and terminates in an application. An application needing a real-time QoS for a flow must somehow invoke a local reservation setup agent. The best way to interface to applications is still to be determined. For example, there might be an explicit API for network resource setup, or the setup might be invoked implicitly as part of the operating system scheduling function. The IP output routine of a host may need no classifier, since the class assignment for a packet can be specified in the local I/O control structure corresponding to the flow.

In routers, integrated service will require changes to both the forwarding path and the background functions. The forwarding path, which may depend upon hardware acceleration for performance, will be the more difficult and costly to change. It will be vital to choose a set of traffic control mechanisms that is general and adaptable to a wide variety of policy requirements and future circumstances, and that can be implemented efficiently.

3. Integrated Services Model

A service model is embedded within the network service interface invoked by applications to define the set of services they can request. While both the underlying network technology and the overlying suite of applications will evolve, the need for compatibility requires that this service interface remain relatively stable (or, more properly, extensible; we do expect to add new services in the future but we also expect that it will be hard to change existing services). Because of its enduring impact, the service model should not be designed in reference to any specific network artifact but rather should be based on fundamental service requirements.

We now briefly describe a proposal for a core set of services for the Internet; this proposed core service model is more fully described in [SCZ93a, SCZ93b]. This core service model addresses those services which relate most directly to the time-of-delivery of packets. We leave the remaining services (such as routing, security, or stream synchronization) for other standardization venues. A service model consists of a set of service commitments; in response to a service request the network commits to deliver some service. These service commitments can be categorized by the entity to whom they are made: they can be made to either individual flows or to collective entities (classes of flows). The service commitments made to individual flows are intended to provide reasonable application performance, and thus are driven by the ergonomic requirements of the applications; these

service commitments relate to the quality of service delivered to an
individual flow. The service commitments made to collective entities
are driven by resource-sharing, or economic, requirements; these
service commitments relate to the aggregate resources made available
to the various entities.

In this section we start by exploring the service requirements of
individual flows and propose a corresponding set of services. We
then discuss the service requirements and services for resource
sharing. Finally, we conclude with some remarks about packet
dropping.

3.1 Quality of Service Requirements

   The core service model is concerned almost exclusively with the
   time-of-delivery of packets. Thus, per-packet delay is the
   central quantity about which the network makes quality of service
   commitments. We make the even more restrictive assumption that
   the only quantity about which we make quantitative service
   commitments are bounds on the maximum and minimum delays.

   The degree to which application performance depends on low delay
   service varies widely, and we can make several qualitative
   distinctions between applications based on the degree of their
   dependence. One class of applications needs the data in each
   packet by a certain time and, if the data has not arrived by then,
   the data is essentially worthless; we call these real-time
   applications. Another class of applications will always wait for
   data to arrive; we call these " elastic" applications. We now
   consider the delay requirements of these two classes separately.

   3.1.1 Real-Time Applications

      An important class of such real-time applications, which are
      the only real-time applications we explicitly consider in the
      arguments that follow, are "playback" applications. In a
      playback application, the source takes some signal, packetizes
      it, and then transmits the packets over the network. The
      network inevitably introduces some variation in the delay of
      the delivered packets. The receiver depacketizes the data and
      then attempts to faithfully play back the signal. This is done
      by buffering the incoming data and then replaying the signal at
      some fixed offset delay from the original departure time; the
      term "playback point" refers to the point in time which is
      offset from the original departure time by this fixed delay.
      Any data that arrives before its associated playback point can
      be used to reconstruct the signal; data arriving after the
      playback point is essentially useless in reconstructing the

real-time signal.

In order to choose a reasonable value for the offset delay, an application needs some "a priori" characterization of the maximum delay its packets will experience. This "a priori" characterization could either be provided by the network in a quantitative service commitment to a delay bound, or through the observation of the delays experienced by the previously arrived packets; the application needs to know what delays to expect, but this expectation need not be constant for the entire duration of the flow.

The performance of a playback application is measured along two dimensions: latency and fidelity. Some playback applications, in particular those that involve interaction between the two ends of a connection such as a phone call, are rather sensitive to the latency; other playback applications, such as transmitting a movie or lecture, are not. Similarly, applications exhibit a wide range of sensitivity to loss of fidelity. We will consider two somewhat artificially dichotomous classes: intolerant applications, which require an absolutely faithful playback, and tolerant applications, which can tolerate some loss of fidelity. We expect that the vast bulk of audio and video applications will be tolerant, but we also suspect that there will be other applications, such as circuit emulation, that are intolerant.

Delay can affect the performance of playback applications in two ways. First, the value of the offset delay, which is determined by predictions about the future packet delays, determines the latency of the application. Second, the delays of individual packets can decrease the fidelity of the playback by exceeding the offset delay; the application then can either change the offset delay in order to play back late packets (which introduces distortion) or merely discard late packets (which creates an incomplete signal). The two different ways of coping with late packets offer a choice between an incomplete signal and a distorted one, and the optimal choice will depend on the details of the application, but the important point is that late packets necessarily decrease fidelity.

Intolerant applications must use a fixed offset delay, since any variation in the offset delay will introduce some distortion in the playback. For a given distribution of packet delays, this fixed offset delay must be larger than the absolute maximum delay, to avoid the possibility of late packets. Such an application can only set its offset delay appropriately if it is given a perfectly reliable upper bound on the maximum delay of each packet. We call a service characterized by a perfectly reliable upper bound on delay " guaranteed service", and propose this as the appropriate service model for intolerant playback applications.

In contrast, tolerant applications need not set their offset delay greater than the absolute maximum delay, since they can tolerate some late packets. Moreover, instead of using a single fixed value for the offset delay, they can attempt to reduce their latency by varying their offset delays in response to the actual packet delays experienced in the recent past. We call applications which vary their offset delays in this manner "adaptive" playback applications.

For tolerant applications we propose a service model called " predictive service" which supplies a fairly reliable, but not perfectly reliable, delay bound. This bound, in contrast to the bound in the guaranteed service, is not based on worst case assumptions on the behavior of other flows. Instead, this bound might be computed with properly conservative predictions about the behavior of other flows. If the network turns out to be wrong and the bound is violated, the application's performance will perhaps suffer, but the users are willing to tolerate such interruptions in service in return for the presumed lower cost of the service. Furthermore, because many of the tolerant applications are adaptive, we augment the predictive service to also give "minimax" service, which is to attempt to minimize the ex post maximum delay. This service is not trying to minimize the delay of every packet, but rather is trying to pull in the tail of the delay distribution.

It is clear that given a choice, with all other things being equal, an application would perform no worse with absolutely reliable bounds than with fairly reliable bounds. Why, then, do we offer predictive service? The key consideration here is efficiency; when one relaxes the service requirements from perfectly to fairly reliable bounds, this increases the level of network utilization that can be sustained, and thus the price of the predictive service will presumably be lower than that of guaranteed service. The predictive service class is motivated by the conjecture that the performance penalty will be small for tolerant applications but the overall efficiency gain will be quite large.

In order to provide a delay bound, the nature of the traffic from the source must be characterized, and there must be some admission control algorithm which insures that a requested flow

can actually be accommodated. A fundamental point of our
overall architecture is that traffic characterization and
admission control are necessary for these real-time delay bound
services. So far we have assumed that an application's data
generation process is an intrinsic property unaffected by the
network. However, there are likely to be many audio and video
applications which can adjust their coding scheme and thus can
alter the resulting data generation process depending on the
network service available. This alteration of the coding
scheme will present a tradeoff between fidelity (of the coding
scheme itself, not of the playback process) and the bandwidth
requirements of the flow. Such "rate-adaptive" playback
applications have the advantage that they can adjust to the
current network conditions not just by resetting their playback
point but also by adjusting the traffic pattern itself. For
rate-adaptive applications, the traffic characterizations used
in the service commitment are not immutable. We can thus
augment the service model by allowing the network to notify
(either implicitly through packet drops or explicitly through
control packets) rate-adaptive applications to change their
traffic characterization.

3.1.2 Elastic Applications

While real-time applications do not wait for late data to
arrive, elastic applications will always wait for data to
arrive. It is not that these applications are insensitive to
delay; to the contrary, significantly increasing the delay of a
packet will often harm the application's performance. Rather,
the key point is that the application typically uses the
arriving data immediately, rather than buffering it for some
later time, and will always choose to wait for the incoming
data rather than proceed without it. Because arriving data can
be used immediately, these applications do not require any a
priori characterization of the service in order for the
application to function. Generally speaking, it is likely that
for a given distribution of packet delays, the perceived
performance of elastic applications will depend more on the
average delay than on the tail of the delay distribution. One
can think of several categories of such elastic applications:
interactive burst (Telnet, X, NFS), interactive bulk transfer
(FTP), and asynchronous bulk transfer (electronic mail, FAX).
The delay requirements of these elastic applications vary from
rather demanding for interactive burst applications to rather
lax for asynchronous bulk transfer, with interactive bulk
transfer being intermediate between them.

An appropriate service model for elastic applications is to
provide "as-soon-as-possible", or ASAP service. (For
compatibility with historical usage, we will use the term
best-effort service when referring to ASAP service.). We
furthermore propose to offer several classes of best-effort
service to reflect the relative delay sensitivities of
different elastic applications. This service model allows
interactive burst applications to have lower delays than
interactive bulk applications, which in turn would have lower
delays than asynchronous bulk applications. In contrast to the
real-time service models, applications using this service are
not subject to admission control.

The taxonomy of applications into tolerant playback, intolerant
playback, and elastic is neither exact nor complete, but was
only used to guide the development of the core service model.
The resulting core service model should be judged not on the
validity of the underlying taxonomy but rather on its ability
to adequately meet the needs of the entire spectrum of
applications. In particular, not all real-time applications
are playback applications; for example, one might imagine a
visualization application which merely displayed the image
encoded in each packet whenever it arrived. However, non-
playback applications can still use either the guaranteed or
predictive real-time service model, although these services are
not specifically tailored to their needs. Similarly, playback
applications cannot be neatly classified as either tolerant or
intolerant, but rather fall along a continuum; offering both
guaranteed and predictive service allows applications to make
their own tradeoff between fidelity, latency, and cost.
Despite these obvious deficiencies in the taxonomy, we expect
that it describes the service requirements of current and
future applications well enough so that our core service model
can adequately meet all application needs.

3.2 Resource-Sharing Requirements and Service Models

The last section considered quality of service commitments; these
commitments dictate how the network must allocate its resources
among the individual flows. This allocation of resources is
typically negotiated on a flow-by-flow basis as each flow requests
admission to the network, and does not address any of the policy
issues that arise when one looks at collections of flows. To
address these collective policy issues, we now discuss resource-
sharing service commitments. Recall that for individual quality
of service commitments we focused on delay as the only quantity of
interest. Here, we postulate that the quantity of primary
interest in resource-sharing is aggregate bandwidth on individual

links. Thus, this component of the service model, called "link-sharing", addresses the question of how to share the aggregate bandwidth of a link among various collective entities according to some set of specified shares. There are several examples that are commonly used to explain the requirement of link-sharing among collective entities.

Multi-entity link-sharing. -- A link may be purchased and used jointly by several organizations, government agencies or the like. They may wish to insure that under overload the link is shared in a controlled way, perhaps in proportion to the capital investment of each entity. At the same time, they might wish that when the link is underloaded, any one of the entities could utilize all the idle bandwidth.

Multi-protocol link-sharing -- In a multi-protocol Internet, it may be desired to prevent one protocol family (DECnet, IP, IPX, OSI, SNA, etc.) from overloading the link and excluding the other families. This is important because different families may have different methods of detecting and responding to congestion, and some methods may be more "aggressive" than others. This could lead to a situation in which one protocol backs off more rapidly than another under congestion, and ends up getting no bandwidth. Explicit control in the router may be required to correct this. Again, one might expect that this control should apply only under overload, while permitting an idle link to be used in any proportion.

Multi-service sharing -- Within a protocol family such as IP, an administrator might wish to limit the fraction of bandwidth allocated to various service classes. For example, an administrator might wish to limit the amount of real-time traffic to some fraction of the link, to avoid preempting elastic traffic such as FTP.

In general terms, the link-sharing service model is to share the aggregate bandwidth according to some specified shares. We can extend this link-sharing service model to a hierarchical version. For instance, a link could be divided between a number of organizations, each of which would divide the resulting allocation among a number of protocols, each of which would be divided among a number of services. Here, the sharing is defined by a tree with shares assigned to each leaf node.

An idealized fluid model of instantaneous link-sharing with proportional sharing of excess is the fluid processor sharing model (introduced in [DKS89] and further explored in [Parekh92] and generalized to the hierarchical case) where at every instant

the available bandwidth is shared between the active entities
(i.e., those having packets in the queue) in proportion to the
assigned shares of the resource. This fluid model exhibits the
desired policy behavior but is, of course, an unrealistic
idealization. We then propose that the actual service model
should be to approximate, as closely as possible, the bandwidth
shares produced by this ideal fluid model. It is not necessary to
require that the specific order of packet departures match those
of the fluid model since we presume that all detailed per-packet
delay requirements of individual flows are addressed through
quality of service commitments and, furthermore, the satisfaction
with the link-sharing service delivered will probably not depend
very sensitively on small deviations from the scheduling implied
by the fluid link-sharing model.

We previously observed that admission control was necessary to
ensure that the real-time service commitments could be met.
Similarly, admission control will again be necessary to ensure
that the link-sharing commitments can be met. For each entity,
admission control must keep the cumulative guaranteed and
predictive traffic from exceeding the assigned link-share.

3.3 Packet Dropping

So far, we have implicitly assumed that all packets within a flow
were equally important. However, in many audio and video streams,
some packets are more valuable than others. We therefore propose
augmenting the service model with a "preemptable" packet service,
whereby some of the packets within a flow could be marked as
preemptable. When the network was in danger of not meeting some
of its quantitative service commitments, it could exercise a
certain packet's "preemptability option" and discard the packet
(not merely delay it, since that would introduce out-of-order
problems). By discarding these preemptable packets, a router can
reduce the delays of the not-preempted packets.

Furthermore, one can define a class of packets that is not subject
to admission control. In the scenario described above where
preemptable packets are dropped only when quantitative service
commitments are in danger of being violated, the expectation is
that preemptable packets will almost always be delivered and thus
they must included in the traffic description used in admission
control. However, we can extend preemptability to the extreme
case of "expendable" packets (the term expendable is used to
connote an extreme degree of preemptability), where the
expectation is that many of these expendable packets may not be
delivered. One can then exclude expendable packets from the
traffic description used in admission control; i.e., the packets

are not considered part of the flow from the perspective of
admission control, since there is no commitment that they will be
delivered.

3.4 Usage Feedback

Another important issue in the service is the model for usage
feedback, also known as "accounting", to prevent abuse of network
resources.   The link-sharing service described earlier can be
used to provide administratively-imposed limits on usage.
However, a more free-market model of network access will require
back-pressure on users for the network resources they reserve.
This is a highly contentious issue, and we are not prepared to say
more about it at this time.

3.5 Reservation Model

The "reservation model" describes how an application negotiates
for a QoS level. The simplest model is that the application asks
for a particular QoS and the network either grants it or refuses.
Often the situation will be more complex. Many applications will
be able to get acceptable service from a range of QoS levels, or
more generally, from anywhere within some region of the multi-
dimensional space of a flowspec.

For example, rather than simply refusing the request, the network
might grant a lower resource level and inform the application of
what QoS has been actually granted. A more complex example is the
"two-pass" reservation model, In this scheme, an "offered"
flowspec is propagated along the multicast distribution tree from
each sender Si to all receivers Rj. Each router along the path
records these values and perhaps adjusts them to reflect available
capacity. The receivers get these offers, generate corresponding
"requested" flowspecs, and propagate them back along the same
routes to the senders. At each node, a local reconciliation must
be performed between the offered and the requested flowspec to
create a reservation, and an appropriately modified requested
flowspec is passed on. This two-pass scheme allows extensive
properties like allowed delay to be distributed across hops in the
path [Tenet90, ST2-90]. Further work is needed to define the
amount of generality, with a corresponding level of complexity,
that is required in the reservation model.

4. Traffic Control Mechanisms

We first survey very briefly the possible traffic control mechanisms.
Then in Section 4.2 we apply a subset of these mechanisms to support
the various services that we have proposed.

4.1 Basic Functions

In the packet forwarding path, there is actually a very limited
set of actions that a router can take. Given a particular packet,
a router must select a route for it; in addition the router can
either forward it or drop it, and the router may reorder it with
respect to other packets waiting to depart. The router can also
hold the packet, even though the link is idle. These are the
building blocks from which we must fashion the desired behavior.

4.1.1 Packet Scheduling

The basic function of packet scheduling is to reorder the
output queue. There are many papers that have been written on
possible ways to manage the output queue, and the resulting
behavior. Perhaps the simplest approach is a priority scheme,
in which packets are ordered by priority, and highest priority
packets always leave first. This has the effect of giving some
packets absolute preference over others; if there are enough of
the higher priority packets, the lower priority class can be
completely prevented from being sent.

An alternative scheduling scheme is round-robin or some
variant, which gives different classes of packets access to a
share of the link. A variant called Weighted Fair Queueing, or
WFQ, has been demonstrated to allocate the total bandwidth of a
link into specified shares.

There are more complex schemes for queue management, most of
which involve observing the service objectives of individual
packets, such as delivery deadline, and ordering packets based
on these criteria.

4.1.2 Packet Dropping

The controlled dropping of packets is as important as their
scheduling.

Most obviously, a router must drop packets when its buffers are
all full. This fact, however, does not determine which packet
should be dropped. Dropping the arriving packet, while simple,
may cause undesired behavior.

In the context of today's Internet, with TCP operating over
best effort IP service, dropping a packet is taken by TCP as a
signal of congestion and causes it to reduce its load on the
network. Thus, picking a packet to drop is the same as picking
a source to throttle. Without going into any particular
algorithm, this simple relation suggests that some specific
dropping controls should be implemented in routers to improve
congestion control.

In the context of real-time services, dropping more directly
relates to achieving the desired quality of service. If a
queue builds up, dropping one packet reduces the delay of all
the packets behind it in the queue. The loss of one can
contribute to the success of many. The problem for the
implementor is to determine when the service objective (the
delay bound) is in danger of being violated. One cannot look
at queue length as an indication of how long packets have sat
in a queue. If there is a priority scheme in place, packets of
lower priority can be pre-empted indefinitely, so even a short
queue may have very old packets in it. While actual time
stamps could be used to measure holding time, the complexity
may be unacceptable.

Some simple dropping schemes, such as combining all the buffers
in a single global pool, and dropping the arriving packet if
the pool is full, can defeat the service objective of a WFQ
scheduling scheme. Thus, dropping and scheduling must be
coordinated.

4.1.3 Packet Classification

The above discussion of scheduling and dropping presumed that
the packet had been classified into some flow or sequence of
packets that should be treated in a specified way. A
preliminary to this sort of processing is the classification
itself. Today a router looks at the destination address and
selects a route. The destination address is not sufficient to
select the class of service a packet must receive; more
information is needed.

One approach would be to abandon the IP datagram model for a
virtual circuit model, in which a circuit is set up with
specific service attributes, and the packet carries a circuit
identifier. This is the approach of ATM as well as protocols
such as ST-II [ST2-90]. Another model, less hostile to IP, is
to allow the classifier to look at more fields in the packet,
such as the source address, the protocol number and the port
fields. Thus, video streams might be recognized by a

particular well-known port field in the UDP header, or a
particular flow might be recognized by looking at both the
source and destination port numbers. It would be possible to
look even deeper into the packets, for example testing a field
in the application layer to select a subset of a
hierarchically-encoded video stream.

The classifier implementation issues are complexity and
processing overhead. Current experience suggests that careful
implementation of efficient algorithms can lead to efficient
classification of IP packets. This result is very important,
since it allows us to add QoS support to existing applications,
such as Telnet, which are based on existing IP headers.

One approach to reducing the overhead of classification would
be to provide a "flow-id" field in the Internet-layer packet
header. This flow-id would be a handle that could be cached
and used to short-cut classification of the packet. There are
a number of variations of this concept, and engineering is
required to choose the best design.

4.1.4 Admission Control

As we stated in the introduction, real-time service depends on
setting up state in the router and making commitments to
certain classes of packets. In order to insure that these
commitments can be met, it is necessary that resources be
explicitly requested, so that the request can be refused if the
resources are not available. The decision about resource
availability is called admission control.

Admission control requires that the router understand the
demands that are currently being made on its assets. The
approach traditionally proposed is to remember the service
parameters of past requests, and make a computation based on
the worst-case bounds on each service. A recent proposal,
which is likely to provide better link utilization, is to
program the router to measure the actual usage by existing
packet flows, and to use this measured information as a basis
of admitting new flows [JCSZ92]. This approach is subject to
higher risk of overload, but may prove much more effective in
using bandwidth.

Note that while the need for admission control is part of the
global service model, the details of the algorithm run in each
router is a local matter. Thus, vendors can compete by
developing and marketing better admission control algorithms,
which lead to higher link loadings with fewer service

overloads.

4.2 Applying the Mechanisms

The various tools described above can be combined to support the services which were discussed in section 3.

o   Guaranteed delay bounds

A theoretical result by Parekh [Parekh92] shows that if the router implements a WFQ scheduling discipline, and if the nature of the traffic source can be characterized (e.g. if it fits within some bound such as a token bucket) then there will be an absolute upper bound on the network delay of the traffic in question. This simple and very powerful result applies not just to one switch, but to general networks of routers. The result is a constructive one; that is, Parekh displays a source behavior which leads to the bound, and then shows that this behavior is the worst possible. This means that the bound he computes is the best there can be, under these assumptions.

o   Link sharing

The same WFQ scheme can provide controlled link sharing. The service objective here is not to bound delay, but to limit overload shares on a link, while allowing any mix of traffic to proceed if there is spare capacity. This use of WFQ is available in commercial routers today, and is used to segregate traffic into classes based on such things as protocol type or application. For example, one can allocate separate shares to TCP, IPX and SNA, and one can assure that network control traffic gets a guaranteed share of the link.

o   Predictive real-time service

This service is actually more subtle than guaranteed service. Its objective is to give a delay bound which is, on the one hand, as low as possible, and on the other hand, stable enough that the receiver can estimate it. The WFQ mechanism leads to a guaranteed bound, but not necessarily a low bound. In fact, mixing traffic into one queue, rather than separating it as in WFQ, leads to lower bounds, so long as the mixed traffic is generally similar (e.g., mixing traffic from multiple video coders makes sense, mixing video and FTP does not).

This suggests that we need a two-tier mechanism, in which the
first tier separates traffic which has different service
objectives, and the second tier schedules traffic within each
first tier class in order to meet its service objective.

4.3 An example: The CSZ scheme

As a proof of concept, a code package has been implemented which
realizes the services discussed above. It actually uses a number
of the basic tools, combined in a way specific to the service
needs. We describe in general terms how it works, to suggest how
services can be realized. We stress that there are other ways of
building a router to meet the same service needs, and there are in
fact other implementations being used today.

At the top level, the CSZ code uses WFQ as an isolation mechanism
to separate guaranteed flows from each other, as well as from the
rest of the traffic. Guaranteed service gets the highest priority
when and only when it needs the access to meets its deadline. WFQ
provides a separate guarantee for each and every guaranteed flow.

Predictive service and best effort service are separated by
priority. Within the predictive service class, a further priority
is used to provide sub-classes with different delay bounds.
Inside each predictive sub-class, simple FIFO queueing is used to
mix the traffic, which seems to produce good overall delay
behavior. This works because the top-tier algorithm has separated
out the best effort traffic such as FTP.

Within the best-effort class, WFQ is used to provide link sharing.
Since there is a possible requirement for nested shares, this WFQ
code can be used recursively. There are thus two different uses
of WFQ in this code, one to segregate the guaranteed classes, and
one to segregate the link shares. They are similar, but differ in
detail.

Within each link share of the best effort class, priority is used
to permit more time-sensitive elastic traffic to precede other
elastic traffic, e.g., to allow interactive traffic to precede
asynchronous bulk transfers.

The CSZ code thus uses both WFQ and priority in an alternating
manner to build a mechanism to support a range of rather
sophisticated service offerings. This discussion is very brief,
and does not touch on a number of significant issues, such as how
the CSZ code fits real time traffic into the link sharing
objectives. But the basic building blocks are very simple, and

very powerful. In particular, while priority has been proposed as
a key to real-time services, WFQ may be the more general and
powerful of the two schemes. It, rather than priority, supports
guaranteed service and link sharing.

5. Reservation Setup Protocol

There are a number of requirements to be met by the design of a
reservation setuop protocol. It should be fundamentally designed for
a multicast environment, and it must accommodate heterogeneous
service needs. It must give flexible control over the manner in
which reservations can be shared along branches of the multicast
delivery trees. It should be designed around the elementary action
of adding one sender and/or receiver to an existing set, or deleting
one. It must be robust and scale well to large multicast groups.
Finally, it must provide for advance reservation of resources, and
for the preemption that this implies. The reservation setup protocol
RSVP has been designed to meet these requirements [RSVP93a, RSVP93b].
This section gives an overview of the design of RSVP.

5.1 RSVP Overview

Figure shows multi-source, multi-destination data delivery for a
particular shared, distributed application. The arrows indicate
data flow from senders S1 and S2 to receivers R1, R2, and R3, and
the cloud represents the distribution mesh created by the
multicast routing protocol. Multicasting distribution replicates
each data packet from a sender Si, for delivery to every receiver
Rj. We treat uncast delivery from S1 to R1 as a special case, and
we call this multicast distribution mesh a session. A session is
defined by the common IP (multicast) destination address of the
receiver(s).

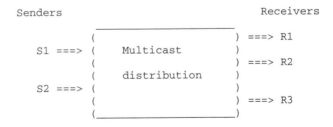

Figure 2: Multicast Distribution Session

5.1.1 Flowspecs and Filter Specs

In general, an RSVP reservation request specifies the amount of resources to be reserved for all, or some subset of, the packets in a particular session. The resource quantity is specified by a flowspec, while the packet subset to receive those resources is specified by a filter spec. Assuming admission control succeeds, the flowspec will be used to parametrize a resource class in the packet scheduler, and the filter spec will be instantiated in the packet classifier to map the appropriate packets into this class. The subset of the classifier state that selects a particular class is referred to in RSVP documentation as a (packet) "filter".

The RSVP protocol mechanisms provide a very general facility for creating and maintaining distributed reservation state across the mesh of multicast delivery paths. These mechanisms treat flowspecs and filter specs as mostly opaque binary data, handing them to the local traffic control machinery for interpretation. Of course, the service model presented to an application must specify how to encode flowspecs and filter specs.

5.1.2 Reservation Styles

RSVP offers several different reservation "styles", which determine the manner in which the resource requirements of multiple receivers are aggregated in the routers. These styles allow the reserved resources to more efficiently meet application requirements. Currently there are three reservation styles, "wildcard", "fixed-filter", and " dynamic-filter". A wildcard reservation uses a filter spec that is not source-specific, so all packets destined for the associated destination (session) may use a common pool of reserved resources. This allows a single resource allocation to be made across all distribution paths for the group. The wildcard reservation style is useful in support of an audio conference, where at most a small number of sources are active simultaneously and may share the resource allocation.

The other two styles use filter specs that select particular sources. A receiver may desire to receive from a fixed set of sources, or instead it may desire the network to switch between different source, by changing its filter spec(s) dymamically. A fixed-filter style reservation cannot be changed during its lifetime without re-invoking admission control. Dynamic-filter reservations do allow a receiver to modify its choice of source(s) over time without additional admission control;

however, this requires that sufficient resources be allocated
to handle the worst case when all downstream receivers take
input from different sources.

5.1.3 Receiver Initiation

An important design question is whether senders or receivers
should have responsibility for initiating reservations. A
sender knows the qualities of the traffic stream it can send,
while a receiver knows what it wants to (or can) receive.
Perhaps the most obvious choice is to let the sender initiate
the reservation. However, this scales poorly for large,
dynamic multicast delivery trees and for heterogeneous
receivers.

Both of these scaling problems are solved by making the
receiver responsible for initiating a reservation. Receiver
initiation handles heterogeneous receivers easily; each
receiver simply asks for a reservation appropriate to itself,
and any differences among reservations from different receivers
are resolved ("merged") within the network by RSVP. Receiver
initiation is also consisent with IP multicast, in which a
multicast group is created implicitly by receivers joining it.

Although receiver-initiated reservation is the natural choice
for multicast sessions, the justification for receiver
initiateion may appear weaker for unicast sessions, where the
sender may be the logical session initiator. However, we
expect that every realtime application will have its higher-
level signalling and control protocol, and this protocol can be
used to signal the receiver to initiate a reservation (and
perhaps indicate the flowspec to be used). For simplicity and
economy, a setup protocol should support only one direction of
initiation, and, and receiver initiation appears to us to be
the clear winner.

RSVP uses receiver-initiation of rservations [RSVP93b]. A
receiver is assumed to learn the senders' offered flowspecs by
a higher-level mechanism ("out of band"), it then generates its
own desired flowspec and propagates it towards the senders,
making reservations in each router along the way.

5.1.4 Soft State

There are two different possible styles for reservation setup
protocols, the "hard state" (HS) approach (also called
"connection-oriented"), and the "soft state" (SS) approach
(also called "connectionless"). In both approaches, multicast

distribution is performed using flow-specific state in each
router along the path. Under the HS approach, this state is
created and deleted in a fully deterministic manner by
cooperation among the routers. Once a host requests a session,
the "network" takes responsibility for creating and later
destroying the necessary state. ST-II is an example of the HS
approach [ST2-90]. Since management of HS session state is
completely deterministic, the HS setup protocol must be
reliable, with acknowledgments and retransmissions. In order
to achieve deterministic cleanup of state after a failure,
there must be some mechanism to detect failures, i.e., an
"up/down" protocol. The router upstream (towards the source)
from a failure takes responsibility for rebuilding the
necessary state on the router(s) along an alternate route.

RSVP takes the SS approach, which regards the reservation state
as cached information that is installed and periodically
refreshed by the end hosts. Unused state is timed out by the
routers. If the route changes, the refresh messages
automatically install the necessary state along the new route.
The SS approach was chosen to obtain the simplicity and
robustness that have been demonstrated by connectionless
protocols such as IP [Clark88].

5.2 Routing and Reservations

There is a fundamental interaction between resource reservation
set up and routing, since reservation requires the installation of
flow state along the route of data packets. If and when a route
changes, there must be some mechanism to set up a reservation
along the new route.

Some have suggested that reservation setup necessarily requires
route set up, i.e., the imposition of a virtual-circuit internet
layer. However, our goal is to simply extend the Internet
architecture, not replace it. The fundamental connectionless
internet layer [Clark88] has been highly successful, and we wish
to retain it as an architectural foundation. We propose instead
to modify somewhat the pure datagram forwarding mechanism of the
present Internet to accomodate "IS".

There are four routing issues faced by a reservation setup
protocol such as RSVP.

1. Find a route that supports resource reservation.

    This is simply "type-of-service" routing, a facility that is
    already available in some modern routing protocols.

2. Find a route that has sufficient unreserved capacity for a
    new flow.

    Early experiments on the ARPANET showed that it is difficult
    to do load-dependent dynamic routing on a packet-by-packet
    basis without instability problems. However, instability
    should not be a problem if load-dependent routing is
    performed only at reservation setup time.

    Two different approaches might be taken to finding a route
    with enough capacity. One could modify the routing
    protocol(s) and interface them to the traffic control
    mechanism, so the route computation can consider the average
    recent load. Alternatively, the routing protocol could be
    (re-)designed to provide multiple alternative routes, and
    reservation setup could be attempted along each in turn.

3. Adapt to a route failure

    When some node or link fails, adaptive routing finds an
    alternate path. The periodic refresh messages of RSVP will
    automatically request a reservation along the new path. Of
    course, this reservation may fail because there is
    insufficienct available capacity on the new path. This is a
    problem of provisioning and network engineering, which cannot
    be solved by the routing or setup protocols.

    There is a problem of timeliness of establishing reservation
    state on the new path. The end-to-end robustness mechanism
    of refreshes is limited in frequency by overhead, which may
    cause a gap in realtime service when an old route breaks and
    a new one is chosen. It should be possible to engineer RSVP
    to sypplement the global refresh mechanism with a local
    repair mechanism, using hints about route changes from the
    routing mechanism.

4. Adapt to a route change (without failure)

    Route changes may occur even without failure in the affected
    path. Although RSVP could use the same repair techniques as

those described in (3), this case raises a problem with the robustness of the QoS guarantees. If it should happen that admission control fails on the new route, the user will see service degradation unnecessarily and capriciously, since the orginal route is still functional.

To avoid this problem, a mechanism called "route pinning" has been suggested. This would modify the routing protocol implementation and the interface to the classifier, so that routes associated with resource reservations would be "pinned". The routing prootocol would not change a pinned route if it was still viable.

It may eventually be possible to fold together the routing and reservation setup problems, but we do not yet understand enough to do that. Furthermore, the reservation protocol needs to coexist with a number of different routing protocols in use in the Internet. Therefore, RSVP is currently designed to work with any current-generation routing protocol without modification. This is a short-term compromise, which may result in an occasional failure to create the best, or even any, real-time session, or an occasional service degradation due to a route change. We expect that future generations of routing protocols will remove this compromise, by including hooks and mechanisms that, in conjunction with RSVP, will solve the problems (1) through (4) just listed. They will support route pinning, notification of RSVP to trigger local repair, and selection of routes with "IS" support and adequate capacity.

The last routing-related issue is provided by mobile hosts. Our conjecture is that mobility is not essentially different from other route changes, so that the mechanism suggested in (3) and (4) will suffice. More study and experimentation is needed to prove or disprove this conjecture.

6. ACKNOWLEDGMENTS

Many Internet researchers have contributed to the work described in this memo. We want to especially acknowledge, Steve Casner, Steve Deering, Deborah Estrin, Sally Floyd, Shai Herzog, Van Jacobson, Sugih Jamin, Craig Partridge, John Wroclawski, and Lixia Zhang. This approach to Internet integrated services was initially discussed and organized in the End-to-End Research Group of the Internet Research Taskforce, and we are grateful to all members of that group for their interesting (and sometimes heated) discussions.

REFERENCES

[CerfKahn74] Cerf, V., and R. Kahn, "A Protocol for Packet Network
     Intercommunication", IEEE Trans on Comm., Vol. Com-22, No. 5, May
     1974.

[Clark88] Clark, D., "The Design Philosophy of the DARPA Internet
     Protocols", ACM SIGCOMM '88, August 1988.

[CSZ92] Clark, D., Shenker, S., and L. Zhang, "Supporting Real-Time
     Applications in an Integrated Services Packet Network: Architecture
     and Mechanisms", Proc. SIGCOMM '92, Baltimore, MD, August 1992.

[DKS89] Demers, A., Keshav, S., and S. Shenker. "Analysis and
     Simulation of a Fair Queueing Algorithm", Journal of
     Internetworking: Research and Experience, 1, pp. 3-26, 1990. Also
     in Proc. ACM SIGCOMM '89, pp 3-12.

[SCZ93a] Shenker, S., Clark, D., and L. Zhang, "A Scheduling Service
     Model and a Scheduling Architecture for an Integrated Services
     Packet Network", submitted to ACM/IEEE Trans. on Networking.

[SCZ93b] Shenker, S., Clark, D., and L. Zhang, "A Service Model for the
     Integrated Services Internet", Work in Progress, October 1993.

[Floyd92] Floyd, S., "Issues in Flexible Resource Management for
     Datagram Networks", Proceedings of the 3rd Workshop on Very High
     Speed Networks, March 1992.

[Jacobson91] Jacobson, V., "Private Communication", 1991.

[JCSZ92] Jamin, S., Shenker, S., Zhang, L., and D. Clark, "An Admission
     Control Algorithm for Predictive Real-Time Service", Extended
     abstract, in Proc. Third International Workshop on Network and
     Operating System Support for Digital Audio and Video, San Diego, CA,
     Nov. 1992, pp. 73-91.

[Parekh92] Parekh, A., "A Generalized Processor Sharing Approach to
     Flow Control in Integrated Services Networks", Technical Report
     LIDS-TR-2089, Laboratory for Information and Decision Systems,
     Massachusetts Institute of Technology, 1992.

[Partridge92] Partridge, C., "A Proposed Flow Specification", RFC 1363,
     BBN, July 1992.

[RSVP93a] Zhang, L., Deering, S., Estrin, D., Shenker, S., and D.
     Zappala, "RSVP: A New Resource ReSerVation Protocol", Accepted for
     publication in IEEE Network, 1993.

[RSVP93b]   Zhang, L., Braden, R., Estrin, D., Herzog, S., and S. Jamin, "Resource ReSerVation Protocol (RSVP) - Version 1 Functional Specification", Work in Progress, 1993.

[ST2-90]   Topolcic, C., "Experimental Internet Stream Protocol: Version 2 (ST-II)", RFC 1190, BBN, October 1990.

[Tenet90]   Ferrari, D., and D. Verma, "A Scheme for Real-Time Channel Establishment in Wide-Area Networks", IEEE JSAC, Vol. 8, No. 3, pp 368-379, April 1990.

Security Considerations

As noted in Section 2.1, the ability to reserve resources will create a requirement for authentication, both of users requesting resource guarantees and of packets that claim to have the right to use those guarantees. These authentication issues are not otherwise addressed in this memo, but are for further study.

Authors' Addresses

   Bob Braden
   USC Information Sciences Institute
   4676 Admiralty Way
   Marina del Rey, CA 90292

   Phone: (310) 822-1511
   EMail: Braden@ISI.EDU

   David Clark
   MIT Laboratory for Computer Science
   545 Technology Square
   Cambridge, MA 02139-1986

   Phone: (617) 253-6003
   EMail: ddc@LCS.MIT.EDU

   Scott Shenker
   Xerox Palo Alto Research Center
   3333 Coyote Hill Road
   Palo Alto, CA 94304

   Phone: (415) 812-4840
   EMail: Shenker@PARC.XEROX.COM

Network Working Group   Y. Katsube
Request for Comments: 2098   K. Nagami
Category: Informational   H. Esaki
                                                 Toshiba R&D Center
                                                     February 1997

Toshiba's Router Architecture Extensions for ATM : Overview

Abstract

   This memo describes a new internetworking architecture which makes
   better use of the property of ATM. IP datagrams are transferred
   along hop-by-hop path via routers, but datagram assembly/disassembly
   and IP header processing are not necessarily carried out at
   individual routers in the proposed architecture. A concept of "Cell
   Switch Router (CSR)" is introduced as a new internetworking
   equipment, which has ATM cell switching capabilities in addition to
   conventional IP datagram forwarding. Proposed architecture can
   provide applications with high-throughput and low-latency ATM pipes
   while retaining current router-based internetworking concept. It
   also provides applications with specific QoS/bandwidth by cooperating
   with internetworking level resource reservation protocols such as
   RSVP.

1. Introduction

   The Internet is growing both in its size and its traffic volume. In
   addition, recent applications often require guaranteed bandwidth and
   QoS rather than best effort. Such changes make the current hop-by-
   hop datagram forwarding paradigm inadequate, then accelerate
   investigations on new internetworking architectures.

   Roughly two distinct approaches can be seen as possible solutions;
   the use of ATM to convey IP datagrams, and the revision of IP to
   support flow concept and resource reservation. Integration or
   interworking of these approaches will be necessary to provide end
   hosts with high throughput and QoS guaranteed internetworking
   services over any datalink platforms as well as ATM.

   New internetworking architecture proposed in this draft is based on
   "Cell Switch Router (CSR)" which has the following properties.

- It makes the best use of ATM's property while retaining current router-based internetworking and routing architecture.

- It takes into account interoperability with future IP that supports flow concept and resource reservations.

Section 2 of this draft explains background and motivations of our proposal. Section 3 describes an overview of the proposed internetworking architecture and its several remarkable features. Section 4 discusses control architectures for CSR, which will need to be further investigated.

2. Background and Motivation

It is considered that the current hop-by-hop best effort datagram forwarding paradigm will not be adequate to support future large scale Internet which accommodates huge amount of traffic with certain QoS requirements. Two major schools of investigations can be seen in IETF whose main purpose is to improve ability of the Internet with regard to its throughput and QoS. One is to utilize ATM technology as much as possible, and the other is to introduce the concept of resource reservation and flow into IP.

1) Utilization of ATM

Although basic properties of ATM; necessity of connection setup, necessity of traffic contract, etc.; is not necessarily suited to conventional IP datagram transmission, its excellent throughput and delay characteristics let us to investigate the realization of IP datagram transmission over ATM.

A typical internetworking architecture is the "Classical IP Model" [RFC1577]. This model allows direct ATM connectivities only between nodes that share the same IP address prefix. IP datagrams should traverse routers whenever they go beyond IP subnet boundaries even though their source and destination are accommodated in the same ATM cloud. Although an ATMARP is introduced which is not based on legacy datalink broadcast but on centralized ATMARP servers, this model does not require drastic changes to the legacy internetworking architectures with regard to the IP datagram forwarding process. This model still has problems of limited throughput and large latency, compared with the ability of ATM, due to IP header processing at every router. It will become more critical when multimedia applications that require much larger bandwidth and lower latency become dominant in the near future.

Another internetworking architecture is "NHRP (Next Hop Resolution
Protocol) Model" [NHRP09]. This model aims at resolving throughput
and latency problems in the Classical IP Model and making the best
use of ATM. ATM connections can be directly established from an
ingress point to an egress point of an ATM cloud even when they do
not share the same IP address prefix. In order to enable it, the
Next Hop Server [KAT95] is introduced which can find an egress point
of the ATM cloud nearest to the given destination and resolves its
ATM address. A sort of query/response protocols between the
server(s) and clients and possibly server and server are specified.
After the ATM address of a desired egress point is resolved, the
client establishes a direct ATM connection to that point through ATM
signaling procedures [ATM3.1]. Once a direct ATM connection has been
set up through this procedure, IP datagrams do not have to experience
hop-by-hop IP processing but can be transmitted over the direct ATM
connection. Therefore, high throughput and low latency
communications become possible even if they go beyond IP subnet
boundaries. It should be noted that the provision of such direct ATM
connections does not mean disappearance of legacy routers which
interconnect distinct ATM-based IP subnets. For example, hop-by-hop
IP datagram forwarding function would still be required in the
following cases:

- When you want to transmit IP datagrams before direct ATM connection
  from an ingress point to an egress point of the ATM cloud is
  established

- When you neither require a certain QoS nor transmit large amount of
  IP datagrams for some communication

- When the direct ATM connection is not allowed by security or policy
  reasons

2) IP level resource reservation and flow support

Apart from investigation on specific datalink technology such as ATM,
resource reservation technologies for desired IP level flows have
been studied and are still under discussion. Their typical examples
are RSVP [RSVP13] and STII [RFC1819].

RSVP itself is not a connection oriented technology since datagrams
can be transmitted regardless of the result of the resource
reservation process. After a resource reservation process from a
receiver (or receivers) to a sender (or senders) is successfully
completed, RSVP-capable routers along the path of the flow reserve
their resources for datagram forwarding according to the requested
flow spec.

STII is regarded as a connection oriented IP which requires
connection setup process from a sender to a receiver (or receivers)
before transmitting datagrams. STII-capable routers along the path
of the requested connection reserve their resources for datagram
forwarding according to the flow spec.

Neither RSVP nor STII restrict underlying datalink networks since
their primary purpose is to let routers provide each IP flow with
desired forwarding quality (by controlling their datagram scheduling
rules). Since various datalink networks will coexist as well as ATM
in the future, these IP level resource reservation technologies would
be necessary in order to provide end-to-end IP flow with desired
bandwidth and QoS.

aking this background into consideration, we should be aware of
several issues which motivate our proposal.

- As of the time of writing, the ATM specific internetworking
  architecture proposed does not take into account interoperability
  with IP level resource reservation or connection setup protocols.
  In particular, operating RSVP in the NHRP-based ATM cloud seems to
  require much effort since RSVP is a soft-state receiver-oriented
  protocol with multicast capability as a default, while ATM with
  NHRP is a hard-state sender-oriented protocol which does not
  support multicast yet.

- Although RSVP or STII-based routers will provide each IP flow with
  a desired bandwidth and QoS, they have some native throughput
  limitations due to the processor-based IP forwarding mechanism
  compared with the hardware switching mechanism of ATM.

The main objective of our proposal is to resolve the above issues.

The proposed internetworking architecture makes the best use of the
property of ATM by extending legacy routers to handle future IP
features such as flow support and resource reservation with the help
of ATM's cell switching capabilities.

3.   Internetworking Architecture Based On the Cell Switch Router (CSR)

3.1 Overview

The Cell Switch Router (CSR) is a key network element of the proposed
internetworking architecture. The CSR provides cell switching
functionality in addition to conventional IP datagram forwarding.
Communications with high throughput and low latency, that are native
properties of ATM, become possible by using this cell switching
functionality even when the communications pass through IP subnetwork

boundaries. In an ATM internet composed of CSRs, VPI/VCI-based cell switching which bypasses datagram assembly/disassembly and IP header processing is possible at every CSR for communications which lend themselves to such (e.g., communications which require certain amount of bandwidth and QoS), while conventional hop-by-hop datagram forwarding based on the IP header is also possible at every CSR for other conventional communications.

By using such cell-level switching capabilities, the CSR is able to concatenate incoming and outgoing ATM VCs, although the concatenation in this case is controlled outside the ATM cloud (ATM's control/ management-plane) unlike conventional ATM switch nodes. That is, the CSR is attached to ATM networks via an ATM-UNI instead of NNI. By carrying out such VPI/VCI concatenations at multiple CSRs consecutively, ATM level connectivity composed of multiple ATM VCs, each of which connects adjacent CSRs (or CSR and hosts/routers), can be provided. We call such an ATM pipe "ATM Bypass-pipe" to differentiate it from "ATM VCC (VC connection)" provided by a single ATM datalink cloud through ATM signaling.

Example network configurations based on CSRs are shown in figure 1. An ATM datalink network may be a large cloud which accommodates multiple IP subnets X, Y and Z. Or several distinct ATM datalinks may accommodate single IP subnet X, Y and Z respectively. The latter configuration would be straightforward in discussing the CSR, but the CSR is also applicable to the former configuration as well. In addition, the CSR would be applicable as a router which interconnects multiple NHRP-based ATM clouds.

Two different kinds of ATM VCs are defined between adjacent CSRs or between CSR and ATM-attached hosts/routers.

1) Default-VC

   It is a general purpose VC used by any communications which select conventional hop-by-hop IP routed paths. All incoming cells received from this VC are assembled to IP datagrams and handled based on their IP headers. VCs set up in the Classical IP Model are classified into this category.

2) Dedicated-VC

   It is used by specific communications (IP flows) which are specified by, for example, any combination of the destination IP address/port, the source IP address/port or IPv6 flow label. It can be concatenated with other Dedicated-VCs which accommodate the same IP flow as it, and can constitute an ATM Bypass-pipe for those IP flows.

Ingress/egress nodes of the Bypass-pipe can be either CSRs or ATM-attached routers/hosts both of which speak a Bypass-pipe control protocol. (we call that "Bypass-capable nodes") On the other hand, intermediate nodes of the Bypass-pipe should be CSRs since they need to have cell switching capabilities as well as to speak the Bypass-pipe control protocol.

The route for a Bypass-pipe follows IP routing information in each CSR. In figure 1, IP datagrams from a source host or router X.1 to a destination host or router Z.1 are transferred over the route X.1 -> CSR1 -> CSR2 -> Z.1 regardless of whether the communication is on a hop-by-hop basis or Bypass-pipe basis. Routes for individual Dedicated-VCs which constitutes the Bypass-pipe X.1 --> Z.1 (X.1 -> CSR1, CSR1 -> CSR2, CSR2 -> Z.1) would be determined based on ATM routing protocols such as PNNI [PNNI1.0], and would be independent of IP level routing.

An example of IP datagram transmission mechanism is as follows.

o The host/router X.1 checks an identifier of each IP datagram, which may be the "destination IP address (prefix)", "source/destination IP address (prefix) pair", "destination IP address and port", "source IP address and Flow label (in IPv6)", and so on. Based on either of those identifiers, it determines over which VC the datagram should be transmitted.

o The CSR1/2 checks the VPI/VCI value of each incoming cell. When the mapping from the incoming interface/VPI/VCI to outgoing interface/VPI/VCI is found in an ATM routing table, it is directly forwarded to the specified interface through an ATM switch module. When the mapping in not found in the ATM routing table (or the table shows an IP module as an output interface), the cell is assembled to an IP datagram and then forwarded to an appropriate outgoing interface/VPI/VCI based on an identifier of the datagram.

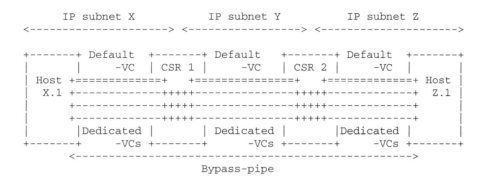

```
          IP subnet X              IP subnet Y              IP subnet Z
    <-------------------->  <----------------->  <-------------------->

   +-------+ Default  +-------+ Default  +-------+ Default  +-------+
   |       |    -VC   | CSR 1 |    -VC   | CSR 2 |    -VC   |       |
   | Host  +===========+      +===========+      +===========+ Host |
   |  X.1  +-----------++++---------------++++-----------+    Z.1  |
   |       +-----------++++---------------++++-----------+          |
   |       +-----------++++---------------++++-----------+          |
   |       |Dedicated |     | Dedicated |     |Dedicated |          |
   +-------+   -VCs  +-------+    -VCs +-------+   -VCs  +-------+
           <---------------------------------------------------->
                             Bypass-pipe
```

Figure 1   Internetworking Architecture based on CSR

3.2 Features

The main feature of the CSR-based internetworking architecture is the
same as that of the NHRP-based architecture in the sense that they
both provide direct ATM level connectivity beyond IP subnet
boundaries. There are, however, several notable differences in the
CSR-based architecture compared with the NHRP-based one as follows.

1) Relationship between IP routing and ATM routing

In the NHRP model, an egress point of the ATM network is first
determined in the next hop resolution phase based on IP level routing
information. Then the actual route for an ATM-VC to the obtained
egress point is determined in the ATM connection setup phase based on
ATM level routing information. Both kinds of routing information
would be calculated according to factors such as network topology and
available bandwidth for the large ATM cloud. The ATM routing will be
based on PNNI phase1 [PNNI1.0] while the IP routing will be based on
OSPF, BGP, IS-IS, etc. We need to manage two different routing
protocols over the large ATM cloud until Integtrated-PNNI [IPNNI96]
which takes both ATM level metric and IP level metric into account
will be phased in in the future.

In the CSR model, IP level routing determines an egress point of the
ATM cloud as well as determines inter-subnet level path to the point
that shows which CSRs it should pass through. ATM level routing
determines an intra-subnet level path for ATM-VCs (both Dedicated-VC
and Default-VC) only between adjacent nodes (CSRs or ATM-attached
hosts/routers). Since the roles of routing are hierarchically
subdivided into inter-subnet level (router level) and intra-subnet
level (ATM SW level), ATM routing does not have to operate all over

the ATM cloud but only in individual IP subnets independent from each
other. This will decrease the amount of information for ATM routing
protocol handling. But an end-to-end ATM path may not be optimal
compared with the NHRP model since the path should go through routers
at subnet boundaries in the CSR model.

2) Dynamic routing and redundancy support

   A CSR-based network can dynamically change routes for Bypass-pipes
   when related IP level routing information changes. Bypass-pipes
   related to the routing changes do not have to be torn down nor
   established from scratch since intermediate CSRs related to IP
   routing changes can follow them and change routes for related
   Bypass-pipes by themselves.

   The same things apply when some error or outage happens in any ATM
   nodes/links/routers on the route of a Bypass-pipe. CSRs that have
   noticed such errors or outages would change routes for related
   Bypass-pipes by themselves.

3) Interoperability with IP level resource reservation protocols in
   multicast environments

   As current NHRP specification assumes application of NHRP to unicast
   environments only, multicast IP flows should still be carried based
   on a hop-by-hop manner with multicast routers. In addition,
   realization of IP level resource reservation protocols such as RSVP
   over NHRP environments requires further investigation.

   The CSR-based internetworking architecture which keeps subnet-by-
   subnet internetworking with regard to any control protocol sequence
   can provide multicast Bypass-pipes without requiring any
   modifications in IP multicast over ATM [IPMC96] or multicast routing
   techniques. In addition, since the CSR can handle RSVP messages
   which are transmitted in a hop-by-hop manner, it can provide Bypass-
   pipes which satisfy QoS requirements by the cooperation of the RSVP
   and the Bypass-pipe control protocol.

4. Control Architecture for CSR

   Several issues with regard to a control architecture for the CSR are
   discussed in this section.

4.1 Network Reference Model

   In order to help understanding discussions in this section, the
   following network reference model is assumed. Source hosts S1, S2,
   and destination hosts D1, D2 are attached to Ethernets, while S3 and

D3 are attached to the ATM. Routers R1 and R5 are attached to
Ethernets only, while R2, R3 and R4 are attached to the ATM. The ATM
datalink for subnet #3 and subnet #4 can either be physically
separated datalinks or be the same datalink. In other words, R3 can
be either one-port or multi-port router.

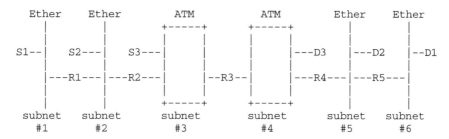

```
    Ether     Ether        ATM         ATM        Ether     Ether
      |         |       +-----+     +-----+         |         |
      |         |       |     |     |     |         |         |
   S1--|     S2---|    S3---|     |     |     |---D3   |---D2   |--D1
      |         |       |     |     |     |         |         |
      |---R1---|---R2---|     |   |--R3--|     |---R4---|---R5---|
      |         |       |     |     |     |         |         |
      |         |       +-----+     +-----+         |         |
    subnet    subnet      subnet      subnet      subnet    subnet
     #1        #2          #3          #4          #5        #6
```

                Figure 2 Network Reference Model

Bypass-pipes can be configured [S3 or R2]-->R3-->[D3 or R4]. That
means that S3, D3, R2, R3 and R4 need to speak Bypass-pipe control
protocol, and means that R3 needs to be the CSR. We use term
"Bypass-capable nodes" for hosts/routers which can speak Bypass-pipe
control protocol but are not necessarily CSRs.

As shown in this reference model, Bypass-pipe can be configured from
host to host (S3-->R3-->D3), router to host (R2-->R3-->D3), host to
router (S3-->R3-->R4), and router to router (R2-->R3-->R4).

4.2 Possible Use of Bypass-pipe

Possible use (or purposes) of Bypass-pipe provided by CSRs, in other
words, possible triggers that initiate Bypass-pipe setup procedure,
is discussed in this subsection.

Following two purposes for Bypass-pipe setup are assumed at present;

a) Provision of low latency path

This indicates cases in which end hosts or routers initiate a
Bypass-pipe setup procedure when they will transmit large amount of
datagrams toward a specific destination. For instance,

  - End hosts or routers initiate Bypass-pipe setup procedures based
    on the measurement of IP datagrams transmitted toward a certain
    destination.

- End hosts or routers initiate Bypass-pipe setup procedures when
  it detects datagrams with certain higher layer protocols such as
  ftp, nntp, http, etc.

Other triggers may be possible depending on the policy in each
network. In any case, the purpose of Bypass-pipe setup in each of
these cases is to reduce IP processing burden at intermediate routers
as well as to provide a communication path with low latency for burst
data transfer, rather than to provide end host applications with
specific bandwidth/QoS.

There would be no rule for determining bandwidth for such kinds of
Bypass-pipes since no explicit information about bandwidth/QoS
requirement by end hosts is available without IP-level resource
reservation protocols such as RSVP. Using UBR VCs as components of
the Bypass-pipe would be the easiest choice although there is no
guarantees for cell loss quality, while using other services such as
CBR/VBR/ABR with an adequate parameter tuning would be possible.

b) Provision of specific bandwidth/QoS requested by hosts

This indicates cases in which routers or end hosts initiate a
Bypass-pipe setup procedure by triggers related to IP-level
bandwidth/QoS request from end hosts. The "resource management
entity" in the host or router, which has received bandwidth/QoS
requests from applications or adjacent nodes may choose to
accommodate the requested IP flow to an existing VC or choose to
allocate a new Dedicated-VC for the requested IP flow. Selecting the
latter choice at each router can correspond to the trigger for
constituting a Bypass-pipe. When both an incoming VC and an outgoing
VC (or VCs) are dedicated to the same IP flow(s), those VCs can be
concatenated at the CSR (ATM cut-through) to constitute a Bypass-
pipe. Bandwidth for the Bypass-pipe (namely, individual VCs
constituting the Bypass-pipe) in this case would be determined based
on the bandwidth/QoS requirements by the end host which is conveyed
by, e.g., RSVP messages. The ATM service classes; e.g., CBR/VBR/ABR;
that would be selected depends on the IP-level service classes
requested by the end hosts.

Bypass-pipe provision for the purpose of b) will surely be beneficial
in the near future when related IP-level resource reservation
protocol will become available as well as when definitions of
individual service classes and flow specs offered to applications
become clear. On the other hand, Bypass-pipe setup for the purpose
of a) may be beneficial right now since it does not require
availability of IP-level resource reservation protocols. In that
sense, a) can be regarded as a kind of short-term use while b) is a
long-term use.

4.3 Variations of Bypass-pipe Control Architecture

A number of variations regarding Bypass-pipe control architecture are introduced. Items which are related to architectural variations are;

   o Ways of providing Dedicated-VCs

   o Channels for Bypass-pipe control message transfer

   o Bypass-pipe control procedures

Each of these items are discussed below.

4.3.1 Ways of Providing Dedicated-VCs

There are roughly three alternatives regarding the way of providing Dedicated-VCs in individual IP subnets as components of a Bypass-pipe.

a) On-demand SVC setup

Dedicated-VCs are set up in individual IP subnets each time you want to set up a Bypass-pipe through the ATM signaling procedure.

b) Picking up one from a bunch of (semi-)PVCs

Several VCs are set up beforehand between CSR and CSR, or CSR and other ATM-attached nodes (hosts/router) in each IP subnet. Unused VC is picked up as a Dedicated-VC from these PVCs in each IP subnet when a Bypass-pipe is set up.

c) Picking up one VCI in PVP/SVP

PVPs or SVPs are set up between CSR and CSR, or CSR and other ATM-attached nodes (hosts/routers) in each IP subnet. PVPs would be set up as a router/host initialization procedure, while SVPs, on the other hand, would be set up through ATM signaling when the first VC (either Default- or Dedicated-) setup request is initiated by either of some peer nodes. Then, Unused VCI value is picked up as a Dedicated-VC in the PVP/SVP in each IP subnet when a Bypass-pipe is set up. The SVP can be released through ATM signaling when no VCI value is in active state.

The best choice will be a) with regard to efficient network resource usage. However, you may go through three steps, ATMARP (for unicast [RFC1577] or multicast [IPMC96] in each IP subnet), SVC setup (in each IP subnet) and exchange of Bypass-pipe control message in this case. Whether a) is practical choice or not will depend on whether

you can allow larger Bypass-pipe setup time due to three-step
procedure mentioned above, or whether you can send datagrams over
Default-VCs in a hop-by-hop manner while waiting for the Bypass-pipe
set up.

In the case of b) or c), the issue of Bypass-pipe setup time will be
improved since SVC setup step can be skipped. In b), each node (CSR
or ATM-attached host/router) should specify some traffic descriptors
even for unused VCs, and the ATM datalink should reserve its desired
resource (such as VCI value and bandwidth) for them. In addition,
the ATM datalink may have to carry out UPC functions for those unused
VCs. Such burden would be reduced when you use UBR-PVCs and set peak
cell rate for each of them equal to link rate, but bandwidth/QoS for
the Bypass-pipe is not provided in this case. In c), on the other
hand, traffic descriptors which should be specified by each node for
the ATM datalink is not each VC's but VP's only. Resource
reservations for individual VCs will be carried out not as a
functionality of the ATM datalink but of each CSR or ATM-attached
host/router if necessary. A functionality which need to be provided
by the ATM datalink is control of VPs' bandwidth only such as UPC and
dynamic bandwidth negotiation if it would be widely available.

4.3.2 Channels for Bypass-pipe Control Message Transfer

There are several alternatives regarding the channels for managing
(setting up, releasing, and possibly changing the route of) a
Bypass-pipe. This subsection explains these alternatives and
discusses their properties.

Three alternatives are discussed, Inband control message, Outband
control message, and use of ATM signaling.

i) Inband Control Message

When setting up a Bypass-pipe, control messages are transmitted over
a Dedicated-VC which will eventually be used as a component of the
Bypass-pipe. These messages are handled at each CSR, and similar
messages are transmitted to the next-hop node over a Dedicated-VC
along the selected route (based on IP routing table). Unlike outband
message protocol described in ii), each message does not have to
indicate a Dedicated-VC which will be used since the message itself
is carried over "that" VC.

The inband control message can be either "datagram dedicated for
Bypass-pipe control" or "actual IP datagram" sent by user
application. Actual IP datagrams can be transmitted over Bypass-pipe
after it has been set up in the former case. In the latter case, on
the other hand, the first (or several) IP datagram(s) received from

an unused Dedicated-VC are analyzed at IP level and transmitted toward adequate next hop over an unused Dedicated-VC. Then incoming Dedicated-VC and outgoing Dedicated-VC are concatenated to construct a Bypass-pipe.

In inband control, Bypass-pipe control messages transmitted after a Bypass-pipe has been set up cannot be identified at intermediate CSRs since those messages are forwarded at cell level there. As a possible solution for this issue, intermediate CSRs can identify Bypass-pipe control messages by marking cell headers, e.g., PTI bit which indicates F5 OAM cell. With regard to Bypass-pipe release, explicit release message may not be necessary if individual CSRs administer the amount of traffic over each Dedicated-VC and deletes concatenation information for an inactive Bypass-pipe with their own decision.

ii) Outband Control Message

When a Bypass-pipe is set up or released, control messages are transmitted over VCs which are different from Dedicated-VCs used as components of the Bypass-pipe. Unlike inband message protocol described in i), each message has to indicate which Dedicated-VCs the message would like to control. Therefore, an identifier that uniquely discriminates a VC, which is not a VPI/VCI that is not identical at both endpoints of the VC, need to be defined and be given at VC initiation phase. However, an issue of control message transmission after a Bypass-pipe has been set up in inband case does not exist.

Four alternatives are possible regarding how to convey Bypass-pipe control messages hop-by-hop over ATM datalink networks.

1) Defines VC for Bypass-pipe control messages only.

2) Uses Default-VC and discriminates Bypass-pipe control messages from user datagrams by an LLC/SANP value in RFC1483 encapsulation.

3) Uses Default-VC and discriminates Bypass-pipe control messages from user datagrams by a protocol field value in IP header.

4) Uses Default-VC and discriminates Bypass-pipe control messages from user datagrams by a port ID in the UDP frame.

When we take into account interoperability with Bypass-incapable routers, 1) will not be a good choice. Whether we select 2) or 3) 4) depends on whether we should consider multiprotocol rather than IP only.

In the case of IP multicast, point-to-multipoint VCs in individual
subnets are concatenated at CSRs consecutively in order to constitute
end-to-end multicast tree. Above four alternatives may require the
same number of point-to-multipoint Defalut-VCs as the number of
requested point-to-multipoint Dedicated-VCs in multicast case. The
fifth alternative which can reduce the necessary number of VCs to
convey control messages in a multicast environment is;

5) Defines point-to-multipoint VC whose leaves are members of
   multicast group 224.0.0.1. All nodes which are members of at
   least one of active multicast group would become leaves of this
   point-to-multipoint VC.

Each upstream node may become a root of the point-to-multipoint VC,
or a sort of multicast server to which each upstream node transmits
cells over a point-to-point VC may become a root of that. In any
case, Bypass-pipe control messages for every multicast group are
transmitted to all nodes which are members of either of the group.
When a downstream node has received control messages which are not
related to a multicast group it belongs, it should discard them by
referring to a destination group address on their IP header.
Donwstream node would still need to use point-to-point VC to send
control messages toward upstream.

iii) Use of ATM Signaling Message

Supposing that ATM signaling messages can convey IP addresses (and
possibly port IDs) of source and destination, it may be possible that
ATM signaling messages be used as Bypass-pipe control messages also.
In that case, an ATM connection setup message indicates a setup of a
Dedicated-VC to an ATM address of a desirable next-hop IP node, and
also indicates a setup of a Bypass-pipe to an IP address (and
possibly port ID) of a target destination node. Information elements
for the Dedicated-VC setup (ATM address of a next-hop node,
bandwidth, QoS, etc.) are handled at ATM nodes, while information
elements for the Bypass-pipe setup (source and destination IP
addresses, possibly their port IDs, or flow label for IPv6, etc.) are
transparently transferred to the next-hop IP node. The next-hop IP
node accepts Dedicated-VC setup and handles such IP level information
elements.

ATM signaling messages can be transferred from receiver to sender as
well as sender to receiver when you set zero Forward Cell Rate and
non-zero Backward Cell Rate as an ATM traffic descriptor information
element in unicast case, or when Leaf Initiated Join capabilities
will become available in multicast case.

Issues in this method are,

- Information elements which specify IP level (and port level)
  information need to be defined, e.g., B-HLI or B-UUI, as an ATM
  signaling specification.

- It would be difficult to support soft-state Bypass-pipe control
  which transmits control messages periodically since ATM signaling
  is a hard-state protocol.

4.3.3 Bypass-pipe Control Procedures

This subsection discusses several items with regard to actual
procedures for Bypass-pipe control.

a) Distributed trigger vs. Centralized (restricted) trigger

The first item to be discussed is whether the functionality of
detecting a trigger of Dedicated-VC/Bypass-pipe control is
distributed to all the nodes (including CSRs and hosts/edge devices)
or restricted to specific nodes.

In the case of the distributed trigger, every node is regarded as
having a capability of detecting a trigger of Bypass-pipe setup or
termination. For example, every node detects datagrams for ftp, and
sets up (or fetches) a Dedicated-VC individually to construct a
Bypass-pipe. After setting up or fetching the Dedicated-VCs,
messages which informs (or requests) the transmission of the IP flow
over the Dedicated-VC are exchanged between adjacent nodes. That
enables peer nodes to share the same knowledge about the mapping
relationship between the IP flow and the Dedicated-VC. There is no
end-to-end message transmission in the Bypass-pipe control procedure
itself, but transmission between adjacent nodes only.

In the case of the centralized (or restricted) trigger, capability of
detecting a trigger of Bypass-pipe setup or termination is restricted
to nodes which are located at "the boundary of the CSR-cloud". The
boundary of the CSR-cloud signifies, for individual IP flows, the
node which is the first-hop or the last-hop CSR-capable node. For
example, a node which detects datagrams for ftp can initiate Bypass-
pipe setup procedure only when its previous hop is non-ATM or CSR-
incapable. In this case, Bypass-pipe control messages are originated
at the boundary of the CSR-cloud, and forwarded hop-by-hop toward
another side of the boundary, which is similar to ATM signaling
messages. The semantics of the messages may be the request of end-
to-end Bypass-pipe setup as well as notification or request of
mapping relationship between the IP flow and the Dedicated-VC.

b) Upstream-initiated control vs. Downstream-initiated control

The second item to be discussed is whether the setup of a Dedicated-
VC and the control procedure for constructing a Bypass-pipe are
initiated by upstream side or downstream side.

In the case of the upstream-initiated control, the upstream node
takes the initiative when setting up a Dedicated-VC for a specific IP
flow and creating the mapping relationship between the IP flow and
the Dedicated-VC. For example, a CSR which detects datagrams for ftp
sets up (or fetches) a Dedicated-VC toward its downstream neighbor
and notifies its downstream neighbor that it will transmit a specific
IP flow over the Dedicated-VC. This means that the downstream node
is requested to receive datagrams from the Dedicated-VC.

In the case of the downstream-initiated control, the downstream node
takes the initiative when setting up a Dedicated-VC for a specific IP
flow and creating the mapping relationship between the IP flow and
the Dedicated-VC. For example, a CSR which detects datagrams for ftp
sets up (or fetches) a Dedicated-VC toward its upstream neighbor and
requests its upstream neighbor to transmit a specific IP flow over
the Dedicated-VC. This means that the upstream node is requested to
transmit the IP flow over the Dedicated-VC.

c) Hard-state management vs. Soft-state management

The third item to be discussed is whether the control (setup,
maintain, and release) of the Bypass-pipe is based on hard-state or
soft-state.

In hard-state management, individual nodes transmit Bypass-pipe
control messages only when they want to notify or request any change
in their neighbors' state. They should wait for an acknowledgement
of the message before they change their internal state. For example,
after setting up a Bypass-pipe, it is maintained until either of a
peer nodes transmits a message to release the Bypass-pipe.

In soft-state management, individual nodes periodically transmit
Bypass-pipe control messages in order to maintain their neighbors'
state. They do not have to wait for an acknowledgement of the
message before they changes its internal state. For example, even
after setting up a Bypass-pipe, either of a peer nodes is required to
periodically transmit refresh messages to its neighbor in order to
maintain the Bypass-pipe.

5. Security Considerations

Security issues are not discussed in this memo.

6. Summary

    Basic concept of Cell Switch Router (CSR) are clarified and control
    architecture for CSR is discussed. A number of methods to control
    Bypass-pipe will be possible each of which has its own advantages and
    disadvantages. Further investigation and discussion will be
    necessary to design control protocol which may depend on the
    requirements by users.

7. References

    [IPMC96] Armitage, G., "Support for Multicast over UNI 3.0/3.1 based
    ATM Networks", RFC 2022, November 1996.

    [ATM3.1] The ATM-Forum, "ATM User-Network Interface Specification,
    v.3.1", Sept. 1994.

    [RSVP13] Braden, R., et al., "Resource ReSerVation Protocol (RSVP),
    Version 1 Functional Specification", Work in Progress.

    [IPNNI96] R. Callon, et al., "Issues and Approaches for Integrated
    PNNI", The ATM Forum Contribution No. 96-0355, April 1996.

    [NHRP09] Luciani, J., et al., "NBMA Next Hop Resolution Protocol
    (NHRP)", Work in Progress.

    [PNNI1.0] The ATM-Forum, "P-NNI Specification Version 1.0", March
    1996.

    [RFC1483] Heinanen, J., "Multiprotocol Encapsulation over ATM
    Adaptation Layer 5", RFC 1483, July 1993.

    [RFC1577] Laubach, M., "Classical IP and ARP over ATM", RFC 1577,
    October 1993.

    [RFC1819] Delgrossi, L, and L. Berger, "Internet STream Protocol
    Version 2 (STII) Protocol Specification Version ST2+", RFC 1819,
    August 1995.

8.   Authors' Addresses

Yasuhiro Katsube
R&D Center, Toshiba
1 Komukai Toshiba-cho, Saiwai-ku, Kawasaki 210
Japan
Phone : +81-44-549-2238
EMail : katsube@isl.rdc.toshiba.co.jp

Ken-ichi Nagami
R&D Center, Toshiba
1 Komukai Toshiba-cho, Saiwai-ku, Kawasaki 210
Japan
Phone : +81-44-549-2238
EMail : nagami@isl.rdc.toshiba.co.jp

Hiroshi Esaki
R&D Center, Toshiba
1 Komukai Toshiba-cho, Saiwai-ku, Kawasaki 210
Japan
Phone : +81-44-549-2238
EMail : hiroshi@isl.rdc.toshiba.co.jp

Network Working Group   Y. Rekhter
Request for Comments: 2105   B. Davie
Category: Informational   D. Katz
                                                          E. Rosen
                                                        G. Swallow
                                              Cisco Systems, Inc.
                                                    February 1997

           Cisco Systems' Tag Switching Architecture Overview

Status of this Memo

IESG Note:

   This protocol is NOT the product of an IETF working group nor is it a
   standards track document. It has not necessarily benefited from the
   widespread and in depth community review that standards track
   documents receive.

Abstract

   This document provides an overview of a novel approach to network
   layer packet forwarding, called tag switching. The two main
   components of the tag switching architecture - forwarding and
   control - are described. Forwarding is accomplished using simple
   label-swapping techniques, while the existing network layer routing
   protocols plus mechanisms for binding and distributing tags are used
   for control. Tag switching can retain the scaling properties of IP,
   and can help improve the scalability of IP networks. While tag
   switching does not rely on ATM, it can straightforwardly be applied
   to ATM switches. A range of tag switching applications and deployment
   scenarios are described.

Table of Contents

1. Introduction

Continuous growth of the Internet demands higher bandwidth within the Internet Service Providers (ISPs). However, growth of the Internet is not the only driving factor for higher bandwidth - demand for higher bandwidth also comes from emerging multimedia applications. Demand for higher bandwidth, in turn, requires higher forwarding performance (packets per second) by routers, for both multicast and unicast traffic.

The growth of the Internet also demands improved scaling properties of the Internet routing system. The ability to contain the volume of routing information maintained by individual routers and the ability to build a hierarchy of routing knowledge are essential to support a high quality, scalable routing system.

We see the need to improve forwarding performance while at the same time adding routing functionality to support multicast, allowing more flexible control over how traffic is routed, and providing the ability to build a hierarchy of routing knowledge. Moreover, it becomes more and more crucial to have a routing system that can support graceful evolution to accommodate new and emerging requirements.

Tag switching is a technology that provides an efficient solution to these challenges. Tag switching blends the flexibility and rich functionality provided by Network Layer routing with the simplicity provided by the label swapping forwarding paradigm. The simplicity of the tag switching forwarding paradigm (label swapping) enables improved forwarding performance, while maintaining competitive price/performance. By associating a wide range of forwarding granularities with a tag, the same forwarding paradigm can be used to support a wide variety of routing functions, such as destination-based routing, multicast, hierarchy of routing knowledge, and flexible routing control. Finally, a combination of simple forwarding, a wide range of forwarding granularities, and the ability to evolve routing functionality while preserving the same forwarding paradigm enables a routing system that can gracefully evolve to accommodate new and emerging requirements.

The rest of the document is organized as follows. Section 2
introduces the main components of tag switching, forwarding and
control. Section 3 describes the forwarding component. Section 4
describes the control component. Section 5 describes how tag
switching could be used with ATM. Section 6 describes the use of tag
switching to help provide a range of qualities of service. Section 7
briefly describes possible deployment scenarios. Section 8 summarizes
the results.

2. Tag Switching components

Tag switching consists of two components: forwarding and control.
The forwarding component uses the tag information (tags) carried by
packets and the tag forwarding information maintained by a tag switch
to perform packet forwarding. The control component is responsible
for maintaining correct tag forwarding information among a group of
interconnected tag switches.

3. Forwarding component

The fundamental forwarding paradigm employed by tag switching is
based on the notion of label swapping. When a packet with a tag is
received by a tag switch, the switch uses the tag as an index in its
Tag Information Base (TIB). Each entry in the TIB consists of an
incoming tag, and one or more sub-entries of the form (outgoing tag,
outgoing interface, outgoing link level information). If the switch
finds an entry with the incoming tag equal to the tag carried in the
packet, then for each (outgoing tag, outgoing interface, outgoing
link level information) in the entry the switch replaces the tag in
the packet with the outgoing tag, replaces the link level information
(e.g MAC address) in the packet with the outgoing link level
information, and forwards the packet over the outgoing interface.

From the above description of the forwarding component we can make
several observations. First, the forwarding decision is based on the
exact match algorithm using a fixed length, fairly short tag as an
index. This enables a simplified forwarding procedure, relative to
longest match forwarding traditionally used at the network layer.
This in turn enables higher forwarding performance (higher packets
per second). The forwarding procedure is simple enough to allow a
straightforward hardware implementation.

A second observation is that the forwarding decision is independent
of the tag's forwarding granularity. For example, the same forwarding
algorithm applies to both unicast and multicast - a unicast entry
would just have a single (outgoing tag, outgoing interface, outgoing

link level information) sub-entry, while a multicast entry may have
one or more (outgoing tag, outgoing interface, outgoing link level
information) sub-entries. (For multi-access links, the outgoing link
level information in this case would include a multicast MAC
address.) This illustrates how with tag switching the same forwarding
paradigm can be used to support different routing functions (e.g.,
unicast, multicast, etc...)

The simple forwarding procedure is thus essentially decoupled from
the control component of tag switching. New routing (control)
functions can readily be deployed without disturbing the forwarding
paradigm. This means that it is not necessary to re-optimize
forwarding performance (by modifying either hardware or software) as
new routing functionality is added.

3.1. Tag encapsulation

Tag information can be carried in a packet in a variety of ways:

   - as a small "shim" tag header inserted between the layer 2 and
   the Network Layer headers;

   - as part of the layer 2 header, if the layer 2 header provides
   adequate semantics (e.g., ATM, as discussed below);

   - as part of the Network Layer header (e.g., using the Flow Label
   field in IPv6 with appropriately modified semantics).

It is therefore possible to implement tag switching over virtually
any media type including point-to-point links, multi-access links,
and ATM.

Observe also that the tag forwarding component is Network Layer
independent. Use of control component(s) specific to a particular
Network Layer protocol enables the use of tag switching with
different Network Layer protocols.

4. Control component

Essential to tag switching is the notion of binding between a tag and
Network Layer routing (routes). To provide good scaling
characteristics, while also accommodating diverse routing
functionality, tag switching supports a wide range of forwarding
granularities. At one extreme a tag could be associated (bound) to a
group of routes (more specifically to the Network Layer Reachability
Information of the routes in the group). At the other extreme a tag
could be bound to an individual application flow (e.g., an RSVP
flow). A tag could also be bound to a multicast tree.

The control component is responsible for creating tag bindings, and
then distributing the tag binding information among tag switches.
The control component is organized as a collection of modules, each
designed to support a particular routing function. To support new
routing functions, new modules can be added. The following describes
some of the modules.

4.1. Destination-based routing

In this section we describe how tag switching can support
destination-based routing. Recall that with destination-based routing
a router makes a forwarding decision based on the destination address
carried in a packet and the information stored in the Forwarding
Information Base (FIB) maintained by the router. A router constructs
its FIB by using the information the router receives from routing
protocols (e.g., OSPF, BGP).

To support destination-based routing with tag switching, a tag
switch, just like a router, participates in routing protocols (e.g.,
OSPF, BGP), and constructs its FIB using the information it receives
from these protocols.

There are three permitted methods for tag allocation and Tag
Information Base (TIB) management: (a) downstream tag allocation, (b)
downstream tag allocation on demand, and (c) upstream tag allocation.
In all cases, a switch allocates tags and binds them to address
prefixes in its FIB. In downstream allocation, the tag that is
carried in a packet is generated and bound to a prefix by the switch
at the downstream end of the link (with respect to the direction of
data flow). In upstream allocation, tags are allocated and bound at
the upstream end of the link. `On demand' allocation means that tags
will only be allocated and distributed by the downstream switch when
it is requested to do so by the upstream switch. Methods (b) and (c)
are most useful in ATM networks (see Section 5). Note that in
downstream allocation, a switch is responsible for creating tag
bindings that apply to incoming data packets, and receives tag
bindings for outgoing packets from its neighbors. In upstream
allocation, a switch is responsible for creating tag bindings for
outgoing tags, i.e. tags that are applied to data packets leaving the
switch, and receives bindings for incoming tags from its neighbors.

The downstream tag allocation scheme operates as follows: for each
route in its FIB the switch allocates a tag, creates an entry in its
Tag Information Base (TIB) with the incoming tag set to the allocated
tag, and then advertises the binding between the (incoming) tag and
the route to other adjacent tag switches. The advertisement could be
accomplished by either piggybacking the binding on top of the
existing routing protocols, or by using a separate Tag Distribution

Protocol [TDP]. When a tag switch receives tag binding information for a route, and that information was originated by the next hop for that route, the switch places the tag (carried as part of the binding information) into the outgoing tag of the TIB entry associated with the route. This creates the binding between the outgoing tag and the route.

With the downstream tag allocation on demand scheme, operation is as follows. For each route in its FIB, the switch identifies the next hop for that route. It then issues a request (via TDP) to the next hop for a tag binding for that route. When the next hop receives the request, it allocates a tag, creates an entry in its TIB with the incoming tag set to the allocated tag, and then returns the binding between the (incoming) tag and the route to the switch that sent the original request. When the switch receives the binding information, the switch creates an entry in its TIB, and sets the outgoing tag in the entry to the value received from the next hop.

The upstream tag allocation scheme is used as follows. If a tag switch has one or more point-to-point interfaces, then for each route in its FIB whose next hop is reachable via one of these interfaces, the switch allocates a tag, creates an entry in its TIB with the outgoing tag set to the allocated tag, and then advertises to the next hop (via TDP) the binding between the (outgoing) tag and the route. When a tag switch that is the next hop receives the tag binding information, the switch places the tag (carried as part of the binding information) into the incoming tag of the TIB entry associated with the route.

Once a TIB entry is populated with both incoming and outgoing tags, the tag switch can forward packets for routes bound to the tags by using the tag switching forwarding algorithm (as described in Section 3).

When a tag switch creates a binding between an outgoing tag and a route, the switch, in addition to populating its TIB, also updates its FIB with the binding information. This enables the switch to add tags to previously untagged packets.

To understand the scaling properties of tag switching in conjunction with destination-based routing, observe that the total number of tags that a tag switch has to maintain can not be greater than the number of routes in the switch's FIB. Moreover, in some cases a single tag could be associated with a group of routes, rather than with a single route. Thus, much less state is required than would be the case if tags were allocated to individual flows.

In general, a tag switch will try to populate its TIB with incoming
and outgoing tags for all routes to which it has reachability, so
that all packets can be forwarded by simple label swapping. Tag
allocation is thus driven by topology (routing), not traffic - it is
the existence of a FIB entry that causes tag allocations, not the
arrival of data packets.

Use of tags associated with routes, rather than flows, also means
that there is no need to perform flow classification procedures for
all the flows to determine whether to assign a tag to a flow. That,
in turn, simplifies the overall scheme, and makes it more robust and
stable in the presence of changing traffic patterns.

Note that when tag switching is used to support destination-based
routing, tag switching does not completely eliminate the need to
perform normal Network Layer forwarding. First of all, to add a tag
to a previously untagged packet requires normal Network Layer
forwarding. This function could be performed by the first hop router,
or by the first router on the path that is able to participate in tag
switching. In addition, whenever a tag switch aggregates a set of
routes (e.g., by using the technique of hierarchical routing), into a
single tag, and the routes do not share a common next hop, the switch
needs to perform Network Layer forwarding for packets carrying that
tag. However, one could observe that the number of places where
routes get aggregated is smaller than the total number of places
where forwarding decisions have to be made. Moreover, quite often
aggregation is applied to only a subset of the routes maintained by a
tag switch. As a result, on average a packet can be forwarded most of
the time using the tag switching algorithm.

4.2. Hierarchy of routing knowledge

The IP routing architecture models a network as a collection of
routing domains. Within a domain, routing is provided via interior
routing (e.g., OSPF), while routing across domains is provided via
exterior routing (e.g., BGP). However, all routers within domains
that carry transit traffic (e.g., domains formed by Internet Service
Providers) have to maintain information provided by not just interior
routing, but exterior routing as well. That creates certain problems.
First of all, the amount of this information is not insignificant.
Thus it places additional demand on the resources required by the
routers. Moreover, increase in the volume of routing information
quite often increases routing convergence time. This, in turn,
degrades the overall performance of the system.

Tag switching allows the decoupling of interior and exterior routing,
so that only tag switches at the border of a domain would be required
to maintain routing information provided by exterior routing, while

all other switches within the domain would just maintain routing
information provided by the domain's interior routing (which is
usually significantly smaller than the exterior routing information).
This, in turn, reduces the routing load on non-border switches, and
shortens routing convergence time.

To support this functionality, tag switching allows a packet to carry
not one but a set of tags, organized as a stack. A tag switch could
either swap the tag at the top of the stack, or pop the stack, or
swap the tag and push one or more tags into the stack.

When a packet is forwarded between two (border) tag switches in
different domains, the tag stack in the packet contains just one tag.
However, when a packet is forwarded within a domain, the tag stack in
the packet contains not one, but two tags (the second tag is pushed
by the domain's ingress border tag switch). The tag at the top of
the stack provides packet forwarding to an appropriate egress border
tag switch, while the next tag in the stack provides correct packet
forwarding at the egress switch. The stack is popped by either the
egress switch or by the penultimate (with respect to the egress
switch) switch.

The control component used in this scenario is fairly similar to the
one used with destination-based routing. In fact, the only essential
difference is that in this scenario the tag binding information is
distributed both among physically adjacent tag switches, and among
border tag switches within a single domain. One could also observe
that the latter (distribution among border switches) could be
trivially accommodated by very minor extensions to BGP (via a
separate Tag Binding BGP attribute).

4.3. Multicast

Essential to multicast routing is the notion of spanning trees.
Multicast routing procedures (e.g., PIM) are responsible for
constructing such trees (with receivers as leafs), while multicast
forwarding is responsible for forwarding multicast packets along such
trees.

To support a multicast forwarding function with tag switching, each
tag switch associates a tag with a multicast tree as follows. When a
tag switch creates a multicast forwarding entry (either for a shared
or for a source-specific tree), and the list of outgoing interfaces
for the entry, the switch also creates local tags (one per outgoing
interface). The switch creates an entry in its TIB and populates
(outgoing tag, outgoing interface, outgoing MAC header) with this
information for each outgoing interface, placing a locally generated
tag in the outgoing tag field. This creates a binding between a

multicast tree and the tags. The switch then advertises over each
outgoing interface associated with the entry the binding between the
tag (associated with this interface) and the tree.

When a tag switch receives a binding between a multicast tree and a
tag from another tag switch, if the other switch is the upstream
neighbor (with respect to the multicast tree), the local switch
places the tag carried in the binding into the incoming tag component
of the TIB entry associated with the tree.

When a set of tag switches are interconnected via a multiple-access
subnetwork, the tag allocation procedure for multicast has to be
coordinated among the switches. In all other cases tag allocation
procedure for multicast could be the same as for tags used with
destination-based routing.

4.4. Flexible routing (explicit routes)

One of the fundamental properties of destination-based routing is
that the only information from a packet that is used to forward the
packet is the destination address. While this property enables highly
scalable routing, it also limits the ability to influence the actual
paths taken by packets. This, in turn, limits the ability to evenly
distribute traffic among multiple links, taking the load off highly
utilized links, and shifting it towards less utilized links. For
Internet Service Providers (ISPs) who support different classes of
service, destination-based routing also limits their ability to
segregate different classes with respect to the links used by these
classes. Some of the ISPs today use Frame Relay or ATM to overcome
the limitations imposed by destination-based routing. Tag switching,
because of the flexible granularity of tags, is able to overcome
these limitations without using either Frame Relay or ATM.

To provide forwarding along the paths that are different from the
paths determined by the destination-based routing, the control
component of tag switching allows installation of tag bindings in tag
switches that do not correspond to the destination-based routing
paths.

5. Tag switching with ATM

Since the tag switching forwarding paradigm is based on label
swapping, and since ATM forwarding is also based on label swapping,
tag switching technology can readily be applied to ATM switches by
implementing the control component of tag switching.

The tag information needed for tag switching can be carried in the
VCI field. If two levels of tagging are needed, then the VPI field
could be used as well, although the size of the VPI field limits the
size of networks in which this would be practical. However, for most
applications of one level of tagging the VCI field is adequate.

To obtain the necessary control information, the switch should be
able (at a minimum) to participate as a peer in Network Layer routing
protocols (e.g., OSPF, BGP). Moreover, if the switch has to perform
routing information aggregation, then to support destination-based
unicast routing the switch should be able to perform Network Layer
forwarding for some fraction of the traffic as well.

Supporting the destination-based routing function with tag switching
on an ATM switch may require the switch to maintain not one, but
several tags associated with a route (or a group of routes with the
same next hop). This is necessary to avoid the interleaving of
packets which arrive from different upstream tag switches, but are
sent concurrently to the same next hop. Either the downstream tag
allocation on demand or the upstream tag allocation scheme could be
used for the tag allocation and TIB maintenance procedures with ATM
switches.

Therefore, an ATM switch can support tag switching, but at the
minimum it needs to implement Network Layer routing protocols, and
the tag switching control component on the switch. It may also need
to support some network layer forwarding.

Implementing tag switching on an ATM switch would simplify
integration of ATM switches and routers - an ATM switch capable of
tag switching would appear as a router to an adjacent router. That
could provide a viable, more scalable alternative to the overlay
model. It also removes the necessity for ATM addressing, routing and
signalling schemes. Because the destination-based forwarding approach
described in section 4.1 is topology driven rather than traffic
driven, application of this approach to ATM switches does not high
call setup rates, nor does it depend on the longevity of flows.

Implementing tag switching on an ATM switch does not preclude the
ability to support a traditional ATM control plane (e.g., PNNI) on
the same switch. The two components, tag switching and the ATM
control plane, would operate in a Ships In the Night mode (with
VPI/VCI space and other resources partitioned so that the components
do not interact).

6. Quality of service

Two mechanisms are needed for providing a range of qualities of
service to packets passing through a router or a tag switch. First,
we need to classify packets into different classes. Second, we need
to ensure that the handling of packets is such that the appropriate
QOS characteristics (bandwidth, loss, etc.) are provided to each
class.

Tag switching provides an easy way to mark packets as belonging to a
particular class after they have been classified the first time.
Initial classification would be done using information carried in the
network layer or higher layer headers. A tag corresponding to the
resultant class would then be applied to the packet. Tagged packets
can then be efficiently handled by the tag switching routers in their
path without needing to be reclassified. The actual packet scheduling
and queueing is largely orthogonal - the key point here is that tag
switching enables simple logic to be used to find the state that
identifies how the packet should be scheduled.

The exact use of tag switching for QOS purposes depends a great deal
on how QOS is deployed. If RSVP is used to request a certain QOS for
a class of packets, then it would be necessary to allocate a tag
corresponding to each RSVP session for which state is installed at a
tag switch. This might be done by TDP or by extension of RSVP.

7. Tag switching migration strategies

Since tag switching is performed between a pair of adjacent tag
switches, and since the tag binding information could be distributed
on a pairwise basis, tag switching could be introduced in a fairly
simple, incremental fashion. For example, once a pair of adjacent
routers are converted into tag switches, each of the switches would
tag packets destined to the other, thus enabling the other switch to
use tag switching. Since tag switches use the same routing protocols
as routers, the introduction of tag switches has no impact on
routers. In fact, a tag switch connected to a router acts just as a
router from the router's perspective.

As more and more routers are upgraded to enable tag switching, the
scope of functionality provided by tag switching widens. For example,
once all the routers within a domain are upgraded to support tag
switching, in becomes possible to start using the hierarchy of
routing knowledge function.

8. Summary

In this document we described the tag switching technology. Tag
switching is not constrained to a particular Network Layer protocol -
it is a multiprotocol solution. The forwarding component of tag
switching is simple enough to facilitate high performance forwarding,
and may be implemented on high performance forwarding hardware such
as ATM switches. The control component is flexible enough to support
a wide variety of routing functions, such as destination-based
routing, multicast routing, hierarchy of routing knowledge, and
explicitly defined routes. By allowing a wide range of forwarding
granularities that could be associated with a tag, we provide both
scalable and functionally rich routing. A combination of a wide range
of forwarding granularities and the ability to evolve the control
component fairly independently from the forwarding component results
in a solution that enables graceful introduction of new routing
functionality to meet the demands of a rapidly evolving computer
networking environment.

9. Security Considerations

Security issues are not discussed in this memo.

10. Intellectual Property Considerations

Cisco Systems may seek patent or other intellectual property
protection for some or all of the technologies disclosed in this
document. If any standards arising from this document are or become
protected by one or more patents assigned to Cisco Systems, Cisco
intends to disclose those patents and license them on reasonable and
non-discriminatory terms.

11. Acknowledgments

Significant contributions to this work have been made by Anthony
Alles, Fred Baker, Paul Doolan, Dino Farinacci, Guy Fedorkow, Jeremy
Lawrence, Arthur Lin, Morgan Littlewood, Keith McCloghrie, and Dan
Tappan.

12. Authors' Addresses

Yakov Rekhter
Cisco Systems, Inc.
170 Tasman Drive
San Jose, CA, 95134

EMail: yakov@cisco.com

Bruce Davie
Cisco Systems, Inc.
250 Apollo Drive
Chelmsford, MA, 01824

EMail: bsd@cisco.com

Dave Katz
Cisco Systems, Inc.
170 Tasman Drive
San Jose, CA, 95134

EMail: dkatz@cisco.com

Eric Rosen
Cisco Systems, Inc.
250 Apollo Drive
Chelmsford, MA, 01824

EMail: erosen@cisco.com

George Swallow
Cisco Systems, Inc.
250 Apollo Drive
Chelmsford, MA, 01824

EMail: swallow@cisco.com

Network Working Group   K. Nagami
Request for Comments: 2129   Y. Katsube
Category: Informational   Y. Shobatake
                                                                A. Mogi
                                                           S. Matsuzawa
                                                              T. Jinmei
                                                               H. Esaki
                                                      Toshiba R&D Center
                                                             April 1997

      Toshiba's Flow Attribute Notification Protocol (FANP) Specification

Status of this Memo

   This memo provides information for the Internet community. This memo
   does not specify an Internet standard of any kind. Distribution of
   this memo is unlimited.

Abstract

   This memo discusses Flow Attribute Notification Protocol (FANP),
   which is a protocol between neighbor nodes for the management of
   cut-through packet forwarding functionalities. In cut-through packet
   forwarding, a router doesn't have to perform conventional IP packet
   processing for received packets. FANP indicates mapping information
   between a datalink connection and a packet flow to the neighbor node
   and helps a pair of nodes manage the mapping information. By using
   FANP, routers (e.g., CSR; Cell Switch Router) can forward incoming
   packets based on their datalink-level connection identifiers,
   bypassing usual IP packet processing. The design policy of the FANP
   is;

        (1) soft-state cut-through path (Dedicated-VC) management
        (2) protocol between neighbor nodes instead of end-to-end
        (3) applicable to any connection oriented datalink platform

1. Background

   Due to the scalability requirement, connection oriented (CO) datalink
   platforms, e.g., ATM and Frame Relay, are going to be used as well as
   connection less (CL) datalink platforms, e.g., Ethernet and FDDI.
   One of the important features of the CO datalink is the presence of a
   datalink-level connection identifier. In the CO datalink, we can
   establish multiple virtual connections (VCs) with their VC
   identifiers among the nodes. When we aggregate packets that have the
   same direction (e.g., having the same destination IP address) into a
   single VC, we can forward the packets in the VC without IP

RFC 2129

processing. With this configuration, routers can decide which node
is the next-hop for the packets based on the VC identifier. CSRs [1]
can forward the incoming packets using an ATM switch engine bypassing
the conventional IP processing. According to the ingress VPI/VCI
value with ingress interface information, CSR determines the egress
interface and egress VPI/VCI value.

In order to configure the cut-through packet forwarding state, a pair
of neighbor nodes have to share the mapping information between the
packet flow and the datalink VC. FANP (Flow Attribute Notification
Protocol) described in this memo is the protocol to configure and
manage the cut-through packet forwarding state.

2.   Protocol Requirements and Future Enhancement

2.1 Protocol Requirements

The followings are the protocol requirements for FANP.

(1) Applicable to various types of CO datalink platforms

(2) Available with various connection types (i.e., SVC, PVC, VP)

(3) Robust operation
    The system should operate correctly even under the following
    conditions.

    (a) VC failure
        Some systems can detect VC failure as the function of
        datalink (e.g., OAM function in the ATM). However, we can
        not assume all nodes in the system can detect VC failure.
        The system has to operate correctly, assuming that every
        node can not detect VC failure.

    (b) Message loss
        Control messages in the FANP may be lost. The system has to
        operate correctly, even when some control messages are lost.

    (c Node failure
        A node may be down without any explicit notification to its
        neighbors. The system has to operate correctly, even with
        node failure.

Though FANP is not the protocol only for ATM, the following
discussion assumes that the datalink is an ATM network.

2.2 Future Enhancement

    The followings are the future enhancements to be done.

        (1) Aggregated flow

            In this memo, we define the flow which contain source and
            destination IP address. As this may require many VC
            resources, we also need a new definition of aggregated flow
            which includes several end-to-end flows. The concrete
            definition of the aggregated flow is for future study.

        (2) Providing multicast service
        (3) Supporting IP level QOS signaling like RSVP
        (4) Supporting IPv6

3. Terminology and Definition

    o VCID (Virtual Connection IDentifier)
      Since VPI/VCI values at the origination and the termination points
      of a VC (and VP) may not be the same, we need an identifier to
      uniquely identify the datalink connection between neighbor nodes.
      We define this identifier as a VCID. Currently, only one type of
      VCID is defined. This VCID contains the ESI (End System
      Identifier) of a source node and the unique identifier within a
      source node.

    o Flow ID (Flow IDentifier)
      IP level packet flow is identified by some parameters in a packet.
      Currently, only one type of flow ID is defined. This flow ID
      contains a source IP address and a destination IP address. Note
      that flow ID used in this specification is not the same as the
      flow-id specified in IPv6.

    o Cut-through packet forwarding
      Packets are forwarded without any IP processing at the router
      using the datalink level information (e.g.,VPI/VCI).
      Internetworking level information (e.g., destination IP address)
      is mapped to the corresponding datalink-level identifier by using
      the FANP.

    o Hop-by-Hop packet forwarding
      Packets are forwarded using IP level information like conventional
      routers. In ATM, cells are re-assembled into packets at the
      router to analyze the IP header.

o Default-VC
  Default-VC is used for hop-by-hop packet forwarding. Cells
  received from the Default-VC are reassembled into IP packets.
  Conventional IP processing is performed for these packets. The
  encapsulation over the Default-VC is LLC for routed non-ISO
  protocols defined by RFC1483 [3].

o Dedicated-VC
  Dedicated-VC is used for the specific IP packet flow identified by
  the flow-ID. When the flow-ID for an incoming VC and an outgoing
  VC are the same at a CSR, it can forward the packets belonging to
  the flow through the cut-through packet forwarding. The
  encapsulation over the Dedicated-VC is LLC for routed non-ISO
  protocols defined by RFC1483 [3].

o Cut-through trigger
  When a FANP capable node receives a trigger packet, it tries to
  establish Dedicated-VC and to notify the mapping information
  between the Dedicated-VC and the IP packet flow which the received
  trigger packet belongs to. Trigger packets are defined by the
  port-ID of TCP/UDP with the local policy of each FANP capable
  node. In general, they would be the port-ID's of sessions with a
  long life-time and/or with large amount of packets; e.g., http,
  ftp and nntp. Future implementation will include other triggers
  such as an arrival of resource reservation request.

4. Protocol Overview

   Figure 1 shows an operational overview of FANP. In the figure, a
   cut-through packet forwarding path is established from host 1 (H1) to
   host 2 (H2) using two Dedicated-VCs. H1 and H2 are connected to
   Ethernets, and R1, R2 and R3 are routers which can speak FANP. R1
   and R3 have both an ATM interface and an Ethernet interface. R2 has
   two ATM interfaces.

   When R1 receives an IP packet from H1, R1 analyzes the payload of the
   received IP packet whether it is a trigger packet or not. When the
   received packet is a trigger packet, R1 fetches a Dedicated-VC to its
   downstream neighbor(R2) and sends FANP messages. FANP is effective
   between the neighboring nodes only. The same procedure would be
   performed between R2 and R3 independently from the procedure between
   R1 and R2. The flow-ID of the packet flow from H1 to H2 is
   represented as id(H1,H2). Here, id(H1,H2) is the set of the IP
   address of H1 and that of H2.

The Dedicated-VC is released when no packet is transferred on it for
a given period. We do not need to explicitly indicate release of the
Dedicated-VC to the neighbor node, since the state management in FANP
is of soft-state, rather than of hard-state.

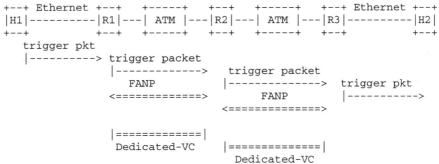

```
+--+ Ethernet +--+   +-----+   +--+   +-----+   +--+ Ethernet +--+
|H1|----------|R1|---| ATM |---|R2|---| ATM |---|R3|----------|H2|
+--+          +--+   +-----+   +--+   +-----+   +--+          +--+
 trigger pkt
 |----------> trigger packet
             |------------->   trigger packet
                FANP         |-------------> trigger pkt
             <=============>      FANP       |----------->
                             <=============>

             |============|
             Dedicated-VC   |=============|
                            Dedicated-VC
```

Figure 1. Trigger packet and FANP initiation

5. Protocol Sequence

FANP has the following five procedures, that are (1) Dedicated-VC
selection, (2) VCID negotiation, (3) flow-ID notification, (4)
Dedicated-VC refresh and (5) Dedicated-VC release. Procedures (2),
(3) and (4) have nothing to do with the kind of the Dedicated-
VC;i.e.,SVC,PVC or VP. On the contrary, the procedures (1) and (5)
with SVC are different from the procedures with PVC and with VP.

The detailed procedures are described in the following subsections.

5.1 Dedicated-VC Selection Procedure

A VC is picked up in order to use as a Dedicated-VC. The ways of
picking up the Dedicated-VC is either of the followings.

(1) A number of VCs are prepared in advance, and registered into an
    un-used VC list. When a Dedicated-VC is needed, one of them is
    picked up from the un-used VC list.

(2) A new VC is established through ATM signaling on demand.

With ATM PVC/VP configuration, a Dedicated-VC is activated by the
procedure (1).

With ATM SVC configuration, a Dedicated-VC is activated by the procedure (1) or (2). When the procedure (1) is used, some number of VCs are prepared in advance through ATM signaling. These VCs are registered into the un-used VC list. When a Dedicated-VC is needed, a VC is picked up from the un-used VC list. When the procedure (2) is used, a Dedicated-VC is established through ATM signaling each time it is required.

The procedure (1) can decrease a time to activate a Dedicated-VC. But the necessary VC resource will increase as it need to prepare additional VCs. Which procedure should be applied to is a matter of local decision in each node, taking the economical requirement and the system responsiveness into account.

A Dedicated-VC is used as a uni-directional VC, although it is generally bi-directional. This means that packets are transferred only from upstream node to downstream node in the Dedicated-VC. The packets from downstream node to upstream node are transferred through the Default-VC or through another Dedicated-VC.

5.2 VCID Negotiation Procedure

After the Dedicated-VC selection procedure, the upstream node transmits the PROPOSE message to the downstream node through the Dedicated-VC. The PROPOSE message contains a VCID for the Dedicated-VC and IP address (target IP address) of downstream node. When the downstream node accepts the PROPOSE message, it transmits the PROPOSE ACK message to the upstream node through the Default-VC. With this procedure, the upstream and the downstream nodes (both end-points of the Dedicated-VC) can share the same indicator "VCID" for the Dedicated-VC. When the downstream node can not accept the proposal from the upstream node with some reason (e.g., policy), the downstream node sends an ERROR message to the upstream node through the Default-VC.

The procedure at the downstream node which has received PROPOSE message is;

1. if(Target IP address of the PROPOSE message isn't equal to my IP address)
   then Goto end.

2. if(The PROPOSE message should be refused)
   then Send an ERROR(refuse by policy) message. Go to end.

3. if(VCID Type in the PROPOSE message isn't known)
   then Send an ERROR(unknown VCID Type) message. Go to end.

RFC 2129

6

4. if(The VCID in the PROPOSE message is the same as the VCID which
   has already been registered for another Dedicated-VC in the node)
   then Delete the registered VCID.
   Release the old Dedicated-VC.

5. if(A VCID is registered for the Dedicated-VC which has received
   the PROPOSE message)
   then Delete the registered VCID.

6. Register the mapping between VCID and I/F, VPI, VCI for the
   Dedicated-VC.

7. if(The mapping is successful)
   then Send a PROPOSE ACK.
   else Send an ERROR(resource unavailable).

The upstream node retransmits the PROPOSE message when it neither
receive PROPOSE ACK message nor ERROR message. When the upstream
node has received neither of the messages even with five
retransmissions of the PROPOSE message, the Dedicated-VC picked up
through the Dedicated-VC selection procedure should be released.
Here, the number of retransmissions (five in this specification)is
recommended value and can be modified in the future.

The purpose of the VCID negotiation procedure is not only to share
the VCID information regarding the Dedicated-VC, but also to confirm
whether the Dedicated-VC is available and whether the neighbor node
operates correctly.

If the VCID negotiation procedure with a neighbor node always fails,
it is considered that the node may not be FANP-capable node.
Therefore the upstream node should not try the VCID negotiation
procedure to that node for a certain time period.

5.3 Flow-ID Notification Procedure

After the VCID negotiation procedure, the upstream node transmits an
OFFER message to the downstream node through the Default-VC. The
OFFER message contains the VCID of the Dedicated-VC, the flow-ID of
the packet flow transferred through the Dedicated-VC and the refresh
interval of a READY message.

When the downstream node receives the OFFER message from the upstream
node, it transmits the READY message to the upstream node through the
Default-VC in order to indicate that the OFFER message issued by the
upstream node is accepted. By the reception of the READY message,
the upstream node realizes that the downstream node can receive IP
packets transferred through the Dedicated-VC.

The upstream node retransmits the OFFER message when it does not
receive a READY message from the downstream node. When the upstream
node has not receive a READY message even with five retransmissions,
the Dedicated-VC should be released. Here, the number of
retransmissions (i.e., five in this specification) is a recommended
value and may be modified in the future.

The node transmits an ERROR message to its neighbor in the following
cases. When the node receives the ERROR message, the Dedicated-VC
should be released.

  (a) unknown VCID: The VCID in the message is unknown.
  (b) unknown VCID Type: The VCID Type is unknown.
  (c) unknown flow-ID Type: the flow-ID Type is unknown.

When the downstream node accepts the OFFER message from the upstream
node, it must send a READY message to the upstream node within the
refresh interval offered by the upstream node. If it can not, the
downstream node sends the ERROR message (this refresh interval is not
supported) to the upstream node. The downstream node should accept
the refresh interval larger than 120 seconds. Therefore the
downstream node shouldn't send the ERROR message (this refresh
interval is not supported) when the refresh interval in the OFFER
message is larger than 120 seconds.

The following describes the procedure of the node which has received
an OFFER message.

  1. if(unknown version in the OFFER message)
     then Discard the message. Goto end.

  2. if(unknown VCID Type in the OFFER message)
     then Send an ERROR (unknown VCID Type) message. Goto end.

  3. if(VCID in the OFFER message has not been registered)
     then Send an ERROR (unknown VCID) message. Goto end.

  4. if(unknown Flow ID Type in the OFFER message)
     then Send an ERROR (unknown Flow ID Type) message. Goto end.

  5. if(refuse Flow ID in the OFFER message)
     then Send an ERROR (refused by policy) message. Goto end.

  6. if(refuse refresh interval in the OFFER message)
     then Send an ERROR(This refresh interval is not supported)
     message. Goto end.

RFC 2129

8

    7. if(the mapping between Flow ID and VCID already exists and
          Flow ID in the OFFER message is different from the registered
          Flow ID for the corresponding VCID)
       then Do Flow-ID removal procedure. Goto end.

    8. Do the procedure of receiving the OFFER message.

    7. if(successful)
       then Send a READY message.
       else Send an ERROR (resource unavailable) message.

    8. end.

The procedure of the node which has received a READY message is
described.

    1. if(unknown version in the READY message)
       then Discard the message. Goto end.

    2. if(unknown VCID Type in the READY message)
       then Send an ERROR (unknown VCID Type) message. Goto end.

    3. if(VCID in the READY message has not been registered)
       then Send an ERROR (unknown VCID) message. Goto end.

    4. if(unknown Flow ID Type in the READY message)
       then Send an ERROR (unknown Flow ID Type) message. Goto end.

    5. if((the mapping between Flow ID and VCID doesn't exist)||
          (the mapping between Flow ID and VCID already exists and
           Flow ID in the READY message is different from registered Flow
           ID for the corresponding VCID))
       then Send an ERROR (unknown VCID) message. Goto end.

    6. Do the procedure of receiving the READY message.

    7. end.

5.4 Flow ID Refresh Procedure

    While the downstream node receives IP packets through the Dedicated-
    VC, it should periodically (with a refresh interval) send the READY
    message to the upstream node. When the downstream node does not
    receive any IP packet during the refresh interval, it does not send
    the READY message to the upstream node.

While the upstream node continues to receive READY messages, it
realizes that it can transmit the IP packets through the Dedicated-
VC. When it does not receive a READY message at all for a
predetermined period (dead interval), it removes the mapping between
the Flow IP and VCID. The dead interval is defined below.

When the upstream node falls into failure without the Flow ID removal
procedure for a Dedicated-VC, its mapping must be removed by the
downstream node. The downstream node removes the mapping between the
Flow ID and VCID for the Dedicated-VC when it does not receive any IP
packet for a "removal period" (=refresh interval times m).

The refresh interval, the dead interval and the removal period should
satisfy the following equation.

   refresh interval < dead interval < removal period (=refresh
   interval times m)

   The recommended values are:
        refresh interval = 2 minutes
        dead interval   = 6 minutes (=refresh interval x 3)
        removal period   = 20 minutes (=refresh interval x 10)

5.5 Flow ID Removal Procedure

When the upstream node realizes that the Dedicated-VC is not used, it
performs a Flow ID removal procedure.

The Flow ID removal procedure differs between the case of PVC/VP
configuration and the case of SVC configuration.

With the PVC/VP configuration, the upstream node issues a REMOVE
message to the downstream node, and the downstream node sends back a
REMOVE ACK message to the upstream node. The upstream node
retransmits REMOVE messages when it does not receive a REMOVE ACK
message. The upstream node assumes that the downstream node is in
failure state when it dose not receive any REMOVE ACK message from
the downstream node even with five REMOVE message retransmissions.

With SVC configuration, two procedures are possible. One is that the
mapping between the Flow ID and the VCID is removed without the
release of the ATM connection, which is the same procedure as the
PVC/VP configuration. The other procedure is that the mapping
between the Flow ID and the VCID is removed by releasing the VC
through ATM signaling. The former procedure can promptly create and
delete the mapping between Flow ID and VCID, since the ATM signaling
does not have to be performed each time. However, an un-used ATM
connections have to be maintained by the node. Which procedure is
applied to is a matter of each CSR's local decision, taking the VC
resource cost and responsiveness into account.

The downstream node may want to remove the mapping between the Flow
ID and the VCID. When the upstream node receives the REMOVE message,
it sends a REMOVE ACK message to the downstream node.

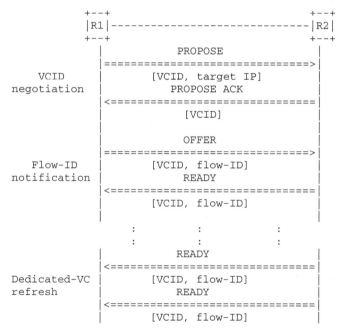

```
               +--+                                 +--+
               |R1|---------------------------------|R2|
               +--+                                 +--+
                  |             PROPOSE                |
                  |================================>|
      VCID        |          [VCID, target IP]         |
   negotiation    |            PROPOSE ACK             |
                  |<================================|
                  |               [VCID]              |
                  |                                   |
                  |              OFFER                 |
                  |================================>|
   Flow-ID        |          [VCID, flow-ID]           |
  notification    |              READY                 |
                  |<================================|
                  |          [VCID, flow-ID]           |
                  |                                   |
                  |       :         :         :       |
                  |       :         :         :       |
                  |              READY                 |
                  |<================================|
  Dedicated-VC    |          [VCID, flow-ID]           |
    refresh       |              READY                 |
                  |<================================|
                  |          [VCID, flow-ID]           |
```

Figure 2. Flow ID notification and refresh procedure

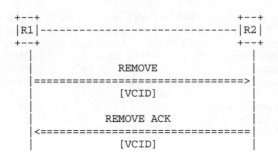

```
     +--+                                    +--+
     |R1|------------------------------|R2|
     +--+                                    +--+
       |                                        |
       |              REMOVE                  |
       |================================>|
       |              [VCID]                   |
       |                                        |
       |            REMOVE ACK             |
       |<===============================|
       |              [VCID]                   |
```

(a) Flow ID removal (independent of ATM signaling)

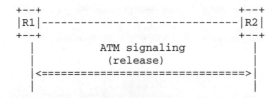

```
     +--+                                    +--+
     |R1|------------------------------|R2|
     +--+                                    +--+
       |           ATM signaling            |
       |              (release)               |
       |<===============================>|
       |                                        |
```

(b) Flow ID removal through ATM signaling

Figure 3. Flow ID removal procedure

6. Message Format

   FANP control procedure includes seven messages described from 6.2 to
   6.8. Among them, a PROPOSE message used for VCID negotiation
   procedure uses an extended ATM ARP message format defined in RFC1577
   [2]. The other messages are encapsulated into IP packets.

   The destination IP address in the IP packet header signifies the
   neighbor node's IP address and the source IP address signifies
   sender's IP address. Currently, the protocol ID for these messages
   is 110(decimal). This protocol ID must be registered by IANA.

   The reserved field in the following packet format must be zero.

6.1 Field Format

6.1.1 VCID field

   VCID type value decides VCID field format. Currently, only type "1"
   is defined. The VCID field format of VCID type 1 is shown below.

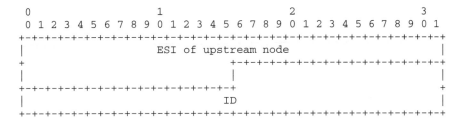
```
0                   1                   2                   3
0 1 2 3 4 5 6 7 8 9 0 1 2 3 4 5 6 7 8 9 0 1 2 3 4 5 6 7 8 9 0 1
+-+-+-+-+-+-+-+-+-+-+-+-+-+-+-+-+-+-+-+-+-+-+-+-+-+-+-+-+-+-+-+-+
|                      ESI of upstream node                     |
+                            +-+-+-+-+-+-+-+-+-+-+-+-+-+-+-+-+-+-+
|                            |                                  |
+-+-+-+-+-+-+-+-+-+-+-+-+-+-+-+                                  +
|                            ID                                 |
+-+-+-+-+-+-+-+-+-+-+-+-+-+-+-+-+-+-+-+-+-+-+-+-+-+-+-+-+-+-+-+-+
```

      ESI field: ESI of upstream node
      ID   : upstream node decides unique identifier.

6.1.2 Flow ID field

   Flow ID type value decides flow-ID field format. Currently, flow-ID
   type "0" and "1" are defined. The flow ID type value "0" signifies
   that the flow ID field is null. When flow ID type value is "1", the
   format shown below is used.

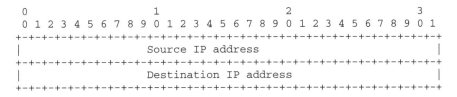
```
0                   1                   2                   3
0 1 2 3 4 5 6 7 8 9 0 1 2 3 4 5 6 7 8 9 0 1 2 3 4 5 6 7 8 9 0 1
+-+-+-+-+-+-+-+-+-+-+-+-+-+-+-+-+-+-+-+-+-+-+-+-+-+-+-+-+-+-+-+-+
|                      Source IP address                        |
+-+-+-+-+-+-+-+-+-+-+-+-+-+-+-+-+-+-+-+-+-+-+-+-+-+-+-+-+-+-+-+-+
|                   Destination IP address                      |
+-+-+-+-+-+-+-+-+-+-+-+-+-+-+-+-+-+-+-+-+-+-+-+-+-+-+-+-+-+-+-+-+
```

      Source IP address   : source IP address of flow
      Destination IP address : destination IP address of flow

6.2 PROPOSE message

   PROPOSE message uses the extended ATM-ARP message format [2] to which
   the VCID type and the VCID field are added. Type & Length fields are
   set to zero, because the messages don't need sender/target ATM
   address. This message is transferred from the upstream node to the
   downstream node through the Dedicated-VC.

   PROPOSE message is transferred from the upstream node to the
   downstream node through the Dedicated-VC.

```
 0                   1                   2                   3
 0 1 2 3 4 5 6 7 8 9 0 1 2 3 4 5 6 7 8 9 0 1 2 3 4 5 6 7 8 9 0 1
+-+-+-+-+-+-+-+-+-+-+-+-+-+-+-+-+-+-+-+-+-+-+-+-+-+-+-+-+-+-+-+-+
| Hardware Type = 0x13          | Protocol Type = 0x0800         |
+-+-+-+-+-+-+-+-+-+-+-+-+-+-+-+-+-+-+-+-+-+-+-+-+-+-+-+-+-+-+-+-+
| Type&Length 1 | Type&Length 2 |       Opereation Code          |
+-+-+-+-+-+-+-+-+-+-+-+-+-+-+-+-+-+-+-+-+-+-+-+-+-+-+-+-+-+-+-+-+
|    Length 1   | Type&Length 3 | Type&Length 4 |   Length 2     |
+-+-+-+-+-+-+-+-+-+-+-+-+-+-+-+-+-+-+-+-+-+-+-+-+-+-+-+-+-+-+-+-+
|                     Sender IP Address                          |
+-+-+-+-+-+-+-+-+-+-+-+-+-+-+-+-+-+-+-+-+-+-+-+-+-+-+-+-+-+-+-+-+
|                     Target IP Address                          |
+-+-+-+-+-+-+-+-+-+-+-+-+-+-+-+-+-+-+-+-+-+-+-+-+-+-+-+-+-+-+-+-+
|   VCID Type   |VCID Length    |         Reserved               |
+-+-+-+-+-+-+-+-+-+-+-+-+-+-+-+-+-+-+-+-+-+-+-+-+-+-+-+-+-+-+-+-+
|                       VCID                                     |
/                                                               /
+-+-+-+-+-+-+-+-+-+-+-+-+-+-+-+-+-+-+-+-+-+-+-+-+-+-+-+-+-+-+-+-+
```

```
Type&Length 1 ; Type & Length of sender ATM number = 0
Type&Length 2 ; Type & Length of sender ATM subnumber = 0
Type&Length 3 ; Type & Length of sender ATM number = 0
Type&Length 4 ; Type & Length of sender ATM subnumber =0
Length 1      ; Source IP address length
Length 2      ; Target IP address length

Operation code
        0x10 = PROPOSE

VCID Type:   Currently , VCID Type = 1 is defined.
VCID Length: Length of VCID field
VCID :       VCID described previous
```

6.3 PROPOSE ACK

   PROPOSE ACK messages is transferred through the Default-VC.

```
 0                   1                   2                   3
 0 1 2 3 4 5 6 7 8 9 0 1 2 3 4 5 6 7 8 9 0 1 2 3 4 5 6 7 8 9 0 1
+-+-+-+-+-+-+-+-+-+-+-+-+-+-+-+-+-+-+-+-+-+-+-+-+-+-+-+-+-+-+-+-+
| Version       |Op code = 1    |         Checksum               |
+-+-+-+-+-+-+-+-+-+-+-+-+-+-+-+-+-+-+-+-+-+-+-+-+-+-+-+-+-+-+-+-+
| VCID type     |Flow-ID type=0 |         Reserved               |
+-+-+-+-+-+-+-+-+-+-+-+-+-+-+-+-+-+-+-+-+-+-+-+-+-+-+-+-+-+-+-+-+
|                       VCID                                     |
/                                                               /
+-+-+-+-+-+-+-+-+-+-+-+-+-+-+-+-+-+-+-+-+-+-+-+-+-+-+-+-+-+-+-+-+
```

RFC 2129

14

Version
    This field indicates the version   number of FANP.   Currently,
    Version = 1

Operation Code

    This field indicates the operation code   of the message. There
    are five operation codes, below.

    operation code = 1 : PROPOSE ACK message

Checksum
    This field is the 16 bits checksum for whole body of FANP message.
    The checksum algorithm is same as the IP header.

VCID Type
    This field indicates the VCID type. Currently, only "1" is
    defined.

6.4 OFFER message

    OFFER message is transferred from an upstream node to a downstream
    node. The following is the message format.

```
 0                   1                   2                   3
 0 1 2 3 4 5 6 7 8 9 0 1 2 3 4 5 6 7 8 9 0 1 2 3 4 5 6 7 8 9 0 1
+-+-+-+-+-+-+-+-+-+-+-+-+-+-+-+-+-+-+-+-+-+-+-+-+-+-+-+-+-+-+-+-+
| Version = 1   | Op Code = 2   |            Checksum           |
+-+-+-+-+-+-+-+-+-+-+-+-+-+-+-+-+-+-+-+-+-+-+-+-+-+-+-+-+-+-+-+-+
| VCID type     |Flow-ID type   |       Refresh Interval        |
+-+-+-+-+-+-+-+-+-+-+-+-+-+-+-+-+-+-+-+-+-+-+-+-+-+-+-+-+-+-+-+-+
|                             VCID                              |
/                                                              /
+-+-+-+-+-+-+-+-+-+-+-+-+-+-+-+-+-+-+-+-+-+-+-+-+-+-+-+-+-+-+-+-+
|                            Flow-ID                            |
/                                                              /
+-+-+-+-+-+-+-+-+-+-+-+-+-+-+-+-+-+-+-+-+-+-+-+-+-+-+-+-+-+-+-+-+
```

Refresh Interval
    This field indicates the interval of refresh timer. The refresh
    interval is represented by second in integer. This field is
    used only in OFFER message. Recommended value is 120 (second).

6.5 READY message

   READY message is transfered from a downstream node to an upstream
   node. This message is transferred when the downstream node receives
   OFFER message. And this message is transferred periodically in each
   refresh interval. The following is the message format.

```
 0                   1                   2                   3
 0 1 2 3 4 5 6 7 8 9 0 1 2 3 4 5 6 7 8 9 0 1 2 3 4 5 6 7 8 9 0 1
+-+-+-+-+-+-+-+-+-+-+-+-+-+-+-+-+-+-+-+-+-+-+-+-+-+-+-+-+-+-+-+-+
| Version = 1   | Op Code = 3   |           Checksum            |
+-+-+-+-+-+-+-+-+-+-+-+-+-+-+-+-+-+-+-+-+-+-+-+-+-+-+-+-+-+-+-+-+
| VCID type     |Flow-ID type   |          Reserved             |
+-+-+-+-+-+-+-+-+-+-+-+-+-+-+-+-+-+-+-+-+-+-+-+-+-+-+-+-+-+-+-+-+
|                            VCID                               |
/                                                               /
+-+-+-+-+-+-+-+-+-+-+-+-+-+-+-+-+-+-+-+-+-+-+-+-+-+-+-+-+-+-+-+-+
|                           Flow-ID                             |
/                                                               /
+-+-+-+-+-+-+-+-+-+-+-+-+-+-+-+-+-+-+-+-+-+-+-+-+-+-+-+-+-+-+-+-+
```

6.6 ERROR message

   ERROR message is transfered from a downstream node to an upstream
   node or from an upstream node to a downstream node. This message is
   transferred when some of the fields in the receive message is unknown
   or refused. When the receive message is the ERROR message, ERROR
   message isn't sent. VCID type ,VCID, Flow ID Type and Flow ID field
   in the ERROR message are filled with the same field in the receive
   message.

   The following is the message format.

```
 0                   1                   2                   3
 0 1 2 3 4 5 6 7 8 9 0 1 2 3 4 5 6 7 8 9 0 1 2 3 4 5 6 7 8 9 0 1
+-+-+-+-+-+-+-+-+-+-+-+-+-+-+-+-+-+-+-+-+-+-+-+-+-+-+-+-+-+-+-+-+
| Version = 1   | Op Code = 4   |           Checksum            |
+-+-+-+-+-+-+-+-+-+-+-+-+-+-+-+-+-+-+-+-+-+-+-+-+-+-+-+-+-+-+-+-+
| VCID type     |Flow-ID type   |         Error code            |
+-+-+-+-+-+-+-+-+-+-+-+-+-+-+-+-+-+-+-+-+-+-+-+-+-+-+-+-+-+-+-+-+
|                            VCID                               |
/                                                               /
+-+-+-+-+-+-+-+-+-+-+-+-+-+-+-+-+-+-+-+-+-+-+-+-+-+-+-+-+-+-+-+-+
|                           Flow-ID                             |
/                                                               /
+-+-+-+-+-+-+-+-+-+-+-+-+-+-+-+-+-+-+-+-+-+-+-+-+-+-+-+-+-+-+-+-+
```

RFC 2129

16

```
  Error Code = 1 : unknown VCID type
             = 2 : unknown Flow-ID type
             = 3 : unknown VCID
             = 4 : resource is unavailable
             = 5 : unavailable refresh interval is offered
             = 6 : refuse by policy
```

6.7 REMOVE message

REMOVE message is transferred from a downstream node to an upstream node or vice versa. This message is transferred to remove the mapping relationship between the flow ID and and the VCID. The node which receives REMOVE message must send REMOVE ACK message, even when VCID in the receive message isn't known .

The following is the message format.

```
 0                   1                   2                   3
 0 1 2 3 4 5 6 7 8 9 0 1 2 3 4 5 6 7 8 9 0 1 2 3 4 5 6 7 8 9 0 1
+-+-+-+-+-+-+-+-+-+-+-+-+-+-+-+-+-+-+-+-+-+-+-+-+-+-+-+-+-+-+-+-+
| Version = 1   | Op Code = 5   |           Checksum            |
+-+-+-+-+-+-+-+-+-+-+-+-+-+-+-+-+-+-+-+-+-+-+-+-+-+-+-+-+-+-+-+-+
| VCID type     |Flow-ID type   |          Reserved             |
+-+-+-+-+-+-+-+-+-+-+-+-+-+-+-+-+-+-+-+-+-+-+-+-+-+-+-+-+-+-+-+-+
|                             VCID                              |
/                                                              /
+-+-+-+-+-+-+-+-+-+-+-+-+-+-+-+-+-+-+-+-+-+-+-+-+-+-+-+-+-+-+-+-+
```

6.8 REMOVE ACK message

REMOVE ACK message is transferred from a downstream node to an upstream node or from an upstream node to a downstream node. The following is the message format.

```
 0                   1                   2                   3
 0 1 2 3 4 5 6 7 8 9 0 1 2 3 4 5 6 7 8 9 0 1 2 3 4 5 6 7 8 9 0 1
+-+-+-+-+-+-+-+-+-+-+-+-+-+-+-+-+-+-+-+-+-+-+-+-+-+-+-+-+-+-+-+-+
| Version = 1   | Op Code = 6   |           Checksum            |
+-+-+-+-+-+-+-+-+-+-+-+-+-+-+-+-+-+-+-+-+-+-+-+-+-+-+-+-+-+-+-+-+
| VCID type     |Flow-ID type   |          Reserved             |
+-+-+-+-+-+-+-+-+-+-+-+-+-+-+-+-+-+-+-+-+-+-+-+-+-+-+-+-+-+-+-+-+
|                             VCID                              |
/                                                              /
+-+-+-+-+-+-+-+-+-+-+-+-+-+-+-+-+-+-+-+-+-+-+-+-+-+-+-+-+-+-+-+-+
```

7. Security Considerations

   Security issues are not discussed in this memo.

8. References

   [1] Katsube, Y., Nagami, K., and H. Esaki, "Router Architecture
       Extensions for ATM; overview", Work in Progress.

   [2] Laubach, M., "Classical IP and ARP over ATM", RFC 1577,
       October 1993.

   [3] Heinanen, J., "Multiprotocol Encapsulation over ATM Adaptation
       Layer 5", RFC 1483, July 1993.

   Ethernet is a registered trademark of Xerox Corp. All other product
   names mentioned herein may be trademarks of their respective
   companies.

9. Authors' Addresses

   Ken-ichi Nagami
   R&D Center, Toshiba
   1 Komukai Toshiba-cho, Saiwai-ku, Kawasaki 210 Japan
   Phone : +81-44-549-2238
   EMail : nagami@isl.rdc.toshiba.co.jp

   Yasuhiro Katsube
   R&D Center, Toshiba
   1 Komukai Toshiba-cho, Saiwai-ku, Kawasaki 210 Japan
   Phone : +81-44-549-2238
   EMail : katsube@isl.rdc.toshiba.co.jp

   Yasuro Shobatake
   R&D Center, Toshiba
   1 Komukai Toshiba-cho, Saiwai-ku, Kawasaki 210 Japan
   Phone : +81-44-549-2238
   Email : masahata@csl.rdc.toshiba.co.jp

   Akiyoshi Mogi
   R&D Center, Toshiba
   1 Komukai Toshiba-cho, Saiwai-ku, Kawasaki 210 Japan
   Phone : +81-44-549-2238
   EMail : mogi@isl.rdc.toshiba.co.jp

RFC 2129

18

Shigeo Matsuzawa
R&D Center, Toshiba
1 Komukai Toshiba-cho, Saiwai-ku, Kawasaki 210 Japan
Phone : +81-44-549-2238
EMail : shigeom@isl.rdc.toshiba.co.jp

Tatsuya Jinmei
R&D Center, Toshiba
1 Komukai Toshiba-cho, Saiwai-ku, Kawasaki 210 Japan
Phone : +81-44-549-2238
EMail : jinmei@isl.rdc.toshiba.co.jp

Hiroshi Esaki
R&D Center, Toshiba
1 Komukai Toshiba-cho, Saiwai-ku, Kawasaki 210 Japan
Phone : +81-44-549-2238
EMail : hiroshi@isl.rdc.toshiba.co.jp

Network Working Group   M. Laubach
Request for Comments: 2225   Com21, Inc.
Category: Standards Track   J. Halpern
Obsoletes: 1626, 1577   Newbridge Networks, Inc.
                                                         April 1998

                    Classical IP and ARP over ATM

Status of this Memo

   This document specifies an Internet standards track protocol for the
   Internet community, and requests discussion and suggestions for
   improvements. Please refer to the current edition of the "Internet
   Official Protocol Standards" (STD 1) for the standardization state
   and status of this protocol. Distribution of this memo is unlimited.

Copyright Notice

Table of Contents

1. ABSTRACT

This memo defines an initial application of classical IP and ARP in
an Asynchronous Transfer Mode (ATM) network environment configured as
a Logical IP Subnetwork (LIS) as described in Section 5. This memo
does not preclude the subsequent development of ATM technology into
areas other than a LIS; specifically, as single ATM networks grow to
replace many Ethernet local LAN segments and as these networks become
globally connected, the application of IP and ARP will be treated
differently. This memo considers only the application of ATM as a
direct replacement for the "wires" and local LAN segments connecting
IP end-stations ("members") and routers operating in the "classical"
LAN-based paradigm. Issues raised by MAC level bridging and LAN
emulation are beyond the scope of this paper.

This memo introduces general ATM technology and nomenclature.
Readers are encouraged to review the ATM Forum and ITU-TS (formerly
CCITT) references for more detailed information about ATM
implementation agreements and standards.

2. ACKNOWLEDGMENT

The authors would like to thank the efforts of the IP over ATM
Working Group of the IETF. Without their substantial, and sometimes
contentious support, of the Classical IP over ATM model, this updated
memo would not have been possible. Section 7, on Default MTU, has
been incorporated directly from Ran Atkinson's RFC 1626, with his
permission. Thanks to Andy Malis for an early review and comments
for rolc and ion related issues.

3. CONVENTIONS

    The key words "MUST", "MUST NOT", "REQUIRED", "SHALL", "SHALL NOT",
    "SHOULD", "SHOULD NOT", "RECOMMENDED", "MAY", and "OPTIONAL" in this
    document are to be interpreted as described in RFC 2119 [20].

4. INTRODUCTION

    The goal of this specification is to allow compatible and
    interoperable implementations for transmitting IP datagrams and ATM
    Address Resolution Protocol (ATMARP) requests and replies over ATM
    Adaptation Layer 5 (AAL5)[2,6].

    This memo specifies the stable foundation baseline operational model
    which will always be available in IP and ARP over ATM
    implementations. Subsequent memos will build upon and refine this
    model. However, in the absence or failure of those extensions,
    operations will default to the specifications contained in this memo.
    Consequently, this memo will not reference these other extensions.

    This memo defines only the operation of IP and address resolution
    over ATM, and is not meant to describe the operation of ATM networks.
    Any reference to virtual connections, permanent virtual connections,
    or switched virtual connections applies only to virtual channel
    connections used to support IP and address resolution over ATM, and
    thus are assumed to be using AAL5. This memo places no restrictions
    or requirements on virtual connections used for other purposes.

    Initial deployment of ATM provides a LAN segment replacement for:

    1) Local area networks (e.g., Ethernets, Token Rings and FDDI).

    2) Local-area backbones between existing (non-ATM) LANs.

    3) Dedicated circuits or frame relay PVCs between IP routers.

    NOTE: In 1), local IP routers with one or more ATM interfaces will be
    able to connect islands of ATM networks. In 3), public or private
    ATM Wide Area networks will be used to connect IP routers, which in
    turn may or may not connect to local ATM networks. ATM WANs and LANs
    may be interconnected.

    Private ATM networks (local or wide area) will use the private ATM
    address structure specified in the ATM Forum UNI 3.1 specification
    [9] or as in the ATM Forum UNI 4.0 specification [19]. This
    structure is modeled after the format of an OSI Network Service
    Access Point Address (NSAPA). A private ATM address uniquely
    identifies an ATM endpoint.

Public networks will use either the address structure specified in
ITU-TS recommendation E.164 or the private network ATM address
structure. An E.164 address uniquely identifies an interface to a
public network.

The characteristics and features of ATM networks are different than
those found in LANs:

o   ATM provides a Virtual Connection (VC) switched environment. VC
     setup may be done on either a Permanent Virtual Connection (PVC)
     or dynamic Switched Virtual Connection (SVC) basis. SVC call
     management signalling is performed via implementations of the UNI
     3.1 protocol [7,9].

o   Data to be passed by a VC is segmented into 53 octet quantities
     called cells (5 octets of ATM header and 48 octets of data).

o   The function of mapping user Protocol Data Units (PDUs) into the
     information field of the ATM cell and vice versa is performed in
     the ATM Adaptation Layer (AAL). When a VC is created a specific
     AAL type is associated with the VC. There are four different AAL
     types, which are referred to individually as "AAL1", "AAL2",
     "AAL3/4", and "AAL5". (NOTE: this memo concerns itself with the
     mapping of IP and ATMARP over AAL5 only. The other AAL types are
     mentioned for introductory purposes only.) The AAL type is known
     by the VC end points via the call setup mechanism and is not
     carried in the ATM cell header. For PVCs the AAL type is
     administratively configured at the end points when the Connection
     (circuit) is set up. For SVCs, the AAL type is communicated
     along the VC path via UNI 3.1 as part of call setup establishment
     and the end points use the signaled information for
     configuration. ATM switches generally do not care about the AAL
     type of VCs. The AAL5 format specifies a packet format with a
     maximum size of (64K - 1) octets of user data. Cells for an AAL5
     PDU are transmitted first to last, the last cell indicating the
     end of the PDU. ATM standards guarantee that on a given VC, cell
     ordering is preserved end-to-end. NOTE: AAL5 provides a non-
     assured data transfer service - it is up to higher-level
     protocols to provide retransmission.

o   ATM Forum signaling defines point-to-point and point-to-
     point Connection setup [9, 19.] Multipoint-to-multipoint not yet
     specified by ITU-TS or ATM Forum.

     An ATM Forum ATM address is either encoded as an NSAP form ATM
     EndSystem Address (AESA) or is an E.164 Public-UNI address [9,
     19]. In some cases, both an AESA and an E.164 Public UNI address
     are needed by an ATMARP client to reach another host or router.

Since the use of AESAs and E.164 public UNI addresses by ATMARP
are analogous to the use of Ethernet addresses, the notion of
"hardware address" is extended to encompass ATM addresses in the
context of ATMARP, even though ATM addresses need not have
hardware significance. ATM Forum NSAP format addresses (AESA)
use the same basic format as U.S. GOSIP OSI NSAPAs [11]. NOTE:
ATM Forum addresses should not be construed as being U.S. GOSIP
NSAPAs. They are not, the administration is different, which
fields get filled out are different, etc. However, in this
document, these will be referred to as NSAPAs.

This memo describes the initial deployment of ATM within "classical"
IP networks as a direct replacement for local area networks
(Ethernets) and for IP links which interconnect routers, either
within or between administrative domains. The "classical" model here
refers to the treatment of the ATM host adapter as a networking
interface to the IP protocol stack operating in a LAN-based paradigm.

Characteristics of the classical model are:

o   The same maximum transmission unit (MTU) size is the default for
    all VCs in a LIS. However, on a VC-by-VC point-to-point basis,
    the MTU size may be negotiated during connection setup using Path
    MTU Discovery to better suit the needs of the cooperating pair of
    IP members or the attributes of the communications path. (Refer
    to Section 7.3)

o   Default LLC/SNAP encapsulation of IP packets.

o   End-to-end IP routing architecture stays the same.

o   IP addresses are resolved to ATM addresses by use of an ATMARP
    service within the LIS - ATMARPs stay within the LIS. From a
    client's perspective, the ATMARP architecture stays faithful to
    the basic ARP model presented in [3].

o   One IP subnet is used for many hosts and routers. Each VC
    directly connects two IP members within the same LIS.

Future memos will describe the operation of IP over ATM when ATM
networks become globally deployed and interconnected.

The deployment of ATM into the Internet community is just beginning
and will take many years to complete. During the early part of this
period, we expect deployment to follow traditional IP subnet
boundaries for the following reasons:

o   Administrators and managers of IP subnetworks will tend to
    initially follow the same models as they currently have deployed.
    The mindset of the community will change slowly over time as ATM
    increases its coverage and builds its credibility.

o   Policy administration practices rely on the security, access,
    routing, and filtering capability of IP Internet gateways: i.e.,
    firewalls. ATM will not be allowed to "back-door" around these
    mechanisms until ATM provides better management capability than
    the existing services and practices.

o   Standards for global IP over ATM will take some time to complete
    and deploy.

This memo details the treatment of the classical model of IP and
ATMARP over ATM. This memo does not preclude the subsequent
treatment of ATM networks within the IP framework as ATM becomes
globally deployed and interconnected; this will be the subject of
future documents. This memo does not address issues related to
transparent data link layer interoperability.

5. IP SUBNETWORK CONFIGURATION

5.1 Background

In the LIS scenario, each separate administrative entity configures
its hosts and routers within a LIS. Each LIS operates and
communicates independently of other LISs on the same ATM network.

In the classical model, hosts communicate directly via ATM to other
hosts within the same LIS using the ATMARP service as the mechanism
for resolving target IP addresses to target ATM endpoint addresses.
The ATMARP service has LIS scope only and serves all hosts in the
LIS. Communication to hosts located outside of the local LIS is
provided via an IP router. This router is an ATM endpoint attached
to the ATM network that is configured as a member of one or more
LISs. This configuration MAY result in a number of disjoint LISs
operating over the same ATM network. Using this model hosts of
differing IP subnets MUST communicate via an intermediate IP router
even though it may be possible to open a direct VC between the two IP
members over the ATM network.

By default, the ATMARP service and the classical LIS routing model
MUST be available to any IP member client in the LIS.

5.2 LIS Configuration Requirements

The requirements for IP members (hosts, routers) operating in an ATM LIS configuration are:

o   All members of the LIS have the same IP network/subnet number and address mask [8].

o   All members within a LIS are directly connected to the ATM network.

o   All members of a LIS MUST have a mechanism for resolving IP addresses to ATM addresses via ATMARP (based on [3]) and vice versa via InATMARP (based on [12]) when using SVCs. Refer to Section 8 "LIS ADDRESS RESOLUTION SERVICES" in this memo.

o   All members of a LIS MUST have a mechanism for resolving VCs to IP addresses via InATMARP (based on [12]) when using PVCs. Refer to Section 8 "LIS ADDRESS RESOLUTION SERVICES" in this memo.

o   All members within a LIS MUST be able to communicate via ATM with all other members in the same LIS; i.e., the Virtual Connection topology underlying the intercommunication among the members is fully meshed.

The following list identifies the set of ATM specific parameters that MUST be implemented in each IP station connected to the ATM network:

o   ATM Hardware Address (atm$ha). The ATM address of the individual IP station.

o   ATMARP Request Address list (atm$arp-req-list): atm$arp-req-list is a list containing one or more ATM addresses of individual ATMARP servers located within the LIS. In an SVC environment, ATMARP servers are used to resolve target IP addresses to target ATM address via an ATMARP request and reply protocol. ATMARP servers MUST have authoritative responsibility for resolving ATMARP requests of all IP members using SVCs located within the LIS.

A LIS MUST have a single ATMARP service entry configured and available to all members of the LIS who use SVCs.

In the case where there is only a single ATMARP server within the LIS, then all ATMARP clients MUST be configured identically to have only one non-null entry in atm$arp-req-list configured with the same address of the single ATMARP service.

If the IP member is operating with PVCs only, then atm$arp-req-list
MUST be configured with all null entries and the client MUST not make
queries to either address resolution service.

Within the restrictions mentioned above and in Section 8, local
administration MUST decide which server address(es) are appropriate
for atm$arp-req-list.

By default, atm$arp-req-list MUST be configured using the MIB [18].

Manual configuration of the addresses and address lists presented in
this section is implementation dependent and beyond the scope of this
document; i.e., this memo does not require any specific configuration
method. This memo does require that these addresses MUST be
configured completely on the client, as appropriate for the LIS,
prior to use by any service or operation detailed in this memo.

5.3 LIS Router Additional Configuration

It is RECOMMENDED that routers providing LIS functionality over the
ATM network also support the ability to interconnect multiple LISs.
Routers that wish to provide interconnection of differing LISs MUST
be able to support multiple sets of these parameters (one set for
each connected LIS) and be able to associate each set of parameters
to a specific IP network/ subnet number. In addition, it is
RECOMMENDED that a router be able to provide this multiple LIS
support with a single physical ATM interface that may have one or
more individual ATM endpoint addresses. NOTE: this does not
necessarily mean different End System Identifiers (ESIs) when NSAPAs
are used. The last octet of an NSAPA is the NSAPA Selector (SEL)
field which can be used to differentiate up to 256 different LISs for
the same ESI. (Refer to Section 5.1.3.1, "Private Networks" in [9].)

6. IP PACKET FORMAT

Implementations MUST support IEEE 802.2 LLC/SNAP encapsulation as
described in [2]. LLC/SNAP encapsulation is the default packet
format for IP datagrams.

This memo recognizes that other encapsulation methods may be used
however, in the absence of other knowledge or agreement, LLC/SNAP
encapsulation is the default.

This memo recognizes that end-to-end signaling within ATM may allow
negotiation of encapsulation method on a per-VC basis.

7. DEFAULT VALUE FOR IP MTU OVER ATM AAL5

   Protocols in wide use throughout the Internet, such as the Network
   File System (NFS), currently use large frame sizes (e.g., 8 KB).
   Empirical evidence with various applications over the Transmission
   Control Protocol (TCP) indicates that larger Maximum Transmission
   Unit (MTU) sizes for the Internet Protocol (IP) tend to give better
   performance. Fragmentation of IP datagrams is known to be highly
   undesirable [16]. It is desirable to reduce fragmentation in the
   network and thereby enhance performance by having the IP Maximum
   Transmission Unit (MTU) for AAL5 be reasonably large. NFS defaults
   to an 8192 byte frame size. Allowing for RPC/XDR, UDP, IP, and LLC
   headers, NFS would prefer a default MTU of at least 8300 octets.
   Routers can sometimes perform better with larger packet sizes because
   most of the performance costs in routers relate to "packets handled"
   rather than "bytes transferred". So, there are a number of good
   reasons to have a reasonably large default MTU value for IP over ATM
   AAL5.

   RFC 1209 specifies the IP MTU over SMDS to be 9180 octets, which is
   larger than 8300 octets but still in the same range [1]. There is no
   good reason for the default MTU of IP over ATM AAL5 to be different
   from IP over SMDS, given that they will be the same magnitude.
   Having the two be the same size will be helpful in interoperability
   and will also help reduce incidence of IP fragmentation.

   Therefore, the default IP MTU for use with ATM AAL5 shall be 9180
   octets. All implementations compliant and conformant with this
   specification shall support at least the default IP MTU value for use
   over ATM AAL5.

7.1 Permanent Virtual Circuits

   Implementations which only support Permanent Virtual Circuits (PVCs)
   will (by definition) not implement any ATM signalling protocol. Such
   implementations shall use the default IP MTU value of 9180 octets
   unless both parties have agreed in advance to use some other IP MTU
   value via some mechanism not specified here.

7.2 Switched Virtual Circuits

   Implementations that support Switched Virtual Circuits (SVCs) MUST
   attempt to negotiate the AAL CPCS-SDU size using the ATM signalling
   protocol. The industry standard ATM signalling protocol uses two
   different parts of the Information Element named "AAL Parameters" to
   exchange information on the MTU over the ATM circuit being setup [9].
   The Forward Maximum CPCS-SDU Size field contains the value over the
   path from the calling party to the called party. The Backwards

Maximum CPCS-SDU Size Identifier field contains the value over the
path from the called party to the calling party. The ATM Forum
specifies the valid values of this identifier as 1 to 65535
inclusive. Note that the ATM Forum's User-to-Network-Interface (UNI)
signalling permits the MTU in one direction to be different from the
MTU in the opposite direction, so the Forward Maximum CPCS-SDU Size
Identifier might have a different value from the Backwards Maximum
CPCS-SDU Size Identifier on the same connection.

If the calling party wishes to use the default MTU it shall still
include the "AAL Parameters" information element with the default
values for the Maximum CPCS-SDU Size as part of the SETUP message of
the ATM signalling protocol [9]. If the calling party desires to use
a different value than the default, it shall include the "AAL
Parameters" information element with the desired value for the
Maximum CPCS-SDU Size as part of the SETUP message of the ATM
Signalling Protocol. The called party will respond using the same
information elements and identifiers in its CONNECT message response
[9].

If the called party receives a SETUP message containing the "Maximum
CPCS-SDU Size" in the AAL Parameters information element, it shall
handle the Forward and Backward Maximum CPCS-SDU Size Identifier as
follows:

a) If it is able to accept the ATM MTU values proposed by the SETUP
    message, it shall include an AAL Parameters information element
    in its response. The Forward and Backwards Maximum CPCS-SDU Size
    fields shall be present and their values shall be equal to the
    corresponding values in the SETUP message.

b) If it wishes a smaller ATM MTU size than that proposed, then it
    shall set the values of the Maximum CPCS-SDU Size in the AAL
    Parameters information elements equal to the desired value in the
    CONNECT message responding to the original SETUP message.

c) If the calling endpoint receives a CONNECT message that does not
    contain the AAL Parameters Information Element, but the
    corresponding SETUP message did contain the AAL Parameters
    Information element (including the forward and backward CPCS-SDU
    Size fields), it shall clear the call with cause "AAL Parameters
    cannot be supported".

d) If either endpoint receives a STATUS message with cause
    "Information Element Non-existent or Not Implemented" or cause
    "Access Information Discarded", and with a diagnostic field

indicating the AAL Parameters Information Element identifier, it
shall clear the call with cause "AAL Parameters cannot be
supported."

e) If either endpoint receives CPCS-SDUs in excess of the negotiated
    MTU size, it may use IP fragmentation or may clear the call with
    cause "AAL Parameters cannot be supported". In this case, an
    error has occurred either due to a fault in an end system or in
    the ATM network. The error should be noted by ATM network
    management for human examination and intervention.

If the called endpoint incorrectly includes the Forward and Backward
Maximum CPCS-SDU Size fields in the CONNECT messages (e.g., because
the original SETUP message did not include these fields) or it sets
these fields to an invalid value, then the calling party shall clear
the call with cause "Invalid Information Element Contents".

7.3 Path MTU Discovery Required

The Path MTU Discovery mechanism is Internet Standard RFC 1191 [17]
and is an important mechanism for reducing IP fragmentation in the
Internet. This mechanism is particularly important because new
subnet ATM uses a default MTU sizes significantly different from
older subnet technologies such as Ethernet and FDDI.

In order to ensure good performance throughout the Internet and also
to permit IP to take full advantage of the potentially larger IP
datagram sizes supported by ATM, all router implementations that
comply or conform with this specification must also implement the IP
Path MTU Discovery mechanism as defined in RFC 1191 and clarified by
RFC 1435 [14]. Host implementations should implement the IP Path MTU
Discovery mechanism as defined in RFC 1191.

8. LIS ADDRESS RESOLUTION SERVICES

8.1 ATM-based ARP and InARP Equivalent Services

Address resolution within an ATM LIS SHALL make use of the ATM
Address Resolution Protocol (ATMARP) (based on [3]) and the Inverse
ATM Address Resolution Protocol (InATMARP) (based on [12]) and as
defined in this memo. ATMARP is the same protocol as the ARP
protocol presented in [3] with extensions needed to support address
resolution in a unicast server ATM environment. InATMARP is the same
protocol as the original InARP protocol presented in [12] but applied
to ATM networks. All IP stations MUST support these protocols as
updated and extended in this memo. Use of these protocols differs
depending on whether PVCs or SVCs are used.

8.2 Permanent Virtual Connections

An IP station MUST have a mechanism (e.g., manual configuration) for determining what PVCs it has, and in particular which PVCs are being used with LLC/SNAP encapsulation. The details of the mechanism are beyond the scope of this memo.

All IP members supporting PVCs are required to use the Inverse ATM Address Resolution Protocol (InATMARP) (refer to [12]) on those VCs using LLC/SNAP encapsulation. In a strict PVC environment, the receiver SHALL infer the relevant VC from the VC on which the InATMARP_Request or response InATMARP_Reply was received. When the ATM source and/or target address is unknown, the corresponding ATM address length in the InATMARP packet MUST be set to zero (0) indicating a null length, and no storage be allocated in the InATMARP packet, otherwise the appropriate address field should be filled in and the corresponding length set appropriately. InATMARP packet format details are presented later in this memo.

Directly from [12]: "When the requesting station receives the In[ATM]ARP_Reply, it may complete the [ATM]ARP table entry and use the provided address information. NOTE: as with [ATM]ARP, information learned via In[ATM]ARP may be aged or invalidated under certain circumstances." IP stations supporting PVCs MUST re-validate ATMARP table entries as part of the table aging process. See the Section 8.5.1 "Client ATMARP Table Aging".

If a client has more than one IP address within the LIS and if using PVCs, when an InATMARP_Request is received an InATMARP_Reply MUST be generated for each such address.

8.3 Switched Virtual Connections

SVCs require support from address resolution services for resolving target IP addresses to target ATM endpoint addresses. All members in the LIS MUST use the same service. This service MUST have authoritative responsibility for resolving the ATMARP requests of all IP members within the LIS.

ATMARP servers do not actively establish connections. They depend on the clients in the LIS to initiate connections for the ATMARP registration procedure and for transmitting ATMARP requests. An individual client connects to the ATMARP server using a point-to-point LLC/SNAP VC. The client sends normal ATMARP request packets to the server. The ATMARP server examines each ATMARP_Request packet for

the source protocol and source hardware address information of the
sending client and uses this information to build its ATMARP table
cache. This information is used to generate replies to any ATMARP
requests it receives.

InATMARP_Request packets MUST specify valid address information for
ATM source number, ATM target number, and source protocol address;
i.e., these fields MUST be non-null in InATMARP_Request packets.

This memo defines the address resolution service in the LIS and
constrains it to consist of a single ATMARP server. Client-server
interaction is defined by using a single server approach as a
reference model.

This memo recognizes the future development of standards and
implementations of multiple-ATMARP-server models that will extend the
operations as defined in this memo to provide a highly reliable
address resolution service.

8.4 ATMARP Single Server Operational Requirements

A single ATMARP server accepts ATM calls/connections from other ATM
end points. After receiving any ATMARP_Request, the server will
examine the source and target address information in the packet and
make note of the VC on which the ATMARP_Request arrived. It will use
this information as necessary to build and update its ATMARP table
entries.

For each ATMARP_Request, then:

1. If the source IP protocol address is the same as the target IP
    protocol address and a table entry exists for that IP address and
    if the source ATM hardware address does not match the table entry
    ATM address and there is an open VC associated with that table
    entry that is not the same as the VC associated with the
    ATMARP_Request, the server MUST return the table entry
    information in the ATMARP_Reply, and MUST raise a "duplicate IP
    address detected" condition to the server's management. The
    table entry is not updated.

2. Otherwise, if the source IP protocol address is the same as the
    target IP protocol address, and either there is no table entry
    for that IP address, or a table entry exists for that IP address
    and there is no open VC associated with that table entry, or if
    the VC associated with that entry is the same as the VC for the
    ATMARP_Request, the server MUST either create a new entry or
    update the old entry as appropriate and return that table entry
    information in the ATMARP Reply.

3. Otherwise, when the source IP protocol address does not match the
    target IP protocol address, the ATMARP server will generate the
    corresponding ATMARP_Reply if it has an entry for the target
    information in its ATMARP table. Otherwise, it will generate a
    negative ATMARP reply (ATMARP_NAK).

4. Additionally, when the source IP protocol address does not match
    the target IP protocol address and when the server receives an
    ATMARP_Request over a VC, where the source IP and ATM address do
    not have a corresponding table entry, the ATMARP server MUST
    create a new table entry for the source information.
    Explanation: this allows old RFC 1577 clients to register with
    this ATMARP service by just issuing requests to it.

5. Additionally, when the source IP protocol address does not match
    the target IP protocol address and where the source IP and ATM
    addresses match the association already in the ATMARP table and
    the ATM address matches that associated with the VC, the server
    MUST update the table timeout on the source ATMARP table entry
    but only if it has been more than 10 minutes since the last
    update. Explanation: if the client is sending ATMARP requests to
    the server over the same VC that it used to register its ATMARP
    entry, the server should examine the ATMARP request and note that
    the client is still "alive" by updating the timeout on the
    client's ATMARP table entry.

6. Additionally, when the source IP protocol address does not match
    the target IP protocol address and where the source IP and ATM
    addresses do not match the association already in the ATMARP
    table, the server MUST NOT update the ATMARP table entry.

An ATMARP server MUST have knowledge of any open VCs it has and their
association with an ATMARP table entry, and in particular, which VCs
support LLC/SNAP encapsulation. In normal operation, active ATMARP
clients will revalidate their entries prior to the server aging
process taking effect.

Server ATMARP table entries are valid for 20 minutes. If an entry
ages beyond 20 minutes without being updated (refreshed) by the
client, that entry is deleted from the table regardless of the state
of any VCs that may be associated with that entry.

8.5 ATMARP Client Operational Requirements

The ATMARP client is responsible for contacting the ATMARP service to
both initially register and subsequently refresh its own ATMARP
information.

The client is also responsible for using the ATMARP service to gain and revalidate ATMARP information about other IP members in the LIS (server selection overview is discussed in Section 8.6). As noted in Section 5.2, ATMARP clients MUST be configured with the ATM address of the appropriate server prior to client ATMARP operation.

IP clients MUST register their ATM endpoint address with their ATMARP server using the ATM address structure appropriate for their ATM network connection: i.e., LISs implemented over ATM LANs following ATM Forum UNI 3.1 should register using Structure 1; LISs implemented over an E.164 "public" ATM network should register using Structure 2. A LIS implemented over a combination of ATM LANs and public ATM networks may need to register using Structure 3. Implementations based on this memo MUST support all three ATM address structures. See Section 8.7.1 for more details regarding the ATMARP Request packet format.

To handle the case when a client has more than one IP address within a LIS, when using an ATMARP server, the client MUST register each such address.

For initial registration and subsequent refreshing of its own information with the ATMARP service, clients MUST:

1. Establish an LLC/SNAP VC connection to a server in the ATMARP service for the purposes of transmitting and receiving ATMARP packets.

    NOTE: in the case of refreshing its own information with the ATMARP service, a client MAY reuse an existing established connection to the ATMARP service provided that the connection was previously used either to initially register its information with the ATMARP service or to refresh its information with the ATMARP service.

2. After establishing a successful connection to the ATMARP service, the client MUST transmit an ATMARP_Request packet, requesting a target ATM address for its own IP address as the target IP protocol address. The client checks the ATMARP_Reply and if the source hardware and protocol addresses match the respective target hardware and protocol addresses, the client is registered with the ATMARP service. If the addresses do not match, the client MAY take action, raise alarms, etc.; however, these actions are beyond the scope of this memo. In the case of a client having more than one IP address in the list, this step MUST be repeated for each IP address.

3. Clients MUST respond to ATMARP_Request and InATMARP_Request
    packets received on any VC appropriately. (Refer to Section 7,
    "Protocol Operation" in RFC 1293 [12].)

    NOTE: for reasons of robustness, clients MUST respond to
    ATMARP_Requests.

4. Generate and transmit address resolution request packets to the
    address resolution service. Respond to address resolution reply
    packets appropriately to build/refresh its own client ATMARP
    table entries.

5. Generate and transmit InATMARP_Request packets as needed and
    process InATMARP_Reply packets appropriately. InATMARP_Reply
    packets should be used to build/refresh its own client ATMARP
    table entries. (Refer to Section 7, "Protocol Operation" in
    [12].) If a client has more than one IP address within the LIS
    when an InATMARP_Request is received an InATMARP_Reply MUST be
    generated for each such address.

The client MUST refresh its ATMARP information with the server at
least once every 15 minutes. This is done by repeating steps 1 and
2.

An ATMARP client MUST have knowledge of any open VCs it has
(permanent or switched), their association with an ATMARP table
entry, and in particular, which VCs support LLC/SNAP encapsulation.

8.5.1 Client ATMARP Table Aging

Client ATMARP table entries are valid for a maximum time of 15
minutes.

When an ATMARP table entry ages, an ATMARP client MUST invalidate the
table entry. If there is no open VC server associated with the
invalidated entry, that entry is deleted. In the case of an
invalidated entry and an open VC, the client MUST revalidate the
entry prior to transmitting any non address resolution traffic on
that VC; this requirement applies to both PVCs and SVCs. NOTE: the
client is permitted to revalidate an ATMARP table entry before it
ages, thus restarting the aging time when the table entry is
successfully revalidated. The client MAY continue to use the open
VC, as long as the table entry has not aged, while revalidation is in
progress.

In the case of an open PVC, the client revalidates the entry by
transmitting an InATMARP_Request and updating the entry on receipt of
an InATMARP_Reply.

In the case of an open SVC, the client revalidates the entry by
querying the address resolution service. If a valid reply is
received (e.g., ATMARP_Reply), the entry is updated. If the address
resolution service cannot resolve the entry (i.e., "host not found"),
the SVC should be closed and the associated table entry removed. If
the address resolution service is not available (i.e., "server
failure") and if the SVC is LLC/SNAP encapsulated, the client MUST
attempt to revalidate the entry by transmitting an InATMARP_Request
on that VC and updating the entry on receipt of an InATMARP_Reply.
If the InATMARP_Request attempt fails to return an InATMARP_Reply,
the SVC should be closed and the associated table entry removed.

If a VC with an associated invalidated ATMARP table entry is closed,
that table entry is removed.

8.5.2 Non-Normal VC Operations

The specific details on client procedures for detecting non-normal VC
connection establishment or closures, or failed communications on an
established VC are beyond the scope of this memo. It is REQUIRED
however, that the client MUST remove the associated ATMARP entry for
a VC that fails to operate properly, as defined by the client, when
the client closes that VC, when it releases its resources for a VC,
or prior to any attempt to reopen that VC. This behavior
specifically REQUIRES that the client MUST refresh its ATMARP table
information prior to any attempt to re-establish communication to an
IP member after a non-normal communications problem has previously
occurred on a VC to that IP member.

8.5.3 Use of ATMARP In Mobile-IP Scenarios

When an ATM LIS is used as the home network in a mobile-IP scenario,
it is RECOMMENDED that the home agent NOT maintain long term
connections with the ATMARP service. The absence of this VC will
permit a mobile node's registration, upon its return to the home
network, to immediately preempt the home agent's previous gratuitous
registration.

8.6 Address Resolution Server Selection

If the client supports PVCs only, the ATMARP server list is empty and
the client MUST not generate any address resolution requests other
than the InATMARP requests on a PVC needed to validate that PVC.

If the client supports SVCs, then the client MUST have a non-NULL
atm$arp-req-list pointing to the ATMARP server(s) which provides
ATMARP service for the LIS.

The client MUST register with a server from atm$arp-req-list.

The client SHALL attempt to communicate with any of the servers until
a successful registration is accomplished. The order in which client
selects servers to attempt registration, is a local matter, as are
the number of retries and timeouts for such attempts.

8.6.1 PVCs to ATMARP Servers

In a mixed PVC and SVC LIS environment, an ATMARP client MAY have a
PVC to an ATMARP server. In this case, this PVC is used for ATMARP
requests and responses as if it were an established SVC. NOTE: if
this PVC is to be used for IP traffic, then the ATMARP server MUST be
prepared to accept and respond appropriately to InATMARP traffic.

8.7 ATMARP Packet Formats

Internet addresses are assigned independently of ATM addresses. Each
host implementation MUST know its own IP and ATM address(es) and MUST
respond to address resolution requests appropriately. IP members
MUST also use ATMARP and InATMARP to resolve IP addresses to ATM
addresses when needed.

NOTE: the ATMARP packet format presented in this memo is general in
nature in that the ATM number and ATM subaddress fields SHOULD map
directly to the corresponding UNI 3.1 fields used for ATM
call/connection setup signalling messages. The IP over ATM Working
Group expects ATM Forum NSAPA numbers (Structure 1) to predominate
over E.164 numbers (Structure 2) as ATM endpoint identifiers within
ATM LANs. The ATM Forum's VC Routing specification is not complete
at this time and therefore its impact on the operational use of ATM
Address Structure 3 is undefined. The ATM Forum will be defining
this relationship in the future. It is for this reason that IP
members need to support all three ATM address structures.

8.7.1 ATMARP/InATMARP Request and Reply Packet Formats

The ATMARP and InATMARP request and reply protocols use the same
hardware type (ar$hrd), protocol type (ar$pro), and operation code
(ar$op) data formats as the ARP and InARP protocols [3,12]. The
location of these three fields within the ATMARP packet are in the
same byte position as those in ARP and InARP packets. A unique
hardware type value has been assigned for ATMARP. In addition,
ATMARP makes use of an additional operation code for ARP_NAK. The
remainder of the ATMARP/InATMARP packet format is different than the
ARP/InARP packet format.

The ATMARP and InATMARP protocols have several fields that have the
following format and values:

```
Data:
    ar$hrd   16 bits  Hardware type
    ar$pro   16 bits  Protocol type
    ar$shtl   8 bits  Type & length (TL) of source ATM number (q)
    ar$sstl   8 bits  Type & length (TL) of source ATM subaddress (r)
    ar$op    16 bits  Operation code (request, reply, or NAK)
    ar$spln   8 bits  Length of source protocol address (s)
    ar$thtl   8 bits  Type & length (TL) of target ATM number (x)
    ar$tstl   8 bits  Type & length (TL) of target ATM subaddress (y)
    ar$tpln   8 bits  Length of target protocol address (z)
    ar$sha   qoctets of source ATM number
    ar$ssa   roctets of source ATM subaddress
    ar$spa   soctets of source protocol address
    ar$tha   xoctets of target ATM number
    ar$tsa   yoctets of target ATM subaddress
    ar$tpa   zoctets of target protocol address

Where:
    ar$hrd  - assigned to ATM Forum address family and is
              19 decimal (0x0013) [4].

    ar$pro  - see Assigned Numbers for protocol type number for
              the protocol using ATMARP. (IP is 0x0800).

    ar$shtl - Type and length of source ATM number.  See
              Section 8.7.4 for TL encoding details.

    ar$sstl - Type and length of source ATM subaddress.  See
              Section 8.7.4 for TL encoding details.

    ar$op   - The operation type value (decimal):

              ATMARP_Request   = ARP_REQUEST   = 1
              ATMARP_Reply     = ARP_REPLY     = 2
              InATMARP_Request = InARP_REQUEST = 8
              InATMARP_Reply   = InARP_REPLY   = 9
              ATMARP_NAK       = ARP_NAK       = 10

    ar$spln - length in octets of the source protocol address. Value
              range is 0 or 4 (decimal).  For IPv4 ar$spln is 4.

    ar$thtl - Type and length of target ATM number.  See
              Section 8.7.4 for TL encoding details.
```

ar$tstl -   Type and length of target ATM subaddress. See
            Section 8.7.4 for TL encoding details.

ar$tpln -   length in octets of the target protocol address. Value
            range is 0 or 4 (decimal). For IPv4 ar$tpln is 4.

ar$sha -   source ATM number (E.164 or ATM Forum NSAPA)

ar$ssa -   source ATM subaddress (ATM Forum NSAPA)

ar$spa -   source protocol address

ar$tha -   target ATM number (E.164 or ATM Forum NSAPA)

ar$tsa -   target ATM subaddress (ATM Forum NSAPA)

ar$tpa -   target protocol address

8.7.2 Receiving Unknown ATMARP packets

   If an ATMARP client receives an ATMARP message with an operation code
   (ar$op) for which it is not coded to support, it MUST gracefully
   discard the message and continue normal operation. An ATMARP client
   is NOT REQUIRED to return any message to the sender of the
   unsupported message.

8.7.3 TL, ATM Number, and ATM Subaddress Encoding

   The encoding of the 8-bit TL (type and length) fields in ATMARP and
   In_ATMARP packets is as follows:

```
   MSB   8     7     6     5     4     3     2     1   LSB
       +-----+-----+-----+-----+-----+-----+-----+-----+
       |  0  | 1/0 |  Octet length of address          |
       +-----+-----+-----+-----+-----+-----+-----+-----+
```

   Where:
     bit.8   (reserved) = 0 (for future use)

     bit.7   (type)   = 0   ATM Forum NSAPA format
                         = 1   E.164 format

     bit.6-1 (length)   = 6 bit unsigned octet length of address
                          (MSB = bit.6, LSB = bit.1) Value
                          range is from 0 to 20 (decimal).

ATM addresses, as defined by the ATM Forum UNI 3.1 signaling
specification [9], include a "Calling Party Number Information
Element" and a "Calling Party Subaddress Information Element". These
Information Elements (IEs) SHOULD map to ATMARP/InATMARP source ATM
number and source ATM subaddress respectively. Furthermore, ATM
Forum defines a "Called Party Number Information Element" and a
"Called Party Subaddress Information Element". These IEs map to
ATMARP/InATMARP target ATM number and target ATM subaddress,
respectively.

The ATM Forum defines three structures for the combined use of number
and subaddress [9]:

```
                        ATM Number        ATM Subaddress
                        --------------    --------------
        Structure 1   ATM Forum NSAPA         null
        Structure 2       E.164               null
        Structure 3       E.164         ATM Forum NSAPA
```

ATMARP and InATMARP requests and replies for ATM address structures 1
and 2 MUST indicate a null or unknown ATM subaddress by setting the
appropriate subaddress length to zero; i.e., ar$sstl.length = 0 or
ar$tstl.length = 0, the corresponding type field (ar$sstl.type or
ar$tstl.type) MUST be ignored and the physical space for the ATM
subaddress buffer MUST not be allocated in the ATMARP packet. For
example, if ar$sstl.length=0, the storage for the source ATM
subaddress is not allocated and the first byte of the source protocol
address ar$spa follows immediately after the last byte of the source
hardware address ar$sha in the packet.

Null or unknown ATM addresses MUST be indicated by setting the
appropriate address length to zero; i.e., ar$shtl.length and
ar$thtl.length is zero and the corresponding type field (ar$sstl.type
or ar$tstl.type) MUST be ignored and the physical space for the ATM
address or ATM subaddress buffer MUST not be allocated in the ATMARP
packet.

8.7.4 ATMARP_NAK Packet Format

The ATMARP_NAK packet format is the same as the received
ATMARP_Request packet format with the operation code set to ARP_NAK,
i.e., the ATMARP_Request packet data is exactly copied (e.g., using
bcopy) for transmission with the ATMARP_Request operation code
changed to ARP_NAK value.

8.7.5 Variable Length Requirements for ATMARP Packets

ATMARP and InATMARP packets are variable in length.

A null or unknown source or target protocol address is indicated by
the corresponding length set to zero: e.g., when ar$spln or ar$tpln
is zero the physical space for the corresponding address structure
MUST not be allocated in the packet.

For backward compatibility with previous implementations, a null IPv4
protocol address may be received with length = 4 and an allocated
address in storage set to the value 0.0.0.0. Receiving stations MUST
be liberal in accepting this format of a null IPv4 address. However,
on transmitting an ATMARP or InATMARP packet, a null IPv4 address
MUST only be indicated by the length set to zero and MUST have no
storage allocated.

8.8 ATMARP/InATMARP Packet Encapsulation

ATMARP and InATMARP packets are to be encoded in AAL5 PDUs using
LLC/SNAP encapsulation. The format of the AAL5 CPCS-SDU payload
field for ATMARP/InATMARP PDUs is:

```
           Payload Format for ATMARP/InATMARP PDUs:
           +-----------------------------+
           |       LLC 0xAA-AA-03        |
           +-----------------------------+
           |       OUI 0x00-00-00        |
           +-----------------------------+
           |      EtherType 0x08-06      |
           +-----------------------------+
           |                             |
           |    ATMARP/InATMARP Packet   |
           |                             |
           +-----------------------------+
```

The LLC value of 0xAA-AA-03 (3 octets) indicates the presence of a
SNAP header.

The OUI value of 0x00-00-00 (3 octets) indicates that the following
two-bytes is an EtherType.

The EtherType value of 0x08-06 (2 octets) indicates ARP [4].

The total size of the LLC/SNAP header is fixed at 8-octets. This
aligns the start of the ATMARP packet on a 64-bit boundary relative
to the start of the AAL5 CPCS-SDU.

The LLC/SNAP encapsulation for ATMARP/InATMARP presented here is
consistent with the treatment of multiprotocol encapsulation of IP
over ATM AAL5 as specified in [2] and in the format of ATMARP over
IEEE 802 networks as specified in [5].

Traditionally, address resolution requests are broadcast to all
directly connected IP members within a LIS. It is conceivable in the
future that larger scaled ATM networks may handle ATMARP requests to
destinations outside the originating LIS, perhaps even globally;
issues raised by ATMARPing outside the LIS or by a global ATMARP
mechanism are beyond the scope of this memo.

9. IP BROADCAST ADDRESS

ATM does not support broadcast addressing, therefore there are no
mappings available from IP broadcast addresses to ATM broadcast
services. Note: this lack of mapping does not restrict members from
transmitting or receiving IP datagrams specifying any of the four
standard IP broadcast address forms as described in [8]. Members,
upon receiving an IP broadcast or IP subnet broadcast for their LIS,
MUST process the packet as if addressed to that station.

This memo recognizes the future development of standards and
implementations that will extend the operations as defined in this
memo to provide an IP broadcast capability for use by the classical
client.

10. IP MULTICAST ADDRESS

ATM does not directly support IP multicast address services,
therefore there are no mappings available from IP multicast addresses
to ATM multicast services. Current IP multicast implementations
(i.e., MBONE and IP tunneling, see [10]) will continue to operate
over ATM based logical IP subnets if operated in the WAN
configuration.

This memo recognizes the future development of ATM multicast service
addressing by the ATM Forum. When available and widely implemented,
the roll-over from the current IP multicast architecture to this new
ATM architecture will be straightforward.

This memo recognizes the future development of standards and
implementations that will extend the operations as defined in this
memo to provide an IP multicast capability for use by the classical
client.

11. SECURITY CONSIDERATIONS

Not all of the security issues relating to IP over ATM are clearly
understood at this time, due to the fluid state of ATM
specifications, newness of the technology, and other factors.

It is believed that ATM and IP facilities for authenticated call
management, authenticated end-to-end communications, and data
encryption will be needed in globally connected ATM networks. Such
future security facilities and their use by IP networks are beyond
the scope of this memo.

There are known security issues relating to host impersonation via
the address resolution protocols used in the Internet [13]. No
special security mechanisms have been added to the address resolution
mechanism defined here for use with networks using IP over ATM.

12. MIB SPECIFICATION

Clients built to this specification MUST implement and provide a
Management Information Base (MIB) as defined in "Definitions of
Managed Objects for Classical IP and ARP Over ATM Using SMIv2" [18].

13. OPEN ISSUES

o   Automatic configuration of client ATM addresses via DHCP [15] or
    via ATM UNI 3.1 Interim Local Management Interface (ILMI)
    services would be a useful extended service addition to this
    document and should be addressed in a separate memo.

o   ATMARP packets are not authenticated. This is a potentially
    serious flaw in the overall system by allowing a mechanism by
    which corrupt information may be introduced into the server
    system.

14. REFERENCES

[1] Piscitello, D., and J. Lawrence, "The Transmission of IP
    Datagrams over the SMDS Service", STD 52, RFC 1209, March 1991.

[2] Heinanen, J., "Multiprotocol Encapsulation over ATM Adaptation
    Layer 5", RFC 1483, July 1993.

[3] Plummer, D., "An Ethernet Address Resolution Protocol - or -
    Converting Network Protocol Addresses to 48.bit Ethernet
    Address for Transmission on Ethernet Hardware", STD 37, RFC
    826, November 1982.

[4] Reynolds, J., and J. Postel, "Assigned Numbers", STD 2, RFC 1700,
    July 1992.

[5] Postel, J., and J. Reynolds, "A Standard for the Transmission
    of IP Datagrams over IEEE 802 Networks", STD 43, RFC 1042,
    February 1988.

[6] CCITT, "Draft Recommendation I.363", CCITT Study Group XVIII, Geneva, 19-29 January 1993.

[7] CCITT, "Draft text for Q.93B", CCITT Study Group XI, 23 September - 2 October 1992.

[8] Braden, R., "Requirements for Internet Hosts -- Communication Layers", STD 3, RFC 1122, October 1989.

[9] ATM Forum, "ATM User-Network Interface (UNI) Specification Version 3.1.", ISBN 0-13-393828-X, Prentice-Hall, Inc., Upper Saddle River, NJ, 07458, September, 1994.

[10] Deering, S., "Host Extensions for IP Multicasting", STD 5, RFC 1112, August 1989.

[11] Colella, R., Gardner, E., and R. Callon, "Guidelines for OSI NSAP Allocation in the Internet", RFC 1237, July 1991.

[12] Bradely, T., and C. Brown, "Inverse Address Resolution Protocol", RFC 1293, January 1992.

[13] Bellovin, Steven M., "Security Problems in the TCP/IP Protocol Suite", ACM Computer Communications Review, Vol. 19, Issue 2, pp. 32-48, 1989.

[14] Knowles, S., "IESG Advice from Experience with Path MTU Discovery", RFC 1435, March 1993.

[15] Droms, R., "Dynamic Host Configuration Protocol", RFC 1541, March 1997.

[16] Kent C., and J. Mogul, "Fragmentation Considered Harmful", Proceedings of the ACM SIGCOMM '87 Workshop on Frontiers in Computer Communications Technology, August 1987.

[17] Mogul, J., and S. Deering, "Path MTU Discovery", RFC 1191, November 1990.

[18] Green, M., Luciani, J., White, K., and T. Kuo, "Definitions of Managed Objects for Classical IP and ARP over ATM Using SMIv2", RFC 2320, April 1998.

[19] ATM Forum, "ATM User-Network Interface (UNI) Specification Version 4.0", ATM Forum specfication af-sig-0061.000, ftp://ftp.atmforum.com/, July, 1996.

     [20] Bradner, S., "Key words for use in RFCs to Indicate Requirement
          Levels", BCP 14, RFC 2119, March 1997.

15. AUTHORS' ADDRESSES

     Mark Laubach
     Com21, Inc.
     750 Tasman Drive
     Milpitas, CA 95035

     Phone: 408.953.9175
     FAX: 408.953.9299
     EMail: laubach@com21.com

     Joel Halpern
     Newbridge Networks, Inc.
     593 Herndon Parkway
     Herndon, VA 22070-5241

     Phone: 703.736.5954
     FAX: 703.736.5959
     EMail: jhalpern@Newbridge.com

APPENDIX A - Update Information

This memo represents an update to RFC 1577 and RFC 1626. The
following changes are included in this memo:

o   Pointer to Classical MIB I-D for setting of variables

o   Single ATMARP server address to ATMARP server list, configurable
     via the MIB.

o   RFC 1626 text replaces MTU section

o   Client registration procedure from In_ATMARP to first
     ATMARP_Request

o   Clarification of variable length ATMARP packet format

o   Clarification of ARP_NAK packet format

o   Clarification of InATMARP packet format for null IPv4 addresses

o   Clarification on ATMARP registration and use of InATMARP_Reply
     for clients having more than one IP address in a LIS

Full Copyright Statement

Network Working Group   J. Luciani
Request for Comments: 2332   Bay Networks
Category: Standards Track   D. Katz
                                                               cisco Systems
                                                            D. Piscitello
                                                       Core Competence, Inc.
                                                                   B. Cole
                                                            Juniper Networks
                                                              N. Doraswamy
                                                               Bay Networks
                                                                 April 1998

RFC 2332 1

NBMA Next Hop Resolution Protocol (NHRP)

Status of this Memo

   This document specifies an Internet standards track protocol for the
   Internet community, and requests discussion and suggestions for
   improvements. Please refer to the current edition of the "Internet
   Official Protocol Standards" (STD 1) for the standardization state
   and status of this protocol. Distribution of this memo is unlimited.

Abstract

   This document describes the NBMA Next Hop Resolution Protocol (NHRP).
   NHRP can be used by a source station (host or router) connected to a
   Non-Broadcast, Multi-Access (NBMA) subnetwork to determine the
   internetworking layer address and NBMA subnetwork addresses of the
   "NBMA next hop" towards a destination station. If the destination is
   connected to the NBMA subnetwork, then the NBMA next hop is the
   destination station itself. Otherwise, the NBMA next hop is the
   egress router from the NBMA subnetwork that is "nearest" to the
   destination station. NHRP is intended for use in a multiprotocol
   internetworking layer environment over NBMA subnetworks.

   Note that while this protocol was developed for use with NBMA
   subnetworks, it is possible, if not likely, that it will be applied
   to BMA subnetworks as well. However, this usage of NHRP is for
   further study.

   This document is intended to be a functional superset of the NBMA
   Address Resolution Protocol (NARP) documented in [1].

Operation of NHRP as a means of establishing a transit path across an
NBMA subnetwork between two routers will be addressed in a separate
document (see [13]).

1. Introduction

   The keywords MUST, MUST NOT, REQUIRED, SHALL, SHALL NOT, SHOULD,
   SHOULD NOT, RECOMMENDED, MAY, and OPTIONAL, when they appear in this
   document, are to be interpreted as described in [15].

   The NBMA Next Hop Resolution Protocol (NHRP) allows a source station
   (a host or router), wishing to communicate over a Non-Broadcast,
   Multi-Access (NBMA) subnetwork, to determine the internetworking
   layer addresses and NBMA addresses of suitable "NBMA next hops"
   toward a destination station. A subnetwork can be non-broadcast
   either because it technically doesn't support broadcasting (e.g., an
   X.25 subnetwork) or because broadcasting is not feasible for one
   reason or another (e.g., an SMDS multicast group or an extended
   Ethernet would be too large). If the destination is connected to the
   NBMA subnetwork, then the NBMA next hop is the destination station
   itself. Otherwise, the NBMA next hop is the egress router from the
   NBMA subnetwork that is "nearest" to the destination station.

   One way to model an NBMA network is by using the notion of logically
   independent IP subnets (LISs). LISs, as defined in [3] and [4], have
   the following properties:

   1) All members of a LIS have the same IP network/subnet number
       and address mask.

   2) All members of a LIS are directly connected to the same
       NBMA subnetwork.

   3) All hosts and routers outside of the LIS are accessed via
       a router.

   4) All members of a LIS access each other directly (without
       routers).

   Address resolution as described in [3] and [4] only resolves the next
   hop address if the destination station is a member of the same LIS as
   the source station; otherwise, the source station must forward
   packets to a router that is a member of multiple LIS's. In multi-LIS

configurations, hop-by-hop address resolution may not be sufficient
to resolve the "NBMA next hop" toward the destination station, and IP
packets may have multiple IP hops through the NBMA subnetwork.

Another way to model NBMA is by using the notion of Local Address
Groups (LAGs) [10]. The essential difference between the LIS and the
LAG models is that while with the LIS model the outcome of the
"local/remote" forwarding decision is driven purely by addressing
information, with the LAG model the outcome of this decision is
decoupled from the addressing information and is coupled with the
Quality of Service and/or traffic characteristics. With the LAG
model any two entities on a common NBMA network could establish a
direct communication with each other, irrespective of the entities'
addresses.

Support for the LAG model assumes the existence of a mechanism that
allows any entity (i.e., host or router) connected to an NBMA network
to resolve an internetworking layer address to an NBMA address for
any other entity connected to the same NBMA network. This resolution
would take place regardless of the address assignments to these
entities. Within the parameters described in this document, NHRP
describes such a mechanism. For example, when the internetworking
layer address is of type IP, once the NBMA next hop has been
resolved, the source may either start sending IP packets to the
destination (in a connectionless NBMA subnetwork such as SMDS) or may
first establish a connection to the destination with the desired
bandwidth (in a connection-oriented NBMA subnetwork such as ATM).

Use of NHRP may be sufficient for hosts doing address resolution when
those hosts are directly connected to an NBMA subnetwork, allowing
for straightforward implementations in NBMA stations. NHRP also has
the capability of determining the egress point from an NBMA
subnetwork when the destination is not directly connected to the NBMA
subnetwork and the identity of the egress router is not learned by
other methods (such as routing protocols). Optional extensions to
NHRP provide additional robustness and diagnosability.

Address resolution techniques such as those described in [3] and [4]
may be in use when NHRP is deployed. ARP servers and services over
NBMA subnetworks may be required to support hosts that are not
capable of dealing with any model for communication other than the
LIS model, and deployed hosts may not implement NHRP but may continue
to support ARP variants such as those described in [3] and [4]. NHRP
is intended to reduce or eliminate the extra router hops required by
the LIS model, and can be deployed in a non-interfering manner with
existing ARP services [14].

The operation of NHRP to establish transit paths across NBMA
subnetworks between two routers requires additional mechanisms to
avoid stable routing loops, and will be described in a separate
document (see [13]).

2. Overview

2.1 Terminology

The term "network" is highly overloaded, and is especially confusing
in the context of NHRP. We use the following terms:

Internetwork layer--the media-independent layer (IP in the case of
TCP/IP networks).

Subnetwork layer--the media-dependent layer underlying the
internetwork layer, including the NBMA technology (ATM, X.25, SMDS,
etc.)

The term "server", unless explicitly stated to the contrary, refers
to a Next Hop Server (NHS). An NHS is an entity performing the
Next Hop Resolution Protocol service within the NBMA cloud. An NHS
is always tightly coupled with a routing entity (router, route
server or edge device) although the converse is not yet guaranteed
until ubiquitous deployment of this functionality occurs. Note
that the presence of intermediate routers that are not coupled with
an NHS entity may preclude the use of NHRP when source and
destination stations on different sides of such routers and thus
such routers may partition NHRP reachability within an NBMA
network.

The term "client", unless explicitly stated to the contrary, refers
to a Next Hop Resolution Protocol client (NHC). An NHC is an
entity which initiates NHRP requests of various types in order to
obtain access to the NHRP service.

The term "station" generally refers to a host or router which
contains an NHRP entity. Occasionally, the term station will
describe a "user" of the NHRP client or service functionality; the
difference in usage is largely semantic.

2.2 Protocol Overview

In this section, we briefly describe how a source S (which
potentially can be either a router or a host) uses NHRP to determine
the "NBMA next hop" to destination D.

For administrative and policy reasons, a physical NBMA subnetwork may
be partitioned into several, disjoint "Logical NBMA subnetworks". A
Logical NBMA subnetwork is defined as a collection of hosts and
routers that share unfiltered subnetwork connectivity over an NBMA
subnetwork. "Unfiltered subnetwork connectivity" refers to the
absence of closed user groups, address screening or similar features
that may be used to prevent direct communication between stations
connected to the same NBMA subnetwork. (Hereafter, unless otherwise
specified, we use the term "NBMA subnetwork" to mean *logical* NBMA
subnetwork.)

Placed within the NBMA subnetwork are one or more entities that
implement the NHRP protocol. Such stations which are capable of
answering NHRP Resolution Requests are known as "Next Hop Servers"
(NHSs). Each NHS serves a set of destination hosts, which may or may
not be directly connected to the NBMA subnetwork. NHSs cooperatively
resolve the NBMA next hop within their logical NBMA subnetwork. In
addition to NHRP, NHSs may support "classical" ARP service; however,
this will be the subject of a separate document [14].

An NHS maintains a cache which contains protocol layer address to
NBMA subnetwork layer address resolution information. This cache can
be constructed from information obtained from NHRP Register packets
(see Section 5.2.3 and 5.2.4), from NHRP Resolution Request/Reply
packets, or through mechanisms outside the scope of this document
(examples of such mechanisms might include ARP[3] and pre-configured
tables). Section 6.2 further describes cache management issues.

For a station within a given LIS to avoid providing NHS
functionality, there must be one or more NHSs within the NBMA
subnetwork which are providing authoritative address resolution
information on its behalf. Such an NHS is said to be "serving" the
station. A station on a LIS that lacks NHS functionality and is a
client of the NHRP service is known as NHRP Client or just NHCs. If
a serving NHS is to be able to supply the address resolution
information for an NHC then NHSs must exist at each hop along all
routed paths between the NHC making the resolution request and the
destination NHC. The last NHRP entity along the routed path is the
serving NHS; that is, NHRP Resolution Requests are not forwarded to
destination NHCs but rather are processed by the serving NHS.

An NHC also maintains a cache of protocol address to NBMA address
resolution information. This cache is populated through information
obtained from NHRP Resolution Reply packets, from manual
configuration, or through mechanisms outside the scope of this
document.

The protocol proceeds as follows. An event occurs triggering station
S to want to resolve the NBMA address of a path to D. This is most
likely to be when a data packet addressed to station D is to be
emitted from station S (either because station S is a host, or
station S is a transit router), but the address resolution could also
be triggered by other means (a routing protocol update packet, for
example). Station S first determines the next hop to station D
through normal routing processes (for a host, the next hop may simply
be the default router; for routers, this is the "next hop" to the
destination internetwork layer address). If the destination's
address resolution information is already available in S's cache then
that information is used to forward the packet. Otherwise, if the
next hop is reachable through one of its NBMA interfaces, S
constructs an NHRP Resolution Request packet (see Section 5.2.1)
containing station D's internetwork layer address as the (target)
destination address, S's own internetwork layer address as the source
address (Next Hop Resolution Request initiator), and station S's NBMA
addressing information. Station S may also indicate that it prefers
an authoritative NHRP Resolution Reply (i.e., station S only wishes
to receive an NHRP Resolution Reply from an NHS serving the
destination NHC). Station S emits the NHRP Resolution Request packet
towards the destination.

If the NHRP Resolution Request is triggered by a data packet then S
may, while awaiting an NHRP Resolution Reply, choose to dispose of
the data packet in one of the following ways:

   (a) Drop the packet
   (b) Retain the packet until the NHRP Resolution Reply arrives
        and a more optimal path is available
   (c) Forward the packet along the routed path toward D

The choice of which of the above to perform is a local policy matter,
though option (c) is the recommended default, since it may allow data
to flow to the destination while the NBMA address is being resolved.
Note that an NHRP Resolution Request for a given destination MUST NOT
be triggered on every packet.

When the NHS receives an NHRP Resolution Request, a check is made to
see if it serves station D. If the NHS does not serve D, the NHS
forwards the NHRP Resolution Request to another NHS. Mechanisms for
determining how to forward the NHRP Resolution Request are discussed
in Section 3.

If this NHS serves D, the NHS resolves station D's NBMA address
information, and generates a positive NHRP Resolution Reply on D's
behalf. NHRP Resolution Replies in this scenario are always marked
as "authoritative". The NHRP Resolution Reply packet contains the

address resolution information for station D which is to be sent back
to S. Note that if station D is not on the NBMA subnetwork, the next
hop internetwork layer address will be that of the egress router
through which packets for station D are forwarded.

A transit NHS receiving an NHRP Resolution Reply may cache the
address resolution information contained therein. To a subsequent
NHRP Resolution Request, this NHS may respond with the cached, "non-
authoritative" address resolution information if the NHS is permitted
to do so (see Sections 5.2.2 and 6.2 for more information on non-
authoritative versus authoritative NHRP Resolution Replies). Non-
authoritative NHRP Resolution Replies are distinguished from
authoritative NHRP Resolution Replies so that if a communication
attempt based on non-authoritative information fails, a source
station can choose to send an authoritative NHRP Resolution Request.
NHSs MUST NOT respond to authoritative NHRP Resolution Requests with
cached information.

If the determination is made that no NHS in the NBMA subnetwork can
reply to the NHRP Resolution Request for D then a negative NHRP
Resolution Reply (NAK) is returned. This occurs when (a) no next-hop
resolution information is available for station D from any NHS, or
(b) an NHS is unable to forward the NHRP Resolution Request (e.g.,
connectivity is lost).

NHRP Registration Requests, NHRP Purge Requests, NHRP Purge Replies,
and NHRP Error Indications follow a routed path in the same fashion
that NHRP Resolution Requests and NHRP Resolution Replies do.
Specifically, "requests" and "indications" follow the routed path
from Source Protocol Address (which is the address of the station
initiating the communication) to the Destination Protocol Address.
"Replies", on the other hand, follow the routed path from the
Destination Protocol Address back to the Source Protocol Address with
the following exceptions: in the case of a NHRP Registration Reply
and in the case of an NHC initiated NHRP Purge Request, the packet is
always returned via a direct VC (see Sections 5.2.4 and 5.2.5); if
one does not exists then one MUST be created.

NHRP Requests and NHRP Replies do NOT cross the borders of a NBMA
subnetwork however further study is being done in this area (see
Section 7). Thus, the internetwork layer data traffic out of and
into an NBMA subnetwork always traverses an internetwork layer router
at its border.

NHRP optionally provides a mechanism to send a NHRP Resolution Reply
which contains aggregated address resolution information. For
example, suppose that router X is the next hop from station S to
station D and that X is an egress router for all stations sharing an

internetwork layer address prefix with station D. When an NHRP
Resolution Reply is generated in response to a NHRP Resolution
Request, the responder may augment the internetwork layer address of
station D with a prefix length (see Section 5.2.0.1). A subsequent
(non-authoritative) NHRP Resolution Request for some destination that
shares an internetwork layer address prefix (for the number of bits
specified in the prefix length) with D may be satisfied with this
cached information. See section 6.2 regarding caching issues.

To dynamically detect subnetwork-layer filtering in NBMA subnetworks
(e.g., X.25 closed user group facility, or SMDS address screens), to
trace the routed path that an NHRP packet takes, or to provide loop
detection and diagnostic capabilities, a "Route Record" may be
included in NHRP packets (see Sections 5.3.2 and 5.3.3). The Route
Record extensions are the NHRP Forward Transit NHS Record Extension
and the NHRP Reverse Transit NHS Record Extension. They contain the
internetwork (and subnetwork layer) addresses of all intermediate
NHSs between source and destination and between destination and
source respectively. When a source station is unable to communicate
with the responder (e.g., an attempt to open an SVC fails), it may
attempt to do so successively with other subnetwork layer addresses
in the NHRP Forward Transit NHS Record Extension until it succeeds
(if authentication policy permits such action). This approach can
find a suitable egress point in the presence of subnetwork-layer
filtering (which may be source/destination sensitive, for instance,
without necessarily creating separate logical NBMA subnetworks) or
subnetwork-layer congestion (especially in connection-oriented
media).

3. Deployment

NHRP Resolution Requests traverse one or more hops within an NBMA
subnetwork before reaching the station that is expected to generate a
response. Each station, including the source station, chooses a
neighboring NHS to which it will forward the NHRP Resolution Request.
The NHS selection procedure typically involves applying a destination
protocol layer address to the protocol layer routing table which
causes a routing decision to be returned. This routing decision is
then used to forward the NHRP Resolution Request to the downstream
NHS. The destination protocol layer address previously mentioned is
carried within the NHRP Resolution Request packet. Note that even
though a protocol layer address was used to acquire a routing
decision, NHRP packets are not encapsulated within a protocol layer
header but rather are carried at the NBMA layer using the
encapsulation described in Section 5.

Each NHS/router examines the NHRP Resolution Request packet on its
way toward the destination. Each NHS which the NHRP packet traverses
on the way to the packet's destination might modify the packet (e.g.,
updating the Forward Record extension). Ignoring error situations,
the NHRP Resolution Request eventually arrives at a station that is
to generate an NHRP Resolution Reply. This responding station
"serves" the destination. The responding station generates an NHRP
Resolution Reply using the source protocol address from within the
NHRP packet to determine where the NHRP Resolution Reply should be
sent.

Rather than use routing to determine the next hop for an NHRP packet,
an NHS may use other applicable means (such as static configuration
information) in order to determine to which neighboring NHSs to
forward the NHRP Resolution Request packet as long as such other
means would not cause the NHRP packet to arrive at an NHS which is
not along the routed path. The use of static configuration
information for this purpose is beyond the scope of this document.

The NHS serving a particular destination must lie along the routed
path to that destination. In practice, this means that all egress
routers must double as NHSs serving the destinations beyond them, and
that hosts on the NBMA subnetwork are served by routers that double
as NHSs. Also, this implies that forwarding of NHRP packets within
an NBMA subnetwork requires a contiguous deployment of NHRP capable
routers. It is important that, in a given LIS/LAG which is using
NHRP, all NHSs within the LIS/LAG have at least some portion of their
resolution databases synchronized so that a packet arriving at one
router/NHS in a given LIS/LAG will be forwarded in the same fashion
as a packet arriving at a different router/NHS for the given LIS/LAG.
One method, among others, is to use the Server Cache Synchronization
Protocol (SCSP) [12]. It is RECOMMENDED that SCSP be the method used
when a LIS/LAG contains two or more router/NHSs.

During migration to NHRP, it cannot be expected that all routers
within the NBMA subnetwork are NHRP capable. Thus, NHRP traffic
which would otherwise need to be forwarded through such routers can
be expected to be dropped due to the NHRP packet not being
recognized. In this case, NHRP will be unable to establish any
transit paths whose discovery requires the traversal of the non-NHRP
speaking routers. If the client has tried and failed to acquire a
cut through path then the client should use the network layer routed
path as a default.

If an NBMA technology offers a group, an anycast, or a multicast
addressing feature then the NHC may be configured with such an
address (appropriate to the routing realm it participates in) which
would be assigned to all NHS serving that routing realm. This

address can then be used for establishing an initial connection to an NHS to transmit a registration request. This address may not be used for sending NHRP requests. The resulting VC may be used for NHRP requests if and only if the registration response is received over that VC, thereby indicating that one happens to have anycast connected to an NHS serving the LIS/LAG. In the case of non-connection oriented networks, or of multicast (rather than anycast) addresses, the addres MUST NOT be used for sending NHRP resolution requests.

When an NHS "serves" an NHC, the NHS MUST send NHRP messages destined for the NHC directly to the NHC. That is, the NHRP message MUST NOT transit through any NHS which is not serving the NHC when the NHRP message is currently at an NHS which does serve the NHC (this, of course, assumes the NHRP message is destined for the NHC). Further, an NHS which serves an NHC SHOULD have a direct NBMA level connection to that NHC (see Section 5.2.3 and 5.2.4 for examples).

With the exception of NHRP Registration Requests (see Section 5.2.3 and 5.2.4 for details of the NHRP Registration Request case), an NHC MUST send NHRP messages over a direct NBMA level connection between the serving NHS and the served NHC.

It may not be desirable to maintain semi-permanent NBMA level connectivity between the NHC and the NHS.   In this case, when NBMA level connectivity is initially setup between the NHS and the NHC (as described in Section 5.2.4), the NBMA address of the NHS should be obtained through the NBMA level signaling technology. This address should be stored for future use in setting up subsequent NBMA level connections. A somewhat more information rich technique to obtain the address information (and more) of the serving NHS would be for the NHC to include the Responder Address extension (see Section 5.3.1) in the NHRP Registration Request and to store the information returned to the NHC in the Responder Address extension which is subsequently included in the NHRP Registration Reply. Note also that, in practice, a client's default router should also be its NHS; thus a client may be able to know the NBMA address of its NHS from the configuration which was already required for the client to be able to communicate. Further, as mentioned in Section 4, NHCs may be configured with the addressing information of one or more NHSs.

4. Configuration

   Next Hop Clients

      An NHC connected to an NBMA subnetwork MAY be configured with the
      Protocol address(es) and NBMA address(es) of its NHS(s). The
      NHS(s) will likely also represent the NHC's default or peer

routers, so their NBMA addresses may be obtained from the NHC's
existing configuration. If the NHC is attached to several
subnetworks (including logical NBMA subnetworks), the NHC should
also be configured to receive routing information from its NHS(s)
and peer routers so that it can determine which internetwork layer
networks are reachable through which subnetworks.

Next Hop Servers

An NHS is configured with knowledge of its own internetwork layer
and NBMA addresses. An NHS MAY also be configured with a set of
internetwork layer address prefixes that correspond to the
internetwork layer addresses of the stations it serves. The NBMA
addresses of the stations served by the NHS may be learned via NHRP
Registration packets.

If a served NHC is attached to several subnetworks, the
router/route-server coresident with the serving NHS may also need
to be configured to advertise routing information to such NHCs.

If an NHS acts as an egress router for stations connected to other
subnetworks than the NBMA subnetwork, the NHS must, in addition to
the above, be configured to exchange routing information between
the NBMA subnetwork and these other subnetworks.

In all cases, routing information is exchanged using conventional
intra-domain and/or inter-domain routing protocols.

5. NHRP Packet Formats

This section describes the format of NHRP packets. In the following,
unless otherwise stated explicitly, the unqualified term "request"
refers generically to any of the NHRP packet types which are
"requests". Further, unless otherwise stated explicitly, the
unqualified term "reply" refers generically to any of the NHRP packet
types which are "replies".

An NHRP packet consists of a Fixed Part, a Mandatory Part, and an
Extensions Part. The Fixed Part is common to all NHRP packet types.
The Mandatory Part MUST be present, but varies depending on packet
type. The Extensions Part also varies depending on packet type, and
need not be present.

The length of the Fixed Part is fixed at 20 octets. The length of
the Mandatory Part is determined by the contents of the extensions
offset field (ar$extoff). If ar$extoff=0x0 then the mandatory part
length is equal to total packet length (ar$pktsz) minus 20 otherwise
the mandatory part length is equal to ar$extoff minus 20. The length

of the Extensions Part is implied by ar$pktsz minus ar$extoff. NHSs
may increase the size of an NHRP packet as a result of extension
processing, but not beyond the offered maximum packet size of the
NBMA network.

NHRP packets are actually members of a wider class of address mapping
and management protocols being developed by the IETF. A specific
encapsulation, based on the native formats used on the particular
NBMA network over which NHRP is carried, indicates the generic IETF
mapping and management protocol. For example, SMDS networks always
use LLC/SNAP encapsulation at the NBMA layer [4], and an NHRP packet
is preceded by the following LLC/SNAP encapsulation:

[0xAA-AA-03] [0x00-00-5E] [0x00-03]

The first three octets are LLC, indicating that SNAP follows. The
SNAP OUI portion is the IANA's OUI, and the SNAP PID portion
identifies the mapping and management protocol. A field in the Fixed
Header following the encapsulation indicates that it is NHRP.

ATM uses either LLC/SNAP encapsulation of each packet (including
NHRP), or uses no encapsulation on VCs dedicated to a single protocol
(see [7]). Frame Relay and X.25 both use NLPID/SNAP encapsulation or
identification of NHRP, using a NLPID of 0x0080 and the same SNAP
contents as above (see [8], [9]).

Fields marked "unused" MUST be set to zero on transmission, and
ignored on receipt.

Most packet types (ar$op.type) have both internetwork layer
protocol-independent fields and protocol-specific fields. The
protocol type/snap fields (ar$pro.type/snap) qualify the format of
the protocol-specific fields.

5.1 NHRP Fixed Header

The Fixed Part of the NHRP packet contains those elements of the NHRP
packet which are always present and do not vary in size with the type
of packet.

```
 0                   1                   2                   3
 0 1 2 3 4 5 6 7 8 9 0 1 2 3 4 5 6 7 8 9 0 1 2 3 4 5 6 7 8 9 0 1
+-+-+-+-+-+-+-+-+-+-+-+-+-+-+-+-+-+-+-+-+-+-+-+-+-+-+-+-+-+-+-+-+
|             ar$afn            |          ar$pro.type          |
+-+-+-+-+-+-+-+-+-+-+-+-+-+-+-+-+-+-+-+-+-+-+-+-+-+-+-+-+-+-+-+-+
|                          ar$pro.snap                          |
+-+-+-+-+-+-+-+-+-+-+-+-+-+-+-+-+-+-+-+-+-+-+-+-+-+-+-+-+-+-+-+-+
|  ar$pro.snap  |   ar$hopcnt   |           ar$pktsz            |
+-+-+-+-+-+-+-+-+-+-+-+-+-+-+-+-+-+-+-+-+-+-+-+-+-+-+-+-+-+-+-+-+
|           ar$chksum           |           ar$extoff           |
+-+-+-+-+-+-+-+-+-+-+-+-+-+-+-+-+-+-+-+-+-+-+-+-+-+-+-+-+-+-+-+-+
| ar$op.version |   ar$op.type  |    ar$shtl    |    ar$sstl     |
+-+-+-+-+-+-+-+-+-+-+-+-+-+-+-+-+-+-+-+-+-+-+-+-+-+-+-+-+-+-+-+-+
```

ar$afn
  Defines the type of "link layer" addresses being carried. This
  number is taken from the 'address family number' list specified in
  [6]. This field has implications to the coding of ar$shtl and
  ar$sstl as described below.

ar$pro.type
  field is a 16 bit unsigned integer representing the following
  number space:

     0x0000 to 0x00FF Protocols defined by the equivalent NLPIDs.
     0x0100 to 0x03FF Reserved for future use by the IETF.
     0x0400 to 0x04FF Allocated for use by the ATM Forum.
     0x0500 to 0x05FF Experimental/Local use.
     0x0600 to 0xFFFF Protocols defined by the equivalent Ethertypes.

  (based on the observations that valid Ethertypes are never smaller
  than 0x600, and NLPIDs never larger than 0xFF.)

ar$pro.snap
  When ar$pro.type has a value of 0x0080, a SNAP encoded extension is
  being used to encode the protocol type. This snap extension is
  placed in the ar$pro.snap field. This is termed the 'long form'
  protocol ID. If ar$pro != 0x0080 then the ar$pro.snap field MUST be
  zero on transmit and ignored on receive. The ar$pro.type field
  itself identifies the protocol being referred to. This is termed
  the 'short form' protocol ID.

  In all cases, where a protocol has an assigned number in the
  ar$pro.type space (excluding 0x0080) the short form MUST be used
  when transmitting NHRP messages; i.e., if Ethertype or NLPID
  codings exist then they are used on transmit rather than the

ethertype.   If both Ethertype and NLPID codings exist then when
transmitting NHRP messages, the Ethertype coding MUST be used (this
is consistent with RFC 1483 coding). So, for example, the
following codings exist for IP:

```
SNAP:       ar$pro.type = 0x00-80, ar$pro.snap = 0x00-00-00-08-00
NLPID:      ar$pro.type = 0x00-CC, ar$pro.snap = 0x00-00-00-00-00
Ethertype: ar$pro.type = 0x08-00, ar$pro.snap = 0x00-00-00-00-00
```

and thus, since the Ethertype coding exists, it is used in
preference.

ar$hopcnt
    The Hop count indicates the maximum number of NHSs that an NHRP
    packet is allowed to traverse before being discarded. This field
    is used in a similar fashion to the way that a TTL is used in an IP
    packet and should be set accordingly. Each NHS decrements the TTL
    as the NHRP packet transits the NHS on the way to the next hop
    along the routed path to the destination. If an NHS receives an
    NHRP packet which it would normally forward to a next hop and that
    packet contains an ar$hopcnt set to zero then the NHS sends an
    error indication message back to the source protocol address
    stating that the hop count has been exceeded (see Section 5.2.7)
    and the NHS drops the packet in error; however, an error
    indication is never sent as a result of receiving an error
    indication. When a responding NHS replies to an NHRP request, that
    NHS places a value in ar$hopcnt as if it were sending a request of
    its own.

ar$pktsz
    The total length of the NHRP packet, in octets (excluding link
    layer encapsulation).

ar$chksum
    The standard IP checksum over the entire NHRP packet starting at
    the fixed header. If the packet is an odd number of bytes in
    length then this calculation is performed as if a byte set to 0x00
    is appended to the end of the packet.

ar$extoff
    This field identifies the existence and location of NHRP
    extensions. If this field is 0 then no extensions exist otherwise
    this field represents the offset from the beginning of the NHRP
    packet (i.e., starting from the ar$afn field) of the first
    extension.

ar$op.version
   This field indicates what version of generic address mapping and
   management protocol is represented by this message.

   0   MARS protocol [11].
   1   NHRP as defined in this document.
   0x02 - 0xEF   Reserved for future use by the IETF.
   0xF0 - 0xFE   Allocated for use by the ATM Forum.
   0xFF   Experimental/Local use.

ar$op.type
   When ar$op.version == 1, this is the NHRP packet type: NHRP
   Resolution Request(1), NHRP Resolution Reply(2), NHRP Registration
   Request(3), NHRP Registration Reply(4), NHRP Purge Request(5), NHRP
   Purge Reply(6), or NHRP Error Indication(7). Use of NHRP packet
   Types in the range 128 to 255 are reserved for research or use in
   other protocol development and will be administered by IANA as
   described in Section 9.

ar$shtl
   Type & length of source NBMA address interpreted in the context of
   the 'address family number'[6] indicated by ar$afn. See below for
   more details.

ar$sstl
   Type & length of source NBMA subaddress interpreted in the context
   of the 'address family number'[6] indicated by ar$afn. When an
   NBMA technology has no concept of a subaddress, the subaddress
   length is always coded ar$sstl = 0 and no storage is allocated for
   the subaddress in the appropriate mandatory part. See below for
   more details.

Subnetwork layer address type/length fields (e.g., ar$shtl, Cli Addr
T/L) and subnetwork layer subaddresses type/length fields (e.g.,
ar$sstl, Cli SAddr T/L) are coded as follows:

```
 7 6 5 4 3 2 1 0
+-+-+-+-+-+-+-+-+
|0|x| length    |
+-+-+-+-+-+-+-+-+
```

The most significant bit is reserved and MUST be set to zero. The
second most significant bit (x) is a flag indicating whether the
address being referred to is in:

   - NSAP format (x = 0).
   - Native E.164 format (x = 1).

For NBMA technologies that use neither NSAP nor E.164 format
addresses, x = 0 SHALL be used to indicate the native form for the
particular NBMA technology.

If the NBMA network is ATM and a subaddress (e.g., Source NBMA
SubAddress, Client NBMA SubAddress) is to be included in any part of
the NHRP packet then ar$afn MUST be set to 0x000F; further, the
subnetwork layer address type/length fields (e.g., ar$shtl, Cli Addr
T/L) and subnetwork layer subaddress type/length fields (e.g.,
ar$sstl, Cli SAddr T/L) MUST be coded as in [11]. If the NBMA
network is ATM and no subaddress field is to be included in any part
of the NHRP packet then ar$afn MAY be set to 0x0003 (NSAP) or 0x0008
(E.164) accordingly.

The bottom 6 bits is an unsigned integer value indicating the length
of the associated NBMA address in octets. If this value is zero the
flag x is ignored.

5.2.0 Mandatory Part

The Mandatory Part of the NHRP packet contains the operation specific
information (e.g., NHRP Resolution Request/Reply, etc.) and variable
length data which is pertinent to the packet type.

5.2.0.1 Mandatory Part Format

Sections 5.2.1 through 5.2.6 have a very similar mandatory part.
This mandatory part includes a common header and zero or more Client
Information Entries (CIEs). Section 5.2.7 has a different format
which is specified in that section.

The common header looks like the following:

```
 0                   1                   2                   3
 0 1 2 3 4 5 6 7 8 9 0 1 2 3 4 5 6 7 8 9 0 1 2 3 4 5 6 7 8 9 0 1
+-+-+-+-+-+-+-+-+-+-+-+-+-+-+-+-+-+-+-+-+-+-+-+-+-+-+-+-+-+-+-+-+
| Src Proto Len | Dst Proto Len |              Flags            |
+-+-+-+-+-+-+-+-+-+-+-+-+-+-+-+-+-+-+-+-+-+-+-+-+-+-+-+-+-+-+-+-+
|                           Request ID                          |
+-+-+-+-+-+-+-+-+-+-+-+-+-+-+-+-+-+-+-+-+-+-+-+-+-+-+-+-+-+-+-+-+
|               Source NBMA Address (variable length)           |
+-+-+-+-+-+-+-+-+-+-+-+-+-+-+-+-+-+-+-+-+-+-+-+-+-+-+-+-+-+-+-+-+
|               Source NBMA Subaddress (variable length)        |
+-+-+-+-+-+-+-+-+-+-+-+-+-+-+-+-+-+-+-+-+-+-+-+-+-+-+-+-+-+-+-+-+
|               Source Protocol Address (variable length)       |
+-+-+-+-+-+-+-+-+-+-+-+-+-+-+-+-+-+-+-+-+-+-+-+-+-+-+-+-+-+-+-+-+
|            Destination  Protocol Address (variable length)    |
+-+-+-+-+-+-+-+-+-+-+-+-+-+-+-+-+-+-+-+-+-+-+-+-+-+-+-+-+-+-+-+-+
```

And the CIEs have the following format:

```
0                   1                   2                   3
0 1 2 3 4 5 6 7 8 9 0 1 2 3 4 5 6 7 8 9 0 1 2 3 4 5 6 7 8 9 0 1
+-+-+-+-+-+-+-+-+-+-+-+-+-+-+-+-+-+-+-+-+-+-+-+-+-+-+-+-+-+-+-+-+
|    Code       | Prefix Length |             unused            |
+-+-+-+-+-+-+-+-+-+-+-+-+-+-+-+-+-+-+-+-+-+-+-+-+-+-+-+-+-+-+-+-+
| Maximum Transmission Unit     |         Holding Time          |
+-+-+-+-+-+-+-+-+-+-+-+-+-+-+-+-+-+-+-+-+-+-+-+-+-+-+-+-+-+-+-+-+
| Cli Addr T/L | Cli SAddr T/L | Cli Proto Len |   Preference   |
+-+-+-+-+-+-+-+-+-+-+-+-+-+-+-+-+-+-+-+-+-+-+-+-+-+-+-+-+-+-+-+-+
|              Client NBMA Address (variable length)            |
+-+-+-+-+-+-+-+-+-+-+-+-+-+-+-+-+-+-+-+-+-+-+-+-+-+-+-+-+-+-+-+-+
|            Client NBMA Subaddress (variable length)           |
+-+-+-+-+-+-+-+-+-+-+-+-+-+-+-+-+-+-+-+-+-+-+-+-+-+-+-+-+-+-+-+-+
|            Client Protocol Address (variable length)          |
+-+-+-+-+-+-+-+-+-+-+-+-+-+-+-+-+-+-+-+-+-+-+-+-+-+-+-+-+-+-+-+-+
                      ...................
+-+-+-+-+-+-+-+-+-+-+-+-+-+-+-+-+-+-+-+-+-+-+-+-+-+-+-+-+-+-+-+-+
|    Code       | Prefix Length |             unused            |
+-+-+-+-+-+-+-+-+-+-+-+-+-+-+-+-+-+-+-+-+-+-+-+-+-+-+-+-+-+-+-+-+
| Maximum Transmission Unit     |         Holding Time          |
+-+-+-+-+-+-+-+-+-+-+-+-+-+-+-+-+-+-+-+-+-+-+-+-+-+-+-+-+-+-+-+-+
| Cli Addr T/L | Cli SAddr T/L | Cli Proto Len |   Preference   |
+-+-+-+-+-+-+-+-+-+-+-+-+-+-+-+-+-+-+-+-+-+-+-+-+-+-+-+-+-+-+-+-+
|              Client NBMA Address (variable length)            |
+-+-+-+-+-+-+-+-+-+-+-+-+-+-+-+-+-+-+-+-+-+-+-+-+-+-+-+-+-+-+-+-+
|            Client NBMA Subaddress (variable length)           |
+-+-+-+-+-+-+-+-+-+-+-+-+-+-+-+-+-+-+-+-+-+-+-+-+-+-+-+-+-+-+-+-+
|            Client Protocol Address (variable length)          |
+-+-+-+-+-+-+-+-+-+-+-+-+-+-+-+-+-+-+-+-+-+-+-+-+-+-+-+-+-+-+-+-+
```

The meanings of the fields are as follows:

Src Proto Len
  This field holds the length in octets of the Source Protocol
  Address.

Dst Proto Len
  This field holds the length in octets of the Destination Protocol
  Address.

Flags
  These flags are specific to the given message type and they are
  explained in each section.

Request ID
   A value which, when coupled with the address of the source,
   provides a unique identifier for the information contained in a
   "request" packet. This value is copied directly from an "request"
   packet into the associated "reply". When a sender of a "request"
   receives "reply", it will compare the Request ID and source address
   information in the received "reply" against that found in its
   outstanding "request" list. When a match is found then the
   "request" is considered to be acknowledged.

   The value is taken from a 32 bit counter that is incremented each
   time a new "request" is transmitted. The same value MUST be used
   when resending a "request", i.e., when a "reply" has not been
   received for a "request" and a retry is sent after an appropriate
   interval.

   It is RECOMMENDED that the initial value for this number be 0. A
   node MAY reuse a sequence number if and only if the reuse of the
   sequence number is not precluded by use of a particular method of
   synchronization (e.g., as described in Appendix A).

The NBMA address/subaddress form specified below allows combined
E.164/NSAPA form of NBMA addressing. For NBMA technologies without a
subaddress concept, the subaddress field is always ZERO length and
ar$sstl = 0.

Source NBMA Address
   The Source NBMA address field is the address of the source station
   which is sending the "request". If the field's length as specified
   in ar$shtl is 0 then no storage is allocated for this address at
   all.

Source NBMA SubAddress
   The Source NBMA subaddress field is the address of the source
   station which is sending the "request". If the field's length as
   specified in ar$sstl is 0 then no storage is allocated for this
   address at all.

For those NBMA technologies which have a notion of "Calling Party
Addresses", the Source NBMA Addresses above are the addresses used
when signaling for an SVC.

"Requests" and "indications" follow the routed path from Source
Protocol Address to the Destination Protocol Address. "Replies", on
the other hand, follow the routed path from the Destination Protocol
Address back to the Source Protocol Address with the following

exceptions: in the case of a NHRP Registration Reply and in the case
of an NHC initiated NHRP Purge Request, the packet is always returned
via a direct VC (see Sections 5.2.4 and 5.2.5).

Source Protocol Address
  This is the protocol address of the station which is sending the
  "request". This is also the protocol address of the station toward
  which a "reply" packet is sent.

Destination Protocol Address
  This is the protocol address of the station toward which a
  "request" packet is sent.

Code
  This field is message specific. See the relevant message sections
  below. In general, this field is a NAK code; i.e., when the field
  is 0 in a reply then the packet is acknowledging a request and if
  it contains any other value the packet contains a negative
  acknowledgment.

Prefix Length
  This field is message specific. See the relevant message sections
  below. In general, however, this fields is used to indicate that
  the information carried in an NHRP message pertains to an
  equivalence class of internetwork layer addresses rather than just
  a single internetwork layer address specified. All internetwork
  layer addresses that match the first "Prefix Length" bit positions
  for the specific internetwork layer address are included in the
  equivalence class. If this field is set to 0x00 then this field
  MUST be ignored and no equivalence information is assumed (note
  that 0x00 is thus equivalent to 0xFF).

Maximum Transmission Unit
  This field gives the maximum transmission unit for the relevant
  client station. If this value is 0 then either the default MTU is
  used or the MTU negotiated via signaling is used if such
  negotiation is possible for the given NBMA.

Holding Time
  The Holding Time field specifies the number of seconds for which
  the Next Hop NBMA information specified in the CIE is considered to
  be valid. Cached information SHALL be discarded when the holding
  time expires. This field must be set to 0 on a NAK.

Cli Addr T/L
Type & length of next hop NBMA address specified in the CIE. This
field is interpreted in the context of the 'address family
number'[6] indicated by ar$afn (e.g., ar$afn=0x0003 for ATM).

Cli SAddr T/L
Type & length of next hop NBMA subaddress specified in the CIE.
This field is interpreted in the context of the 'address family
number'[6] indicated by ar$afn (e.g., ar$afn=0x0015 for ATM makes
the address an E.164 and the subaddress an ATM Forum NSAP address).
When an NBMA technology has no concept of a subaddress, the
subaddress is always null with a length of 0. When the address
length is specified as 0 no storage is allocated for the address.

Cli Proto Len
This field holds the length in octets of the Client Protocol
Address specified in the CIE.

Preference
This field specifies the preference for use of the specific CIE
relative to other CIEs. Higher values indicate higher preference.
Action taken when multiple CIEs have equal or highest preference
value is a local matter.

Client NBMA Address
This is the client's NBMA address.

Client NBMA SubAddress
This is the client's NBMA subaddress.

Client Protocol Address
This is the client's internetworking layer address specified.

Note that an NHS may cache source address binding information from an
NHRP Resolution Request if and only if the conditions described in
Section 6.2 are met for the NHS. In all other cases, source address
binding information appearing in an NHRP message MUST NOT be cached.

5.2.1 NHRP Resolution Request

The NHRP Resolution Request packet has a Type code of 1. Its
mandatory part is coded as described in Section 5.2.0.1 and the
message specific meanings of the fields are as follows:

Flags - The flags field is coded as follows:

```
 0                   1
 0 1 2 3 4 5 6 7 8 9 0 1 2 3 4 5
+-+-+-+-+-+-+-+-+-+-+-+-+-+-+-+-+
|Q|A|D|U|S|        unused        |
+-+-+-+-+-+-+-+-+-+-+-+-+-+-+-+-+
```

Q

  Set if the station sending the NHRP Resolution Request is a
  router; clear if the it is a host.

A

  This bit is set in a NHRP Resolution Request if only
  authoritative next hop information is desired and is clear
  otherwise. See the NHRP Resolution Reply section below for
  further details on the "A" bit and its usage.

D

  Unused (clear on transmit)

U

  This is the Uniqueness bit. This bit aids in duplicate address
  detection. When this bit is set in an NHRP Resolution Request
  and one or more entries exist in the NHS cache which meet the
  requirements of the NHRP Resolution Request then only the CIE in
  the NHS's cache with this bit set will be returned. Note that
  even if this bit was set at registration time, there may still be
  multiple CIEs that might fulfill the NHRP Resolution Request
  because an entire subnet can be registered through use of the
  Prefix Length in the CIE and the address of interest might be
  within such a subnet. If the "uniqueness" bit is set and the
  responding NHS has one or more cache entries which match the
  request but no such cache entry has the "uniqueness" bit set,
  then the NHRP Resolution Reply returns with a NAK code of "13 -
  Binding Exists But Is Not Unique" and no CIE is included. If a
  client wishes to receive non- unique Next Hop Entries, then
  the client must have the "uniqueness" bit set to zero in its NHRP
  Resolution Request. Note that when this bit is set in an NHRP
  Registration Request, only a single CIE may be specified in the
  NHRP Registration Request and that CIE must have the Prefix
  Length field set to 0xFF.

S

  Set if the binding between the Source Protocol Address and the
  Source NBMA information in the NHRP Resolution Request is
  guaranteed to be stable and accurate (e.g., these addresses are
  those of an ingress router which is connected to an ethernet stub
  network or the NHC is an NBMA attached host).

Zero or one CIEs (see Section 5.2.0.1) may be specified in an NHRP
Resolution Request. If one is specified then that entry carries the
pertinent information for the client sourcing the NHRP Resolution
Request. Usage of the CIE in the NHRP Resolution Request is
described below:

   Prefix Length
      If a CIE is specified in the NHRP Resolution Request then the
      Prefix Length field may be used to qualify the widest acceptable
      prefix which may be used to satisfy the NHRP Resolution Request.
      In the case of NHRP Resolution Request/Reply, the Prefix Length
      specifies the equivalence class of addresses which match the
      first "Prefix Length" bit positions of the Destination Protocol
      Address. If the "U" bit is set in the common header then this
      field MUST be set to 0xFF.

   Maximum Transmission Unit
      This field gives the maximum transmission unit for the source
      station. A possible use of this field in the NHRP Resolution
      Request packet is for the NHRP Resolution Requester to ask for a
      target MTU.

   Holding Time
      The Holding Time specified in the one CIE permitted to be
      included in an NHRP Resolution Request is the amount of time
      which the source address binding information in the NHRP
      Resolution Request is permitted to cached by transit and
      responding NHSs. Note that this field may only have a non-zero
      value if the S bit is set.

   All other fields in the CIE MUST be ignored and SHOULD be set to 0.

   The Destination Protocol Address in the common header of the
   Mandatory Part of this message contains the protocol address of the
   station for which resolution is desired. An NHC MUST send the NHRP
   Resolution Request directly to one of its serving NHSs (see Section 3
   for more information).

5.2.2 NHRP Resolution Reply

   The NHRP Resolution Reply packet has a Type code of 2. CIEs
   correspond to Next Hop Entries in an NHS's cache which match the
   criteria in the NHRP Resolution Request. Its mandatory part is coded
   as described in Section 5.2.0.1. The message specific meanings of
   the fields are as follows:

   Flags - The flags field is coded as follows:

```
 0                   1
 0 1 2 3 4 5 6 7 8 9 0 1 2 3 4 5
+-+-+-+-+-+-+-+-+-+-+-+-+-+-+-+-+
|Q|A|D|U|S|          unused          |
+-+-+-+-+-+-+-+-+-+-+-+-+-+-+-+-+
```

Q
   Copied from the NHRP Resolution Request. Set if the NHRP
   Resolution Requester is a router; clear if it is a host.

A
   Set if the next hop CIE in the NHRP Resolution Reply is
   authoritative; clear if the NHRP Resolution Reply is non-
   authoritative.

   When an NHS receives a NHRP Resolution Request for authoritative
   information for which it is the authoritative source, it MUST
   respond with a NHRP Resolution Reply containing all and only
   those next hop CIEs which are contained in the NHS's cache which
   both match the criteria of the NHRP Resolution Request and are
   authoritative cache entries. An NHS is an authoritative source
   for a NHRP Resolution Request if the information in the NHS's
   cache matches the NHRP Resolution Request criteria and that
   information was obtained through a NHRP Registration Request or
   through synchronization with an NHS which obtained this
   information through a NHRP Registration Request. An
   authoritative cache entry is one which is obtained through a NHRP
   Registration Request or through synchronization with an NHS which
   obtained this information through a NHRP Registration Request.

   An NHS obtains non-authoritative CIEs through promiscuous
   listening to NHRP packets other than NHRP Registrations which are
   directed at it. A NHRP Resolution Request which indicates a
   request for non-authoritative information should cause a NHRP
   Resolution Reply which contains all entries in the replying NHS's
   cache (i.e., both authoritative and non-authoritative) which
   match the criteria specified in the request.

D
   Set if the association between destination and the associate next
   hop information included in all CIEs of the NHRP Resolution Reply
   is guaranteed to be stable for the lifetime of the information
   (the holding time). This is the case if the Next Hop protocol
   address in a CIE identifies the destination (though it may be
   different in value than the Destination address if the
   destination system has multiple addresses) or if the destination
   is not connected directly to the NBMA subnetwork but the egress
   router to that destination is guaranteed to be stable (such as

when the destination is immediately adjacent to the egress router
through a non-NBMA interface).

U

This is the Uniqueness bit. See the NHRP Resolution Request
section above for details. When this bit is set, only one CIE is
included since only one unique binding should exist in an NHS's
cache.

S

Copied from NHRP Resolution Request message.

One or more CIEs are specified in the NHRP Resolution Reply. Each CIE
contains NHRP next hop information which the responding NHS has
cached and which matches the parameters specified in the NHRP
Resolution Request. If no match is found by the NHS issuing the NHRP
Resolution Reply then a single CIE is enclosed with the a CIE Code
set appropriately (see below) and all other fields MUST be ignored
and SHOULD be set to 0. In order to facilitate the use of NHRP by
minimal client implementations, the first CIE MUST contain the next
hop with the highest preference value so that such an implementation
need parse only a single CIE.

Code
    If this field is set to zero then this packet contains a
    positively acknowledged NHRP Resolution Reply. If this field
    contains any other value then this message contains an NHRP
    Resolution Reply NAK which means that an appropriate
    internetworking layer to NBMA address binding was not available
    in the responding NHS's cache. If NHRP Resolution Reply contains
    a Client Information Entry with a NAK Code other than 0 then it
    MUST NOT contain any other CIE. Currently defined NAK Codes are
    as follows:

4 - Administratively Prohibited

    An NHS may refuse an NHRP Resolution Request attempt for
    administrative reasons (due to policy constraints or routing
    state). If so, the NHS MUST send an NHRP Resolution Reply
    which contains a NAK code of 4.

5 - Insufficient Resources

    If an NHS cannot serve a station due to a lack of resources
    (e.g., can't store sufficient information to send a purge if
    routing changes), the NHS MUST reply with a NAKed NHRP
    Resolution Reply which contains a NAK code of 5.

12 - No Internetworking Layer Address to NBMA Address Binding
     Exists

   This code states that there were absolutely no internetworking
   layer address to NBMA address bindings found in the responding
   NHS's cache.

13 - Binding Exists But Is Not Unique

   This code states that there were one or more internetworking
   layer address to NBMA address bindings found in the responding
   NHS's cache, however none of them had the uniqueness bit set.

Prefix Length
   In the case of NHRP Resolution Reply, the Prefix Length specifies
   the equivalence class of addresses which match the first "Prefix
   Length" bit positions of the Destination Protocol Address.

Holding Time
   The Holding Time specified in a CIE of an NHRP Resolution Reply
   is the amount of time remaining before the expiration of the
   client information which is cached at the replying NHS. It is
   not the value which was registered by the client.

The remainder of the fields for the CIE for each next hop are
filled out as they were defined when the next hop was registered
with the responding NHS (or one of the responding NHS's
synchronized servers) via the NHRP Registration Request.

Load-splitting may be performed when more than one Client Information
Entry is returned to a requester when equal preference values are
specified. Also, the alternative addresses may be used in case of
connectivity failure in the NBMA subnetwork (such as a failed call
attempt in connection-oriented NBMA subnetworks).

Any extensions present in the NHRP Resolution Request packet MUST be
present in the NHRP Resolution Reply even if the extension is non-
Compulsory.

If an unsolicited NHRP Resolution Reply packet is received, an Error
Indication of type Invalid NHRP Resolution Reply Received SHOULD be
sent in response.

When an NHS that serves a given NHC receives an NHRP Resolution Reply
destined for that NHC then the NHS must MUST send the NHRP Resolution
Reply directly to the NHC (see Section 3).

5.2.3 NHRP Registration Request

The NHRP Registration Request is sent from a station to an NHS to
notify the NHS of the station's NBMA information. It has a Type code
of 3. Each CIE corresponds to Next Hop information which is to be
cached at an NHS. The mandatory part of an NHRP Registration Request
is coded as described in Section 5.2.0.1. The message specific
meanings of the fields are as follows:

Flags - The flags field is coded as follows:

```
    0                     1
    0 1 2 3 4 5 6 7 8 9 0 1 2 3 4 5
   +-+-+-+-+-+-+-+-+-+-+-+-+-+-+-+-+
   |U|          unused             |
   +-+-+-+-+-+-+-+-+-+-+-+-+-+-+-+-+
```

   U
      This is the Uniqueness bit. When set in an NHRP Registration
      Request, this bit indicates that the registration of the protocol
      address is unique within the confines of the set of synchronized
      NHSs. This "uniqueness" qualifier MUST be stored in the NHS/NHC
      cache. Any attempt to register a binding between the protocol
      address and an NBMA address when this bit is set MUST be rejected
      with a Code of "14 - Unique Internetworking Layer Address Already
      Registered" if the replying NHS already has a cache entry for the
      protocol address and the cache entry has the "uniqueness" bit
      set. A registration of a CIE's information is rejected when the
      CIE is returned with the Code field set to anything other than
      0x00. See the description of the uniqueness bit in NHRP
      Resolution Request section above for further details. When this
      bit is set only, only one CIE MAY be included in the NHRP
      Registration Request.

   Request ID
      The request ID has the same meaning as described in Section
      5.2.0.1. However, the request ID for NHRP Registrations which is
      maintained at each client MUST be kept in non-volatile memory so
      that when a client crashes and reregisters there will be no
      inconsistency in the NHS's database. In order to reduce the
      overhead associated with updating non-volatile memory, the actual
      updating need not be done with every increment of the Request ID
      but could be done, for example, every 50 or 100 increments. In
      this scenario, when a client crashes and reregisters it knows to
      add 100 to the value of the Request ID in the non-volatile memory
      before using the Request ID for subsequent registrations.

One or more CIEs are specified in the NHRP Registration Request.
Each CIE contains next hop information which a client is attempting
to register with its servers. Generally, all fields in CIEs enclosed
in NHRP Registration Requests are coded as described in Section
5.2.0.1. However, if a station is only registering itself with the
NHRP Registration Request then it MAY code the Cli Addr T/L, Cli
SAddr T/L, and Cli Proto Len as zero which signifies that the client
address information is to be taken from the source information in the
common header (see Section 5.2.0.1). Below, further clarification is
given for some fields in a CIE in the context of a NHRP Registration
Request.

    Code
        This field is set to 0x00 in NHRP Registration Requests.

    Prefix Length

        This field may be used in a NHRP Registration Request to register
        equivalence information for the Client Protocol Address specified
        in the CIE of an NHRP Registration Request In the case of NHRP
        Registration Request, the Prefix Length specifies the equivalence
        class of addresses which match the first "Prefix Length" bit
        positions of the Client Protocol Address. If the "U" bit is set
        in the common header then this field MUST be set to 0xFF.

The NHRP Registration Request is used to register an NHC's NHRP
information with its NHSs. If an NHC is configured with the protocol
address of a serving NHS then the NHC may place the NHS's protocol
address in the Destination Protocol Address field of the NHRP
Registration Request common header otherwise the NHC must place its
own protocol address in the Destination Protocol Address field.

When an NHS receives an NHRP Registration Request which has the
Destination Protocol Address field set to an address which belongs to
a LIS/LAG for which the NHS is serving then if the Destination
Protocol Address field is equal to the Source Protocol Address field
(which would happen if the NHC put its protocol address in the
Destination Protocol Address) or the Destination Protocol Address
field is equal to the protocol address of the NHS then the NHS
processes the NHRP Registration Request after doing appropriate error
checking (including any applicable policy checking).

When an NHS receives an NHRP Registration Request which has the
Destination Protocol Address field set to an address which does not
belong to a LIS/LAG for which the NHS is serving then the NHS
forwards the packet down the routed path toward the appropriate
LIS/LAG.

When an NHS receives an NHRP Registration Request which has the
Destination Protocol Address field set to an address which belongs to
a LIS/LAG for which the NHS is serving then if the Destination
Protocol Address field does not equal the Source Protocol Address
field and the Destination Protocol Address field does not equal the
protocol address of the NHS then the NHS forwards the message to the
appropriate NHS within the LIS/LAG as specified by Destination
Protocol Address field.

It is possible that a misconfigured station will attempt to register
with the wrong NHS (i.e., one that cannot serve it due to policy
constraints or routing state). If this is the case, the NHS MUST
reply with a NAK-ed Registration Reply of type Can't Serve This
Address.

If an NHS cannot serve a station due to a lack of resources, the NHS
MUST reply with a NAK-ed Registration Reply of type Registration
Overflow.

In order to keep the registration entry from being discarded, the
station MUST re-send the NHRP Registration Request packet often
enough to refresh the registration, even in the face of occasional
packet loss. It is recommended that the NHRP Registration Request
packet be sent at an interval equal to one-third of the Holding Time
specified therein.

5.2.4 NHRP Registration Reply

The NHRP Registration Reply is sent by an NHS to a client in response
to that client's NHRP Registration Request. If the Code field of a
CIE in the NHRP Registration Reply has anything other than zero in it
then the NHRP Registration Reply is a NAK otherwise the reply is an
ACK. The NHRP Registration Reply has a Type code of 4.

An NHRP Registration Reply is formed from an NHRP Registration
Request by changing the type code to 4, updating the CIE Code field,
and filling in the appropriate extensions if they exist. The message
specific meanings of the fields are as follows:

Attempts to register the information in the CIEs of an NHRP
Registration Request may fail for various reasons. If this is the
case then each failed attempt to register the information in a CIE of
an NHRP Registration Request is logged in the associated NHRP
Registration Reply by setting the CIE Code field to the appropriate
error code as shown below:

CIE Code

0 - Successful Registration

The information in the CIE was successfully registered with the NHS.

4 - Administratively Prohibited

An NHS may refuse an NHRP Registration Request attempt for administrative reasons (due to policy constraints or routing state). If so, the NHS MUST send an NHRP Registration Reply which contains a NAK code of 4.

5 - Insufficient Resources

If an NHS cannot serve a station due to a lack of resources, the NHS MUST reply with a NAKed NHRP Registration Reply which contains a NAK code of 5.

14 - Unique Internetworking Layer Address Already Registered
If a client tries to register a protocol address to NBMA address binding with the uniqueness bit on and the protocol address already exists in the NHS's cache then if that cache entry also has the uniqueness bit on then this NAK Code is returned in the CIE in the NHRP Registration Reply.

Due to the possible existence of asymmetric routing, an NHRP Registration Reply may not be able to merely follow the routed path back to the source protocol address specified in the common header of the NHRP Registration Reply. As a result, there MUST exist a direct NBMA level connection between the NHC and its NHS on which to send the NHRP Registration Reply before NHRP Registration Reply may be returned to the NHC. If such a connection does not exist then the NHS must setup such a connection to the NHC by using the source NBMA information supplied in the common header of the NHRP Registration Request.

5.2.5 NHRP Purge Request

The NHRP Purge Request packet is sent in order to invalidate cached information in a station. The NHRP Purge Request packet has a type code of 5. The mandatory part of an NHRP Purge Request is coded as described in Section 5.2.0.1. The message specific meanings of the fields are as follows:

Flags - The flags field is coded as follows:

```
 0                   1
 0 1 2 3 4 5 6 7 8 9 0 1 2 3 4 5
+-+-+-+-+-+-+-+-+-+-+-+-+-+-+-+-+
|N|         unused              |
+-+-+-+-+-+-+-+-+-+-+-+-+-+-+-+-+
```

N
   When set, this bit tells the receiver of the NHRP Purge Request
   that the requester does not expect to receive an NHRP Purge
   Reply. If an unsolicited NHRP Purge Reply is received by a
   station where that station is identified in the Source Protocol
   Address of the packet then that packet must be ignored.

One or more CIEs are specified in the NHRP Purge Request. Each CIE
contains next hop information which is to be purged from an NHS/NHC
cache. Generally, all fields in CIEs enclosed in NHRP Purge Requests
are coded as described in Section 5.2.0.1. Below, further
clarification is given for some fields in a CIE in the context of a
NHRP Purge Request.

Code
   This field is set to 0x00 in NHRP Purge Requests.

Prefix Length

   In the case of NHRP Purge Requests, the Prefix Length specifies
   the equivalence class of addresses which match the first "Prefix
   Length" bit positions of the Client Protocol Address specified in
   the CIE. All next hop information which contains a protocol
   address which matches an element of this equivalence class is to
   be purged from the receivers cache.

The Maximum Transmission Unit and Preference fields of the CIE are
coded as zero. The Holding Time should be coded as zero but there
may be some utility in supplying a "short" holding time to be
applied to the matching next hop information before that
information would be purged; this usage is for further study. The
Client Protocol Address field and the Cli Proto Len field MUST be
filled in. The Client Protocol Address is filled in with the
protocol address to be purged from the receiving station's cache
while the Cli Proto Len is set the length of the purged client's
protocol address. All remaining fields in the CIE MAY be set to
zero although the client NBMA information (and associated length
fields) MAY be specified to narrow the scope of the NHRP Purge
Request if requester desires. However, the receiver of an NHRP
Purge Request may choose to ignore the Client NBMA information if
it is supplied.

An NHRP Purge Request packet is sent from an NHS to a station to cause it to delete previously cached information. This is done when the information may be no longer valid (typically when the NHS has previously provided next hop information for a station that is not directly connected to the NBMA subnetwork, and the egress point to that station may have changed).

An NHRP Purge Request packet may also be sent from an NHC to an NHS with which the NHC had previously registered. This allows for an NHC to invalidate its registration with NHRP before it would otherwise expire via the holding timer. If an NHC does not have knowledge of a protocol address of a serving NHS then the NHC must place its own protocol address in the Destination Protocol Address field and forward the packet along the routed path. Otherwise, the NHC must place the protocol address of a serving NHS in this field.

Serving NHSs may need to send one or more new NHRP Purge Requests as a result of receiving a purge from one of their served NHCs since the NHS may have previously responded to NHRP Resolution Requests for that NHC's NBMA information. These purges are "new" in that they are sourced by the NHS and not the NHC; that is, for each NHC that previously sent a NHRP Resolution Request for the purged NHC NBMA information, an NHRP Purge Request is sent which contains the Source Protocol/NBMA Addresses of the NHS and the Destination Protocol Address of the NHC which previously sent an NHRP Resolution Request prior to the purge.

The station sending the NHRP Purge Request MAY periodically retransmit the NHRP Purge Request until either NHRP Purge Request is acknowledged or until the holding time of the information being purged has expired. Retransmission strategies for NHRP Purge Requests are a local matter.

When a station receives an NHRP Purge Request, it MUST discard any previously cached information that matches the information in the CIEs.

An NHRP Purge Reply MUST be returned for the NHRP Purge Request even if the station does not have a matching cache entry assuming that the "N" bit is off in the NHRP Purge Request.

If the station wishes to reestablish communication with the destination shortly after receiving an NHRP Purge Request, it should make an authoritative NHRP Resolution Request in order to avoid any stale cache entries that might be present in intermediate NHSs (See section 6.2.2.). It is recommended that authoritative NHRP Resolution Requests be made for the duration of the holding time of the old information.

5.2.6 NHRP Purge Reply

   The NHRP Purge Reply packet is sent in order to assure the sender of
   an NHRP Purge Request that all cached information of the specified
   type has been purged from the station sending the reply. The NHRP
   Purge Reply has a type code of 6.

   An NHRP Purge Reply is formed from an NHRP Purge Request by merely
   changing the type code in the request to 6. The packet is then
   returned to the requester after filling in the appropriate extensions
   if they exist.

5.2.7 NHRP Error Indication

   The NHRP Error Indication is used to convey error indications to the
   sender of an NHRP packet. It has a type code of 7. The Mandatory
   Part has the following format:

```
 0                   1                   2                   3
 0 1 2 3 4 5 6 7 8 9 0 1 2 3 4 5 6 7 8 9 0 1 2 3 4 5 6 7 8 9 0 1
+-+-+-+-+-+-+-+-+-+-+-+-+-+-+-+-+-+-+-+-+-+-+-+-+-+-+-+-+-+-+-+-+
| Src Proto Len | Dst Proto Len |             unused            |
+-+-+-+-+-+-+-+-+-+-+-+-+-+-+-+-+-+-+-+-+-+-+-+-+-+-+-+-+-+-+-+-+
|          Error Code           |         Error Offset          |
+-+-+-+-+-+-+-+-+-+-+-+-+-+-+-+-+-+-+-+-+-+-+-+-+-+-+-+-+-+-+-+-+
|            Source NBMA Address (variable length)             |
+-+-+-+-+-+-+-+-+-+-+-+-+-+-+-+-+-+-+-+-+-+-+-+-+-+-+-+-+-+-+-+-+
|          Source NBMA Subaddress (variable length)            |
+-+-+-+-+-+-+-+-+-+-+-+-+-+-+-+-+-+-+-+-+-+-+-+-+-+-+-+-+-+-+-+-+
|          Source Protocol Address (variable length)           |
+-+-+-+-+-+-+-+-+-+-+-+-+-+-+-+-+-+-+-+-+-+-+-+-+-+-+-+-+-+-+-+-+
|        Destination  Protocol Address (variable length)       |
+-+-+-+-+-+-+-+-+-+-+-+-+-+-+-+-+-+-+-+-+-+-+-+-+-+-+-+-+-+-+-+-+
|       Contents of NHRP Packet in error (variable length)     |
+-+-+-+-+-+-+-+-+-+-+-+-+-+-+-+-+-+-+-+-+-+-+-+-+-+-+-+-+-+-+-+-+
```

   Src Proto Len
     This field holds the length in octets of the Source Protocol
     Address.

   Dst Proto Len
     This field holds the length in octets of the Destination Protocol
     Address.

Error Code
    An error code indicating the type of error detected, chosen from
    the following list:

    1 - Unrecognized Extension

        When the Compulsory bit of an extension in NHRP packet is set,
        the NHRP packet cannot be processed unless the extension has
        been processed. The responder MUST return an NHRP Error
        Indication of type Unrecognized Extension if it is incapable of
        processing the extension. However, if a transit NHS (one which
        is not going to generate a reply) detects an unrecognized
        extension, it SHALL ignore the extension.

    3 - NHRP Loop Detected

        A Loop Detected error is generated when it is determined that
        an NHRP packet is being forwarded in a loop.

    6 - Protocol Address Unreachable

        This error occurs when a packet it moving along the routed path
        and it reaches a point such that the protocol address of
        interest is not reachable.

    7 - Protocol Error

        A generic packet processing error has occurred (e.g., invalid
        version number, invalid protocol type, failed checksum, etc.)

    8 - NHRP SDU Size Exceeded

        If the SDU size of the NHRP packet exceeds the MTU size of the
        NBMA network then this error is returned.

    9 - Invalid Extension

        If an NHS finds an extension in a packet which is inappropriate
        for the packet type, an error is sent back to the sender with
        Invalid Extension as the code.

    10 - Invalid NHRP Resolution Reply Received

        If a client receives a NHRP Resolution Reply for a Next Hop
        Resolution Request which it believes it did not make then an
        error packet is sent to the station making the reply with an
        error code of Invalid Reply Received.

        11 - Authentication Failure

            If a received packet fails an authentication test then this
            error is returned.

        15 - Hop Count Exceeded

            The hop count which was specified in the Fixed Header of an
            NHRP message has been exceeded.

    Error Offset
        The offset in octets into the original NHRP packet in which an
        error was detected. This offset is calculated starting from the
        NHRP Fixed Header.

    Source NBMA Address
        The Source NBMA address field is the address of the station which
        observed the error.

    Source NBMA SubAddress
        The Source NBMA subaddress field is the address of the station
        which observed the error. If the field's length as specified in
        ar$sstl is 0 then no storage is allocated for this address at all.

    Source Protocol Address
        This is the protocol address of the station which issued the Error
        packet.

    Destination Protocol Address
        This is the protocol address of the station which sent the packet
        which was found to be in error.

    An NHRP Error Indication packet SHALL NEVER be generated in response
    to another NHRP Error Indication packet. When an NHRP Error
    Indication packet is generated, the offending NHRP packet SHALL be
    discarded. In no case should more than one NHRP Error Indication
    packet be generated for a single NHRP packet.

    If an NHS sees its own Protocol and NBMA Addresses in the Source NBMA
    and Source Protocol address fields of a transiting NHRP Error
    Indication packet then the NHS will quietly drop the packet and do
    nothing (this scenario would occur when the NHRP Error Indication
    packet was itself in a loop).

    Note that no extensions may be added to an NHRP Error Indication.

5.3 Extensions Part

   The Extensions Part, if present, carries one or more extensions in
   {Type, Length, Value} triplets.

   Extensions have the following format:

```
0                   1                   2                   3
0 1 2 3 4 5 6 7 8 9 0 1 2 3 4 5 6 7 8 9 0 1 2 3 4 5 6 7 8 9 0 1
+-+-+-+-+-+-+-+-+-+-+-+-+-+-+-+-+-+-+-+-+-+-+-+-+-+-+-+-+-+-+-+-+
|C|u|          Type             |             Length             |
+-+-+-+-+-+-+-+-+-+-+-+-+-+-+-+-+-+-+-+-+-+-+-+-+-+-+-+-+-+-+-+-+
|                          Value...                             |
+-+-+-+-+-+-+-+-+-+-+-+-+-+-+-+-+-+-+-+-+-+-+-+-+-+-+-+-+-+-+-+-+
```

   C
     "Compulsory." If clear, and the NHS does not recognize the type
     code, the extension may safely be ignored. If set, and the NHS
     does not recognize the type code, the NHRP "request" is considered
     to be in error. (See below for details.)

   u
     Unused and must be set to zero.

   Type
     The extension type code (see below). The extension type is not
     qualified by the Compulsory bit, but is orthogonal to it.

   Length
     The length in octets of the value (not including the Type and
     Length fields; a null extension will have only an extension header
     and a length of zero).

   When extensions exist, the extensions list is terminated by the Null
   TLV, having Type = 0 and Length = 0.

   Extensions may occur in any order, but any particular extension type
   may occur only once in an NHRP packet unless explicitly stated to the
   contrary in the extensions definition. For example, the vendor-
   private extension may occur multiple times in a packet in order to
   allow for extensions which do not share the same vendor ID to be
   represented. It is RECOMMENDED that a given vendor include no more
   than one Vendor Private Extension.

   An NHS MUST NOT change the order of extensions. That is, the order
   of extensions placed in an NHRP packet by an NHC (or by an NHS when
   an NHS sources a packet) MUST be preserved as the packet moves
   between NHSs. Minimal NHC implementations MUST only recognize, but

not necessarily parse, the Vendor Private extension and the End Of
Extensions extension. Extensions are only present in a "reply" if
they were present in the corresponding "request" with the exception
of Vendor Private extensions. The previous statement is not intended
to preclude the creation of NHS-only extensions which might be added
to and removed from NHRP packets by the same NHS; such extensions
MUST not be propagated to NHCs.

The Compulsory bit provides for a means to add to the extension set.
If the bit is set in an extension then the station responding to the
NHRP message which contains that extension MUST be able to understand
the extension (in this case, the station responding to the message is
the station that would issue an NHRP reply in response to a NHRP
request). As a result, the responder MUST return an NHRP Error
Indication of type Unrecognized Extension. If the Compulsory bit is
clear then the extension can be safely ignored; however, if an
ignored extension is in a "request" then it MUST be returned,
unchanged, in the corresponding "reply" packet type.

If a transit NHS (one which is not going to generate a "reply")
detects an unrecognized extension, it SHALL ignore the extension. If
the Compulsory bit is set, the transit NHS MUST NOT cache the
information contained in the packet and MUST NOT identify itself as
an egress router (in the Forward Record or Reverse Record
extensions). Effectively, this means, if a transit NHS encounters an
extension which it cannot process and which has the Compulsory bit
set then that NHS MUST NOT participate in any way in the protocol
exchange other than acting as a forwarding agent.

The NHRP extension Type space is subdivided to encourage use outside
the IETF.

     0x0000 - 0x0FFF   Reserved for NHRP.
     0x1000 - 0x11FF   Allocated to the ATM Forum.
     0x1200 - 0x37FF   Reserved for the IETF.
     0x3800 - 0x3FFF   Experimental use.

IANA will administer the ranges reserved for the IETF as described in
Section 9. Values in the 'Experimental use' range have only local
significance.

5.3.0 The End Of Extensions

     Compulsory = 1
     Type = 0
     Length = 0

When extensions exist, the extensions list is terminated by the End
Of Extensions/Null TLV.

5.3.1 Responder Address Extension

    Compulsory = 1
    Type = 3
    Length = variable

This extension is used to determine the address of the NHRP
responder; i.e., the entity that generates the appropriate "reply"
packet for a given "request" packet. In the case of an NHRP
Resolution Request, the station responding may be different (in the
case of cached replies) than the system identified in the Next Hop
field of the NHRP Resolution Reply. Further, this extension may aid
in detecting loops in the NHRP forwarding path.

This extension uses a single CIE with the extension specific meanings
of the fields set as follows:

The Prefix Length fields MUST be set to 0 and ignored.

CIE Code
    5 - Insufficient Resources
        If the responder to an NHRP Resolution Request is an egress point
        for the target of the address resolution request (i.e., it is one
        of the stations identified in the list of CIEs in an NHRP
        Resolution Reply) and the Responder Address extension is included
        in the NHRP Resolution Request and insufficient resources to
        setup a cut-through VC exist at the responder then the Code field
        of the Responder Address Extension is set to 5 in order to tell
        the client that a VC setup attempt would in all likelihood be
        rejected; otherwise this field MUST be coded as a zero. NHCs MAY
        use this field to influence whether they attempt to setup a cut-
        through to the egress router.

Maximum Transmission Unit
    This field gives the maximum transmission unit preferred by the
    responder. If this value is 0 then either the default MTU is used
    or the MTU negotiated via signaling is used if such negotiation is
    possible for the given NBMA.

Holding Time
    The Holding Time field specifies the number of seconds for which
    the NBMA information of the responser is considered to be valid.
    Cached information SHALL be discarded when the holding time
    expires.

"Client Address" information is actually "Responder Address"
information for this extension. Thus, for example, Cli Addr T/L is
the responder NBMA address type and length field.

If a "requester" desires this information, the "requester" SHALL
include this extension with a value of zero. Note that this implies
that no storage is allocated for the Holding Time and Type/Length
fields until the "Value" portion of the extension is filled out.

If an NHS is generating a "reply" packet in response to a "request"
containing this extension, the NHS SHALL include this extension,
containing its protocol address in the "reply". If an NHS has more
than one protocol address, it SHALL use the same protocol address
consistently in all of the Responder Address, Forward Transit NHS
Record, and Reverse Transit NHS Record extensions. The choice of
which of several protocol address to include in this extension is a
local matter.

If an NHRP Resolution Reply packet being forwarded by an NHS contains
a protocol address of that NHS in the Responder Address Extension
then that NHS SHALL generate an NHRP Error Indication of type "NHRP
Loop Detected" and discard the NHRP Resolution Reply.

If an NHRP Resolution Reply packet is being returned by an
intermediate NHS based on cached data, it SHALL place its own address
in this extension (differentiating it from the address in the Next
Hop field).

5.3.2 NHRP Forward Transit NHS Record Extension

    Compulsory = 1
    Type = 4
    Length = variable

The NHRP Forward Transit NHS record contains a list of transit NHSs
through which a "request" has traversed. Each NHS SHALL append to
the extension a Forward Transit NHS element (as specified below)
containing its Protocol address. The extension length field and the
ar$chksum fields SHALL be adjusted appropriately.

The responding NHS, as described in Section 5.3.1, SHALL NOT update
this extension.

In addition, NHSs that are willing to act as egress routers for
packets from the source to the destination SHALL include information
about their NBMA Address.

This extension uses a single CIE per NHS Record element with the
extension specific meanings of the fields set as follows:

The Prefix Length fields MUST be set to 0 and ignored.

CIE Code
    5 - Insufficient Resources
        If an NHRP Resolution Request contains an NHRP Forward Transit
        NHS Record Extension and insufficient resources to setup a cut-
        through VC exist at the current transit NHS then the CIE Code
        field for NHRP Forward Transit NHS Record Extension is set to 5
        in order to tell the client that a VC setup attempt would in all
        likelihood be rejected; otherwise this field MUST be coded as a
        zero. NHCs MAY use this field to influence whether they attempt
        to setup a cut-through as described in Section 2.2. Note that
        the NHRP Reverse Transit NHS Record Extension MUST always have
        this field set to zero.

Maximum Transmission Unit
    This field gives the maximum transmission unit preferred by the
    transit NHS. If this value is 0 then either the default MTU is
    used or the MTU negotiated via signaling is used if such
    negotiation is possible for the given NBMA.

Holding Time
    The Holding Time field specifies the number of seconds for which
    the NBMA information of the transit NHS is considered to be valid.
    Cached information SHALL be discarded when the holding time
    expires.

"Client Address" information is actually "Forward Transit NHS
Address" information for this extension. Thus, for example, Cli Addr
T/L is the transit NHS NBMA address type and length field.

If a "requester" wishes to obtain this information, it SHALL include
this extension with a length of zero. Note that this implies that no
storage is allocated for the Holding Time and Type/Length fields
until the "Value" portion of the extension is filled out.

If an NHS has more than one Protocol address, it SHALL use the same
Protocol address consistently in all of the Responder Address,
Forward NHS Record, and Reverse NHS Record extensions. The choice of
which of several Protocol addresses to include in this extension is a
local matter.

If a "request" that is being forwarded by an NHS contains the
Protocol Address of that NHS in one of the Forward Transit NHS
elements then the NHS SHALL generate an NHRP Error Indication of type
"NHRP Loop Detected" and discard the "request".

5.3.3 NHRP Reverse Transit NHS Record Extension

   Compulsory = 1
   Type = 5
   Length = variable

The NHRP Reverse Transit NHS record contains a list of transit NHSs
through which a "reply" has traversed. Each NHS SHALL append a
Reverse Transit NHS element (as specified below) containing its
Protocol address to this extension. The extension length field and
ar$chksum SHALL be adjusted appropriately.

The responding NHS, as described in Section 5.3.1, SHALL NOT update
this extension.

In addition, NHSs that are willing to act as egress routers for
packets from the source to the destination SHALL include information
about their NBMA Address.

This extension uses a single CIE per NHS Record element with the
extension specific meanings of the fields set as follows:

The CIE Code and Prefix Length fields MUST be set to 0 and ignored.

Maximum Transmission Unit
   This field gives the maximum transmission unit preferred by the
   transit NHS. If this value is 0 then either the default MTU is
   used or the MTU negotiated via signaling is used if such
   negotiation is possible for the given NBMA.

Holding Time
   The Holding Time field specifies the number of seconds for which
   the NBMA information of the transit NHS is considered to be valid.
   Cached information SHALL be discarded when the holding time
   expires.

"Client Address" information is actually "Reverse Transit NHS
Address" information for this extension. Thus, for example, Cli Addr
T/L is the transit NHS NBMA address type and length field.

If a "requester" wishes to obtain this information, it SHALL include
this extension with a length of zero. Note that this implies that no
storage is allocated for the Holding Time and Type/Length fields
until the "Value" portion of the extension is filled out.

If an NHS has more than one Protocol address, it SHALL use the same
Protocol address consistently in all of the Responder Address,
Forward NHS Record, and Reverse NHS Record extensions. The choice of
which of several Protocol addresses to include in this extension is a
local matter.

If a "reply" that is being forwarded by an NHS contains the Protocol
Address of that NHS in one of the Reverse Transit NHS elements then
the NHS SHALL generate an NHRP Error Indication of type "NHRP Loop
Detected" and discard the "reply".

Note that this information may be cached at intermediate NHSs; if
so, the cached value SHALL be used when generating a reply.

5.3.4 NHRP Authentication Extension

Compulsory = 1 Type = 7 Length = variable

The NHRP Authentication Extension is carried in NHRP packets to
convey authentication information between NHRP speakers. The
Authentication Extension may be included in any NHRP "request" or
"reply" only.

The authentication is always done pairwise on an NHRP hop-by-hop
basis; i.e., the authentication extension is regenerated at each
hop. If a received packet fails the authentication test, the station
SHALL generate an Error Indication of type "Authentication Failure"
and discard the packet. Note that one possible authentication failure
is the lack of an Authentication Extension; the presence or absence
of the Authentication Extension is a local matter.

5.3.4.1 Header Format

The authentication header has the following format:

```
 0                   1                   2                   3
 0 1 2 3 4 5 6 7 8 9 0 1 2 3 4 5 6 7 8 9 0 1 2 3 4 5 6 7 8 9 0 1
+-+-+-+-+-+-+-+-+-+-+-+-+-+-+-+-+-+-+-+-+-+-+-+-+-+-+-+-+-+-+-+-+
|   Reserved                    | Security Parameter Index (SPI)|
+-+-+-+-+-+-+-+-+-+-+-+-+-+-+-+-+-+-+-+-+-+-+-+-+-+-+-+-+-+-+-+-+
|                       Src Addr...                             |
+-+-+-+-+-+-+-+-+-+-+-+-+-+-+-+-+-+-+-+-+-+-+-+-+-+-+-+-+-+-+-+-+
|                                                               |
+-+-+-+-+-+-+-+-+-+-+ Authentication Data... -+-+-+-+-+-+-+-+-+-+
|                                                               |
+-+-+-+-+-+-+-+-+-+-+-+-+-+-+-+-+-+-+-+-+-+-+-+-+-+-+-+-+-+-+-+-+
```

Security Parameter Index (SPI) can be thought of as an index into a
table that maintains the keys and other information such as hash
algorithm. Src and Dst communicate either offline using manual keying
or online using a key management protocol to populate this table. The
sending NHRP entity always allocates the SPI and the parameters
associated with it.

Src Addr a variable length field is the address assigned to the
outgoing interface. The length of the addr is obtained from the
source protocol length field in the mandatory part of the NHRP
header. The tuple <spi, src addr> uniquely identifies the key and
other parameters that are used in authentication.

The length of the authentication data field is dependent on the hash
algorithm used. The data field contains the keyed hash calculated
over the entire NHRP payload. The authentication data field is zeroed
out before the hash is calculated.

5.3.4.2 SPI and Security Parameters Negotiation

SPI's can be negotiated either manually or using an Internet Key
Management protocol. Manual keying MUST be supported. The following
parameters are associated with the tuple <SPI, src>- lifetime,
Algorithm, Key. Lifetime indicates the duration in seconds for which
the key is valid. In case of manual keying, this duration can be
infinite. Also, in order to better support manual keying, there may
be multiple tuples active at the same time (Dst being the same).

Algorithm specifies the hash algorithm agreed upon by the two
entities. HMAC-MD5-128 [16] is the default algorithm. Other
algorithms MAY be supported by defining new values. IANA will assign
the numbers to identify the algorithm being used as described in
Section 9.

Any Internet standard key management protocol MAY so be used to
negotiate the SPI and parameters.

5.3.4.3 Message Processing

At the time of adding the authentication extension header, src looks
up in a table to fetch the SPI and the security parameters based on
the outgoing interface address. If there are no entries in the table
and if there is support for key management, the src initiates the key
management protocol to fetch the necessary parameters. The src
constructs the Authentication Extension payload and calculates the
hash by zeroing authentication data field. The result replaces in the
zeroed authentication data field. The src address field in the
payload is the IP address assigned to the outgoing interface.

If key management is not supported and authentication is mandatory,
the packet is dropped and this information is logged.

On the receiving end, dst fetches the parameters based on the SPI and
the ip address in the authentication extension payload. The
authentication data field is extracted before zeroing out to
calculate the hash. It computes the hash on the entire payload and if
the hash does not match, then an "abnormal event" has occurred.

5.3.4.4 Security Considerations

It is important that the keys chosen are strong as the security of
the entire system depends on the keys being chosen properly and the
correct implementation of the algorithms.

The security is performed on a hop by hop basis. The data received
can be trusted only so much as one trusts all the entities in the
path traversed. A chain of trust is established amongst NHRP entities
in the path of the NHRP Message . If the security in an NHRP entity
is compromised, then security in the entire NHRP domain is
compromised.

Data integrity covers the entire NHRP payload. This guarantees that
the message was not modified and the source is authenticated as well.
If authentication extension is not used or if the security is
compromised, then NHRP entities are liable to both spoofing attacks,
active attacks and passive attacks.

There is no mechanism to encrypt the messages. It is assumed that a
standard layer 3 confidentiality mechanism will be used to encrypt
and decrypt messages. It is recommended to use an Internet standard
key management protocol to negotiate the keys between the neighbors.
Transmitting the keys in clear text, if other methods of negotiation
is used, compromises the security completely.

Any NHS is susceptible to Denial of Service (DOS) attacks that cause
it to become overloaded, preventing legitimate packets from being
acted upon properly. A rogue host can send request and registration
packets to the first hop NHS. If the authentication option is not
used, the registration packet is forwarded along the routed path
requiring processing along each NHS. If the authentication option is
used, then only the first hop NHS is susceptible to DOS attacks
(i.e., unauthenticated packets will be dropped rather than forwarded
on). If security of any host is compromised (i.e., the keys it is
using to communicate with an NHS become known), then a rogue host can
send NHRP packets to the first hop NHS of the host whose keys were
compromised, which will then forward them along the routed path as in
the case of unauthenticated packets. However, this attack requires
that the rogue host to have the same first hop NHS as that of the
compromised host. Finally, it should be noted that denial of service
attacks that cause routers on the routed path to expend resources
processing NHRP packets are also susceptable to attacks that flood
packets at the same destination as contained in an NHRP packet's
Destination Protocol Address field.

5.3.5 NHRP Vendor-Private Extension

        Compulsory = 0
        Type = 8
        Length = variable

The NHRP Vendor-Private Extension is carried in NHRP packets to
convey vendor-private information or NHRP extensions between NHRP
speakers.

```
    0                   1                   2                   3
    0 1 2 3 4 5 6 7 8 9 0 1 2 3 4 5 6 7 8 9 0 1 2 3 4 5 6 7 8 9 0 1
   +-+-+-+-+-+-+-+-+-+-+-+-+-+-+-+-+-+-+-+-+-+-+-+-+-+-+-+-+-+-+-+-+
   |                   Vendor ID                | Data....         |
   +-+-+-+-+-+-+-+-+-+-+-+-+-+-+-+-+-+-+-+-+-+-+-+-+-+-+-+-+-+-+-+-+
```

Vendor ID
   802 Vendor ID as assigned by the IEEE [6]

Data
   The remaining octets after the Vendor ID in the payload are
   vendor-dependent data.

This extension may be added to any "request" or "reply" packet and it
is the only extension that may be included multiple times. If the
receiver does not handle this extension, or does not match the Vendor

ID in the extension then the extension may be completely ignored by
the receiver. If a Vendor Private Extension is included in a
"request" then it must be copied to the corresponding "reply".

6. Protocol Operation

   In this section, we discuss certain operational considerations of
   NHRP.

6.1 Router-to-Router Operation

   In practice, the initiating and responding stations may be either
   hosts or routers. However, there is a possibility under certain
   conditions that a stable routing loop may occur if NHRP is used
   between two routers. In particular, attempting to establish an NHRP
   path across a boundary where information used in route selection is
   lost may result in a routing loop. Such situations include the loss
   of BGP path vector information, the interworking of multiple routing
   protocols with dissimilar metrics (e.g, RIP and OSPF), etc. In such
   circumstances, NHRP should not be used. This situation can be
   avoided if there are no "back door" paths between the entry and
   egress router outside of the NBMA subnetwork. Protocol mechanisms to
   relax these restrictions are under investigation.

   In general it is preferable to use mechanisms, if they exist, in
   routing protocols to resolve the egress point when the destination
   lies outside of the NBMA subnetwork, since such mechanisms will be
   more tightly coupled to the state of the routing system and will
   probably be less likely to create loops.

6.2 Cache Management Issues

   The management of NHRP caches in the source station, the NHS serving
   the destination, and any intermediate NHSs is dependent on a number
   of factors.

6.2.1 Caching Requirements

   Source Stations

      Source stations MUST cache all received NHRP Resolution Replies
      that they are actively using. They also must cache "incomplete"
      entries, i.e., those for which a NHRP Resolution Request has been
      sent but those for which an NHRP Resolution Reply has not been
      received. This is necessary in order to preserve the Request ID

for retries, and provides the state necessary to avoid triggering
NHRP Resolution Requests for every data packet sent to the
destination.

Source stations MUST purge expired information from their caches.
Source stations MUST purge the appropriate cached information upon
receipt of an NHRP Purge Request packet.

When a station has a co-resident NHC and NHS, the co-resident NHS
may reply to NHRP Resolution Requests from the co-resident NHC with
information which the station cached as a result of the co-resident
NHC making its own NHRP Resolution Requests as long as the co-
resident NHS follows the rules for Transit NHSs as seen below.

Serving NHSs

The NHS serving the destination (the one which responds
authoritatively to NHRP Resolution Requests) SHOULD cache protocol
address information from all NHRP Resolution Requests to which it
has responded if the information in the NHRP Resolution Reply has
the possibility of changing during its lifetime (so that an NHRP
Purge Request packet can be issued). The internetworking to NBMA
binding information provided by the source station in the NHRP
Resolution Request may also be cached if and only if the "S" bit is
set, the NHRP Resolution Request has included a CIE with the
Holding Time field set greater than zero (this is the valid Holding
Time for the source binding), and only for non-authoritative use
for a period not to exceed the Holding Time.

Transit NHSs

A Transit NHS (lying along the NHRP path between the source station
and the responding NHS) may cache source binding information
contained in NHRP Resolution Request packets that it forwards if
and only if the "S" bit is set, the NHRP Resolution Request has
included a CIE with the Holding Time field set greater than zero
(this is the valid Holding Time for the source binding), and only
for non-authoritative use for a period not to exceed the Holding
Time.

A Transit NHS may cache destination information contained in NHRP
Resolution Reply CIE if only if the D bit is set and then only for
non-authoritative use for a period not to exceed the Holding Time
value contained in the CIE. A Transit NHS MUST NOT cache source
binding information contained in an NHRP Resolution Reply.

Further, a transit NHS MUST discard any cached information when the
prescribed time has expired. It may return cached information in
response to non-authoritative NHRP Resolution Requests only.

6.2.2 Dynamics of Cached Information

  NBMA-Connected Destinations

  NHRP's most basic function is that of simple NBMA address
  resolution of stations directly attached to the NBMA subnetwork.
  These mappings are typically very static, and appropriately chosen
  holding times will minimize problems in the event that the NBMA
  address of a station must be changed. Stale information will cause
  a loss of connectivity, which may be used to trigger an
  authoritative NHRP Resolution Request and bypass the old data. In
  the worst case, connectivity will fail until the cache entry times
  out.

  This applies equally to information marked in NHRP Resolution
  Replies as being "stable" (via the "D" bit).

  Destinations Off of the NBMA Subnetwork

  If the source of an NHRP Resolution Request is a host and the
  destination is not directly attached to the NBMA subnetwork, and
  the route to that destination is not considered to be "stable," the
  destination mapping may be very dynamic (except in the case of a
  subnetwork where each destination is only singly homed to the NBMA
  subnetwork). As such the cached information may very likely become
  stale. The consequence of stale information in this case will be a
  suboptimal path (unless the internetwork has partitioned or some
  other routing failure has occurred).

6.3 Use of the Prefix Length field of a CIE

  A certain amount of care needs to be taken when using the Prefix
  Length field of a CIE, in particular with regard to the prefix length
  advertised (and thus the size of the equivalence class specified by
  it). Assuming that the routers on the NBMA subnetwork are exchanging
  routing information, it should not be possible for an NHS to create a
  black hole by advertising too large of a set of destinations, but
  suboptimal routing (e.g., extra internetwork layer hops through the
  NBMA) can result. To avoid this situation an NHS that wants to send
  the Prefix Length MUST obey the following rule:

  The NHS examines the Network Layer Reachability Information (NLRI)
  associated with the route that the NHS would use to forward towards
  the destination (as specified by the Destination internetwork layer

address in the NHRP Resolution Request), and extracts from this
NLRI the shortest address prefix such that: (a) the Destination
internetwork layer address (from the NHRP Resolution Request) is
covered by the prefix, (b) the NHS does not have any routes with
NLRI which form a subset of what is covered by the prefix. The
prefix may then be used in the CIE.

The Prefix Length field of the CIE should be used with restraint, in
order to avoid NHRP stations choosing suboptimal transit paths when
overlapping prefixes are available. This document specifies the use
of the prefix length only when all the destinations covered by the
prefix are "stable". That is, either:

  (a) All destinations covered by the prefix are on the NBMA network,
      or
  (b) All destinations covered by the prefix are directly attached to
      the NHRP responding station.

Use of the Prefix Length field of the CIE in other circumstances is
outside the scope of this document.

6.4 Domino Effect

One could easily imagine a situation where a router, acting as an
ingress station to the NBMA subnetwork, receives a data packet, such
that this packet triggers an NHRP Resolution Request. If the router
forwards this data packet without waiting for an NHRP transit path to
be established, then when the next router along the path receives the
packet, the next router may do exactly the same - originate its own
NHRP Resolution Request (as well as forward the packet). In fact
such a data packet may trigger NHRP Resolution Request generation at
every router along the path through an NBMA subnetwork. We refer to
this phenomena as the NHRP "domino" effect.

The NHRP domino effect is clearly undesirable. At best it may result
in excessive NHRP traffic. At worst it may result in an excessive
number of virtual circuits being established unnecessarily.
Therefore, it is important to take certain measures to avoid or
suppress this behavior. NHRP implementations for NHSs MUST provide a
mechanism to address this problem. One possible strategy to address
this problem would be to configure a router in such a way that NHRP
Resolution Request generation by the router would be driven only by
the traffic the router receives over its non-NBMA interfaces
(interfaces that are not attached to an NBMA subnetwork). Traffic
received by the router over its NBMA-attached interfaces would not
trigger NHRP Resolution Requests. Such a router avoids the NHRP
domino effect through administrative means.

7. NHRP over Legacy BMA Networks

There would appear to be no significant impediment to running NHRP
over legacy broadcast subnetworks. There may be issues around
running NHRP across multiple subnetworks. Running NHRP on broadcast
media has some interesting possibilities; especially when setting up
a cut-through for inter-ELAN inter-LIS/LAG traffic when one or both
end stations are legacy attached. This use for NHRP requires further
research.

8. Discussion

The result of an NHRP Resolution Request depends on how routing is
configured among the NHSs of an NBMA subnetwork. If the destination
station is directly connected to the NBMA subnetwork and the routed
path to it lies entirely within the NBMA subnetwork, the NHRP
Resolution Replies always return the NBMA address of the destination
station itself rather than the NBMA address of some egress router.
On the other hand, if the routed path exits the NBMA subnetwork, NHRP
will be unable to resolve the NBMA address of the destination, but
rather will return the address of the egress router. For
destinations outside the NBMA subnetwork, egress routers and routers
in the other subnetworks should exchange routing information so that
the optimal egress router may be found.

In addition to NHSs, an NBMA station could also be associated with
one or more regular routers that could act as "connectionless
servers" for the station. The station could then choose to resolve
the NBMA next hop or just send the packets to one of its
connectionless servers. The latter option may be desirable if
communication with the destination is short-lived and/or doesn't
require much network resources. The connectionless servers could, of
course, be physically integrated in the NHSs by augmenting them with
internetwork layer switching functionality.

9. IANA Considerations

IANA will take advice from the Area Director appointed designated
subject matter expert, in order to assign numbers from the various
number spaces described herein. In the event that the Area Director
appointed designated subject matter expert is unavailable, the
relevant IESG Area Director will appoint another expert. Any and all
requests for value assignment within a given number space will be
accepted when the usage of the value assignment documented. Possible
forms of documentantion include, but is not limited to, RFCs or the
product of another cooperative standards body (e.g., the MPOA and
LANE subworking group of the ATM Forum).

References

[1] Heinanen, J., and R. Govindan, "NBMA Address Resolution Protocol (NARP)", RFC 1735, December 1994.

[2] Plummer, D., "Address Resolution Protocol", STD 37, RFC 826, November 1982.

[3] Laubach, M., and J. Halpern, "Classical IP and ARP over ATM", RFC 2225, April 1998.

[4] Piscitello,, D., and J. Lawrence, "Transmission of IP datagrams over the SMDS service", RFC 1209, March 1991.

[5] Protocol Identification in the Network Layer, ISO/IEC TR 9577:1990.

[6] Reynolds, J., and J. Postel, "Assigned Numbers", STD 2, RFC 1700, October 1994.

[7] Heinanen, J., "Multiprotocol Encapsulation over ATM Adaptation Layer 5", RFC 1483, July 1993.

[8] Malis, A., Robinson, D., and R. Ullmann, "Multiprotocol Interconnect on X.25 and ISDN in the Packet Mode", RFC 1356, August 1992.

[9] Bradley, T., Brown, C., and A. Malis, "Multiprotocol Interconnect over Frame Relay", RFC 1490, July 1993.

[10] Rekhter, Y., and D. Kandlur, ""Local/Remote" Forwarding Decision in Switched Data Link Subnetworks", RFC 1937, May 1996.

[11] Armitage, G., "Support for Multicast over UNI 3.0/3.1 based ATM Networks", RFC 2022, November 1996.

[12] Luciani, J., Armitage, G., and J. Halpern, "Server Cache Synchronization Protocol (SCSP) - NBMA", RFC 2334, April 1998.

[13] Rekhter, Y., "NHRP for Destinations off the NBMA Subnetwork", Work In Progress.

[14] Luciani, J., et. al., "Classical IP and ARP over ATM to NHRP Transition", Work In Progress.

[15] Bradner, S., "Key words for use in RFCs to Indicate Requirement Levels", BCP 14, RFC 2119, March 1997.

[16] Krawczyk, H., Bellare, M., and R. Canetti, "HMAC: Keyed Hashing for Message Authentication", RFC 2104, February 1997.

Acknowledgments

We would like to thank (in no particular order) Thomas Narten of IBM for his comments in the role of Internet AD, Juha Heinanen of Telecom Finland and Ramesh Govidan of ISI for their work on NBMA ARP and the original NHRP draft, which served as the basis for this work. Russell Gardo of IBM, John Burnett of Adaptive, Dennis Ferguson of ANS, Andre Fredette of Bay Networks, Joel Halpern of Newbridge, Paul Francis of NTT, Tony Li, Bryan Gleeson, and Yakov Rekhter of cisco, and Grenville Armitage of Bellcore should also be acknowledged for comments and suggestions that improved this work substantially. We would also like to thank the members of the ION working group of the IETF, whose review and discussion of this document have been invaluable.

Authors' Addresses

James V. Luciani   Dave Katz
Bay Networks   cisco Systems
3 Federal Street   170 W. Tasman Dr.
Mail Stop: BL3-03   San Jose, CA 95134 USA
Billerica, MA 01821   Phone: +1 408 526 8284
Phone: +1 978 916 4734   EMail: dkatz@cisco.com
EMail: luciani@baynetworks.com

David Piscitello   Bruce Cole
Core Competence   Juniper Networks
1620 Tuckerstown Road   3260 Jay St.
Dresher, PA 19025 USA   Santa Clara, CA 95054
Phone: +1 215 830 0692   Phone: +1 408 327 1900
EMail: dave@corecom.com   EMail: bcole@jnx.com

Naganand Doraswamy
Bay Networks, Inc.
3 Federal Street
Mail Stop: B13-03
Billerica, MA 01801
Phone: +1 978 916 1323
EMail: naganand@baynetworks.com

Full Copyright Statement

Network Working Group   D. Cansever
Request for Comments: 2333   GTE Laboratories, Inc.
Category: Standards Track   April 1998

NHRP Protocol Applicability Statement

Status of this Memo

Copyright Notice

Abstract

   As required by the Routing Protocol Criteria [RFC 1264], this memo
   discusses the applicability of the Next Hop Resolution Protocol
   (NHRP) in routing of IP datagrams over Non-Broadcast Multiple Access
   (NBMA) networks, such as ATM, SMDS and X.25.

1. Protocol Documents

   The NHRP protocol description is defined in [1]. The NHRP MIB
   description is defined in [2].

2. Introduction

   This document summarizes the key features of NHRP and discusses the
   environments for which the protocol is well suited. For the purposes
   of description, NHRP can be considered a generalization of Classical
   IP and ARP over ATM which is defined in [3] and of the Transmission
   of IP Datagrams over the SMDS Service, defined in [4]. This
   generalization occurs in 2 distinct directions.

   Firstly, NHRP avoids the need to go through extra hops of routers
   when the Source and Destination belong to different Logical Internet
   Subnets (LIS). Of course, [3] and [4] specify that when the source
   and destination belong to different LISs, the source station must
   forward data packets to a router that is a member of multiple LISs,
   even though the source and destination stations may be on the same
   logical NBMA network. If the source and destination stations belong
   to the same logical NBMA network, NHRP provides the source station

with an inter-LIS address resolution mechanism at the end of which both stations can exchange packets without having to use the services of intermediate routers. This feature is also referred to as "short-cut" routing. If the destination station is not part of the logical NBMA network, NHRP provides the source with the NBMA address of the current egress router towards the destination.

The second generalization is that NHRP is not specific to a particular NBMA technology. Of course, [3] assumes an ATM network and [4] assumes an SMDS network at their respective subnetwork layers.

NHRP is specified for resolving the destination NBMA addresses of IP datagrams over IP subnets within a large NBMA cloud. NHRP has been designed to be extensible to network layer protocols other than IP, possibly subject to other network layer protocol specific additions.

As an important application of NHRP, the Multiprotocol Over ATM (MPOA) Working Group of the ATM Forum has decided to adopt and to integrate NHRP into its MPOA Protocol specification [5]. As such, NHRP will be used in resolving the ATM addresses of MPOA packets destined outside the originating subnet.

3. Key Features

NHRP provides a mechanism to obtain the NBMA network address of the destination, or of a router along the path to the destination. NHRP is not a routing protocol, but may make use of routing information. This is further discussed in Section 5.

The most prominent feature of NHRP is that it avoids extra router hops in an NBMA with multiple LISs. To this goal, NHRP provides the source with the NBMA address of the destination, if the destination is directly attached to the NBMA. If the destination station is not attached to the NBMA, then NHRP provides the source with the NBMA address of an exit router that has connectivity to the destination. In general, there may be multiple exit routers that have connectivity to the destination. If NHRP uses the services of a dynamic routing algorithm in fulfilling its function, which is necessary for robust and scalable operation, then the exit router identified by NHRP reflects the selection made by the network layer dynamic routing protocol. In general, the selection made by the routing protocol would often reflect a desirable attribute, such as identifying the exit router that induces the least number of hops in the original routed path.

NHRP is defined for avoiding extra hops in the delivery of IP packets
with a single destination. As such, it is not intended for direct
use in a point-to-multipoint communication setting. However,
elements of NHRP may be used in certain multicast scenarios for the
purpose of providing short cut routing. Such an effort is discussed
in [6]. In this case, NHRP would avoid intermediate routers in the
multicast path. The scalability of providing short-cut paths in a
multicast environment is an open issue.

NHRP can be used in host-host, host-router and router-host
communications. When used in router-router communication, NHRP (as
defined in [1]) can produce persistent routing loops if the
underlying routing protocol looses information critical to loop
suppression. This may occur when there is a change in router metrics
across the autonomous system boundaries. NHRP for router-router
communication that avoids persistent forwarding loops will be
addressed in a separate document.

A special case of router-router communication where loops will not
occur is when the destination host is directly adjacent to the non-
NBMA interface of the egress router. If it is believed that the
adjacency of the destination station to the egress router is a stable
topological configuration, then NHRP can safely be used in this
router-router communication scenario. If the NHRP Request has the Q
bit set, indicating that the requesting party is a router, and if the
destination station is directly adjacent to the egress router as a
stable topological configuration, then the egress router can issue a
corresponding NHRP reply. If the destination is not adjacent to the
egress router, and if Q bit is set in the Request, then a safe mode
of operation for the egress router would be to issue a negative NHRP
Reply (NAK) for this particular request, thereby enforce data packets
to follow the routed path.

As a result of having inter-LIS address resolution capability, NHRP
allows the communicating parties to exchange packets by fully
utilizing the particular features of the NBMA network. One such
example is the use of QoS guarantees when the NMBA network is ATM.

Here, due to short-cut routing, ATM provided QoS guarantees can be
implemented without having to deal with the issues of re-assembling
and re-segmenting IP packets at each network layer hop.

NHRP protocol can be viewed as a client-server interaction. An NHRP
Client is the one who issues an NHRP Request. An NHRP Server is the
one who issues a reply to an NHRP request, or the one who forwards a
received NHRP request to another Server. Of course, an NHRP entity
may act both as a Client and a Server.

4. Use of NHRP

In general, issuing an NHRP request is an application dependent
action [7]. For applications that do not have particular QoS
requirements, and that are executed within a short period of time, an
NBMA short-cut may not be a necessity. In situations where there is a
"cost" associated with NBMA short-cuts, such applications may be
better served by network layer hop-by-hop routing. Here, "cost" may
be understood in a monetary context, or as additional strain on the
equipment that implements short-cuts. Therefore, there is a trade-off
between the "cost" of a short-cut path and its utility to the user.
Reference [7] proposes that this trade-off should be addressed at the
application level. In an environment consisting of LANs and routers
that are interconnected via dedicated links, the basic routing
decision is whether to forward a packet to a router, or to broadcast
it locally. Such a decision on local vs. remote is based on the
destination address. When routing IP packets over an NBMA network,
where there is potentially a direct Source to Destination
connectivity with QoS options, the decision on local vs. remote is no
longer as fundamentally important as in the case where packets have
to traverse routers that are interconnected via dedicated links.
Thus, in an NBMA network with QoS options, the basic decision becomes
the one of short-cut vs. hop-by-hop network layer routing. In this
case, the relevant criterion becomes applications' QoS requirements
[7]. NHRP is particularly applicable for environments where the
decision on local vs. remote is superseded by the decision on short-
cut vs. hop-by-hop network layer routing.

Let us assume that the trade-off is in favor of a short-cut NBMA
route. Generally, an NHRP request can be issued by a variety of NHRP
aware entities, including hosts and routers with NBMA interfaces. If
an IP packet traverses multiple hops before a short-cut path has been
established, then there is a chance that multiple short-cut paths
could be formed. In order to avoid such an undesirable situation, a
useful operation rule is to authorize only the following entities to
issue an NHRP request and to perform short-cut routing.

   i)   The host that originates the IP packet, if the host has an NBMA
        interface.
   ii) The first router along the routing path of the IP packet such
        that the next hop is reachable through the NBMA interface of
        that particular router.
   iii) A policy router within an NBMA network through which the IP
        packet has to traverse.

5. Protocol Scalability

   As previously indicated, NHRP is defined for the delivery of IP
   packets with a single destination. Thus, this discussion is confined
   to a unicast setting. The scalability of NHRP can be analyzed at
   three distinct levels:

      o Client level
      o LIS level
      o Domain level

   At the the Client level, the scalability of NHRP is affected by the
   processing and memory limitations of the NIC that provides interface
   to the NBMA network. When the NBMA network is connection oriented,
   such as ATM, NIC limitations may bound the scalability of NHRP in
   certain applications. For example, a server that handles hundreds of
   requests per second using an ATM interface may be bounded by the
   performance characteristics of the corresponding NIC. Similarly,
   when the NHRP Client resides at an NBMA interface of a router, memory
   and processing limitations of router's NIC may bound the scalability
   of NHRP. This is because routers generally deal with an aggregation
   of traffic from multiple sources, which in turn creates a potentially
   large number of SVCCs out of the router's NBMA interface.

   At the LIS level, the main issue is to maintain and deliver a sizable
   number of NBMA to Network layer address mappings within large LISs.
   To this goal, NHRP implementations can use the services of the Server
   Cache Synchronization Protocol (SCSP) [8] that allows multiple
   synchronized NHSs within an LIS, and hence resolve the associated
   scalability issue.

   At the NHRP Domain level, network layer routing is used in resolving
   the NBMA address of a destination outside the LIS. As such, the
   scalability of NHRP is closely tied to the scalability of the network
   layer routing protocol used by NHRP. Dynamic network layer routing
   protocols are proven to scale well. Thus, when used in conjunction
   with dynamic routing algorithms, at the NHRP domain level, NHRP
   should scale in the same order as the routing algorithm, subject to
   the assumption that all the routers along the path are NHRP aware.
   If an NHRP Request is processed by a router that does not implement
   NHRP, it will be silently discarded. Then, short-cuts cannot be
   implemented and connectivity will be provided on a hop-by-hop basis.

   Thus, when NHRP is implemented in conjunction with dynamic network
   layer routing, a scaling requirement for NHRP is that virtually all
   the routers within a logical NBMA network should be NHRP aware.

One can also use static routing in conjunction with NHRP. Then, not
all the routers in the NBMA network need to be NHRP aware. That is,
since the routers that need to process NHRP control messages are
specified by static routing, routers that are not included in the
manually defined static paths do not have to be NHRP aware. Of
course, static routing does not scale, and if the destination is off
the NBMA network, then the use of static routing could result in
persistently suboptimal routes. Use of static routing also has
fairly negative failure modes.

6. Discussion

NHRP does not replace existing routing protocols. In general, routing
protocols are used to determine the proper path from a source host or
router, or intermediate router, to a particular destination. If the
routing protocol indicates that the proper path is via an interface
to an NBMA network, then NHRP may be used at the NBMA interface to
resolve the destination IP address into the corresponding NBMA
address. Of course, the use of NHRP is subject to considerations
discussed in Section 4.

Assuming that NHRP is applicable and the destination address has been
resolved, packets are forwarded using the particular data forwarding
and path determination mechanisms of the underlying NBMA network.
Here, the sequence of events are such that route determination is
performed by IP routing, independent of NHRP. Then, NHRP is used to
create a short-cut track upon the path determined by the IP routing
protocol. Therefore, NHRP "shortens" the routed path. NHRP (as
defined in [1]) is not sufficient to suppress persistent forwarding
loops when used for router-router communication if the underlying
routing protocol looses information critical to loop suppression [9].
Work is in progress [10] to augment NHRP to enable its use for the
router-router communication without persistent forwarding loops.

When the routed path keeps changing on some relatively short time
scale, such as seconds, this situation will have an effect on the
operation of NHRP. In certain router-router operations, changes in
the routed path could create persistent routing loops. In host-
router, or router-host communications, frequent changes in routed
paths could result in inefficiencies such as frequent creation of
short-cut paths which are short lived.

7. Security Considerations

NHRP is an address resolution protocol, and SCSP is a database
synchronization protocol. As such, they are possibly subject to
server (for NHRP) or peer (for SCSP) spoofing and denial of service
attacks. They both provide authentication mechanisms to allow their

use in environments in which spoofing is a concern. Details can be
found in sections 5.3.4 in [1] and B.3.1 in [8]. There are no
additional security constraints or concerns raised in this document
that are not already discussed in the referenced sections.

References

   [1] Luciani, J., Katz, D., Piscitello, D., Cole, B., and
       N. Doraswamy, "NMBA Next Hop Resolution Protocol (NHRP)", RFC
       2332, April 1998.

   [2] Greene, M., and J. Luciani, "NHRP Management Information Base",
       Work in Progress.

   [3] Laubach, M., and J. Halpern, "Classical IP and ARP over ATM", RFC
       2225, April 1998.

   [4] Lawrance, J., and D. Piscitello, "The Transmission of IP
       datagrams over the SMDS service", RFC 1209, March 1991.

   [5] Multiprotocol Over ATM Version 1.0, ATM Forum Document
       af-mpoa-0087.000

   [6] Rekhter, Y., and D. Farinacci, "Support for Sparse Mode PIM over
       ATM", Work in Progress.

   [7] Rekhter, Y., and D. Kandlur, "Local/Remote" Forwarding Decision
       in Switched Data Link Subnetworks", RFC 1937, May 1996.

   [8] Luciani, J., Armitage, G., Halpern, J., and N. Doraswamy, "Server
       Cache Synchronization Protocol (SCSP) - NBMA", RFC 2334, April
       1998.

   [9] Cole, R., Shur, D., and C. Villamizar, "IP over ATM: A Framework
       Document", RFC 1932, April 1996.

   [10] Rekhter, Y., "NHRP for Destinations off the NBMA Subnetwork",
        Work in Progress.

Acknowledgements

   The author acknowledges valuable contributions and comments from many
   participants of the ION Working Group, in particular from Joel
   Halpern of Newbridge Networks, David Horton of Centre for Information
   Technology Research, Andy Malis of Nexion, Yakov Rekhter and George
   Swallow of Cisco Systems and Curtis Villamizar of ANS.

Author's Address

   Derya H. Cansever
   GTE Laboratories Inc.
   40 Sylvan Rd. MS 51
   Waltham MA 02254

   Phone: +1 617 466 4086
   EMail: dcansever@gte.com

RFC 2333

8

Full Copyright Statement

9

RFC 2333

Network Working Group   T. Li
Request for Comments: 2430   Juniper Networks
Category: Informational   Y. Rekhter
                                                           Cisco Systems
                                                            October 1998

                        A Provider Architecture for
                Differentiated Services and Traffic Engineering
                                  (PASTE)

Status of this Memo

Copyright Notice

1.0 Abstract

   This document describes the Provider Architecture for Differentiated
   Services and Traffic Engineering (PASTE) for Internet Service
   Providers (ISPs). Providing differentiated services in ISPs is a
   challenge because the scaling problems presented by the sheer number
   of flows present in large ISPs makes the cost of maintaining per-flow
   state unacceptable. Coupled with this, large ISPs need the ability
   to perform traffic engineering by directing aggregated flows of
   traffic along specific paths.

   PASTE addresses these issues by using Multiprotocol Label Switching
   (MPLS) [1] and the Resource Reservation Protocol (RSVP) [2] to create
   a scalable traffic management architecture that supports
   differentiated services. This document assumes that the reader has
   at least some familiarity with both of these technologies.

2.0 Terminology

   In common usage, a packet flow, or a flow, refers to a unidirectional
   stream of packets, distributed over time. Typically a flow has very
   fine granularity and reflects a single interchange between hosts,
   such as a TCP connection. An aggregated flow is a number of flows
   that share forwarding state and a single resource reservation along a
   sequence of routers.

One mechanism for supporting aggregated flows is Multiprotocol Label
Switching (MPLS). In MPLS, packets are tunneled by wrapping them in
a minimal header [3]. Each such header contains a label, that
carries both forwarding and resource reservation semantics. MPLS
defines mechanisms to install label-based forwarding information
along a series of Label Switching Routers (LSRs) to construct a Label
Switched Path (LSP). LSPs can also be associated with resource
reservation information.

One protocol for constructing such LSPs is the Resource Reservation
Protocol (RSVP) [4]. When used with the Explicit Route Object (ERO)
[5], RSVP can be used to construct an LSP along an explicit route
[6].

To support differentiated services, packets are divided into separate
traffic classes. For conceptual purposes, we will discuss three
different traffic classes: Best Effort, Priority, and Network
Control. The exact number of subdivisions within each class is to be
defined.

Network Control traffic primarily consists of routing protocols and
network management traffic. If Network Control traffic is dropped,
routing protocols can fail or flap, resulting in network instability.
Thus, Network Control must have very low drop preference. However,
Network Control traffic is generally insensitive to moderate delays
and requires a relatively small amount of bandwidth. A small
bandwidth guarantee is sufficient to insure that Network Control
traffic operates correctly.

Priority traffic is likely to come in many flavors, depending on the
application. Particular flows may require bandwidth guarantees,
jitter guarantees, or upper bounds on delay. For the purposes of
this memo, we will not distinguish the subdivisions of priority
traffic. All priority traffic is assumed to have an explicit
resource reservation.

Currently, the vast majority of traffic in ISPs is Best Effort
traffic. This traffic is, for the most part, delay insensitive and
reasonably adaptive to congestion.

When flows are aggregated according to their traffic class and then
the aggregated flow is placed inside a LSP, we call the result a
traffic trunk, or simply a trunk. The traffic class of a packet is
orthogonal to the LSP that it is on, so many different trunks, each
with its own traffic class, may share an LSP if they have different
traffic classes.

3.0 Introduction

   The next generation of the Internet presents special challenges that
   must be addressed by a single, coordinated architecture. While this
   architecture allows for distinction between ISPs, it also defines a
   framework within which ISPs may provide end-to-end differentiated
   services in a coordinated and reliable fashion. With such an
   architecture, an ISP would be able to craft common agreements for the
   handling of differentiated services in a consistent fashion,
   facilitating end-to-end differentiated services via a composition of
   these agreements. Thus, the goal of this document is to describe an
   architecture for providing differentiated services within the ISPs of
   the Internet, while including support for other forthcoming needs
   such as traffic engineering. While this document addresses the needs
   of the ISPs, its applicability is not limited to the ISPs. The same
   architecture could be used in any large, multiprovider catenet
   needing differentiated services.

   This document only discusses unicast services. Extensions to the
   architecture to support multicast are a subject for future research.

   One of the primary considerations in any ISP architecture is
   scalability. Solutions that have state growth proportional to the
   size of the Internet result in growth rates exceeding Moore's law,
   making such solutions intractable in the long term. Thus, solutions
   that use mechanisms with very limited growth rates are strongly
   preferred.

   Discussions of differentiated services to date have frequently
   resulted in solutions that require per-flow state or per-flow
   queuing. As the number of flows in an ISP within the "default-free
   zone of the Internet" scales with the size of the Internet, the
   growth rate is difficult to support and argues strongly for a
   solution with lower state requirements. Simultaneously, supporting
   differentiated services is a significant benefit to most ISPs. Such
   support would allow providers to offer special services such as
   priority for bandwidth for mission critical services for users
   willing to pay a service premium. Customers would contract with ISPs
   for these services under Service Level Agreements (SLAs). Such an
   agreement may specify the traffic volume, how the traffic is handled,
   either in an absolute or relative manner, and the compensation that
   the ISP receives.

   Differentiated services are likely to be deployed across a single ISP
   to support applications such as a single enterprise's Virtual Private
   Network (VPN). However, this is only the first wave of service
   implementation. Closely following this will be the need for
   differentiated services to support extranets, enterprise VPNs that

span ISPs, or industry interconnection networks such as the ANX [7].
Because such applications span enterprises and thus span ISPs, there
is a clear need for inter-domain SLAs. This document discusses the
technical architecture that would allow the creation of such inter-
domain SLAs.

Another important consideration in this architecture is the advent of
traffic engineering within ISPs. Traffic engineering is the ability
to move trunks away from the path selected by the ISP's IGP and onto
a different path. This allows an ISP to route traffic around known
points of congestion in its network, thereby making more efficient
use of the available bandwidth. In turn, this makes the ISP more
competitive within its market by allowing the ISP to pass lower costs
and better service on to its customers.

Finally, the need to provide end-to-end differentiated services
implies that the architecture must support consistent inter-provider
differentiated services. Most flows in the Internet today traverse
multiple ISPs, making a consistent description and treatment of
priority flows across ISPs a necessity.

4.0 Components of the Architecture

The Differentiated Services Backbone architecture is the integration
of several different mechanisms that, when used in a coordinated way,
achieve the goals outlined above. This section describes each of the
mechanisms used in some detail. Subsequent sections will then detail
the interoperation of these mechanisms.

4.1 Traffic classes

As described above, packets may fall into a variety of different
traffic classes. For ISP operations, it is essential that packets be
accurately classified before entering the ISP and that it is very
easy for an ISP device to determine the traffic class for a
particular packet.

The traffic class of MPLS packets can be encoded in the three bits
reserved for CoS within the MPLS label header. In addition, traffic
classes for IPv4 packets can be classified via the IPv4 ToS byte,
possibly within the three precedence bits within that byte. Note
that the consistent interpretation of the traffic class, regardless
of the bits used to indicate this class, is an important feature of
PASTE.

In this architecture it is not overly important to control which
packets entering the ISP have a particular traffic class. From the
ISP's perspective, each Priority packet should involve some economic
premium for delivery. As a result the ISP need not pass judgment as
to the appropriateness of the traffic class for the application.

It is important that any Network Control traffic entering an ISP be
handled carefully. The contents of such traffic must also be
carefully authenticated. Currently, there is no need for traffic
generated external to a domain to transit a border router of the ISP.

4.2 Trunks

As described above, traffic of a single traffic class that is
aggregated into a single LSP is called a traffic trunk, or simply a
trunk. Trunks are essential to the architecture because they allow
the overhead in the infrastructure to be decoupled from the size of
the network and the amount of traffic in the network. Instead, as
the traffic scales up, the amount of traffic in the trunks increases;
not the number of trunks.

The number of trunks within a given topology has a worst case of one
trunk per traffic class from each entry router to each exit router.
If there are N routers in the topology and C classes of service, this
would be (N * (N-1) * C) trunks. Fortunately, instantiating this
many trunks is not always necessary.

Trunks with a single exit point which share a common internal path
can be merged to form a single sink tree. The computation necessary
to determine if two trunks can be merged is straightforward. If,
when a trunk is being established, it intersects an existing trunk
with the same traffic class and the same remaining explicit route,
the new trunk can be spliced into the existing trunk at the point of
intersection. The splice itself is straightforward: both incoming
trunks will perform a standard label switching operation, but will
result in the same outbound label. Since each sink tree created this
way touches each router at most once and there is one sink tree per
exit router, the result is N * C sink trees.

The number of trunks or sink trees can also be reduced if multiple
trunks or sink trees for different classes follow the same path.
This works because the traffic class of a trunk or sink tree is
orthogonal to the path defined by its LSP. Thus, two trunks with
different traffic classes can share a label for any part of the
topology that is shared and ends in the exit router. Thus, the
entire topology can be overlaid with N trunks.

Further, if Best Effort trunks and individual Best Effort flows are
treated identically, there is no need to instantiate any Best Effort
trunk that would follow the IGP computed path. This is because the
packets can be directly forwarded without an LSP. However, traffic
engineering may require Best Effort trunks to be treated differently
from the individual Best Effort flows, thus requiring the
instantiation of LSPs for Best Effort trunks. Note that Priority
trunks must be instantiated because end-to-end RSVP packets to
support the aggregated Priority flows must be tunneled.

Trunks can also be aggregated with other trunks by adding a new label
to the stack of labels for each trunk, effectively bundling the
trunks into a single tunnel. For the purposes of this document, this
is also considered a trunk, or if we need to be specific, this will
be called an aggregated trunk. Two trunks can be aggregated if they
share a portion of their path. There is no requirement on the exact
length of the common portion of the path, and thus the exact
requirements for forming an aggregated trunk are beyond the scope of
this document. Note that traffic class (i.e., QoS indication) is
propagated when an additional label is added to a trunk, so trunks of
different classes may be aggregated.

Trunks can be terminated at any point, resulting in a deaggregation
of traffic. The obvious consequence is that there needs to be
sufficient switching capacity at the point of deaggregation to deal
with the resultant traffic.

High reliability for a trunk can be provided through the use of one
or more backup trunks. Backup trunks can be initiated either by the
same router that would initiate the primary trunk or by another
backup router. The status of the primary trunk can be ascertained by
the router that initiated the backup trunk (note that this may be
either the same or a different router as the router that initiated
the primary trunk) through out of band information, such as the IGP.
If a backup trunk is established and the primary trunk returns to
service, the backup trunk can be deactivated and the primary trunk
used instead.

4.3 RSVP

Originally RSVP was designed as a protocol to install state
associated with resource reservations for individual flows
originated/destined to hosts, where path was determined by
destination-based routing. Quoting directly from the RSVP
specifications, "The RSVP protocol is used by a host, on behalf of an
application data stream, to request a specific quality of service
(QoS) from the network for particular data streams or flows"
[RFC2205].

The usage of RSVP in PASTE is quite different from the usage of RSVP
as it was originally envisioned by its designers. The first
difference is that RSVP is used in PASTE to install state that
applies to a collection of flows that all share a common path and
common pool of reserved resources. The second difference is that
RSVP is used in PASTE to install state related to forwarding,
including label switching information, in addition to resource
reservations. The third difference is that the path that this state
is installed along is no longer constrained by the destination-based
routing.

The key factor that makes RSVP suitable for PASTE is the set of
mechanisms provided by RSVP. Quoting from the RSVP specifications,
"RSVP protocol mechanisms provide a general facility for creating and
maintaining distributed reservation state across a mesh of multicast
or unicast delivery paths." Moreover, RSVP provides a straightforward
extensibility mechanism by allowing for the creation of new RSVP
Objects. This flexibility allows us to also use the mechanisms
provided by RSVP to create and maintain distributed state for
information other than pure resource reservation, as well as allowing
the creation of forwarding state in conjunction with resource
reservation state.

The original RSVP design, in which "RSVP itself transfers and
manipulates QoS control parameters as opaque data, passing them to
the appropriate traffic control modules for interpretation" can thus
be extended to include explicit route parameters and label binding
parameters. Just as with QoS parameters, RSVP can transfer and
manipulate explicit route parameters and label binding parameters as
opaque data, passing explicit route parameters to the appropriate
forwarding module, and label parameters to the appropriate MPLS
module.

Moreover, an RSVP session in PASTE is not constrained to be only
between a pair of hosts, but is also used between pairs of routers
that act as the originator and the terminator of a traffic trunk.

Using RSVP in PASTE helps consolidate procedures for several tasks:
(a) procedures for establishing forwarding along an explicit route,
(b) procedures for establishing a label switched path, and (c) RSVP's
existing procedures for resource reservation. In addition, these
functions can be cleanly combined in any manner. The main advantage
of this consolidation comes from an observation that the above three
tasks are not independent, but inter-related. Any alternative that
accomplished each of these functions via independent sets of
procedures, would require additional coordination between functions,
adding more complexity to the system.

4.4 Traffic Engineering

The purpose of traffic engineering is to give the ISP precise control over the flow of traffic within its network. Traffic engineering is necessary because standard IGPs compute the shortest path across the ISP's network based solely on the metric that has been administratively assigned to each link. This computation does not take into account the loading of each link. If the ISP's network is not a full mesh of physical links, the result is that there may not be an obvious way to assign metrics to the existing links such that no congestion will occur given known traffic patterns. Traffic engineering can be viewed as assistance to the routing infrastructure that provides additional information in routing traffic along specific paths, with the end goal of more efficient utilization of networking resources.

Traffic engineering is performed by directing trunks along explicit paths within the ISP's topology. This diverts the traffic away from the shortest path computed by the IGP and presumably onto uncongested links, eventually arriving at the same destination. Specification of the explicit route is done by enumerating an explicit list of the routers in the path. Given this list, traffic engineering trunks can be constructed in a variety of ways. For example, a trunk could be manually configured along the explicit path. This would involve configuring each router along the path with state information for forwarding the particular label. Such techniques are currently used for traffic engineering in some ISPs today.

Alternately, a protocol such as RSVP can be used with an Explicit Route Object (ERO) so that the first router in the path can establish the trunk. The computation of the explicit route is beyond the scope of this document but may include considerations of policy, static and dynamic bandwidth allocation, congestion in the topology and manually configured alternatives.

4.5 Resource reservation

Priority traffic has certain requirements on capacity and traffic handling. To provide differentiated services, the ISP's infrastructure must know of, and support these requirements. The mechanism used to communicate these requirements dynamically is RSVP. The flow specification within RSVP can describe many characteristics of the flow or trunk. An LSR receiving RSVP information about a flow or trunk has the ability to look at this information and either accept or reject the reservation based on its local policy. This policy is likely to include constraints about the traffic handling functions that can be supported by the network and the aggregate capacity that the network is willing to provide for Priority traffic.

4.6 Inter-Provider SLAs (IPSs)

   Trunks that span multiple ISPs are likely to be based on legal
   agreements and some other external considerations. As a result, one
   of the common functions that we would expect to see in this type of
   architecture is a bilateral agreement between ISPs to support
   differentiated services. In addition to the obvious compensation,
   this agreement is likely to spell out the acceptable traffic handling
   policies and capacities to be used by both parties.

   Documents similar to this exist today on behalf of Best Effort
   traffic and are known as peering agreements. Extending a peering
   agreement to support differentiated services would effectively create
   an Inter-Provider SLA (IPS). Such agreements may include the types
   of differentiated services that one ISP provides to the other ISP, as
   well as the upper bound on the amount of traffic associated with each
   such service that the ISP would be willing to accept and carry from
   the other ISP. Further, an IPS may limit the types of differentiated
   services and an upper bound on the amount of traffic that may
   originate from a third party ISP and be passed from one signer of the
   IPS to the other.

   If the expected costs associated with the IPS are not symmetric, the
   parties may agree that one ISP will provide the other ISP with
   appropriate compensation. Such costs may be due to inequality of
   traffic exchange, costs in delivering the exchanged traffic, or the
   overhead involved in supporting the protocols exchanged between the
   two ISPs.

   Note that the PASTE architecture provides a technical basis to
   establish IPSs, while the procedures necessary to create such IPSs
   are outside the scope of PASTE.

4.7 Traffic shaping and policing

   To help support IPSs, special facilities must be available at the
   interconnect between ISPs. These mechanisms are necessary to insure
   that the network transmitting a trunk of Priority traffic does so
   within the agreed traffic characterization and capacity. A
   simplistic example of such a mechanism might be a token bucket
   system, implemented on a per-trunk basis. Similarly, there need to
   be mechanisms to insure, on a per trunk basis, that an ISP receiving
   a trunk receives only the traffic that is in compliance with the
   agreement between ISPs.

4.8 Multilateral IPSs

Trunks may span multiple ISPs. As a result, establishing a
particular trunk may require more than two ISPs. The result would be
a multilateral IPS. This type of agreement is unusual with respect
to existing Internet business practices in that it requires multiple
participating parties for a useful result. This is also challenging
because without a commonly accepted service level definition, there
will need to be a multilateral definition, and this definition may
not be compatible used in IPSs between the same parties.

Because this new type of agreement may be a difficulty, it may in
some cases be simpler for certain ISPs to establish aggregated trunks
through other ISPs and then contract with customers to aggregate
their trunks. In this way, trunks can span multiple ISPs without
requiring multilateral IPSs.

Either or both of these two alternatives are possible and acceptable
within this architecture, and the choice is left for the the
participants to make on a case-by-case basis.

5.0 The Provider Architecture for differentiated Services and Traffic
    Engineering (PASTE)

The Provider Architecture for differentiated Services and Traffic
Engineering (PASTE) is based on the usage of MPLS and RSVP as
mechanisms to establish differentiated service connections across
ISPs. This is done in a scalable way by aggregating differentiated
flows into traffic class specific MPLS tunnels, also known as traffic
trunks.

Such trunks can be given an explicit route by an ISP to define the
placement of the trunk within the ISP's infrastructure, allowing the
ISP to traffic engineer its own network. Trunks can also be
aggregated and merged, which helps the scalability of the
architecture by minimizing the number of individual trunks that
intermediate systems must support.

Special traffic handling operations, such as specific queuing
algorithms or drop computations, can be supported by a network on a
per-trunk basis, allowing these services to scale with the number of
trunks in the network.

Agreements for handling of trunks between ISPs require both legal
documentation and conformance mechanisms on both sides of the
agreement. As a trunk is unidirectional, it is sufficient for the
transmitter to monitor and shape outbound traffic, while the receiver
polices the traffic profile.

Trunks can either be aggregated across other ISPs or can be the
subject of a multilateral agreement for the carriage of the trunk.
RSVP information about individual flows is tunneled in the trunk to
provide an end-to-end reservation. To insure that the return RSVP
traffic is handled properly, each trunk must also have another tunnel
running in the opposite direction. Note that the reverse tunnel may
be a different trunk or it may be an independent tunnel terminating
at the same routers as the trunk. Routing symmetry between a trunk
and its return is not assumed.

RSVP already contains the ability to do local path repair. In the
event of a trunk failure, this capability, along with the ability to
specify abstractions in the ERO, allows RSVP to re-establish the
trunk in many failure scenarios.

6.0 Traffic flow in the PASTE architecture

As an example of the operation of this architecture, we consider an
example of a single differentiated flow. Suppose that a user wishes
to make a telephone call using a Voice over IP service. While this
call is full duplex, we can consider the data flow in each direction
in a half duplex fashion because the architecture operates
symmetrically.

Suppose that the data packets for this voice call are created at a
node S and need to traverse to node D. Because this is a voice call,
the data packets are encoded as Priority packets. If there is more
granularity within the traffic classes, these packets might be
encoded as wanting low jitter and having low drop preference.
Initially this is encoded into the precedence bits of the IPv4 ToS
byte.

6.1 Propagation of RSVP messages

To establish the flow to node D, node S first generates an RSVP PATH
message which describes the flow in more detail. For example, the
flow might require 3kbps of bandwidth, be insensitive to jitter of
less than 50ms, and require a delay of less than 200ms. This message
is passed through node S's local network and eventually appears in
node S's ISP. Suppose that this is ISP F.

ISP F has considerable latitude in its options at this point. The
requirement on F is to place the flow into a trunk before it exits
F's infrastructure. One thing that F might do is to perform the
admission control function at the first hop router. At this point, F
would determine if it had the capacity and capability of carrying the
flow across its own infrastructure to an exit router E. If the
admission control decision is negative, the first hop router can

inform node S using RSVP. Alternately, it can propagate the RSVP
PATH message along the path to exit router E. This is simply normal
operation of RSVP on a differentiated flow.

At exit router E, there is a trunk that ISP F maintains that transits
ISP X, Y, and Z and terminates in ISP L. Based on BGP path
information or on out of band information, Node D is known to be a
customer of ISP L. Exit router E matches the flow requirements in
the RSVP PATH message to the characteristics (e.g., remaining
capacity) of the trunk to ISP L. Assuming that the requirements are
compatible, it then notes that the flow should be aggregated into the
trunk.

To insure that the flow reservation happens end to end, the RSVP PATH
message is then encapsulated into the trunk itself, where it is
transmitted to ISP L. It eventually reaches the end of the trunk,
where it is decapsulated by router U. PATH messages are then
propagated all the way to the ultimate destination D.

Note that the end-to-end RSVP RESV messages must be carefully handled
by router U. The RESV messages from router U to E must return via a
tunnel back to router E.

RSVP is also used by exit router E to initialize and maintain the
trunk to ISP L. The RSVP messages for this trunk are not placed
within the trunk itself but the end-to-end RSVP messages are. The
existence of multiple overlapping RSVP sessions in PASTE is
straightforward, but requires explicit enumeration when discussing
particular RSVP sessions.

6.2 Propagation of user data

Data packets created by S flow through ISP F's network following the
flow reservation and eventually make it to router E. At that point,
they are given an MPLS label and placed in the trunk. Normal MPLS
switching will propagate this packet across ISP X's network. Note
that the same traffic class still applies because the class encoding
is propagated from the precedence bits of the IPv4 header to the CoS
bits in the MPLS label. As the packet exits ISP X's network, it can
be aggregated into another trunk for the express purpose of
transiting ISP Y.

Again, label switching is used to bring the packet across ISP Y's
network and then the aggregated trunk terminates at a router in ISP
Z's network. This router deaggregates the trunk, and forwards the
resulting trunk towards ISP L. This trunk transits ISP Z and
terminates in ISP L at router U. At this point, the data packets are
removed from the trunk and forwarded along the path computed by RSVP.

6.3 Trunk establishment and maintenance

In this example, there are two trunks in use. One trunk runs from
ISP F, through ISPs X, Y and Z, and then terminates in ISP L. The
other aggregated trunk begins in ISP X, transits ISP Y and terminates
in ISP Z.

The first trunk may be established based on a multilateral agreement
between ISPs F, X, Z and L. Note that ISP Y is not part of this
multilateral agreement, and ISP X is contractually responsible for
providing carriage of the trunk into ISP Z. Also per this agreement,
the tunnel is maintained by ISP F and is initialized and maintained
through the use of RSVP and an explicit route object that lists ISP's
X, Z, and L. Within this explicit route, ISP X and ISP L are given
as strict hops, thus constraining the path so that there may not be
other ISPs intervening between the pair of ISPs F and X and the pair
Z and L. However, no constraint is placed on the path between ISPs X
and Z. Further, there is no constraint placed on which router
terminates the trunk within L's infrastructure.

Normally this trunk is maintained by one of ISP F's routers adjacent
to ISP X. For robustness, ISP F has a second router adjacent to ISP
X, and that provides a backup trunk.

The second trunk may be established by a bilateral agreement between
ISP X and Y. ISP Z is not involved. The second trunk is constrained
so that it terminates on the last hop router within Y's
infrastructure. This tunnel is initialized and maintained through
the use of RSVP and an explicit route that lists the last hop router
within ISP Y's infrastructure. In order to provide redundancy in the
case of the failure of the last hop router, there are multiple
explicit routes configured into ISP X's routers. These routers can
select one working explicit route from their configured list.
Further, in order to provide redundancy against the failure of X's
primary router, X provides a backup router with a backup trunk.

6.4 Robustness

Note that in this example, there are no single points of failure once
the traffic is within ISP F's network. Each trunk has a backup trunk
to protect against the failure of the primary trunk. To protect
against the failure of any particular router, each trunk can be
configured with multiple explicit route objects that terminate at one
of several acceptable routers.

7.0 Security Considerations

Because Priority traffic intrinsically has more 'value' than Best
Effort traffic, the ability to inject Priority traffic into a network
must be carefully controlled. Further, signaling concerning Priority
traffic has to be authenticated because it is likely that the
signaling information will result in specific accounting and
eventually billing for the Priority services. ISPs are cautioned to
insure that the Priority traffic that they accept is in fact from a
known previous hop. Note that this is a simple requirement to
fulfill at private peerings, but it is much more difficult at public
interconnects. For this reason, exchanging Priority traffic at
public interconnects should be done with great care.

RSVP traffic needs to be authenticated. This can possibly be done
through the use of the Integrity Object.

8.0 Conclusion

The Provider Architecture for differentiated Services and Traffic
Engineering (PASTE) provides a robust, scalable means of deploying
differentiated services in the Internet. It provides scalability by
aggregating flows into class specific MPLS tunnels. These tunnels,
also called trunks, can in turn be aggregated, thus leading to a
hierarchical aggregation of traffic.

Trunk establishment and maintenance is done with RSVP, taking
advantage of existing work in differentiated services. Explicit
routes within the RSVP signaling structure allow providers to perform
traffic engineering by placing trunks on particular links in their
network.

The result is an architecture that is sufficient to scale to meet ISP
needs and can provide differentiated services in the large, support
traffic engineering, and continue to grow with the Internet.

8.1 Acknowledgments

Inspiration and comments about this document came from Noel Chiappa,
Der-Hwa Gan, Robert Elz, Lisa Bourgeault, and Paul Ferguson.

9.0 References

[1] Rosen, E., Viswanathan, A., and R. Callon, "A Proposed
    Architecture for MPLS", Work in Progress.

[2] Braden, R., Zhang, L., Berson, S., Herzog, S., and S. Jamin,
    "Resource ReSerVation Protocol (RSVP) -- Version 1 Functional
    Specification", RFC 2205, September 1997.

[3] Rosen, E., Rekhter, Y., Tappan, D., Farinacci, D., Fedorkow,, G.,
    Li, T., and A. Conta, "MPLS Label Stack Encoding", Work in
    Progress.

[4] Davie, B., Rekhter, Y., Rosen, E., Viswanathan, A., and V.
    Srinivasan, "Use of Label Switching With RSVP", Work in Progress.

[5] Gan, D.-H., Guerin, R., Kamat, S., Li, T., and E. Rosen, "Setting
    up Reservations on Explicit Paths using RSVP", Work in Progress.

[6] Davie, B., Li, T., Rosen, E., and Y. Rekhter, "Explicit Route
    Support in MPLS", Work in Progress.

[7] http://www.anxo.com/

10.0 Authors' Addresses

Tony Li
Juniper Networks, Inc.
385 Ravendale Dr.
Mountain View, CA 94043

Phone: +1 650 526 8006
Fax: +1 650 526 8001
EMail: tli@juniper.net

Yakov Rekhter
cisco Systems, Inc.
170 W. Tasman Dr.
San Jose, CA 95134

EMail: yakov@cisco.com

11. Full Copyright Statement

Network Working Group   K. Nichols
Request for Comments: 2474   Cisco Systems
Obsoletes: 1455, 1349   S. Blake
Category: Standards Track   Torrent Networking Technologies
                                                          F. Baker
                                                    Cisco Systems
                                                         D. Black
                                                  EMC Corporation
                                                    December 1998

        Definition of the Differentiated Services Field (DS Field)
                     in the IPv4 and IPv6 Headers

Status of this Memo

   This document specifies an Internet standards track protocol for the
   Internet community, and requests discussion and suggestions for
   improvements. Please refer to the current edition of the "Internet
   Official Protocol Standards" (STD 1) for the standardization state
   and status of this protocol. Distribution of this memo is unlimited.

Copyright Notice

Abstract

   Differentiated services enhancements to the Internet protocol are
   intended to enable scalable service discrimination in the Internet
   without the need for per-flow state and signaling at every hop. A
   variety of services may be built from a small, well-defined set of
   building blocks which are deployed in network nodes. The services
   may be either end-to-end or intra-domain; they include both those
   that can satisfy quantitative performance requirements (e.g., peak
   bandwidth) and those based on relative performance (e.g., "class"
   differentiation). Services can be constructed by a combination of:

   - setting bits in an IP header field at network boundaries
     (autonomous system boundaries, internal administrative boundaries,
     or hosts),
   - using those bits to determine how packets are forwarded by the
     nodes inside the network, and
   - conditioning the marked packets at network boundaries in accordance
     with the requirements or rules of each service.

RFC 2474

2

The requirements or rules of each service must be set through
administrative policy mechanisms which are outside the scope of this
document. A differentiated services-compliant network node includes
a classifier that selects packets based on the value of the DS field,
along with buffer management and packet scheduling mechanisms capable
of delivering the specific packet forwarding treatment indicated by
the DS field value. Setting of the DS field and conditioning of the
temporal behavior of marked packets need only be performed at network
boundaries and may vary in complexity.

This document defines the IP header field, called the DS (for
differentiated services) field. In IPv4, it defines the layout of
the TOS octet; in IPv6, the Traffic Class octet. In addition, a base
set of packet forwarding treatments, or per-hop behaviors, is
defined.

For a more complete understanding of differentiated services, see
also the differentiated services architecture [ARCH].

Table of Contents

1. Introduction

    Differentiated services are intended to provide a framework and
    building blocks to enable deployment of scalable service
    discrimination in the Internet. The differentiated services approach
    aims to speed deployment by separating the architecture into two
    major components, one of which is fairly well-understood and the
    other of which is just beginning to be understood. In this, we are
    guided by the original design of the Internet where the decision was
    made to separate the forwarding and routing components. Packet
    forwarding is the relatively simple task that needs to be performed
    on a per-packet basis as quickly as possible. Forwarding uses the
    packet header to find an entry in a routing table that determines the
    packet's output interface. Routing sets the entries in that table
    and may need to reflect a range of transit and other policies as well
    as to keep track of route failures. Routing tables are maintained as
    a background process to the forwarding task. Further, routing is the
    more complex task and it has continued to evolve over the past 20
    years.

    Analogously, the differentiated services architecture contains two
    main components. One is the fairly well-understood behavior in the
    forwarding path and the other is the more complex and still emerging
    background policy and allocation component that configures parameters
    used in the forwarding path. The forwarding path behaviors include
    the differential treatment an individual packet receives, as
    implemented by queue service disciplines and/or queue management
    disciplines. These per-hop behaviors are useful and required in
    network nodes to deliver differentiated treatment of packets no
    matter how we construct end-to-end or intra-domain services. Our
    focus is on the general semantics of the behaviors rather than the
    specific mechanisms used to implement them since these behaviors will
    evolve less rapidly than the mechanisms.

    Per-hop behaviors and mechanisms to select them on a per-packet basis
    can be deployed in network nodes today and it is this aspect of the
    differentiated services architecture that is being addressed first.
    In addition, the forwarding path may require that some monitoring,
    policing, and shaping be done on the network traffic designated for
    "special" treatment in order to enforce requirements associated with
    the delivery of the special treatment. Mechanisms for this kind of
    traffic conditioning are also fairly well-understood. The wide
    deployment of such traffic conditioners is also important to enable
    the construction of services, though their actual use in constructing
    services may evolve over time.

The configuration of network elements with respect to which packets
get special treatment and what kinds of rules are to be applied to
the use of resources is much less well-understood. Nevertheless, it
is possible to deploy useful differentiated services in networks by
using simple policies and static configurations. As described in
[ARCH], there are a number of ways to compose per-hop behaviors and
traffic conditioners to create services. In the process, additional
experience is gained that will guide more complex policies and
allocations. The basic behaviors in the forwarding path can remain
the same while this component of the architecture evolves.
Experiences with the construction of such services will continue for
some time, thus we avoid standardizing this construction as it is
premature. Further, much of the details of service construction are
covered by legal agreements between different business entities and
we avoid this as it is very much outside the scope of the IETF.

This document concentrates on the forwarding path component. In the
packet forwarding path, differentiated services are realized by
mapping the codepoint contained in a field in the IP packet header to
a particular forwarding treatment, or per-hop behavior (PHB), at each
network node along its path. The codepoints may be chosen from a set
of mandatory values defined later in this document, from a set of
recommended values to be defined in future documents, or may have
purely local meaning. PHBs are expected to be implemented by
employing a range of queue service and/or queue management
disciplines on a network node's output interface queue: for example
weighted round-robin (WRR) queue servicing or drop-preference queue
management.

Marking is performed by traffic conditioners at network boundaries,
including the edges of the network (first-hop router or source host)
and administrative boundaries. Traffic conditioners may include the
primitives of marking, metering, policing and shaping (these
mechanisms are described in [ARCH]). Services are realized by the
use of particular packet classification and traffic conditioning
mechanisms at boundaries coupled with the concatenation of per-hop
behaviors along the transit path of the traffic. A goal of the
differentiated services architecture is to specify these building
blocks for future extensibility, both of the number and type of the
building blocks and of the services built from them.

Terminology used in this memo is defined in Sec. 2. The
differentiated services field definition (DS field) is given in Sec.
3. In Sec. 4, we discuss the desire for partial backwards
compatibility with current use of the IPv4 Precedence field. As a
solution, we introduce Class Selector Codepoints and Class Selector

Compliant PHBs. Sec. 5 presents guidelines for per-hop behavior
standardization. Sec. 6 discusses guidelines for allocation of
codepoints. Sec. 7 covers security considerations.

This document is a concise description of the DS field and its uses.
It is intended to be read along with the differentiated services
architecture [ARCH].

The key words "MUST", "MUST NOT", "REQUIRED", "SHALL", "SHALL NOT",
"SHOULD", "SHOULD NOT", "RECOMMENDED", "MAY", and "OPTIONAL" in this
document are to be interpreted as described in [RFC2119].

2. Terminology Used in This Document

Behavior Aggregate: a collection of packets with the same codepoint
crossing a link in a particular direction. The terms "aggregate" and
"behavior aggregate" are used interchangeably in this document.

Classifier: an entity which selects packets based on the content of
packet headers according to defined rules.

Class Selector Codepoint: any of the eight codepoints in the range '
xxx000' (where 'x' may equal '0' or '1'). Class Selector Codepoints
are discussed in Sec. 4.2.2.

Class Selector Compliant PHB: a per-hop behavior satisfying the Class
Selector PHB Requirements specified in Sec. 4.2.2.2.

Codepoint: a specific value of the DSCP portion of the DS field.
Recommended codepoints SHOULD map to specific, standardized PHBs.
Multiple codepoints MAY map to the same PHB.

Differentiated Services Boundary: the edge of a DS domain, where
classifiers and traffic conditioners are likely to be deployed. A
differentiated services boundary can be further sub-divided into
ingress and egress nodes, where the ingress/egress nodes are the
downstream/upstream nodes of a boundary link in a given traffic
direction. A differentiated services boundary typically is found at
the ingress to the first-hop differentiated services-compliant router
(or network node) that a host's packets traverse, or at the egress of
the last-hop differentiated services-compliant router or network node
that packets traverse before arriving at a host. This is sometimes
referred to as the boundary at a leaf router. A differentiated
services boundary may be co-located with a host, subject to local
policy. Also DS boundary.

Differentiated Services-Compliant: in compliance with the
requirements specified in this document. Also DS-compliant.

Differentiated Services Domain: a contiguous portion of the Internet
over which a consistent set of differentiated services policies are
administered in a coordinated fashion. A differentiated services
domain can represent different administrative domains or autonomous
systems, different trust regions, different network technologies
(e.g., cell/frame), hosts and routers, etc. Also DS domain.

Differentiated Services Field: the IPv4 header TOS octet or the IPv6
Traffic Class octet when interpreted in conformance with the
definition given in this document. Also DS field.

Mechanism: The implementation of one or more per-hop behaviors
according to a particular algorithm.

Microflow: a single instance of an application-to-application flow of
packets which is identified by source address, destination address,
protocol id, and source port, destination port (where applicable).

Per-hop Behavior (PHB): a description of the externally observable
forwarding treatment applied at a differentiated services-compliant
node to a behavior aggregate. The description of a PHB SHOULD be
sufficiently detailed to allow the construction of predictable
services, as documented in [ARCH].

Per-hop Behavior Group: a set of one or more PHBs that can only be
meaningfully specified and implemented simultaneously, due to a
common constraint applying to all PHBs in the set such as a queue
servicing or queue management policy. Also PHB Group.

Traffic Conditioning: control functions that can be applied to a
behavior aggregate, application flow, or other operationally useful
subset of traffic, e.g., routing updates. These MAY include
metering, policing, shaping, and packet marking. Traffic
conditioning is used to enforce agreements between domains and to
condition traffic to receive a differentiated service within a domain
by marking packets with the appropriate codepoint in the DS field and
by monitoring and altering the temporal characteristics of the
aggregate where necessary. See [ARCH].

Traffic Conditioner: an entity that performs traffic conditioning
functions and which MAY contain meters, policers, shapers, and
markers. Traffic conditioners are typically deployed in DS boundary
nodes (i.e., not in interior nodes of a DS domain).

Service: a description of the overall treatment of (a subset of) a
customer's traffic across a particular domain, across a set of
interconnected DS domains, or end-to-end. Service descriptions are
covered by administrative policy and services are constructed by

applying traffic conditioning to create behavior aggregates which
experience a known PHB at each node within the DS domain. Multiple
services can be supported by a single per-hop behavior used in
concert with a range of traffic conditioners.

To summarize, classifiers and traffic conditioners are used to select
which packets are to be added to behavior aggregates. Aggregates
receive differentiated treatment in a DS domain and traffic
conditioners MAY alter the temporal characteristics of the aggregate
to conform to some requirements. A packet's DS field is used to
designate the packet's behavior aggregate and is subsequently used to
determine which forwarding treatment the packet receives. A behavior
aggregate classifier which can select a PHB, for example a
differential output queue servicing discipline, based on the
codepoint in the DS field SHOULD be included in all network nodes in
a DS domain. The classifiers and traffic conditioners at DS
boundaries are configured in accordance with some service
specification, a matter of administrative policy outside the scope of
this document.

Additional differentiated services definitions are given in [ARCH].

3. Differentiated Services Field Definition

A replacement header field, called the DS field, is defined, which is
intended to supersede the existing definitions of the IPv4 TOS octet
[RFC791] and the IPv6 Traffic Class octet [IPv6].

Six bits of the DS field are used as a codepoint (DSCP) to select the
PHB a packet experiences at each node. A two-bit currently unused
(CU) field is reserved and its definition and interpretation are
outside the scope of this document. The value of the CU bits are
ignored by differentiated services-compliant nodes when determining
the per-hop behavior to apply to a received packet.

The DS field structure is presented below:

```
    0   1   2   3   4   5   6   7
  +---+---+---+---+---+---+---+---+
  |         DSCP          |  CU   |
  +---+---+---+---+---+---+---+---+

    DSCP: differentiated services codepoint
    CU:   currently unused
```

In a DSCP value notation 'xxxxxx' (where 'x' may equal '0' or '1')
used in this document, the left-most bit signifies bit 0 of the DS
field (as shown above), and the right-most bit signifies bit 5.

Implementors should note that the DSCP field is six bits wide. DS-
compliant nodes MUST select PHBs by matching against the entire 6-bit
DSCP field, e.g., by treating the value of the field as a table index
which is used to select a particular packet handling mechanism which
has been implemented in that device. The value of the CU field MUST
be ignored by PHB selection. The DSCP field is defined as an
unstructured field to facilitate the definition of future per-hop
behaviors.

With some exceptions noted below, the mapping of codepoints to PHBs
MUST be configurable. A DS-compliant node MUST support the logical
equivalent of a configurable mapping table from codepoints to PHBs.
PHB specifications MUST include a recommended default codepoint,
which MUST be unique for codepoints in the standard space (see Sec.
6). Implementations should support the recommended codepoint-to-PHB
mappings in their default configuration. Operators may choose to use
different codepoints for a PHB, either in addition to or in place of
the recommended default. Note that if operators do so choose, re-
marking of DS fields may be necessary at administrative boundaries
even if the same PHBs are implemented on both sides of the boundary.

See [ARCH] for further discussion of re-marking.

The exceptions to general configurability are for codepoints 'xxx000'
and are noted in Secs. 4.2.2 and 4.3.

Packets received with an unrecognized codepoint SHOULD be forwarded
as if they were marked for the Default behavior (see Sec. 4), and
their codepoints should not be changed. Such packets MUST NOT cause
the network node to malfunction.

The structure of the DS field shown above is incompatible with the
existing definition of the IPv4 TOS octet in [RFC791]. The
presumption is that DS domains protect themselves by deploying re-
marking boundary nodes, as should networks using the RFC 791
Precedence designations. Correct operational procedure SHOULD follow
[RFC791], which states: "If the actual use of these precedence
designations is of concern to a particular network, it is the
responsibility of that network to control the access to, and use of,
those precedence designations." Validating the value of the DS field
at DS boundaries is sensible in any case since an upstream node can
easily set it to any arbitrary value. DS domains that are not
isolated by suitably configured boundary nodes may deliver
unpredictable service.

Nodes MAY rewrite the DS field as needed to provide a desired local
or end-to-end service. Specifications of DS field translations at DS
boundaries are the subject of service level agreements between
providers and users, and are outside the scope of this document.
Standardized PHBs allow providers to build their services from a
well-known set of packet forwarding treatments that can be expected
to be present in the equipment of many vendors.

4. Historical Codepoint Definitions and PHB Requirements

The DS field will have a limited backwards compatibility with current
practice, as described in this section. Backwards compatibility is
addressed in two ways. First, there are per-hop behaviors that are
already in widespread use (e.g., those satisfying the IPv4 Precedence
queueing requirements specified in [RFC1812]), and we wish to permit
their continued use in DS-compliant nodes. In addition, there are
some codepoints that correspond to historical use of the IP
Precedence field and we reserve these codepoints to map to PHBs that
meet the general requirements specified in Sec. 4.2.2.2, though the
specific differentiated services PHBs mapped to by those codepoints
MAY have additional specifications.

No attempt is made to maintain backwards compatibility with the "DTR"
or TOS bits of the IPv4 TOS octet, as defined in [RFC791].

4.1 A Default PHB

A "default" PHB MUST be available in a DS-compliant node. This is
the common, best-effort forwarding behavior available in existing
routers as standardized in [RFC1812]. When no other agreements are
in place, it is assumed that packets belong to this aggregate. Such
packets MAY be sent into a network without adhering to any particular
rules and the network will deliver as many of these packets as
possible and as soon as possible, subject to other resource policy
constraints. A reasonable implementation of this PHB would be a
queueing discipline that sends packets of this aggregate whenever the
output link is not required to satisfy another PHB. A reasonable
policy for constructing services would ensure that the aggregate was
not "starved". This could be enforced by a mechanism in each node
that reserves some minimal resources (e.g, buffers, bandwidth) for
Default behavior aggregates. This permits senders that are not
differentiated services-aware to continue to use the network in the
same manner as today. The impact of the introduction of
differentiated services into a domain on the service expectations of
its customers and peers is a complex matter involving policy
decisions by the domain and is outside the scope of this document.
The RECOMMENDED codepoint for the Default PHB is the bit pattern '
000000'; the value '000000' MUST map to a PHB that meets these

specifications. The codepoint chosen for Default behavior is
compatible with existing practice [RFC791]. Where a codepoint is not
mapped to a standardized or local use PHB, it SHOULD be mapped to the
Default PHB.

A packet initially marked for the Default behavior MAY be re-marked
with another codepoint as it passes a boundary into a DS domain so
that it will be forwarded using a different PHB within that domain,
possibly subject to some negotiated agreement between the peering
domains.

4.2 Once and Future IP Precedence Field Use

We wish to maintain some form of backward compatibility with present
uses of the IP Precedence Field: bits 0-2 of the IPv4 TOS octet.
Routers exist that use the IP Precedence field to select different
per-hop forwarding treatments in a similar way to the use proposed
here for the DSCP field. Thus, a simple prototype differentiated
services architecture can be quickly deployed by appropriately
configuring these routers. Further, IP systems today understand the
location of the IP Precedence field, and thus if these bits are used
in a similar manner as DS-compliant equipment is deployed,
significant failures are not likely during early deployment. In
other words, strict DS-compliance need not be ubiquitous even within
a single service provider's network if bits 0-2 of the DSCP field are
employed in a manner similar to, or subsuming, the deployed uses of
the IP Precedence field.

4.2.1 IP Precedence History and Evolution in Brief

The IP Precedence field is something of a forerunner of the DS field.
IP Precedence, and the IP Precedence Field, were first defined in
[RFC791]. The values that the three-bit IP Precedence Field might
take were assigned to various uses, including network control
traffic, routing traffic, and various levels of privilege. The least
level of privilege was deemed "routine traffic". In [RFC791], the
notion of Precedence was defined broadly as "An independent measure
of the importance of this datagram." Not all values of the IP
Precedence field were assumed to have meaning across boundaries, for
instance "The Network Control precedence designation is intended to
be used within a network only. The actual use and control of that
designation is up to each network." [RFC791]

Although early BBN IMPs implemented the Precedence feature, early
commercial routers and UNIX IP forwarding code generally did not. As
networks became more complex and customer requirements grew,
commercial router vendors developed ways to implement various kinds
of queueing services including priority queueing, which were

generally based on policies encoded in filters in the routers, which examined IP addresses, IP protocol numbers, TCP or UDP ports, and other header fields. IP Precedence was and is among the options such filters can examine.

In short, IP Precedence is widely deployed and widely used, if not in exactly the manner intended in [RFC791]. This was recognized in [RFC1122], which states that while the use of the IP Precedence field is valid, the specific assignment of the priorities in [RFC791] were merely historical.

4.2.2 Subsuming IP Precedence into Class Selector Codepoints

A specification of the packet forwarding treatments selected by the IP Precedence field today would have to be quite general; probably not specific enough to build predictable services from in the differentiated services framework. To preserve partial backwards compatibility with known current uses of the IP Precedence field without sacrificing future flexibility, we have taken the approach of describing minimum requirements on a set of PHBs that are compatible with most of the deployed forwarding treatments selected by the IP Precedence field. In addition, we give a set of codepoints that MUST map to PHBs meeting these minimum requirements. The PHBs mapped to by these codepoints MAY have a more detailed list of specifications in addition to the required ones stated here. Other codepoints MAY map to these same PHBs. We refer to this set of codepoints as the Class Selector Codepoints, and the minimum requirements for PHBs that these codepoints may map to are called the Class Selector PHB Requirements.

4.2.2.1 The Class Selector Codepoints

A specification of the packet forwarding treatments selected by the The DS field values of 'xxx000|xx', or DSCP = 'xxx000' and CU subfield unspecified, are reserved as a set of Class Selector Codepoints. PHBs which are mapped to by these codepoints MUST satisfy the Class Selector PHB requirements in addition to preserving the Default PHB requirement on codepoint '000000' (Sec. 4.1).

4.2.2.2 The Class Selector PHB Requirements

We refer to a Class Selector Codepoint with a larger numerical value than another Class Selector Codepoint as having a higher relative order while a Class Selector Codepoint with a smaller numerical value than another Class Selector Codepoint is said to have a lower relative order. The set of PHBs mapped to by the eight Class Selector Codepoints MUST yield at least two independently forwarded classes of traffic, and PHBs selected by a Class Selector Codepoint

SHOULD give packets a probability of timely forwarding that is not
lower than that given to packets marked with a Class Selector
codepoint of lower relative order, under reasonable operating
conditions and traffic loads. A discarded packet is considered to be
an extreme case of untimely forwarding. In addition, PHBs selected
by codepoints '11x000' MUST give packets a preferential forwarding
treatment by comparison to the PHB selected by codepoint '000000' to
preserve the common usage of IP Precedence values '110' and '111' for
routing traffic.

Further, PHBs selected by distinct Class Selector Codepoints SHOULD
be independently forwarded; that is, packets marked with different
Class Selector Codepoints MAY be re-ordered. A network node MAY
enforce limits on the amount of the node's resources that can be
utilized by each of these PHBs.

PHB groups whose specification satisfy these requirements are
referred to as Class Selector Compliant PHBs.

The Class Selector PHB Requirements on codepoint '000000' are
compatible with those listed for the Default PHB in Sec. 4.1.

4.2.2.3 Using the Class Selector PHB Requirements for IP Precedence
         Compatibility

A DS-compliant network node can be deployed with a set of one or more
Class Selector Compliant PHB groups. This document states that the
set of codepoints 'xxx000' MUST map to such a set of PHBs. As it is
also possible to map multiple codepoints to the same PHB, the vendor
or the network administrator MAY configure the network node to map
codepoints to PHBs irrespective of bits 3-5 of the DSCP field to
yield a network that is compatible with historical IP Precedence use.
Thus, for example, codepoint '011010' would map to the same PHB as
codepoint '011000'.

4.2.2.4 Example Mechanisms for Implementing Class Selector Compliant
         PHB Groups

Class Selector Compliant PHBs can be realized by a variety of
mechanisms, including strict priority queueing, weighted fair
queueing (WFQ), WRR, or variants [RPS, HPFQA, DRR], or Class-Based
Queuing [CBQ]. The distinction between PHBs and mechanisms is
described in more detail in Sec. 5.

It is important to note that these mechanisms might be available
through other PHBs (standardized or not) that are available in a
particular vendor's equipment. For example, future documents may
standardize a Strict Priority Queueing PHB group for a set of

recommended codepoints. A network administrator might configure
those routers to select the Strict Priority Queueing PHBs with
codepoints 'xxx000' in conformance with the requirements of this
document.

As a further example, another vendor might employ a CBQ mechanism in
its routers. The CBQ mechanism could be used to implement the Strict
Priority Queueing PHBs as well as a set of Class Selector Compliant
PHBs with a wider range of features than would be available in a set
of PHBs that did no more than meet the minimum Class Selector PHB
requirements.

4.3 Summary

This document defines codepoints 'xxx000' as the Class Selector
codepoints, where PHBs selected by these codepoints MUST meet the
Class Selector PHB Requirements described in Sec. 4.2.2.2. This is
done to preserve a useful level of backward compatibility with
current uses of the IP Precedence field in the Internet without
unduly limiting future flexibility. In addition, codepoint '000000'
is used as the Default PHB value for the Internet and, as such, is
not configurable. The remaining seven non-zero Class Selector
codepoints are configurable only to the extent that they map to PHBs
that meet the requirements in Sec. 4.2.2.2.

5. Per-Hop Behavior Standardization Guidelines

The behavioral characteristics of a PHB are to be standardized, and
not the particular algorithms or the mechanisms used to implement
them. A node may have a (possibly large) set of parameters that can
be used to control how packets are scheduled onto an output interface
(e.g., N separate queues with settable priorities, queue lengths,
round-robin weights, drop algorithm, drop preference weights and
thresholds, etc). To illustrate the distinction between a PHB and a
mechanism, we point out that Class Selector Compliant PHBs might be
implemented by several mechanisms, including: strict priority
queueing, WFQ, WRR, or variants [HPFQA, RPS, DRR], or CBQ [CBQ], in
isolation or in combination.

PHBs may be specified individually, or as a group (a single PHB is a
special case of a PHB group). A PHB group usually consists of a set
of two or more PHBs that can only be meaningfully specified and
implemented simultaneously, due to a common constraint applying to
each PHB within the group, such as a queue servicing or queue
management policy. A PHB group specification SHOULD describe
conditions under which a packet might be re-marked to select another
PHB within the group. It is RECOMMENDED that PHB implementations do
not introduce any packet re-ordering within a microflow. PHB group

specifications MUST identify any possible packet re-ordering
implications which may occur for each individual PHB, and which may
occur if different packets within a microflow are marked for
different PHBs within the group.

Only those per-hop behaviors that are not described by an existing
PHB standard, and have been implemented, deployed, and shown to be
useful, SHOULD be standardized. Since current experience with
differentiated services is quite limited, it is premature to
hypothesize the exact specification of these per-hop behaviors.

Each standardized PHB MUST have an associated RECOMMENDED codepoint,
allocated out of a space of 32 codepoints (see Sec. 6). This
specification has left room in the codepoint space to allow for
evolution, thus the defined space ('xxx000') is intentionally sparse.

Network equipment vendors are free to offer whatever parameters and
capabilities are deemed useful or marketable. When a particular,
standardized PHB is implemented in a node, a vendor MAY use any
algorithm that satisfies the definition of the PHB according to the
standard. The node's capabilities and its particular configuration
determine the different ways that packets can be treated.

Service providers are not required to use the same node mechanisms or
configurations to enable service differentiation within their
networks, and are free to configure the node parameters in whatever
way that is appropriate for their service offerings and traffic
engineering objectives. Over time certain common per-hop behaviors
are likely to evolve (i.e., ones that are particularly useful for
implementing end-to-end services) and these MAY be associated with
particular EXP/LU PHB codepoints in the DS field, allowing use across
domain boundaries (see Sec. 6). These PHBs are candidates for future
standardization.

It is RECOMMENDED that standardized PHBs be specified in accordance
with the guidelines set out in [ARCH].

6. IANA Considerations

The DSCP field within the DS field is capable of conveying 64
distinct codepoints. The codepoint space is divided into three pools
for the purpose of codepoint assignment and management: a pool of 32
RECOMMENDED codepoints (Pool 1) to be assigned by Standards Action as
defined in [CONS], a pool of 16 codepoints (Pool 2) to be reserved
for experimental or Local Use (EXP/LU) as defined in [CONS], and a
pool of 16 codepoints (Pool 3) which are initially available for
experimental or local use, but which should be preferentially

utilized for standardized assignments if Pool 1 is ever exhausted.
The pools are defined in the following table (where 'x' refers to
either '0' or '1'):

```
Pool          Codepoint space        Assignment Policy
----          ---------------        -----------------

 1              xxxxx0               Standards Action
 2              xxxx11               EXP/LU
 3              xxxx01               EXP/LU (*)
```

(*) may be utilized for future Standards Action allocations as
    necessary

This document assigns eight RECOMMENDED codepoints ('xxx000') which
are drawn from Pool 1 above. These codepoints MUST be mapped, not to
specific PHBs, but to PHBs that meet "at least" the requirements set
forth in Sec. 4.2.2.2 to provide a minimal level of backwards
compatibility with IP Precedence as defined in [RFC791] and as
deployed in some current equipment.

7. Security Considerations

   This section considers security issues raised by the introduction of
   differentiated services, primarily the potential for denial-of-
   service attacks, and the related potential for theft of service by
   unauthorized traffic (Section 7.1). Section 7.2 addresses the
   operation of differentiated services in the presence of IPsec
   including its interaction with IPsec tunnel mode and other tunnelling
   protocols. See [ARCH] for more extensive treatment of the security
   concerns raised by the overall differentiated services architecture.

7.1 Theft and Denial of Service

   The primary goal of differentiated services is to allow different
   levels of service to be provided for traffic streams on a common
   network infrastructure. A variety of techniques may be used to
   achieve this, but the end result will be that some packets receive
   different (e.g., better) service than others. The mapping of network
   traffic to the specific behaviors that result in different (e.g.,
   better or worse) service is indicated primarily by the DS codepoint,
   and hence an adversary may be able to obtain better service by
   modifying the codepoint to values indicating behaviors used for
   enhanced services or by injecting packets with such codepoint values.
   Taken to its limits, such theft-of-service becomes a denial-of-
   service attack when the modified or injected traffic depletes the
   resources available to forward it and other traffic streams.

The defense against this class of theft- and denial-of-service
attacks consists of the combination of traffic conditioning at DS
domain boundaries with security and integrity of the network
infrastructure within a DS domain. DS domain boundary nodes MUST
ensure that all traffic entering the domain is marked with codepoint
values appropriate to the traffic and the domain, remarking the
traffic with new codepoint values if necessary. These DS boundary
nodes are the primary line of defense against theft- and denial-of-
service attacks based on modified codepoints, as success of any such
attack indicates that the codepoints used by the attacking traffic
were inappropriate. An important instance of a boundary node is that
any traffic-originating node within a DS domain is the initial
boundary node for that traffic. Interior nodes in a DS domain rely
on DS codepoints to associate traffic with the forwarding PHBs, and
are NOT REQUIRED to check codepoint values before using them. As a
result, the interior nodes depend on the correct operation of the DS
domain boundary nodes to prevent the arrival of traffic with
inappropriate codepoints or in excess of provisioned levels that
would disrupt operation of the domain.

7.2 IPsec and Tunnelling Interactions

The IPsec protocol, as defined in [ESP, AH], does not include the IP
header's DS field in any of its cryptographic calculations (in the
case of tunnel mode, it is the outer IP header's DS field that is not
included). Hence modification of the DS field by a network node has
no effect on IPsec's end-to-end security, because it cannot cause any
IPsec integrity check to fail. As a consequence, IPsec does not
provide any defense against an adversary's modification of the DS
field (i.e., a man-in-the-middle attack), as the adversary's
modification will also have no effect on IPsec's end-to-end security.

IPsec's tunnel mode provides security for the encapsulated IP
header's DS field. A tunnel mode IPsec packet contains two IP
headers: an outer header supplied by the tunnel ingress node and an
encapsulated inner header supplied by the original source of the
packet. When an IPsec tunnel is hosted (in whole or in part) on a
differentiated services network, the intermediate network nodes
operate on the DS field in the outer header. At the tunnel egress
node, IPsec processing includes removing the outer header and
forwarding the packet (if required) using the inner header. The
IPsec protocol REQUIRES that the inner header's DS field not be
changed by this decapsulation processing to ensure that modifications
to the DS field cannot be used to launch theft- or denial-of-service
attacks across an IPsec tunnel endpoint. This document makes no
change to that requirement. If the inner IP header has not been
processed by a DS boundary node for the tunnel egress node's DS

domain, the tunnel egress node is the boundary node for traffic exiting the tunnel, and hence MUST ensure that the resulting traffic has appropriate DS codepoints.

When IPsec tunnel egress decapsulation processing includes a sufficiently strong cryptographic integrity check of the encapsulated packet (where sufficiency is determined by local security policy), the tunnel egress node can safely assume that the DS field in the inner header has the same value as it had at the tunnel ingress node. An important consequence is that otherwise insecure links within a DS domain can be secured by a sufficiently strong IPsec tunnel. This analysis and its implications apply to any tunnelling protocol that performs integrity checks, but the level of assurance of the inner header's DS field depends on the strength of the integrity check performed by the tunnelling protocol. In the absence of sufficient assurance for a tunnel that may transit nodes outside the current DS domain (or is otherwise vulnerable), the encapsulated packet MUST be treated as if it had arrived at a boundary from outside the DS domain.

8. Acknowledgements

The authors would like to acknowledge the Differentiated Services Working Group for discussions which helped shape this document.

9. References

[AH]   Kent, S. and R. Atkinson, "IP Authentication Header", RFC 2402, November 1998.

[ARCH]   Blake, S., Black, D., Carlson, M., Davies, E., Wang, Z. and W. Weiss, "An Architecture for Differentiated Services", RFC 2475, December 1998.

[CBQ]   S. Floyd and V. Jacobson, "Link-sharing and Resource Management Models for Packet Networks", IEEE/ACM Transactions on Networking, Vol. 3 no. 4, pp. 365-386, August 1995.

[CONS]   Narten, T. and H. Alvestrand, "Guidelines for Writing an IANA Considerations Section in RFCs", RFC 2434, October 1998.

[DRR]   M. Shreedhar and G. Varghese, Efficient Fair Queueing using Deficit Round Robin", Proc. ACM SIGCOMM 95, 1995.

[ESP]   Kent, S. and R. Atkinson, "IP Encapsulating Security
              Payload (ESP)", RFC 2406, November 1998.

[HPFQA]   J. Bennett and Hui Zhang, "Hierarchical Packet Fair
              Queueing Algorithms", Proc. ACM SIGCOMM 96, August 1996.

[IPv6]   Deering, S. and R. Hinden, "Internet Protocol, Version 6
              (IPv6) Specification", RFC 2460, December 1998.

[RFC791]   Postel, J., Editor, "Internet Protocol", STD 5, RFC 791,
              September 1981.

[RFC1122]   Braden, R., "Requirements for Internet hosts -
              communication layers", STD 3, RFC 1122, October 1989.

[RFC1812]   Baker, F., Editor, "Requirements for IP Version 4
              Routers", RFC 1812, June 1995.

[RFC2119]   Bradner, S., "Key words for use in RFCs to Indicate
              Requirement Levels", BCP 14, RFC 2119, March 1997.

[RPS]   D. Stiliadis and A. Varma, "Rate-Proportional Servers: A
              Design Methodology for Fair Queueing Algorithms", IEEE/
              ACM Trans. on Networking, April 1998.

Authors' Addresses

    Kathleen Nichols
    Cisco Systems
    170 West Tasman Drive
    San Jose, CA   95134-1706

    Phone: +1-408-525-4857
    EMail: kmn@cisco.com

    Steven Blake
    Torrent Networking Technologies
    3000 Aerial Center, Suite 140
    Morrisville, NC   27560

    Phone: +1-919-468-8466 x232
    EMail: slblake@torrentnet.com

    Fred Baker
    Cisco Systems
    519 Lado Drive
    Santa Barbara, CA   93111

    Phone: +1-408-526-4257
    EMail: fred@cisco.com

    David L. Black
    EMC Corporation
    35 Parkwood Drive
    Hopkinton, MA   01748

    Phone: +1-508-435-1000 x76140
    EMail: black_david@emc.com

Full Copyright Statement

Network Working Group   S. Blake
Request for Comments: 2475   Torrent Networking Technologies
Category: Informational   D. Black
                                                     EMC Corporation
                                                          M. Carlson
                                                    Sun Microsystems
                                                          E. Davies
                                                           Nortel UK
                                                            Z. Wang
                                         Bell Labs Lucent Technologies
                                                           W. Weiss
                                                 Lucent Technologies
                                                       December 1998

An Architecture for Differentiated Services

Status of this Memo

Copyright Notice

Abstract

   This document defines an architecture for implementing scalable
   service differentiation in the Internet. This architecture achieves
   scalability by aggregating traffic classification state which is
   conveyed by means of IP-layer packet marking using the DS field
   [DSFIELD]. Packets are classified and marked to receive a particular
   per-hop forwarding behavior on nodes along their path. Sophisticated
   classification, marking, policing, and shaping operations need only
   be implemented at network boundaries or hosts. Network resources are
   allocated to traffic streams by service provisioning policies which
   govern how traffic is marked and conditioned upon entry to a
   differentiated services-capable network, and how that traffic is
   forwarded within that network. A wide variety of services can be
   implemented on top of these building blocks.

Table of Contents

1. Introduction

1.1 Overview

    This document defines an architecture for implementing scalable
    service differentiation in the Internet. A "Service" defines some
    significant characteristics of packet transmission in one direction
    across a set of one or more paths within a network. These

characteristics may be specified in quantitative or statistical terms of throughput, delay, jitter, and/or loss, or may otherwise be specified in terms of some relative priority of access to network resources. Service differentiation is desired to accommodate heterogeneous application requirements and user expectations, and to permit differentiated pricing of Internet service.

This architecture is composed of a number of functional elements implemented in network nodes, including a small set of per-hop forwarding behaviors, packet classification functions, and traffic conditioning functions including metering, marking, shaping, and policing. This architecture achieves scalability by implementing complex classification and conditioning functions only at network boundary nodes, and by applying per-hop behaviors to aggregates of traffic which have been appropriately marked using the DS field in the IPv4 or IPv6 headers [DSFIELD]. Per-hop behaviors are defined to permit a reasonably granular means of allocating buffer and bandwidth resources at each node among competing traffic streams. Per-application flow or per-customer forwarding state need not be maintained within the core of the network. A distinction is maintained between:

o the service provided to a traffic aggregate,

o the conditioning functions and per-hop behaviors used to realize services,

o the DS field value (DS codepoint) used to mark packets to select a per-hop behavior, and

o the particular node implementation mechanisms which realize a per-hop behavior.

Service provisioning and traffic conditioning policies are sufficiently decoupled from the forwarding behaviors within the network interior to permit implementation of a wide variety of service behaviors, with room for future expansion.

This architecture only provides service differentiation in one direction of traffic flow and is therefore asymmetric. Development of a complementary symmetric architecture is a topic of current research but is outside the scope of this document; see for example [EXPLICIT].

Sect. 1.2 is a glossary of terms used within this document. Sec. 1.3 lists requirements addressed by this architecture, and Sec. 1.4 provides a brief comparison to other approaches for service differentiation. Sec. 2 discusses the components of the architecture

in detail. Sec. 3 proposes guidelines for per-hop behavior
specifications. Sec. 4 discusses interoperability issues with nodes
and networks which do not implement differentiated services as
defined in this document and in [DSFIELD]. Sec. 5 discusses issues
with multicast service delivery. Sec. 6 addresses security and
tunnel considerations.

1.2 Terminology

This section gives a general conceptual overview of the terms used in
this document. Some of these terms are more precisely defined in
later sections of this document.

Behavior Aggregate (BA)   a DS behavior aggregate.

BA classifier   a classifier that selects packets based
                           only on the contents of the DS field.

Boundary link   a link connecting the edge nodes of two
                           domains.

Classifier   an entity which selects packets based on
                           the content of packet headers according to
                           defined rules.

DS behavior aggregate   a collection of packets with the same DS
                           codepoint crossing a link in a particular
                           direction.

DS boundary node   a DS node that connects one DS domain to a
                           node either in another DS domain or in a
                           domain that is not DS-capable.

DS-capable   capable of implementing differentiated
                           services as described in this architecture;
                           usually used in reference to a domain
                           consisting of DS-compliant nodes.

DS codepoint   a specific value of the DSCP portion of the
                           DS field, used to select a PHB.

DS-compliant   enabled to support differentiated services
                           functions and behaviors as defined in
                           [DSFIELD], this document, and other
                           differentiated services documents; usually
                           used in reference to a node or device.

DS domain   a DS-capable domain; a contiguous set of
                             nodes which operate with a common set of
                             service provisioning policies and PHB
                             definitions.

DS egress node   a DS boundary node in its role in handling
                             traffic as it leaves a DS domain.

DS ingress node   a DS boundary node in its role in handling
                             traffic as it enters a DS domain.

DS interior node   a DS node that is not a DS boundary node.

DS field   the IPv4 header TOS octet or the IPv6
                             Traffic Class octet when interpreted in
                             conformance with the definition given in
                             [DSFIELD]. The bits of the DSCP field
                             encode the DS codepoint, while the
                             remaining bits are currently unused.

DS node   a DS-compliant node.

DS region   a set of contiguous DS domains which can
                             offer differentiated services over paths
                             across those DS domains.

Downstream DS domain   the DS domain downstream of traffic flow on
                             a boundary link.

Dropper   a device that performs dropping.

Dropping   the process of discarding packets based on
                             specified rules; policing.

Legacy node   a node which implements IPv4 Precedence as
                             defined in [RFC791,RFC1812] but which is
                             otherwise not DS-compliant.

Marker   a device that performs marking.

Marking   the process of setting the DS codepoint in
                             a packet based on defined rules; pre-
                             marking, re-marking.

Mechanism   a specific algorithm or operation (e.g.,
                             queueing discipline) that is implemented in
                             a node to realize a set of one or more per-
                             hop behaviors.

Meter	a device that performs metering.
Metering	the process of measuring the temporal properties (e.g., rate) of a traffic stream selected by a classifier. The instantaneous state of this process may be used to affect the operation of a marker, shaper, or dropper, and/or may be used for accounting and measurement purposes.
Microflow	a single instance of an application-to-application flow of packets which is identified by source address, source port, destination address, destination port and protocol id.
MF Classifier	a multi-field (MF) classifier which selects packets based on the content of some arbitrary number of header fields; typically some combination of source address, destination address, DS field, protocol ID, source port and destination port.
Per-Hop-Behavior (PHB)	the externally observable forwarding behavior applied at a DS-compliant node to a DS behavior aggregate.
PHB group	a set of one or more PHBs that can only be meaningfully specified and implemented simultaneously, due to a common constraint applying to all PHBs in the set such as a queue servicing or queue management policy. A PHB group provides a service building block that allows a set of related forwarding behaviors to be specified together (e.g., four dropping priorities). A single PHB is a special case of a PHB group.
Policing	the process of discarding packets (by a dropper) within a traffic stream in accordance with the state of a corresponding meter enforcing a traffic profile.
Pre-mark	to set the DS codepoint of a packet prior to entry into a downstream DS domain.

Provider DS domain   the DS-capable provider of services to a
source domain.

Re-mark   to change the DS codepoint of a packet,
usually performed by a marker in accordance
with a TCA.

Service   the overall treatment of a defined subset
of a customer's traffic within a DS domain
or end-to-end.

Service Level Agreement   a service contract between a customer and a
(SLA)   service provider that specifies the
forwarding service a customer should
receive. A customer may be a user
organization (source domain) or another DS
domain (upstream domain). A SLA may
include traffic conditioning rules which
constitute a TCA in whole or in part.

Service Provisioning   a policy which defines how traffic
Policy   conditioners are configured on DS boundary
nodes and how traffic streams are mapped to
DS behavior aggregates to achieve a range
of services.

Shaper   a device that performs shaping.

Shaping   the process of delaying packets within a
traffic stream to cause it to conform to
some defined traffic profile.

Source domain   a domain which contains the node(s)
originating the traffic receiving a
particular service.

Traffic conditioner   an entity which performs traffic
conditioning functions and which may
contain meters, markers, droppers, and
shapers. Traffic conditioners are typically
deployed in DS boundary nodes only. A
traffic conditioner may re-mark a traffic
stream or may discard or shape packets to
alter the temporal characteristics of the
stream and bring it into compliance with a
traffic profile.

Traffic conditioning   control functions performed to enforce
                                rules specified in a TCA, including
                                metering, marking, shaping, and policing.

Traffic Conditioning   an agreement specifying classifier rules
Agreement (TCA)   and any corresponding traffic profiles and
                                metering, marking, discarding and/or
                                shaping rules which are to apply to the
                                traffic streams selected by the classifier.
                                A TCA encompasses all of the traffic
                                conditioning rules explicitly specified
                                within a SLA along with all of the rules
                                implicit from the relevant service
                                requirements and/or from a DS domain's
                                service provisioning policy.

Traffic profile   a description of the temporal properties
                                of a traffic stream such as rate and burst
                                size.

Traffic stream   an administratively significant set of one
                                or more microflows which traverse a path
                                segment. A traffic stream may consist of
                                the set of active microflows which are
                                selected by a particular classifier.

Upstream DS domain   the DS domain upstream of traffic flow on a
                                boundary link.

1.3 Requirements

The history of the Internet has been one of continuous growth in the
number of hosts, the number and variety of applications, and the
capacity of the network infrastructure, and this growth is expected
to continue for the foreseeable future. A scalable architecture for
service differentiation must be able to accommodate this continued
growth.

The following requirements were identified and are addressed in this
architecture:

o should accommodate a wide variety of services and provisioning
   policies, extending end-to-end or within a particular (set of)
   network(s),

o should allow decoupling of the service from the particular
   application in use,

o should work with existing applications without the need for
  application programming interface changes or host software
  modifications (assuming suitable deployment of classifiers,
  markers, and other traffic conditioning functions),

o should decouple traffic conditioning and service provisioning
  functions from forwarding behaviors implemented within the core
  network nodes,

o should not depend on hop-by-hop application signaling,

o should require only a small set of forwarding behaviors whose
  implementation complexity does not dominate the cost of a network
  device, and which will not introduce bottlenecks for future high-
  speed system implementations,

o should avoid per-microflow or per-customer state within core
  network nodes,

o should utilize only aggregated classification state within the
  network core,

o should permit simple packet classification implementations in core
  network nodes (BA classifier),

o should permit reasonable interoperability with non-DS-compliant
  network nodes,

o should accommodate incremental deployment.

1.4 Comparisons with Other Approaches

   The differentiated services architecture specified in this document
   can be contrasted with other existing models of service
   differentiation. We classify these alternative models into the
   following categories: relative priority marking, service marking,
   label switching, Integrated Services/RSVP, and static per-hop
   classification.

   Examples of the relative priority marking model include IPv4
   Precedence marking as defined in [RFC791], 802.5 Token Ring priority
   [TR], and the default interpretation of 802.1p traffic classes
   [802.1p]. In this model the application, host, or proxy node selects
   a relative priority or "precedence" for a packet (e.g., delay or
   discard priority), and the network nodes along the transit path apply
   the appropriate priority forwarding behavior corresponding to the
   priority value within the packet's header. Our architecture can be
   considered as a refinement to this model, since we more clearly

specify the role and importance of boundary nodes and traffic
conditioners, and since our per-hop behavior model permits more
general forwarding behaviors than relative delay or discard priority.

An example of a service marking model is IPv4 TOS as defined in
[RFC1349]. In this example each packet is marked with a request for
a "type of service", which may include "minimize delay", "maximize
throughput", "maximize reliability", or "minimize cost". Network
nodes may select routing paths or forwarding behaviors which are
suitably engineered to satisfy the service request. This model is
subtly different from our architecture. Note that we do not describe
the use of the DS field as an input to route selection. The TOS
markings defined in [RFC1349] are very generic and do not span the
range of possible service semantics. Furthermore, the service
request is associated with each individual packet, whereas some
service semantics may depend on the aggregate forwarding behavior of
a sequence of packets. The service marking model does not easily
accommodate growth in the number and range of future services (since
the codepoint space is small) and involves configuration of the
"TOS->forwarding behavior" association in each core network node.
Standardizing service markings implies standardizing service
offerings, which is outside the scope of the IETF. Note that
provisions are made in the allocation of the DS codepoint space to
allow for locally significant codepoints which may be used by a
provider to support service marking semantics [DSFIELD].

Examples of the label switching (or virtual circuit) model include
Frame Relay, ATM, and MPLS [FRELAY, ATM]. In this model path
forwarding state and traffic management or QoS state is established
for traffic streams on each hop along a network path. Traffic
aggregates of varying granularity are associated with a label
switched path at an ingress node, and packets/cells within each label
switched path are marked with a forwarding label that is used to
lookup the next-hop node, the per-hop forwarding behavior, and the
replacement label at each hop. This model permits finer granularity
resource allocation to traffic streams, since label values are not
globally significant but are only significant on a single link;
therefore resources can be reserved for the aggregate of packets/
cells received on a link with a particular label, and the label
switching semantics govern the next-hop selection, allowing a traffic
stream to follow a specially engineered path through the network.
This improved granularity comes at the cost of additional management
and configuration requirements to establish and maintain the label
switched paths. In addition, the amount of forwarding state
maintained at each node scales in proportion to the number of edge
nodes of the network in the best case (assuming multipoint-to-point

label switched paths), and it scales in proportion with the square of
the number of edge nodes in the worst case, when edge-edge label
switched paths with provisioned resources are employed.

The Integrated Services/RSVP model relies upon traditional datagram
forwarding in the default case, but allows sources and receivers to
exchange signaling messages which establish additional packet
classification and forwarding state on each node along the path
between them [RFC1633, RSVP]. In the absence of state aggregation,
the amount of state on each node scales in proportion to the number
of concurrent reservations, which can be potentially large on high-
speed links. This model also requires application support for the
RSVP signaling protocol. Differentiated services mechanisms can be
utilized to aggregate Integrated Services/RSVP state in the core of
the network [Bernet].

A variant of the Integrated Services/RSVP model eliminates the
requirement for hop-by-hop signaling by utilizing only "static"
classification and forwarding policies which are implemented in each
node along a network path. These policies are updated on
administrative timescales and not in response to the instantaneous
mix of microflows active in the network. The state requirements for
this variant are potentially worse than those encountered when RSVP
is used, especially in backbone nodes, since the number of static
policies that might be applicable at a node over time may be larger
than the number of active sender-receiver sessions that might have
installed reservation state on a node. Although the support of large
numbers of classifier rules and forwarding policies may be
computationally feasible, the management burden associated with
installing and maintaining these rules on each node within a backbone
network which might be traversed by a traffic stream is substantial.

Although we contrast our architecture with these alternative models
of service differentiation, it should be noted that links and nodes
employing these techniques may be utilized to extend differentiated
services behaviors and semantics across a layer-2 switched
infrastructure (e.g., 802.1p LANs, Frame Relay/ATM backbones)
interconnecting DS nodes, and in the case of MPLS may be used as an
alternative intra-domain implementation technology. The constraints
imposed by the use of a specific link-layer technology in particular
regions of a DS domain (or in a network providing access to DS
domains) may imply the differentiation of traffic on a coarser grain
basis. Depending on the mapping of PHBs to different link-layer
services and the way in which packets are scheduled over a restricted
set of priority classes (or virtual circuits of different category
and capacity), all or a subset of the PHBs in use may be supportable
(or may be indistinguishable).

2. Differentiated Services Architectural Model

The differentiated services architecture is based on a simple model
where traffic entering a network is classified and possibly
conditioned at the boundaries of the network, and assigned to
different behavior aggregates. Each behavior aggregate is identified
by a single DS codepoint. Within the core of the network, packets
are forwarded according to the per-hop behavior associated with the
DS codepoint. In this section, we discuss the key components within
a differentiated services region, traffic classification and
conditioning functions, and how differentiated services are achieved
through the combination of traffic conditioning and PHB-based
forwarding.

2.1 Differentiated Services Domain

A DS domain is a contiguous set of DS nodes which operate with a
common service provisioning policy and set of PHB groups implemented
on each node. A DS domain has a well-defined boundary consisting of
DS boundary nodes which classify and possibly condition ingress
traffic to ensure that packets which transit the domain are
appropriately marked to select a PHB from one of the PHB groups
supported within the domain. Nodes within the DS domain select the
forwarding behavior for packets based on their DS codepoint, mapping
that value to one of the supported PHBs using either the recommended
codepoint->PHB mapping or a locally customized mapping [DSFIELD].
Inclusion of non-DS-compliant nodes within a DS domain may result in
unpredictable performance and may impede the ability to satisfy
service level agreements (SLAs).

A DS domain normally consists of one or more networks under the same
administration; for example, an organization's intranet or an ISP.
The administration of the domain is responsible for ensuring that
adequate resources are provisioned and/or reserved to support the
SLAs offered by the domain.

2.1.1 DS Boundary Nodes and Interior Nodes

A DS domain consists of DS boundary nodes and DS interior nodes. DS
boundary nodes interconnect the DS domain to other DS or non-DS-
capable domains, whilst DS interior nodes only connect to other DS
interior or boundary nodes within the same DS domain.

Both DS boundary nodes and interior nodes must be able to apply the
appropriate PHB to packets based on the DS codepoint; otherwise
unpredictable behavior may result. In addition, DS boundary nodes
may be required to perform traffic conditioning functions as defined
by a traffic conditioning agreement (TCA) between their DS domain and

the peering domain which they connect to (see Sec. 2.3.3).

Interior nodes may be able to perform limited traffic conditioning
functions such as DS codepoint re-marking. Interior nodes which
implement more complex classification and traffic conditioning
functions are analogous to DS boundary nodes (see Sec. 2.3.4.4).

A host in a network containing a DS domain may act as a DS boundary
node for traffic from applications running on that host; we therefore
say that the host is within the DS domain. If a host does not act as
a boundary node, then the DS node topologically closest to that host
acts as the DS boundary node for that host's traffic.

2.1.2 DS Ingress Node and Egress Node

DS boundary nodes act both as a DS ingress node and as a DS egress
node for different directions of traffic. Traffic enters a DS domain
at a DS ingress node and leaves a DS domain at a DS egress node. A
DS ingress node is responsible for ensuring that the traffic entering
the DS domain conforms to any TCA between it and the other domain to
which the ingress node is connected. A DS egress node may perform
traffic conditioning functions on traffic forwarded to a directly
connected peering domain, depending on the details of the TCA between
the two domains. Note that a DS boundary node may act as a DS
interior node for some set of interfaces.

2.2 Differentiated Services Region

A differentiated services region (DS Region) is a set of one or more
contiguous DS domains. DS regions are capable of supporting
differentiated services along paths which span the domains within the
region.

The DS domains in a DS region may support different PHB groups
internally and different codepoint->PHB mappings. However, to permit
services which span across the domains, the peering DS domains must
each establish a peering SLA which defines (either explicitly or
implicitly) a TCA which specifies how transit traffic from one DS
domain to another is conditioned at the boundary between the two DS
domains.

It is possible that several DS domains within a DS region may adopt a
common service provisioning policy and may support a common set of
PHB groups and codepoint mappings, thus eliminating the need for
traffic conditioning between those DS domains.

2.3 Traffic Classification and Conditioning

Differentiated services are extended across a DS domain boundary by
establishing a SLA between an upstream network and a downstream DS
domain. The SLA may specify packet classification and re-marking
rules and may also specify traffic profiles and actions to traffic
streams which are in- or out-of-profile (see Sec. 2.3.2). The TCA
between the domains is derived (explicitly or implicitly) from this
SLA.

The packet classification policy identifies the subset of traffic
which may receive a differentiated service by being conditioned and/
or mapped to one or more behavior aggregates (by DS codepoint re-
marking) within the DS domain.

Traffic conditioning performs metering, shaping, policing and/or re-
marking to ensure that the traffic entering the DS domain conforms to
the rules specified in the TCA, in accordance with the domain's
service provisioning policy. The extent of traffic conditioning
required is dependent on the specifics of the service offering, and
may range from simple codepoint re-marking to complex policing and
shaping operations. The details of traffic conditioning policies
which are negotiated between networks is outside the scope of this
document.

2.3.1 Classifiers

Packet classifiers select packets in a traffic stream based on the
content of some portion of the packet header. We define two types of
classifiers. The BA (Behavior Aggregate) Classifier classifies
packets based on the DS codepoint only. The MF (Multi-Field)
classifier selects packets based on the value of a combination of one
or more header fields, such as source address, destination address,
DS field, protocol ID, source port and destination port numbers, and
other information such as incoming interface.

Classifiers are used to "steer" packets matching some specified rule
to an element of a traffic conditioner for further processing.
Classifiers must be configured by some management procedure in
accordance with the appropriate TCA.

The classifier should authenticate the information which it uses to
classify the packet (see Sec. 6).

Note that in the event of upstream packet fragmentation, MF
classifiers which examine the contents of transport-layer header
fields may incorrectly classify packet fragments subsequent to the
first. A possible solution to this problem is to maintain

fragmentation state; however, this is not a general solution due to
the possibility of upstream fragment re-ordering or divergent routing
paths. The policy to apply to packet fragments is outside the scope
of this document.

2.3.2 Traffic Profiles

A traffic profile specifies the temporal properties of a traffic
stream selected by a classifier. It provides rules for determining
whether a particular packet is in-profile or out-of-profile. For
example, a profile based on a token bucket may look like:

   codepoint=X, use token-bucket r, b

The above profile indicates that all packets marked with DS codepoint
X should be measured against a token bucket meter with rate r and
burst size b. In this example out-of-profile packets are those
packets in the traffic stream which arrive when insufficient tokens
are available in the bucket. The concept of in- and out-of-profile
can be extended to more than two levels, e.g., multiple levels of
conformance with a profile may be defined and enforced.

Different conditioning actions may be applied to the in-profile
packets and out-of-profile packets, or different accounting actions
may be triggered. In-profile packets may be allowed to enter the DS
domain without further conditioning; or, alternatively, their DS
codepoint may be changed. The latter happens when the DS codepoint
is set to a non-Default value for the first time [DSFIELD], or when
the packets enter a DS domain that uses a different PHB group or
codepoint->PHB mapping policy for this traffic stream. Out-of-
profile packets may be queued until they are in-profile (shaped),
discarded (policed), marked with a new codepoint (re-marked), or
forwarded unchanged while triggering some accounting procedure.
Out-of-profile packets may be mapped to one or more behavior
aggregates that are "inferior" in some dimension of forwarding
performance to the BA into which in-profile packets are mapped.

Note that a traffic profile is an optional component of a TCA and its
use is dependent on the specifics of the service offering and the
domain's service provisioning policy.

2.3.3 Traffic Conditioners

A traffic conditioner may contain the following elements: meter,
marker, shaper, and dropper. A traffic stream is selected by a
classifier, which steers the packets to a logical instance of a
traffic conditioner. A meter is used (where appropriate) to measure
the traffic stream against a traffic profile. The state of the meter

with respect to a particular packet (e.g., whether it is in- or out-of-profile) may be used to affect a marking, dropping, or shaping action.

When packets exit the traffic conditioner of a DS boundary node the DS codepoint of each packet must be set to an appropriate value.

Fig. 1 shows the block diagram of a classifier and traffic conditioner. Note that a traffic conditioner may not necessarily contain all four elements. For example, in the case where no traffic profile is in effect, packets may only pass through a classifier and a marker.

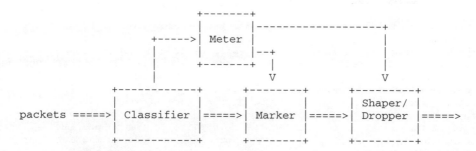

Fig. 1: Logical View of a Packet Classifier and Traffic Conditioner

2.3.3.1 Meters

Traffic meters measure the temporal properties of the stream of packets selected by a classifier against a traffic profile specified in a TCA. A meter passes state information to other conditioning functions to trigger a particular action for each packet which is either in- or out-of-profile (to some extent).

2.3.3.2 Markers

Packet markers set the DS field of a packet to a particular codepoint, adding the marked packet to a particular DS behavior aggregate. The marker may be configured to mark all packets which are steered to it to a single codepoint, or may be configured to mark a packet to one of a set of codepoints used to select a PHB in a PHB group, according to the state of a meter. When the marker changes the codepoint in a packet it is said to have "re-marked" the packet.

2.3.3.3 Shapers

   Shapers delay some or all of the packets in a traffic stream in order
   to bring the stream into compliance with a traffic profile. A shaper
   usually has a finite-size buffer, and packets may be discarded if
   there is not sufficient buffer space to hold the delayed packets.

2.3.3.4 Droppers

   Droppers discard some or all of the packets in a traffic stream in
   order to bring the stream into compliance with a traffic profile.
   This process is know as "policing" the stream. Note that a dropper
   can be implemented as a special case of a shaper by setting the
   shaper buffer size to zero (or a few) packets.

2.3.4 Location of Traffic Conditioners and MF Classifiers

   Traffic conditioners are usually located within DS ingress and egress
   boundary nodes, but may also be located in nodes within the interior
   of a DS domain, or within a non-DS-capable domain.

2.3.4.1 Within the Source Domain

   We define the source domain as the domain containing the node(s)
   which originate the traffic receiving a particular service. Traffic
   sources and intermediate nodes within a source domain may perform
   traffic classification and conditioning functions. The traffic
   originating from the source domain across a boundary may be marked by
   the traffic sources directly or by intermediate nodes before leaving
   the source domain. This is referred to as initial marking or "pre-
   marking".

   Consider the example of a company that has the policy that its CEO's
   packets should have higher priority. The CEO's host may mark the DS
   field of all outgoing packets with a DS codepoint that indicates
   "higher priority". Alternatively, the first-hop router directly
   connected to the CEO's host may classify the traffic and mark the
   CEO's packets with the correct DS codepoint. Such high priority
   traffic may also be conditioned near the source so that there is a
   limit on the amount of high priority traffic forwarded from a
   particular source.

   There are some advantages to marking packets close to the traffic
   source. First, a traffic source can more easily take an
   application's preferences into account when deciding which packets
   should receive better forwarding treatment. Also, classification of

packets is much simpler before the traffic has been aggregated with
packets from other sources, since the number of classification rules
which need to be applied within a single node is reduced.

Since packet marking may be distributed across multiple nodes, the
source DS domain is responsible for ensuring that the aggregated
traffic towards its provider DS domain conforms to the appropriate
TCA. Additional allocation mechanisms such as bandwidth brokers or
RSVP may be used to dynamically allocate resources for a particular
DS behavior aggregate within the provider's network [2BIT, Bernet].
The boundary node of the source domain should also monitor
conformance to the TCA, and may police, shape, or re-mark packets as
necessary.

2.3.4.2 At the Boundary of a DS Domain

Traffic streams may be classified, marked, and otherwise conditioned
on either end of a boundary link (the DS egress node of the upstream
domain or the DS ingress node of the downstream domain). The SLA
between the domains should specify which domain has responsibility
for mapping traffic streams to DS behavior aggregates and
conditioning those aggregates in conformance with the appropriate
TCA. However, a DS ingress node must assume that the incoming
traffic may not conform to the TCA and must be prepared to enforce
the TCA in accordance with local policy.

When packets are pre-marked and conditioned in the upstream domain,
potentially fewer classification and traffic conditioning rules need
to be supported in the downstream DS domain. In this circumstance
the downstream DS domain may only need to re-mark or police the
incoming behavior aggregates to enforce the TCA. However, more
sophisticated services which are path- or source-dependent may
require MF classification in the downstream DS domain's ingress
nodes.

If a DS ingress node is connected to an upstream non-DS-capable
domain, the DS ingress node must be able to perform all necessary
traffic conditioning functions on the incoming traffic.

2.3.4.3 In non-DS-Capable Domains

Traffic sources or intermediate nodes in a non-DS-capable domain may
employ traffic conditioners to pre-mark traffic before it reaches the
ingress of a downstream DS domain. In this way the local policies
for classification and marking may be concealed.

2.3.4.4 In Interior DS Nodes

   Although the basic architecture assumes that complex classification
   and traffic conditioning functions are located only in a network's
   ingress and egress boundary nodes, deployment of these functions in
   the interior of the network is not precluded. For example, more
   restrictive access policies may be enforced on a transoceanic link,
   requiring MF classification and traffic conditioning functionality in
   the upstream node on the link. This approach may have scaling
   limits, due to the potentially large number of classification and
   conditioning rules that might need to be maintained.

2.4 Per-Hop Behaviors

   A per-hop behavior (PHB) is a description of the externally
   observable forwarding behavior of a DS node applied to a particular
   DS behavior aggregate. "Forwarding behavior" is a general concept in
   this context. For example, in the event that only one behavior
   aggregate occupies a link, the observable forwarding behavior (i.e.,
   loss, delay, jitter) will often depend only on the relative loading
   of the link (i.e., in the event that the behavior assumes a work-
   conserving scheduling discipline). Useful behavioral distinctions
   are mainly observed when multiple behavior aggregates compete for
   buffer and bandwidth resources on a node. The PHB is the means by
   which a node allocates resources to behavior aggregates, and it is on
   top of this basic hop-by-hop resource allocation mechanism that
   useful differentiated services may be constructed.

   The most simple example of a PHB is one which guarantees a minimal
   bandwidth allocation of X% of a link (over some reasonable time
   interval) to a behavior aggregate. This PHB can be fairly easily
   measured under a variety of competing traffic conditions. A slightly
   more complex PHB would guarantee a minimal bandwidth allocation of X%
   of a link, with proportional fair sharing of any excess link
   capacity. In general, the observable behavior of a PHB may depend on
   certain constraints on the traffic characteristics of the associated
   behavior aggregate, or the characteristics of other behavior
   aggregates.

   PHBs may be specified in terms of their resource (e.g., buffer,
   bandwidth) priority relative to other PHBs, or in terms of their
   relative observable traffic characteristics (e.g., delay, loss).
   These PHBs may be used as building blocks to allocate resources and
   should be specified as a group (PHB group) for consistency. PHB
   groups will usually share a common constraint applying to each PHB
   within the group, such as a packet scheduling or buffer management
   policy. The relationship between PHBs in a group may be in terms of
   absolute or relative priority (e.g., discard priority by means of

deterministic or stochastic thresholds), but this is not required
(e.g., N equal link shares). A single PHB defined in isolation is a
special case of a PHB group.

PHBs are implemented in nodes by means of some buffer management and
packet scheduling mechanisms. PHBs are defined in terms of behavior
characteristics relevant to service provisioning policies, and not in
terms of particular implementation mechanisms. In general, a variety
of implementation mechanisms may be suitable for implementing a
particular PHB group. Furthermore, it is likely that more than one
PHB group may be implemented on a node and utilized within a domain.
PHB groups should be defined such that the proper resource allocation
between groups can be inferred, and integrated mechanisms can be
implemented which can simultaneously support two or more groups. A
PHB group definition should indicate possible conflicts with
previously documented PHB groups which might prevent simultaneous
operation.

As described in [DSFIELD], a PHB is selected at a node by a mapping
of the DS codepoint in a received packet. Standardized PHBs have a
recommended codepoint. However, the total space of codepoints is
larger than the space available for recommended codepoints for
standardized PHBs, and [DSFIELD] leaves provisions for locally
configurable mappings. A codepoint->PHB mapping table may contain
both 1->1 and N->1 mappings. All codepoints must be mapped to some
PHB; in the absence of some local policy, codepoints which are not
mapped to a standardized PHB in accordance with that PHB's
specification should be mapped to the Default PHB.

2.5 Network Resource Allocation

The implementation, configuration, operation and administration of
the supported PHB groups in the nodes of a DS Domain should
effectively partition the resources of those nodes and the inter-node
links between behavior aggregates, in accordance with the domain's
service provisioning policy. Traffic conditioners can further
control the usage of these resources through enforcement of TCAs and
possibly through operational feedback from the nodes and traffic
conditioners in the domain. Although a range of services can be
deployed in the absence of complex traffic conditioning functions
(e.g., using only static marking policies), functions such as
policing, shaping, and dynamic re-marking enable the deployment of
services providing quantitative performance metrics.

The configuration of and interaction between traffic conditioners and
interior nodes should be managed by the administrative control of the
domain and may require operational control through protocols and a
control entity. There is a wide range of possible control models.

The precise nature and implementation of the interaction between
these components is outside the scope of this architecture. However,
scalability requires that the control of the domain does not require
micro-management of the network resources. The most scalable control
model would operate nodes in open-loop in the operational timeframe,
and would only require administrative-timescale management as SLAs
are varied. This simple model may be unsuitable in some
circumstances, and some automated but slowly varying operational
control (minutes rather than seconds) may be desirable to balance the
utilization of the network against the recent load profile.

3. Per-Hop Behavior Specification Guidelines

   Basic requirements for per-hop behavior standardization are given in
   [DSFIELD]. This section elaborates on that text by describing
   additional guidelines for PHB (group) specifications. This is
   intended to help foster implementation consistency. Before a PHB
   group is proposed for standardization it should satisfy these
   guidelines, as appropriate, to preserve the integrity of this
   architecture.

   G.1: A PHB standard must specify a recommended DS codepoint selected
   from the codepoint space reserved for standard mappings [DSFIELD].
   Recommended codepoints will be assigned by the IANA. A PHB proposal
   may recommend a temporary codepoint from the EXP/LU space to
   facilitate inter-domain experimentation. Determination of a packet's
   PHB must not require inspection of additional packet header fields
   beyond the DS field.

   G.2: The specification of each newly proposed PHB group should
   include an overview of the behavior and the purpose of the behavior
   being proposed. The overview should include a problem or problems
   statement for which the PHB group is targeted. The overview should
   include the basic concepts behind the PHB group. These concepts
   should include, but are not restricted to, queueing behavior, discard
   behavior, and output link selection behavior. Lastly, the overview
   should specify the method by which the PHB group solves the problem
   or problems specified in the problem statement.

   G.3: A PHB group specification should indicate the number of
   individual PHBs specified. In the event that multiple PHBs are
   specified, the interactions between these PHBs and constraints that
   must be respected globally by all the PHBs within the group should be
   clearly specified. As an example, the specification must indicate
   whether the probability of packet reordering within a microflow is
   increased if different packets in that microflow are marked for
   different PHBs within the group.

G.4: When proper functioning of a PHB group is dependent on
constraints such as a provisioning restriction, then the PHB
definition should describe the behavior when these constraints are
violated. Further, if actions such as packet discard or re-marking
are required when these constraints are violated, then these actions
should be specifically stipulated.

G.5: A PHB group may be specified for local use within a domain in
order to provide some domain-specific functionality or domain-
specific services. In this event, the PHB specification is useful
for providing vendors with a consistent definition of the PHB group.
However, any PHB group which is defined for local use should not be
considered for standardization, but may be published as an
Informational RFC. In contrast, a PHB group which is intended for
general use will follow a stricter standardization process.
Therefore all PHB proposals should specifically state whether they
are to be considered for general or local use.

It is recognized that PHB groups can be designed with the intent of
providing host-to-host, WAN edge-to-WAN edge, and/or domain edge-to-
domain edge services. Use of the term "end-to-end" in a PHB
definition should be interpreted to mean "host-to-host" for
consistency.

Other PHB groups may be defined and deployed locally within domains,
for experimental or operational purposes. There is no requirement
that these PHB groups must be publicly documented, but they should
utilize DS codepoints from one of the EXP/LU pools as defined in
[DSFIELD].

G.6: It may be possible or appropriate for a packet marked for a PHB
within a PHB group to be re-marked to select another PHB within the
group; either within a domain or across a domain boundary. Typically
there are three reasons for such PHB modification:

a. The codepoints associated with the PHB group are collectively
   intended to carry state about the network,
b. Conditions exist which require PHB promotion or demotion of a
   packet (this assumes that PHBs within the group can be ranked in
   some order),
c. The boundary between two domains is not covered by a SLA. In this
   case the codepoint/PHB to select when crossing the boundary link
   will be determined by the local policy of the upstream domain.

A PHB specification should clearly state the circumstances under
which packets marked for a PHB within a PHB group may, or should be
modified (e.g., promoted or demoted) to another PHB within the group.
If it is undesirable for a packet's PHB to be modified, the

specification should clearly state the consequent risks when the PHB
is modified.   A possible risk to changing a packet's PHB, either
within or outside a PHB group, is a higher probability of packet re-
ordering within a microflow. PHBs within a group may carry some
host-to-host, WAN edge-to-WAN edge, and/or domain edge-to-domain edge
semantics which may be difficult to duplicate if packets are re-
marked to select another PHB from the group (or otherwise).

For certain PHB groups, it may be appropriate to reflect a state
change in the node by re-marking packets to specify another PHB from
within the group. If a PHB group is designed to reflect the state of
a network, the PHB definition must adequately describe the
relationship between the PHBs and the states they reflect. Further,
if these PHBs limit the forwarding actions a node can perform in some
way, these constraints may be specified as actions the node should,
or must perform.

G.7: A PHB group specification should include a section defining the
implications of tunneling on the utility of the PHB group. This
section should specify the implications for the utility of the PHB
group of a newly created outer header when the original DS field of
the inner header is encapsulated in a tunnel. This section should
also discuss what possible changes should be applied to the inner
header at the egress of the tunnel, when both the codepoints from the
inner header and the outer header are accessible (see Sec. 6.2).

G.8: The process of specifying PHB groups is likely to be
incremental in nature. When new PHB groups are proposed, their known
interactions with previously specified PHB groups should be
documented. When a new PHB group is created, it can be entirely new
in scope or it can be an extension to an existing PHB group. If the
PHB group is entirely independent of some or all of the existing PHB
specifications, a section should be included in the PHB specification
which details how the new PHB group can co-exist with those PHB
groups already standardized. For example, this section might
indicate the possibility of packet re-ordering within a microflow for
packets marked by codepoints associated with two separate PHB groups.
If concurrent operation of two (or more) different PHB groups in the
same node is impossible or detrimental this should be stated. If the
concurrent operation of two (or more) different PHB groups requires
some specific behaviors by the node when packets marked for PHBs from
these different PHB groups are being processed by the node at the
same time, these behaviors should be stated.

Care should be taken to avoid circularity in the definitions of PHB
groups.

If the proposed PHB group is an extension to an existing PHB group, a section should be included in the PHB group specification which details how this extension interoperates with the behavior being extended. Further, if the extension alters or more narrowly defines the existing behavior in some way, this should also be clearly indicated.

G.9: Each PHB specification should include a section specifying minimal conformance requirements for implementations of the PHB group. This conformance section is intended to provide a means for specifying the details of a behavior while allowing for implementation variation to the extent permitted by the PHB specification. This conformance section can take the form of rules, tables, pseudo-code, or tests.

G.10: A PHB specification should include a section detailing the security implications of the behavior. This section should include a discussion of the re-marking of the inner header's codepoint at the egress of a tunnel and its effect on the desired forwarding behavior.

Further, this section should also discuss how the proposed PHB group could be used in denial-of-service attacks, reduction of service contract attacks, and service contract violation attacks. Lastly, this section should discuss possible means for detecting such attacks as they are relevant to the proposed behavior.

G.11: A PHB specification should include a section detailing configuration and management issues which may affect the operation of the PHB and which may impact candidate services that might utilize the PHB.

G.12: It is strongly recommended that an appendix be provided with each PHB specification that considers the implications of the proposed behavior on current and potential services. These services could include but are not restricted to be user-specific, device-specific, domain-specific or end-to-end services. It is also strongly recommended that the appendix include a section describing how the services are verified by users, devices, and/or domains.

G.13: It is recommended that an appendix be provided with each PHB specification that is targeted for local use within a domain, providing guidance for PHB selection for packets which are forwarded into a peer domain which does not support the PHB group.

G.14: It is recommended that an appendix be provided with each PHB
specification which considers the impact of the proposed PHB group on
existing higher-layer protocols. Under some circumstances PHBs may
allow for possible changes to higher-layer protocols which may
increase or decrease the utility of the proposed PHB group.

G.15: It is recommended that an appendix be provided with each PHB
specification which recommends mappings to link-layer QoS mechanisms
to support the intended behavior of the PHB across a shared-medium or
switched link-layer. The determination of the most appropriate
mapping between a PHB and a link-layer QoS mechanism is dependent on
many factors and is outside the scope of this document; however, the
specification should attempt to offer some guidance.

4.   Interoperability with Non-Differentiated Services-Compliant Nodes

We define a non-differentiated services-compliant node (non-DS-
compliant node) as any node which does not interpret the DS field as
specified in [DSFIELD] and/or does not implement some or all of the
standardized PHBs (or those in use within a particular DS domain).
This may be due to the capabilities or configuration of the node. We
define a legacy node as a special case of a non-DS-compliant node
which implements IPv4 Precedence classification and forwarding as
defined in [RFC791, RFC1812], but which is otherwise not DS-
compliant. The precedence values in the IPv4 TOS octet are
compatible by intention with the Class Selector Codepoints defined in
[DSFIELD], and the precedence forwarding behaviors defined in
[RFC791, RFC1812] comply with the Class Selector PHB Requirements
also defined in [DSFIELD]. A key distinction between a legacy node
and a DS-compliant node is that the legacy node may or may not
interpret bits 3-6 of the TOS octet as defined in [RFC1349] (the
"DTRC" bits); in practice it will not interpret these bit as
specified in [DSFIELD]. We assume that the use of the TOS markings
defined in [RFC1349] is deprecated. Nodes which are non-DS-compliant
and which are not legacy nodes may exhibit unpredictable forwarding
behaviors for packets with non-zero DS codepoints.

Differentiated services depend on the resource allocation mechanisms
provided by per-hop behavior implementations in nodes. The quality
or statistical assurance level of a service may break down in the
event that traffic transits a non-DS-compliant node, or a non-DS-
capable domain.

We will examine two separate cases. The first case concerns the use
of non-DS-compliant nodes within a DS domain. Note that PHB
forwarding is primarily useful for allocating scarce node and link
resources in a controlled manner. On high-speed, lightly loaded
links, the worst-case packet delay, jitter, and loss may be

negligible, and the use of a non-DS-compliant node on the upstream
end of such a link may not result in service degradation. In more
realistic circumstances, the lack of PHB forwarding in a node may
make it impossible to offer low-delay, low-loss, or provisioned
bandwidth services across paths which traverse the node. However,
use of a legacy node may be an acceptable alternative, assuming that
the DS domain restricts itself to using only the Class Selector
Codepoints defined in [DSFIELD], and assuming that the particular
precedence implementation in the legacy node provides forwarding
behaviors which are compatible with the services offered along paths
which traverse that node. Note that it is important to restrict the
codepoints in use to the Class Selector Codepoints, since the legacy
node may or may not interpret bits 3-5 in accordance with [RFC1349],
thereby resulting in unpredictable forwarding results.

The second case concerns the behavior of services which traverse
non-DS-capable domains. We assume for the sake of argument that a
non-DS-capable domain does not deploy traffic conditioning functions
on domain boundary nodes; therefore, even in the event that the
domain consists of legacy or DS-compliant interior nodes, the lack of
traffic enforcement at the boundaries will limit the ability to
consistently deliver some types of services across the domain. A DS
domain and a non-DS-capable domain may negotiate an agreement which
governs how egress traffic from the DS-domain should be marked before
entry into the non-DS-capable domain. This agreement might be
monitored for compliance by traffic sampling instead of by rigorous
traffic conditioning. Alternatively, where there is knowledge that
the non-DS-capable domain consists of legacy nodes, the upstream DS
domain may opportunistically re-mark differentiated services traffic
to one or more of the Class Selector Codepoints. Where there is no
knowledge of the traffic management capabilities of the downstream
domain, and no agreement in place, a DS domain egress node may choose
to re-mark DS codepoints to zero, under the assumption that the non-
DS-capable domain will treat the traffic uniformly with best-effort
service.

In the event that a non-DS-capable domain peers with a DS domain,
traffic flowing from the non-DS-capable domain should be conditioned
at the DS ingress node of the DS domain according to the appropriate
SLA or policy.

5. Multicast Considerations

Use of differentiated services by multicast traffic introduces a
number of issues for service provisioning. First, multicast packets
which enter a DS domain at an ingress node may simultaneously take
multiple paths through some segments of the domain due to multicast
packet replication. In this way they consume more network resources

than unicast packets. Where multicast group membership is dynamic,
it is difficult to predict in advance the amount of network resources
that may be consumed by multicast traffic originating from an
upstream network for a particular group. A consequence of this
uncertainty is that it may be difficult to provide quantitative
service guarantees to multicast senders. Further, it may be
necessary to reserve codepoints and PHBs for exclusive use by unicast
traffic, to provide resource isolation from multicast traffic.

The second issue is the selection of the DS codepoint for a multicast
packet arriving at a DS ingress node. Because that packet may exit
the DS domain at multiple DS egress nodes which peer with multiple
downstream domains, the DS codepoint used should not result in the
request for a service from a downstream DS domain which is in
violation of a peering SLA. When establishing classifier and traffic
conditioner state at an DS ingress node for an aggregate of traffic
receiving a differentiated service which spans across the egress
boundary of the domain, the identity of the adjacent downstream
transit domain and the specifics of the corresponding peering SLA can
be factored into the configuration decision (subject to routing
policy and the stability of the routing infrastructure). In this way
peering SLAs with downstream DS domains can be partially enforced at
the ingress of the upstream domain, reducing the classification and
traffic conditioning burden at the egress node of the upstream
domain. This is not so easily performed in the case of multicast
traffic, due to the possibility of dynamic group membership. The
result is that the service guarantees for unicast traffic may be
impacted. One means of addressing this problem is to establish a
separate peering SLA for multicast traffic, and to either utilize a
particular set of codepoints for multicast packets, or to implement
the necessary classification and traffic conditioning mechanisms in
the DS egress nodes to provide preferential isolation for unicast
traffic in conformance with the peering SLA with the downstream
domain.

6. Security and Tunneling Considerations

This section addresses security issues raised by the introduction of
differentiated services, primarily the potential for denial-of-
service attacks, and the related potential for theft of service by
unauthorized traffic (Sec. 6.1). In addition, the operation of
differentiated services in the presence of IPsec and its interaction
with IPsec are also discussed (Sec. 6.2), as well as auditing
requirements (Sec. 6.3). This section considers issues introduced by
the use of both IPsec and non-IPsec tunnels.

6.1 Theft and Denial of Service

The primary goal of differentiated services is to allow different
levels of service to be provided for traffic streams on a common
network infrastructure. A variety of resource management techniques
may be used to achieve this, but the end result will be that some
packets receive different (e.g., better) service than others. The
mapping of network traffic to the specific behaviors that result in
different (e.g., better or worse) service is indicated primarily by
the DS field, and hence an adversary may be able to obtain better
service by modifying the DS field to codepoints indicating behaviors
used for enhanced services or by injecting packets with the DS field
set to such codepoints. Taken to its limits, this theft of service
becomes a denial-of-service attack when the modified or injected
traffic depletes the resources available to forward it and other
traffic streams. The defense against such theft- and denial-of-
service attacks consists of the combination of traffic conditioning
at DS boundary nodes along with security and integrity of the network
infrastructure within a DS domain.

As described in Sec. 2, DS ingress nodes must condition all traffic
entering a DS domain to ensure that it has acceptable DS codepoints.
This means that the codepoints must conform to the applicable TCA(s)
and the domain's service provisioning policy. Hence, the ingress
nodes are the primary line of defense against theft- and denial-of-
service attacks based on modified DS codepoints (e.g., codepoints to
which the traffic is not entitled), as success of any such attack
constitutes a violation of the applicable TCA(s) and/or service
provisioning policy. An important instance of an ingress node is
that any traffic-originating node in a DS domain is the ingress node
for that traffic, and must ensure that all originated traffic carries
acceptable DS codepoints.

Both a domain's service provisioning policy and TCAs may require the
ingress nodes to change the DS codepoint on some entering packets
(e.g., an ingress router may set the DS codepoint of a customer's
traffic in accordance with the appropriate SLA). Ingress nodes must
condition all other inbound traffic to ensure that the DS codepoints
are acceptable; packets found to have unacceptable codepoints must
either be discarded or must have their DS codepoints modified to
acceptable values before being forwarded. For example, an ingress
node receiving traffic from a domain with which no enhanced service
agreement exists may reset the DS codepoint to the Default PHB
codepoint [DSFIELD]. Traffic authentication may be required to
validate the use of some DS codepoints (e.g., those corresponding to
enhanced services), and such authentication may be performed by
technical means (e.g., IPsec) and/or non-technical means (e.g., the
inbound link is known to be connected to exactly one customer site).

An inter-domain agreement may reduce or eliminate the need for
ingress node traffic conditioning by making the upstream domain
partly or completely responsible for ensuring that traffic has DS
codepoints acceptable to the downstream domain. In this case, the
ingress node may still perform redundant traffic conditioning checks
to reduce the dependence on the upstream domain (e.g., such checks
can prevent theft-of-service attacks from propagating across the
domain boundary). If such a check fails because the upstream domain
is not fulfilling its responsibilities, that failure is an auditable
event; the generated audit log entry should include the date/time the
packet was received, the source and destination IP addresses, and the
DS codepoint that caused the failure. In practice, the limited gains
from such checks need to be weighed against their potential
performance impact in determining what, if any, checks to perform
under these circumstances.

Interior nodes in a DS domain may rely on the DS field to associate
differentiated services traffic with the behaviors used to implement
enhanced services. Any node doing so depends on the correct
operation of the DS domain to prevent the arrival of traffic with
unacceptable DS codepoints. Robustness concerns dictate that the
arrival of packets with unacceptable DS codepoints must not cause the
failure (e.g., crash) of network nodes. Interior nodes are not
responsible for enforcing the service provisioning policy (or
individual SLAs) and hence are not required to check DS codepoints
before using them. Interior nodes may perform some traffic
conditioning checks on DS codepoints (e.g., check for DS codepoints
that are never used for traffic on a specific link) to improve
security and robustness (e.g., resistance to theft-of-service attacks
based on DS codepoint modifications). Any detected failure of such a
check is an auditable event and the generated audit log entry should
include the date/time the packet was received, the source and
destination IP addresses, and the DS codepoint that caused the
failure. In practice, the limited gains from such checks need to be
weighed against their potential performance impact in determining
what, if any, checks to perform at interior nodes.

Any link that cannot be adequately secured against modification of DS
codepoints or traffic injection by adversaries should be treated as a
boundary link (and hence any arriving traffic on that link is treated
as if it were entering the domain at an ingress node). Local
security policy provides the definition of "adequately secured," and
such a definition may include a determination that the risks and
consequences of DS codepoint modification and/or traffic injection do
not justify any additional security measures for a link. Link
security can be enhanced via physical access controls and/or software
means such as tunnels that ensure packet integrity.

6.2 IPsec and Tunneling Interactions

The IPsec protocol, as defined in [ESP, AH], does not include the IP
header's DS field in any of its cryptographic calculations (in the
case of tunnel mode, it is the outer IP header's DS field that is not
included). Hence modification of the DS field by a network node has
no effect on IPsec's end-to-end security, because it cannot cause any
IPsec integrity check to fail. As a consequence, IPsec does not
provide any defense against an adversary's modification of the DS
field (i.e., a man-in-the-middle attack), as the adversary's
modification will also have no effect on IPsec's end-to-end security.
In some environments, the ability to modify the DS field without
affecting IPsec integrity checks may constitute a covert channel; if
it is necessary to eliminate such a channel or reduce its bandwidth,
the DS domains should be configured so that the required processing
(e.g., set all DS fields on sensitive traffic to a single value) can
be performed at DS egress nodes where traffic exits higher security
domains.

IPsec's tunnel mode provides security for the encapsulated IP
header's DS field. A tunnel mode IPsec packet contains two IP
headers: an outer header supplied by the tunnel ingress node and an
encapsulated inner header supplied by the original source of the
packet. When an IPsec tunnel is hosted (in whole or in part) on a
differentiated services network, the intermediate network nodes
operate on the DS field in the outer header. At the tunnel egress
node, IPsec processing includes stripping the outer header and
forwarding the packet (if required) using the inner header.   If
the inner IP header has not been processed by a DS ingress node for
the tunnel egress node's DS domain, the tunnel egress node is the DS
ingress node for traffic exiting the tunnel, and hence must carry out
the corresponding traffic conditioning responsibilities (see Sec.
6.1). If the IPsec processing includes a sufficiently strong
cryptographic integrity check of the encapsulated packet (where
sufficiency is determined by local security policy), the tunnel
egress node can safely assume that the DS field in the inner header
has the same value as it had at the tunnel ingress node. This allows
a tunnel egress node in the same DS domain as the tunnel ingress
node, to safely treat a packet passing such an integrity check as if
it had arrived from another node within the same DS domain, omitting
the DS ingress node traffic conditioning that would otherwise be
required. An important consequence is that otherwise insecure links
internal to a DS domain can be secured by a sufficiently strong IPsec
tunnel.

This analysis and its implications apply to any tunneling protocol
that performs integrity checks, but the level of assurance of the
inner header's DS field depends on the strength of the integrity

check performed by the tunneling protocol. In the absence of
sufficient assurance for a tunnel that may transit nodes outside the
current DS domain (or is otherwise vulnerable), the encapsulated
packet must be treated as if it had arrived at a DS ingress node from
outside the domain.

The IPsec protocol currently requires that the inner header's DS
field not be changed by IPsec decapsulation processing at a tunnel
egress node. This ensures that an adversary's modifications to the
DS field cannot be used to launch theft- or denial-of-service attacks
across an IPsec tunnel endpoint, as any such modifications will be
discarded at the tunnel endpoint. This document makes no change to
that IPsec requirement.

If the IPsec specifications are modified in the future to permit a
tunnel egress node to modify the DS field in an inner IP header based
on the DS field value in the outer header (e.g., copying part or all
of the outer DS field to the inner DS field), then additional
considerations would apply. For a tunnel contained entirely within a
single DS domain and for which the links are adequately secured
against modifications of the outer DS field, the only limits on inner
DS field modifications would be those imposed by the domain's service
provisioning policy. Otherwise, the tunnel egress node performing
such modifications would be acting as a DS ingress node for traffic
exiting the tunnel and must carry out the traffic conditioning
responsibilities of an ingress node, including defense against theft-
and denial-of-service attacks (See Sec. 6.1). If the tunnel enters
the DS domain at a node different from the tunnel egress node, the
tunnel egress node may depend on the upstream DS ingress node having
ensured that the outer DS field values are acceptable. Even in this
case, there are some checks that can only be performed by the tunnel
egress node (e.g., a consistency check between the inner and outer DS
codepoints for an encrypted tunnel). Any detected failure of such a
check is an auditable event and the generated audit log entry should
include the date/time the packet was received, the source and
destination IP addresses, and the DS codepoint that was unacceptable.

An IPsec tunnel can be viewed in at least two different ways from an
architectural perspective. If the tunnel is viewed as a logical
single hop "virtual wire", the actions of intermediate nodes in
forwarding the tunneled traffic should not be visible beyond the ends
of the tunnel and hence the DS field should not be modified as part
of decapsulation processing. In contrast, if the tunnel is viewed as
a multi-hop participant in forwarding traffic, then modification of
the DS field as part of tunnel decapsulation processing may be
desirable. A specific example of the latter situation occurs when a
tunnel terminates at an interior node of a DS domain at which the
domain administrator does not wish to deploy traffic conditioning

logic (e.g., to simplify traffic management). This could be
supported by using the DS codepoint in the outer IP header (which was
subject to traffic conditioning at the DS ingress node) to reset the
DS codepoint in the inner IP header, effectively moving DS ingress
traffic conditioning responsibilities from the IPsec tunnel egress
node to the appropriate upstream DS ingress node (which must already
perform that function for unencapsulated traffic).

6.3 Auditing

Not all systems that support differentiated services will implement
auditing. However, if differentiated services support is
incorporated into a system that supports auditing, then the
differentiated services implementation should also support auditing.
If such support is present the implementation must allow a system
administrator to enable or disable auditing for differentiated
services as a whole, and may allow such auditing to be enabled or
disabled in part.

For the most part, the granularity of auditing is a local matter.
However, several auditable events are identified in this document and
for each of these events a minimum set of information that should be
included in an audit log is defined. Additional information (e.g.,
packets related to the one that triggered the auditable event) may
also be included in the audit log for each of these events, and
additional events, not explicitly called out in this specification,
also may result in audit log entries. There is no requirement for
the receiver to transmit any message to the purported sender in
response to the detection of an auditable event, because of the
potential to induce denial of service via such action.

7. Acknowledgements

This document has benefitted from earlier drafts by Steven Blake,
David Clark, Ed Ellesson, Paul Ferguson, Juha Heinanen, Van Jacobson,
Kalevi Kilkki, Kathleen Nichols, Walter Weiss, John Wroclawski, and
Lixia Zhang.

The authors would like to acknowledge the following individuals for
their helpful comments and suggestions: Kathleen Nichols, Brian
Carpenter, Konstantinos Dovrolis, Shivkumar Kalyana, Wu-chang Feng,
Marty Borden, Yoram Bernet, Ronald Bonica, James Binder, Borje
Ohlman, Alessio Casati, Scott Brim, Curtis Villamizar, Hamid Ould-
Brahi, Andrew Smith, John Renwick, Werner Almesberger, Alan O'Neill,
James Fu, and Bob Braden.

8. References

[802.1p]   ISO/IEC Final CD 15802-3 Information technology - Tele-
              communications and information exchange between systems -
              Local and metropolitan area networks - Common
              specifications - Part 3: Media Access Control (MAC)
              bridges, (current draft available as IEEE P802.1D/D15).

[AH]   Kent, S. and R. Atkinson, "IP Authentication Header", RFC
              2402, November 1998.

[ATM]   ATM Traffic Management Specification Version 4.0 <af-tm-
              0056.000>, ATM Forum, April 1996.

[Bernet]   Y. Bernet, R. Yavatkar, P. Ford, F. Baker, L. Zhang, K.
              Nichols, and M. Speer, "A Framework for Use of RSVP with
              Diff-serv Networks", Work in Progress.

[DSFIELD]   Nichols, K., Blake, S., Baker, F. and D. Black,
              "Definition of the Differentiated Services Field (DS
              Field) in the IPv4 and IPv6 Headers", RFC 2474, December
              1998.

[EXPLICIT]   D. Clark and W. Fang, "Explicit Allocation of Best Effort
              Packet Delivery Service", IEEE/ACM Trans. on Networking,
              vol. 6, no. 4, August 1998, pp. 362-373.

[ESP]   Kent, S. and R. Atkinson, "IP Encapsulating Security
              Payload (ESP)", RFC 2406, November 1998.

[FRELAY]   ANSI T1S1, "DSSI Core Aspects of Frame Rely", March 1990.

[RFC791]   Postel, J., Editor, "Internet Protocol", STD 5, RFC 791,
              September 1981.

[RFC1349]   Almquist, P., "Type of Service in the Internet Protocol
              Suite", RFC 1349, July 1992.

[RFC1633]   Braden, R., Clark, D. and S. Shenker, "Integrated
              Services in the Internet Architecture: An Overview", RFC
              1633, July 1994.

[RFC1812]   Baker, F., Editor, "Requirements for IP Version 4
              Routers", RFC 1812, June 1995.

[RSVP]   Braden, B., Zhang, L., Berson S., Herzog, S. and S.
              Jamin, "Resource ReSerVation Protocol (RSVP) -- Version 1
              Functional Specification", RFC 2205, September 1997.

[2BIT]   K. Nichols, V. Jacobson, and L. Zhang, "A Two-bit
            Differentiated Services Architecture for the Internet",
            ftp://ftp.ee.lbl.gov/papers/dsarch.pdf, November 1997.

[TR]   ISO/IEC 8802-5 Information technology -
            Telecommunications and information exchange between
            systems - Local and metropolitan area networks - Common
            specifications - Part 5: Token Ring Access Method and
            Physical Layer Specifications, (also ANSI/IEEE Std 802.5-
            1995), 1995.

Authors' Addresses

    Steven Blake
    Torrent Networking Technologies
    3000 Aerial Center, Suite 140
    Morrisville, NC   27560

    Phone: +1-919-468-8466 x232
    EMail: slblake@torrentnet.com

    David L. Black
    EMC Corporation
    35 Parkwood Drive
    Hopkinton, MA   01748

    Phone: +1-508-435-1000 x76140
    EMail: black_david@emc.com

    Mark A. Carlson
    Sun Microsystems, Inc.
    2990 Center Green Court South
    Boulder, CO   80301

    Phone: +1-303-448-0048 x115
    EMail: mark.carlson@sun.com

    Elwyn Davies
    Nortel UK
    London Road
    Harlow, Essex CM17 9NA, UK

    Phone: +44-1279-405498
    EMail: elwynd@nortel.co.uk

Zheng Wang
Bell Labs Lucent Technologies
101 Crawfords Corner Road
Holmdel, NJ   07733

EMail: zhwang@bell-labs.com

Walter Weiss
Lucent Technologies
300 Baker Avenue, Suite 100
Concord, MA   01742-2168

EMail: wweiss@lucent.com

Full Copyright Statement

Network Working Group   K. Ramakrishnan
Request for Comments: 2481   AT&T Labs Research
Category: Experimental   S. Floyd
                                                                    LBNL
                                                            January 1999

     A Proposal to add Explicit Congestion Notification (ECN) to IP

Status of this Memo

Copyright Notice

Abstract

   This note describes a proposed addition of ECN (Explicit Congestion
   Notification) to IP. TCP is currently the dominant transport
   protocol used in the Internet. We begin by describing TCP's use of
   packet drops as an indication of congestion. Next we argue that with
   the addition of active queue management (e.g., RED) to the Internet
   infrastructure, where routers detect congestion before the queue
   overflows, routers are no longer limited to packet drops as an
   indication of congestion. Routers could instead set a Congestion
   Experienced (CE) bit in the packet header of packets from ECN-capable
   transport protocols. We describe when the CE bit would be set in the
   routers, and describe what modifications would be needed to TCP to
   make it ECN-capable. Modifications to other transport protocols
   (e.g., unreliable unicast or multicast, reliable multicast, other
   reliable unicast transport protocols) could be considered as those
   protocols are developed and advance through the standards process.

1. Conventions and Acronyms

   The keywords MUST, MUST NOT, REQUIRED, SHALL, SHALL NOT, SHOULD,
   SHOULD NOT, RECOMMENDED, MAY, and OPTIONAL, when they appear in this
   document, are to be interpreted as described in [B97].

2. Introduction

TCP's congestion control and avoidance algorithms are based on the notion that the network is a black-box [Jacobson88, Jacobson90]. The network's state of congestion or otherwise is determined by end-systems probing for the network state, by gradually increasing the load on the network (by increasing the window of packets that are outstanding in the network) until the network becomes congested and a packet is lost. Treating the network as a "black-box" and treating loss as an indication of congestion in the network is appropriate for pure best-effort data carried by TCP which has little or no sensitivity to delay or loss of individual packets. In addition, TCP's congestion management algorithms have techniques built-in (such as Fast Retransmit and Fast Recovery) to minimize the impact of losses from a throughput perspective.

However, these mechanisms are not intended to help applications that are in fact sensitive to the delay or loss of one or more individual packets. Interactive traffic such as telnet, web-browsing, and transfer of audio and video data can be sensitive to packet losses (using an unreliable data delivery transport such as UDP) or to the increased latency of the packet caused by the need to retransmit the packet after a loss (for reliable data delivery such as TCP).

Since TCP determines the appropriate congestion window to use by gradually increasing the window size until it experiences a dropped packet, this causes the queues at the bottleneck router to build up. With most packet drop policies at the router that are not sensitive to the load placed by each individual flow, this means that some of the packets of latency-sensitive flows are going to be dropped. Active queue management mechanisms detect congestion before the queue overflows, and provide an indication of this congestion to the end nodes. The advantages of active queue management are discussed in RFC 2309 [RFC2309]. Active queue management avoids some of the bad properties of dropping on queue overflow, including the undesirable synchronization of loss across multiple flows. More importantly, active queue management means that transport protocols with congestion control (e.g., TCP) do not have to rely on buffer overflow as the only indication of congestion. This can reduce unnecessary queueing delay for all traffic sharing that queue.

Active queue management mechanisms may use one of several methods for indicating congestion to end-nodes. One is to use packet drops, as is currently done. However, active queue management allows the router to separate policies of queueing or dropping packets from the policies for indicating congestion. Thus, active queue management allows routers to use the Congestion Experienced (CE) bit in a packet header as an indication of congestion, instead of relying solely on packet drops.

3. Assumptions and General Principles

In this section, we describe some of the important design principles and assumptions that guided the design choices in this proposal.

(1) Congestion may persist over different time-scales. The time scales that we are concerned with are congestion events that may last longer than a round-trip time.

(2) The number of packets in an individual flow (e.g., TCP connection or an exchange using UDP) may range from a small number of packets to quite a large number. We are interested in managing the congestion caused by flows that send enough packets so that they are still active when network feedback reaches them.

(3) New mechanisms for congestion control and avoidance need to co-exist and cooperate with existing mechanisms for congestion control. In particular, new mechanisms have to co-exist with TCP's current methods of adapting to congestion and with routers' current practice of dropping packets in periods of congestion.

(4) Because ECN is likely to be adopted gradually, accommodating migration is essential. Some routers may still only drop packets to indicate congestion, and some end-systems may not be ECN-capable. The most viable strategy is one that accommodates incremental deployment without having to resort to "islands" of ECN-capable and non-ECN-capable environments.

(5) Asymmetric routing is likely to be a normal occurrence in the Internet. The path (sequence of links and routers) followed by data packets may be different from the path followed by the acknowledgment packets in the reverse direction.

(6) Many routers process the "regular" headers in IP packets more efficiently than they process the header information in IP options. This suggests keeping congestion experienced information in the regular headers of an IP packet.

(7) It must be recognized that not all end-systems will cooperate in mechanisms for congestion control. However, new mechanisms shouldn't make it easier for TCP applications to disable TCP congestion control. The benefit of lying about participating in new mechanisms such as ECN-capability should be small.

4. Random Early Detection (RED)

Random Early Detection (RED) is a mechanism for active queue management that has been proposed to detect incipient congestion [FJ93], and is currently being deployed in the Internet backbone [RFC2309]. Although RED is meant to be a general mechanism using one

of several alternatives for congestion indication, in the current
environment of the Internet RED is restricted to using packet drops
as a mechanism for congestion indication. RED drops packets based on
the average queue length exceeding a threshold, rather than only when
the queue overflows. However, when RED drops packets before the
queue actually overflows, RED is not forced by memory limitations to
discard the packet.

RED could set a Congestion Experienced (CE) bit in the packet header
instead of dropping the packet, if such a bit was provided in the IP
header and understood by the transport protocol. The use of the CE
bit would allow the receiver(s) to receive the packet, avoiding the
potential for excessive delays due to retransmissions after packet
losses. We use the term 'CE packet' to denote a packet that has the
CE bit set.

5. Explicit Congestion Notification in IP

We propose that the Internet provide a congestion indication for
incipient congestion (as in RED and earlier work [RJ90]) where the
notification can sometimes be through marking packets rather than
dropping them. This would require an ECN field in the IP header with
two bits. The ECN-Capable Transport (ECT) bit would be set by the
data sender to indicate that the end-points of the transport protocol
are ECN-capable. The CE bit would be set by the router to indicate
congestion to the end nodes. Routers that have a packet arriving at
a full queue would drop the packet, just as they do now.

Bits 6 and 7 in the IPv4 TOS octet are designated as the ECN field.
Bit 6 is designated as the ECT bit, and bit 7 is designated as the CE
bit. The IPv4 TOS octet corresponds to the Traffic Class octet in
IPv6. The definitions for the IPv4 TOS octet [RFC791] and the IPv6
Traffic Class octet are intended to be superseded by the DS
(Differentiated Services) Field [DIFFSERV]. Bits 6 and 7 are listed
in [DIFFSERV] as Currently Unused. Section 19 gives a brief history
of the TOS octet.

Because of the unstable history of the TOS octet, the use of the ECN
field as specified in this document cannot be guaranteed to be
backwards compatible with all past uses of these two bits. The
potential dangers of this lack of backwards compatibility are
discussed in Section 19.

Upon the receipt by an ECN-Capable transport of a single CE packet,
the congestion control algorithms followed at the end-systems MUST be
essentially the same as the congestion control response to a *single*
dropped packet. For example, for ECN-Capable TCP the source TCP is
required to halve its congestion window for any window of data

containing either a packet drop or an ECN indication. However, we
would like to point out some notable exceptions in the reaction of
the source TCP, related to following the shorter-time-scale details
of particular implementations of TCP. For TCP's response to an ECN
indication, we do not recommend such behavior as the slow-start of
Tahoe TCP in response to a packet drop, or Reno TCP's wait of roughly
half a round-trip time during Fast Recovery.

One reason for requiring that the congestion-control response to the
CE packet be essentially the same as the response to a dropped packet
is to accommodate the incremental deployment of ECN in both end-
systems and in routers. Some routers may drop ECN-Capable packets
(e.g., using the same RED policies for congestion detection) while
other routers set the CE bit, for equivalent levels of congestion.
Similarly, a router might drop a non-ECN-Capable packet but set the
CE bit in an ECN-Capable packet, for equivalent levels of congestion.
Different congestion control responses to a CE bit indication and to
a packet drop could result in unfair treatment for different flows.

An additional requirement is that the end-systems should react to
congestion at most once per window of data (i.e., at most once per
roundtrip time), to avoid reacting multiple times to multiple
indications of congestion within a roundtrip time.

For a router, the CE bit of an ECN-Capable packet should only be set
if the router would otherwise have dropped the packet as an
indication of congestion to the end nodes. When the router's buffer
is not yet full and the router is prepared to drop a packet to inform
end nodes of incipient congestion, the router should first check to
see if the ECT bit is set in that packet's IP header. If so, then
instead of dropping the packet, the router MAY instead set the CE bit
in the IP header.

An environment where all end nodes were ECN-Capable could allow new
criteria to be developed for setting the CE bit, and new congestion
control mechanisms for end-node reaction to CE packets. However,
this is a research issue, and as such is not addressed in this
document.

When a CE packet is received by a router, the CE bit is left
unchanged, and the packet transmitted as usual. When severe
congestion has occurred and the router's queue is full, then the
router has no choice but to drop some packet when a new packet
arrives. We anticipate that such packet losses will become
relatively infrequent when a majority of end-systems become ECN-
Capable and participate in TCP or other compatible congestion control
mechanisms. In an adequately-provisioned network in such an ECN-
Capable environment, packet losses should occur primarily during

transients or in the presence of non-cooperating sources.

We expect that routers will set the CE bit in response to incipient congestion as indicated by the average queue size, using the RED algorithms suggested in [FJ93, RFC2309]. To the best of our knowledge, this is the only proposal currently under discussion in the IETF for routers to drop packets proactively, before the buffer overflows. However, this document does not attempt to specify a particular mechanism for active queue management, leaving that endeavor, if needed, to other areas of the IETF. While ECN is inextricably tied up with active queue management at the router, the reverse does not hold; active queue management mechanisms have been developed and deployed independently from ECN, using packet drops as indications of congestion in the absence of ECN in the IP architecture.

6. Support from the Transport Protocol

ECN requires support from the transport protocol, in addition to the functionality given by the ECN field in the IP packet header. The transport protocol might require negotiation between the endpoints during setup to determine that all of the endpoints are ECN-capable, so that the sender can set the ECT bit in transmitted packets. Second, the transport protocol must be capable of reacting appropriately to the receipt of CE packets. This reaction could be in the form of the data receiver informing the data sender of the received CE packet (e.g., TCP), of the data receiver unsubscribing to a layered multicast group (e.g., RLM [MJV96]), or of some other action that ultimately reduces the arrival rate of that flow to that receiver.

This document only addresses the addition of ECN Capability to TCP, leaving issues of ECN and other transport protocols to further research. For TCP, ECN requires three new mechanisms: negotiation between the endpoints during setup to determine if they are both ECN-capable; an ECN-Echo flag in the TCP header so that the data receiver can inform the data sender when a CE packet has been received; and a Congestion Window Reduced (CWR) flag in the TCP header so that the data sender can inform the data receiver that the congestion window has been reduced. The support required from other transport protocols is likely to be different, particular for unreliable or reliable multicast transport protocols, and will have to be determined as other transport protocols are brought to the IETF for standardization.

6.1. TCP

The following sections describe in detail the proposed use of ECN in
TCP. This proposal is described in essentially the same form in
[Floyd94]. We assume that the source TCP uses the standard congestion
control algorithms of Slow-start, Fast Retransmit and Fast Recovery
[RFC 2001].

This proposal specifies two new flags in the Reserved field of the
TCP header. The TCP mechanism for negotiating ECN-Capability uses
the ECN-Echo flag in the TCP header. (This was called the ECN Notify
flag in some earlier documents.) Bit 9 in the Reserved field of the
TCP header is designated as the ECN-Echo flag. The location of the
6-bit Reserved field in the TCP header is shown in Figure 3 of RFC
793 [RFC793].

To enable the TCP receiver to determine when to stop setting the
ECN-Echo flag, we introduce a second new flag in the TCP header, the
Congestion Window Reduced (CWR) flag. The CWR flag is assigned to
Bit 8 in the Reserved field of the TCP header.

The use of these flags is described in the sections below.

6.1.1. TCP Initialization

In the TCP connection setup phase, the source and destination TCPs
exchange information about their desire and/or capability to use ECN.
Subsequent to the completion of this negotiation, the TCP sender sets
the ECT bit in the IP header of data packets to indicate to the
network that the transport is capable and willing to participate in
ECN for this packet. This will indicate to the routers that they may
mark this packet with the CE bit, if they would like to use that as a
method of congestion notification. If the TCP connection does not
wish to use ECN notification for a particular packet, the sending TCP
sets the ECT bit equal to 0 (i.e., not set), and the TCP receiver
ignores the CE bit in the received packet.

When a node sends a TCP SYN packet, it may set the ECN-Echo and CWR
flags in the TCP header. For a SYN packet, the setting of both the
ECN-Echo and CWR flags are defined as an indication that the sending
TCP is ECN-Capable, rather than as an indication of congestion or of
response to congestion. More precisely, a SYN packet with both the
ECN-Echo and CWR flags set indicates that the TCP implementation
transmitting the SYN packet will participate in ECN as both a sender
and receiver. As a receiver, it will respond to incoming data
packets that have the CE bit set in the IP header by setting the
ECN-Echo flag in outgoing TCP Acknowledgement (ACK) packets. As a
sender, it will respond to incoming packets that have the ECN-Echo

flag set by reducing the congestion window when appropriate.

When a node sends a SYN-ACK packet, it may set the ECN-Echo flag, but it does not set the CWR flag. For a SYN-ACK packet, the pattern of the ECN-Echo flag set and the CWR flag not set in the TCP header is defined as an indication that the TCP transmitting the SYN-ACK packet is ECN-Capable.

There is the question of why we chose to have the TCP sending the SYN set two ECN-related flags in the Reserved field of the TCP header for the SYN packet, while the responding TCP sending the SYN-ACK sets only one ECN-related flag in the SYN-ACK packet. This asymmetry is necessary for the robust negotiation of ECN-capability with deployed TCP implementations. There exists at least one TCP implementation in which TCP receivers set the Reserved field of the TCP header in ACK packets (and hence the SYN-ACK) simply to reflect the Reserved field of the TCP header in the received data packet. Because the TCP SYN packet sets the ECN-Echo and CWR flags to indicate ECN-capability, while the SYN-ACK packet sets only the ECN-Echo flag, the sending TCP correctly interprets a receiver's reflection of its own flags in the Reserved field as an indication that the receiver is not ECN-capable.

6.1.2. The TCP Sender

For a TCP connection using ECN, data packets are transmitted with the ECT bit set in the IP header (set to a "1"). If the sender receives an ECN-Echo ACK packet (that is, an ACK packet with the ECN-Echo flag set in the TCP header), then the sender knows that congestion was encountered in the network on the path from the sender to the receiver. The indication of congestion should be treated just as a congestion loss in non-ECN-Capable TCP. That is, the TCP source halves the congestion window "cwnd" and reduces the slow start threshold "ssthresh". The sending TCP does NOT increase the congestion window in response to the receipt of an ECN-Echo ACK packet.

A critical condition is that TCP does not react to congestion indications more than once every window of data (or more loosely, more than once every round-trip time). That is, the TCP sender's congestion window should be reduced only once in response to a series of dropped and/or CE packets from a single window of data, In addition, the TCP source should not decrease the slow-start threshold, ssthresh, if it has been decreased within the last round trip time. However, if any retransmitted packets are dropped or have the CE bit set, then this is interpreted by the source TCP as a new instance of congestion.

After the source TCP reduces its congestion window in response to a
CE packet, incoming acknowledgements that continue to arrive can
"clock out" outgoing packets as allowed by the reduced congestion
window. If the congestion window consists of only one MSS (maximum
segment size), and the sending TCP receives an ECN-Echo ACK packet,
then the sending TCP should in principle still reduce its congestion
window in half. However, the value of the congestion window is
bounded below by a value of one MSS. If the sending TCP were to
continue to send, using a congestion window of 1 MSS, this results in
the transmission of one packet per round-trip time. We believe it is
desirable to still reduce the sending rate of the TCP sender even
further, on receipt of an ECN-Echo packet when the congestion window
is one. We use the retransmit timer as a means to reduce the rate
further in this circumstance. Therefore, the sending TCP should also
reset the retransmit timer on receiving the ECN-Echo packet when the
congestion window is one. The sending TCP will then be able to send
a new packet when the retransmit timer expires.

[Floyd94] discusses TCP's response to ECN in more detail. [Floyd98]
discusses the validation test in the ns simulator, which illustrates
a wide range of ECN scenarios. These scenarios include the following:
an ECN followed by another ECN, a Fast Retransmit, or a Retransmit
Timeout; a Retransmit Timeout or a Fast Retransmit followed by an
ECN, and a congestion window of one packet followed by an ECN.

TCP follows existing algorithms for sending data packets in response
to incoming ACKs, multiple duplicate acknowledgements, or retransmit
timeouts [RFC2001].

6.1.3. The TCP Receiver

When TCP receives a CE data packet at the destination end-system, the
TCP data receiver sets the ECN-Echo flag in the TCP header of the
subsequent ACK packet. If there is any ACK withholding implemented,
as in current "delayed-ACK" TCP implementations where the TCP
receiver can send an ACK for two arriving data packets, then the
ECN-Echo flag in the ACK packet will be set to the OR of the CE bits
of all of the data packets being acknowledged. That is, if any of
the received data packets are CE packets, then the returning ACK has
the ECN-Echo flag set.

To provide robustness against the possibility of a dropped ACK packet
carrying an ECN-Echo flag, the TCP receiver must set the ECN-Echo
flag in a series of ACK packets. The TCP receiver uses the CWR flag
to determine when to stop setting the ECN-Echo flag.

When an ECN-Capable TCP reduces its congestion window for any reason
(because of a retransmit timeout, a Fast Retransmit, or in response
to an ECN Notification), the TCP sets the CWR flag in the TCP header
of the first data packet sent after the window reduction. If that
data packet is dropped in the network, then the sending TCP will have
to reduce the congestion window again and retransmit the dropped
packet. Thus, the Congestion Window Reduced message is reliably
delivered to the data receiver.

After a TCP receiver sends an ACK packet with the ECN-Echo bit set,
that TCP receiver continues to set the ECN-Echo flag in ACK packets
until it receives a CWR packet (a packet with the CWR flag set).
After the receipt of the CWR packet, acknowledgements for subsequent
non-CE data packets do not have the ECN-Echo flag set. If another CE
packet is received by the data receiver, the receiver would once
again send ACK packets with the ECN-Echo flag set. While the receipt
of a CWR packet does not guarantee that the data sender received the
ECN-Echo message, this does indicate that the data sender reduced its
congestion window at some point *after* it sent the data packet for
which the CE bit was set.

We have already specified that a TCP sender reduces its congestion
window at most once per window of data. This mechanism requires some
care to make sure that the sender reduces its congestion window at
most once per ECN indication, and that multiple ECN messages over
several successive windows of data are properly reported to the ECN
sender. This is discussed further in [Floyd98].

6.1.4. Congestion on the ACK-path

For the current generation of TCP congestion control algorithms, pure
acknowledgement packets (e.g., packets that do not contain any
accompanying data) should be sent with the ECT bit off. Current TCP
receivers have no mechanisms for reducing traffic on the ACK-path in
response to congestion notification. Mechanisms for responding to
congestion on the ACK-path are areas for current and future research.
(One simple possibility would be for the sender to reduce its
congestion window when it receives a pure ACK packet with the CE bit
set). For current TCP implementations, a single dropped ACK generally
has only a very small effect on the TCP's sending rate.

7. Summary of changes required in IP and TCP

Two bits need to be specified in the IP header, the ECN-Capable
Transport (ECT) bit and the Congestion Experienced (CE) bit. The ECT
bit set to "0" indicates that the transport protocol will ignore the

CE bit. This is the default value for the ECT bit. The ECT bit set
to "1" indicates that the transport protocol is willing and able to
participate in ECN.

The default value for the CE bit is "0". The router sets the CE bit
to "1" to indicate congestion to the end nodes. The CE bit in a
packet header should never be reset by a router from "1" to "0".

TCP requires three changes, a negotiation phase during setup to
determine if both end nodes are ECN-capable, and two new flags in the
TCP header, from the "reserved" flags in the TCP flags field. The
ECN-Echo flag is used by the data receiver to inform the data sender
of a received CE packet. The Congestion Window Reduced flag is used
by the data sender to inform the data receiver that the congestion
window has been reduced.

8. Non-relationship to ATM's EFCI indicator or Frame Relay's FECN

Since the ATM and Frame Relay mechanisms for congestion indication
have typically been defined without any notion of average queue size
as the basis for determining that an intermediate node is congested,
we believe that they provide a very noisy signal. The TCP-sender
reaction specified in this draft for ECN is NOT the appropriate
reaction for such a noisy signal of congestion notification. It is
our expectation that ATM's EFCI and Frame Relay's FECN mechanisms
would be phased out over time within the ATM network. However, if
the routers that interface to the ATM network have a way of
maintaining the average queue at the interface, and use it to come to
a reliable determination that the ATM subnet is congested, they may
use the ECN notification that is defined here.

We emphasize that a *single* packet with the CE bit set in an IP
packet causes the transport layer to respond, in terms of congestion
control, as it would to a packet drop. As such, the CE bit is not a
good match to a transient signal such as one based on the
instantaneous queue size. However, experiments in techniques at
layer 2 (e.g., in ATM switches or Frame Relay switches) should be
encouraged. For example, using a scheme such as RED (where packet
marking is based on the average queue length exceeding a threshold),
layer 2 devices could provide a reasonably reliable indication of
congestion. When all the layer 2 devices in a path set that layer's
own Congestion Experienced bit (e.g., the EFCI bit for ATM, the FECN
bit in Frame Relay) in this reliable manner, then the interface
router to the layer 2 network could copy the state of that layer 2
Congestion Experienced bit into the CE bit in the IP header. We
recognize that this is not the current practice, nor is it in current
standards. However, encouraging experimentation in this manner may

provide the information needed to enable evolution of existing layer 2 mechanisms to provide a more reliable means of congestion indication, when they use a single bit for indicating congestion.

9. Non-compliance by the End Nodes

This section discusses concerns about the vulnerability of ECN to non-compliant end-nodes (i.e., end nodes that set the ECT bit in transmitted packets but do not respond to received CE packets). We argue that the addition of ECN to the IP architecture would not significantly increase the current vulnerability of the architecture to unresponsive flows.

Even for non-ECN environments, there are serious concerns about the damage that can be done by non-compliant or unresponsive flows (that is, flows that do not respond to congestion control indications by reducing their arrival rate at the congested link). For example, an end-node could "turn off congestion control" by not reducing its congestion window in response to packet drops. This is a concern for the current Internet. It has been argued that routers will have to deploy mechanisms to detect and differentially treat packets from non-compliant flows. It has also been argued that techniques such as end-to-end per-flow scheduling and isolation of one flow from another, differentiated services, or end-to-end reservations could remove some of the more damaging effects of unresponsive flows.

It has been argued that dropping packets in itself may be an adequate deterrent for non-compliance, and that the use of ECN removes this deterrent. We would argue in response that (1) ECN-capable routers preserve packet-dropping behavior in times of high congestion; and (2) even in times of high congestion, dropping packets in itself is not an adequate deterrent for non-compliance.

First, ECN-Capable routers will only mark packets (as opposed to dropping them) when the packet marking rate is reasonably low. During periods where the average queue size exceeds an upper threshold, and therefore the potential packet marking rate would be high, our recommendation is that routers drop packets rather then set the CE bit in packet headers.

During the periods of low or moderate packet marking rates when ECN would be deployed, there would be little deterrent effect on unresponsive flows of dropping rather than marking those packets. For example, delay-insensitive flows using reliable delivery might have an incentive to increase rather than to decrease their sending rate in the presence of dropped packets. Similarly, delay-sensitive flows using unreliable delivery might increase their use of FEC in response to an increased packet drop rate, increasing rather than decreasing

their sending rate. For the same reasons, we do not believe that
packet dropping itself is an effective deterrent for non-compliance
even in an environment of high packet drop rates.

Several methods have been proposed to identify and restrict non-
compliant or unresponsive flows. The addition of ECN to the network
environment would not in any way increase the difficulty of designing
and deploying such mechanisms. If anything, the addition of ECN to
the architecture would make the job of identifying unresponsive flows
slightly easier. For example, in an ECN-Capable environment routers
are not limited to information about packets that are dropped or have
the CE bit set at that router itself; in such an environment routers
could also take note of arriving CE packets that indicate congestion
encountered by that packet earlier in the path.

10. Non-compliance in the Network

The breakdown of effective congestion control could be caused not
only by a non-compliant end-node, but also by the loss of the
congestion indication in the network itself. This could happen
through a rogue or broken router that set the ECT bit in a packet
from a non-ECN-capable transport, or "erased" the CE bit in arriving
packets. As one example, a rogue or broken router that "erased" the
CE bit in arriving CE packets would prevent that indication of
congestion from reaching downstream receivers. This could result in
the failure of congestion control for that flow and a resulting
increase in congestion in the network, ultimately resulting in
subsequent packets dropped for this flow as the average queue size
increased at the congested gateway.

The actions of a rogue or broken router could also result in an
unnecessary indication of congestion to the end-nodes. These actions
can include a router dropping a packet or setting the CE bit in the
absence of congestion. From a congestion control point of view,
setting the CE bit in the absence of congestion by a non-compliant
router would be no different than a router dropping a packet
unecessarily. By "erasing" the ECT bit of a packet that is later
dropped in the network, a router's actions could result in an
unnecessary packet drop for that packet later in the network.

Concerns regarding the loss of congestion indications from
encapsulated, dropped, or corrupted packets are discussed below.

10.1. Encapsulated packets

   Some care is required to handle the CE and ECT bits appropriately
   when packets are encapsulated and de-encapsulated for tunnels.

   When a packet is encapsulated, the following rules apply regarding
   the ECT bit. First, if the ECT bit in the encapsulated ('inside')
   header is a 0, then the ECT bit in the encapsulating ('outside')
   header MUST be a 0. If the ECT bit in the inside header is a 1, then
   the ECT bit in the outside header SHOULD be a 1.

   When a packet is de-encapsulated, the following rules apply regarding
   the CE bit. If the ECT bit is a 1 in both the inside and the outside
   header, then the CE bit in the outside header MUST be ORed with the
   CE bit in the inside header. (That is, in this case a CE bit of 1 in
   the outside header must be copied to the inside header.) If the ECT
   bit in either header is a 0, then the CE bit in the outside header is
   ignored. This requirement for the treatment of de-encapsulated
   packets does not currently apply to IPsec tunnels.

   A specific example of the use of ECN with encapsulation occurs when a
   flow wishes to use ECN-capability to avoid the danger of an
   unnecessary packet drop for the encapsulated packet as a result of
   congestion at an intermediate node in the tunnel. This functionality
   can be supported by copying the ECN field in the inner IP header to
   the outer IP header upon encapsulation, and using the ECN field in
   the outer IP header to set the ECN field in the inner IP header upon
   decapsulation. This effectively allows routers along the tunnel to
   cause the CE bit to be set in the ECN field of the unencapsulated IP
   header of an ECN-capable packet when such routers experience
   congestion.

10.2. IPsec Tunnel Considerations

   The IPsec protocol, as defined in [ESP, AH], does not include the IP
   header's ECN field in any of its cryptographic calculations (in the
   case of tunnel mode, the outer IP header's ECN field is not
   included). Hence modification of the ECN field by a network node has
   no effect on IPsec's end-to-end security, because it cannot cause any
   IPsec integrity check to fail. As a consequence, IPsec does not
   provide any defense against an adversary's modification of the ECN
   field (i.e., a man-in-the-middle attack), as the adversary's
   modification will also have no effect on IPsec's end-to-end security.
   In some environments, the ability to modify the ECN field without
   affecting IPsec integrity checks may constitute a covert channel; if
   it is necessary to eliminate such a channel or reduce its bandwidth,
   then the outer IP header's ECN field can be zeroed at the tunnel
   ingress and egress nodes.

The IPsec protocol currently requires that the inner header's ECN
field not be changed by IPsec decapsulation processing at a tunnel
egress node. This ensures that an adversary's modifications to the
ECN field cannot be used to launch theft- or denial-of-service
attacks across an IPsec tunnel endpoint, as any such modifications
will be discarded at the tunnel endpoint. This document makes no
change to that IPsec requirement. As a consequence of the current
specification of the IPsec protocol, we suggest that experiments with
ECN not be carried out for flows that will undergo IPsec tunneling at
the present time.

If the IPsec specifications are modified in the future to permit a
tunnel egress node to modify the ECN field in an inner IP header
based on the ECN field value in the outer header (e.g., copying part
or all of the outer ECN field to the inner ECN field), or to permit
the ECN field of the outer IP header to be zeroed during
encapsulation, then experiments with ECN may be used in combination
with IPsec tunneling.

This discussion of ECN and IPsec tunnel considerations draws heavily
on related discussions and documents from the Differentiated Services
Working Group.

10.3. Dropped or Corrupted Packets

An additional issue concerns a packet that has the CE bit set at one
router and is dropped by a subsequent router. For the proposed use
for ECN in this paper (that is, for a transport protocol such as TCP
for which a dropped data packet is an indication of congestion), end
nodes detect dropped data packets, and the congestion response of the
end nodes to a dropped data packet is at least as strong as the
congestion response to a received CE packet.

However, transport protocols such as TCP do not necessarily detect
all packet drops, such as the drop of a "pure" ACK packet; for
example, TCP does not reduce the arrival rate of subsequent ACK
packets in response to an earlier dropped ACK packet. Any proposal
for extending ECN-Capability to such packets would have to address
concerns raised by CE packets that were later dropped in the network.

Similarly, if a CE packet is dropped later in the network due to
corruption (bit errors), the end nodes should still invoke congestion
control, just as TCP would today in response to a dropped data
packet. This issue of corrupted CE packets would have to be
considered in any proposal for the network to distinguish between
packets dropped due to corruption, and packets dropped due to
congestion or buffer overflow.

11. A summary of related work.

[Floyd94] considers the advantages and drawbacks of adding ECN to the
TCP/IP architecture. As shown in the simulation-based comparisons,
one advantage of ECN is to avoid unnecessary packet drops for short
or delay-sensitive TCP connections. A second advantage of ECN is in
avoiding some unnecessary retransmit timeouts in TCP. This paper
discusses in detail the integration of ECN into TCP's congestion
control mechanisms. The possible disadvantages of ECN discussed in
the paper are that a non-compliant TCP connection could falsely
advertise itself as ECN-capable, and that a TCP ACK packet carrying
an ECN-Echo message could itself be dropped in the network. The
first of these two issues is discussed in Section 8 of this document,
and the second is addressed by the proposal in Section 5.1.3 for a
CWR flag in the TCP header.

[CKLTZ97] reports on an experimental implementation of ECN in IPv6.
The experiments include an implementation of ECN in an existing
implementation of RED for FreeBSD. A number of experiments were run
to demonstrate the control of the average queue size in the router,
the performance of ECN for a single TCP connection as a congested
router, and fairness with multiple competing TCP connections. One
conclusion of the experiments is that dropping packets from a bulk-
data transfer can degrade performance much more severely than marking
packets.

Because the experimental implementation in [CKLTZ97] predates some of
the developments in this document, the implementation does not
conform to this document in all respects. For example, in the
experimental implementation the CWR flag is not used, but instead the
TCP receiver sends the ECN-Echo bit on a single ACK packet.

[K98] and [CKLTZ98] build on [CKLTZ97] to further analyze the
benefits of ECN for TCP. The conclusions are that ECN TCP gets
moderately better throughput than non-ECN TCP; that ECN TCP flows are
fair towards non-ECN TCP flows; and that ECN TCP is robust with two-
way traffic, congestion in both directions, and with multiple
congested gateways. Experiments with many short web transfers show
that, while most of the short connections have similar transfer times
with or without ECN, a small percentage of the short connections have
very long transfer times for the non-ECN experiments as compared to
the ECN experiments. This increased transfer time is particularly
dramatic for those short connections that have their first packet
dropped in the non-ECN experiments, and that therefore have to wait
six seconds for the retransmit timer to expire.

The ECN Web Page [ECN] has pointers to other implementations of ECN
in progress.

12. Conclusions

   Given the current effort to implement RED, we believe this is the
   right time for router vendors to examine how to implement congestion
   avoidance mechanisms that do not depend on packet drops alone. With
   the increased deployment of applications and transports sensitive to
   the delay and loss of a single packet (e.g., realtime traffic, short
   web transfers), depending on packet loss as a normal congestion
   notification mechanism appears to be insufficient (or at the very
   least, non-optimal).

13. Acknowledgements

   Many people have made contributions to this RFC. In particular, we
   would like to thank Kenjiro Cho for the proposal for the TCP
   mechanism for negotiating ECN-Capability, Kevin Fall for the proposal
   of the CWR bit, Steve Blake for material on IPv4 Header Checksum
   Recalculation, Jamal Hadi Salim for discussions of ECN issues, and
   Steve Bellovin, Jim Bound, Brian Carpenter, Paul Ferguson, Stephen
   Kent, Greg Minshall, and Vern Paxson for discussions of security
   issues. We also thank the Internet End-to-End Research Group for
   ongoing discussions of these issues.

14. References

   [AH]   Kent, S. and R. Atkinson, "IP Authentication Header",
                RFC 2402, November 1998.

   [B97]   Bradner, S., "Key words for use in RFCs to Indicate
                Requirement Levels", BCP 14, RFC 2119, March 1997.

   [CKLT98]   Chen, C., Krishnan, H., Leung, S., Tang, N., and Zhang,
                L., "Implementing ECN for TCP/IPv6", presentation to the
                ECN BOF at the L.A. IETF, March 1998, URL
                "http://www.cs.ucla.edu/~hari/ecn-ietf.ps".

   [DIFFSERV]   Nichols, K., Blake, S., Baker, F. and D. Black,
                "Definition of the Differentiated Services Field (DS
                Field) in the IPv4 and IPv6 Headers", RFC 2474, December
                1998.

   [ECN]   "The ECN Web Page", URL "http://www-
                nrg.ee.lbl.gov/floyd/ecn.html".

   [ESP]   Kent, S. and R. Atkinson, "IP Encapsulating Security
                Payload", RFC 2406, November 1998.

[FJ93]   Floyd, S., and Jacobson, V., "Random Early Detection
              gateways for Congestion Avoidance", IEEE/ACM
              Transactions on Networking, V.1 N.4, August 1993, p.
              397-413. URL "ftp://ftp.ee.lbl.gov/papers/early.pdf".

[Floyd94]   Floyd, S., "TCP and Explicit Congestion Notification",
              ACM Computer Communication Review, V. 24 N. 5, October
              1994, p. 10-23. URL
              "ftp://ftp.ee.lbl.gov/papers/tcp_ecn.4.ps.Z".

[Floyd97]   Floyd, S., and Fall, K., "Router Mechanisms to Support
              End-to-End Congestion Control", Technical report,
              February 1997. URL "http://www-
              nrg.ee.lbl.gov/floyd/end2end-paper.html".

[Floyd98]   Floyd, S., "The ECN Validation Test in the NS
              Simulator", URL "http://www-mash.cs.berkeley.edu/ns/",
              test tcl/test/test-all-ecn.

[K98]   Krishnan, H., "Analyzing Explicit Congestion
              Notification (ECN) benefits for TCP", Master's thesis,
              UCLA, 1998, URL
              "http://www.cs.ucla.edu/~hari/software/ecn/
              ecn_report.ps.gz".

[FRED]   Lin, D., and Morris, R., "Dynamics of Random Early
              Detection", SIGCOMM '97, September 1997. URL
              "http://www.inria.fr/rodeo/sigcomm97/program.html#ab078".

[Jacobson88] V. Jacobson, "Congestion Avoidance and Control", Proc.
              ACM SIGCOMM '88, pp. 314-329. URL
              "ftp://ftp.ee.lbl.gov/papers/congavoid.ps.Z".

[Jacobson90] V. Jacobson, "Modified TCP Congestion Avoidance
              Algorithm", Message to end2end-interest mailing list,
              April 1990. URL
              "ftp://ftp.ee.lbl.gov/email/vanj.90apr30.txt".

[MJV96]   S. McCanne, V. Jacobson, and M. Vetterli, "Receiver-
              driven Layered Multicast", SIGCOMM '96, August 1996, pp.
              117-130.

[RFC791]   Postel, J., "Internet Protocol", STD 5, RFC 791,
              September 1981.

[RFC793]   Postel, J., "Transmission Control Protocol", STD 7, RFC
              793, September 1981.

[RFC1141]   Mallory, T. and A. Kullberg, "Incremental Updating of
             the Internet Checksum", RFC 1141, January 1990.

[RFC1349]   Almquist, P., "Type of Service in the Internet Protocol
             Suite", RFC 1349, July 1992.

[RFC1455]   Eastlake, D., "Physical Link Security Type of Service",
             RFC 1455, May 1993.

[RFC2001]   Stevens, W., "TCP Slow Start, Congestion Avoidance, Fast
             Retransmit, and Fast Recovery Algorithms", RFC 2001,
             January 1997.

[RFC2309]   Braden, B., Clark, D., Crowcroft, J., Davie, B.,
             Deering, S., Estrin, D., Floyd, S., Jacobson, V.,
             Minshall, G., Partridge, C., Peterson, L., Ramakrishnan,
             K., Shenker, S., Wroclawski, J. and L. Zhang,
             "Recommendations on Queue Management and Congestion
             Avoidance in the Internet", RFC 2309, April 1998.

[RJ90]   K. K. Ramakrishnan and Raj Jain, "A Binary Feedback
             Scheme for Congestion Avoidance in Computer Networks",
             ACM Transactions on Computer Systems, Vol.8, No.2, pp.
             158-181, May 1990.

15. Security Considerations

    Security considerations have been discussed in Section 9.

16. IPv4 Header Checksum Recalculation

    IPv4 header checksum recalculation is an issue with some high-end
    router architectures using an output-buffered switch, since most if
    not all of the header manipulation is performed on the input side of
    the switch, while the ECN decision would need to be made local to the
    output buffer. This is not an issue for IPv6, since there is no IPv6
    header checksum. The IPv4 TOS octet is the last byte of a 16-bit
    half-word.

    RFC 1141 [RFC1141] discusses the incremental updating of the IPv4
    checksum after the TTL field is decremented. The incremental
    updating of the IPv4 checksum after the CE bit was set would work as
    follows: Let HC be the original header checksum, and let HC' be the
    new header checksum after the CE bit has been set. Then for header
    checksums calculated with one's complement subtraction, HC' would be
    recalculated as follows:

```
HC' = { HC - 1      HC > 1
      { 0x0000      HC = 1
```

For header checksums calculated on two's complement machines, HC'
would be recalculated as follows after the CE bit was set:

```
HC' = { HC - 1      HC > 0
      { 0xFFFE      HC = 0
```

17. The motivation for the ECT bit.

The need for the ECT bit is motivated by the fact that ECN will be
deployed incrementally in an Internet where some transport protocols
and routers understand ECN and some do not. With the ECT bit, the
router can drop packets from flows that are not ECN-capable, but can
instead set the CE bit in flows that *are* ECN-capable. Because the
ECT bit allows an end node to have the CE bit set in a packet
instead of having the packet dropped, an end node might have some
incentive to deploy ECN.

If there was no ECT indication, then the router would have to set the
CE bit for packets from both ECN-capable and non-ECN-capable flows.
In this case, there would be no incentive for end-nodes to deploy
ECN, and no viable path of incremental deployment from a non-ECN
world to an ECN-capable world. Consider the first stages of such an
incremental deployment, where a subset of the flows are ECN-capable.
At the onset of congestion, when the packet dropping/marking rate
would be low, routers would only set CE bits, rather than dropping
packets. However, only those flows that are ECN-capable would
understand and respond to CE packets. The result is that the ECN-
capable flows would back off, and the non-ECN-capable flows would be
unaware of the ECN signals and would continue to open their
congestion windows.

In this case, there are two possible outcomes: (1) the ECN-capable
flows back off, the non-ECN-capable flows get all of the bandwidth,
and congestion remains mild, or (2) the ECN-capable flows back off,
the non-ECN-capable flows don't, and congestion increases until the
router transitions from setting the CE bit to dropping packets.
While this second outcome evens out the fairness, the ECN-capable
flows would still receive little benefit from being ECN-capable,
because the increased congestion would drive the router to packet-
dropping behavior.

A flow that advertised itself as ECN-Capable but does not respond to
CE bits is functionally equivalent to a flow that turns off
congestion control, as discussed in Sections 8 and 9.

Thus, in a world when a subset of the flows are ECN-capable, but
where ECN-capable flows have no mechanism for indicating that fact to
the routers, there would be less effective and less fair congestion
control in the Internet, resulting in a strong incentive for end
nodes not to deploy ECN.

18. Why use two bits in the IP header?

Given the need for an ECT indication in the IP header, there still
remains the question of whether the ECT (ECN-Capable Transport) and
CE (Congestion Experienced) indications should be overloaded on a
single bit. This overloaded-one-bit alternative, explored in
[Floyd94], would involve a single bit with two values. One value,
"ECT and not CE", would represent an ECN-Capable Transport, and the
other value, "CE or not ECT", would represent either Congestion
Experienced or a non-ECN-Capable transport.

One difference between the one-bit and two-bit implementations
concerns packets that traverse multiple congested routers. Consider
a CE packet that arrives at a second congested router, and is
selected by the active queue management at that router for either
marking or dropping. In the one-bit implementation, the second
congested router has no choice but to drop the CE packet, because it
cannot distinguish between a CE packet and a non-ECT packet. In the
two-bit implementation, the second congested router has the choice of
either dropping the CE packet, or of leaving it alone with the CE bit
set.

Another difference between the one-bit and two-bit implementations
comes from the fact that with the one-bit implementation, receivers
in a single flow cannot distinguish between CE and non-ECT packets.
Thus, in the one-bit implementation an ECN-capable data sender would
have to unambiguously indicate to the receiver or receivers whether
each packet had been sent as ECN-Capable or as non-ECN-Capable. One
possibility would be for the sender to indicate in the transport
header whether the packet was sent as ECN-Capable. A second
possibility that would involve a functional limitation for the one-
bit implementation would be for the sender to unambiguously indicate
that it was going to send *all* of its packets as ECN-Capable or as
non-ECN-Capable. For a multicast transport protocol, this
unambiguous indication would have to be apparent to receivers joining
an on-going multicast session.

Another advantage of the two-bit approach is that it is somewhat more
robust. The most critical issue, discussed in Section 8, is that the
default indication should be that of a non-ECN-Capable transport. In
a two-bit implementation, this requirement for the default value
simply means that the ECT bit should be `OFF' by default. In the

one-bit implementation, this means that the single overloaded bit
should by default be in the "CE or not ECT" position. This is less
clear and straightforward, and possibly more open to incorrect
implementations either in the end nodes or in the routers.

In summary, while the one-bit implementation could be a possible
implementation, it has the following significant limitations relative
to the two-bit implementation. First, the one-bit implementation has
more limited functionality for the treatment of CE packets at a
second congested router. Second, the one-bit implementation requires
either that extra information be carried in the transport header of
packets from ECN-Capable flows (to convey the functionality of the
second bit elsewhere, namely in the transport header), or that
senders in ECN-Capable flows accept the limitation that receivers
must be able to determine a priori which packets are ECN-Capable and
which are not ECN-Capable. Third, the one-bit implementation is
possibly more open to errors from faulty implementations that choose
the wrong default value for the ECN bit. We believe that the use of
the extra bit in the IP header for the ECT-bit is extremely valuable
to overcome these limitations.

19. Historical definitions for the IPv4 TOS octet

RFC 791 [RFC791] defined the ToS (Type of Service) octet in the IP
header. In RFC 791, bits 6 and 7 of the ToS octet are listed as
"Reserved for Future Use", and are shown set to zero. The first two
fields of the ToS octet were defined as the Precedence and Type of
Service (TOS) fields.

```
     0     1     2     3     4     5     6     7
  +-----+-----+-----+-----+-----+-----+-----+-----+
  |   PRECEDENCE    |       TOS       |  0  |  0  |    RFC 791
  +-----+-----+-----+-----+-----+-----+-----+-----+
```

RFC 1122 included bits 6 and 7 in the TOS field, though it did not
discuss any specific use for those two bits:

```
     0     1     2     3     4     5     6     7
  +-----+-----+-----+-----+-----+-----+-----+-----+
  |   PRECEDENCE    |             TOS             |    RFC 1122
  +-----+-----+-----+-----+-----+-----+-----+-----+
```

The IPv4 TOS octet was redefined in RFC 1349 [RFC1349] as follows:

```
     0     1     2     3     4     5     6     7
  +-----+-----+-----+-----+-----+-----+-----+-----+
  |   PRECEDENCE    |        TOS        | MBZ |      RFC 1349
  +-----+-----+-----+-----+-----+-----+-----+-----+
```

Bit 6 in the TOS field was defined in RFC 1349 for "Minimize Monetary
Cost". In addition to the Precedence and Type of Service (TOS)
fields, the last field, MBZ (for "must be zero") was defined as
currently unused. RFC 1349 stated that "The originator of a datagram
sets [the MBZ] field to zero (unless participating in an Internet
protocol experiment which makes use of that bit)."

RFC 1455 [RFC 1455] defined an experimental standard that used all
four bits in the TOS field to request a guaranteed level of link
security.

RFC 1349 is obsoleted by "Definition of the Differentiated Services
Field (DS Field) in the IPv4 and IPv6 Headers" [DIFFSERV], in which
bits 6 and 7 of the DS field are listed as Currently Unused (CU).
The first six bits of the DS field are defined as the Differentiated
Services CodePoint (DSCP):

```
         0     1     2     3     4     5     6     7
      +-----+-----+-----+-----+-----+-----+-----+-----+
      |             DSCP                  |    CU     |
      +-----+-----+-----+-----+-----+-----+-----+-----+
```

Because of this unstable history, the definition of the ECN field in
this document cannot be guaranteed to be backwards compatible with
all past uses of these two bits. The damage that could be done by a
non-ECN-capable router would be to "erase" the CE bit for an ECN-
capable packet that arrived at the router with the CE bit set, or set
the CE bit even in the absence of congestion. This has been
discussed in Section 10 on "Non-compliance in the Network".

The damage that could be done in an ECN-capable environment by a
non-ECN-capable end-node transmitting packets with the ECT bit set
has been discussed in Section 9 on "Non-compliance by the End Nodes".

AUTHORS' ADDRESSES

    K. K. Ramakrishnan
    AT&T Labs. Research

    Phone: +1 (973) 360-8766
    EMail: kkrama@research.att.com
    URL: http://www.research.att.com/info/kkrama

    Sally Floyd
    Lawrence Berkeley National Laboratory

    Phone: +1 (510) 486-7518
    EMail: floyd@ee.lbl.gov
    URL: http://www-nrg.ee.lbl.gov/floyd/

Full Copyright Statement

25

RFC 2481

Network Working Group   E. Rosen
Request for Comments: 2547   Y. Rekhter
Category: Informational   Cisco Systems, Inc.
                                                            March 1999

BGP/MPLS VPNs

Status of this Memo

Copyright Notice

Abstract

This document describes a method by which a Service Provider with an
IP backbone may provide VPNs (Virtual Private Networks) for its
customers. MPLS (Multiprotocol Label Switching) is used for
forwarding packets over the backbone, and BGP (Border Gateway
Protocol) is used for distributing routes over the backbone. The
primary goal of this method is to support the outsourcing of IP
backbone services for enterprise networks. It does so in a manner
which is simple for the enterprise, while still scalable and flexible
for the Service Provider, and while allowing the Service Provider to
add value. These techniques can also be used to provide a VPN which
itself provides IP service to customers.

Table of Contents

1. Introduction

1.1. Virtual Private Networks

   Consider a set of "sites" which are attached to a common network
   which we may call the "backbone". Let's apply some policy to create a
   number of subsets of that set, and let's impose the following rule:
   two sites may have IP interconnectivity over that backbone only if at
   least one of these subsets contains them both.

   The subsets we have created are "Virtual Private Networks" (VPNs).
   Two sites have IP connectivity over the common backbone only if there
   is some VPN which contains them both. Two sites which have no VPN in
   common have no connectivity over that backbone.

   If all the sites in a VPN are owned by the same enterprise, the VPN
   is a corporate "intranet". If the various sites in a VPN are owned
   by different enterprises, the VPN is an "extranet". A site can be in
   more than one VPN; e.g., in an intranet and several extranets. We
   regard both intranets and extranets as VPNs. In general, when we use
   the term VPN we will not be distinguishing between intranets and
   extranets.

   We wish to consider the case in which the backbone is owned and
   operated by one or more Service Providers (SPs). The owners of the
   sites are the "customers" of the SPs. The policies that determine

whether a particular collection of sites is a VPN are the policies of
the customers. Some customers will want the implementation of these
policies to be entirely the responsibility of the SP. Other
customers may want to implement these policies themselves, or to
share with the SP the responsibility for implementing these policies.
In this document, we are primarily discussing mechanisms that may be
used to implement these policies. The mechanisms we describe are
general enough to allow these policies to be implemented either by
the SP alone, or by a VPN customer together with the SP. Most of the
discussion is focused on the former case, however.

The mechanisms discussed in this document allow the implementation of
a wide range of policies. For example, within a given VPN, we can
allow every site to have a direct route to every other site ("full
mesh"), or we can restrict certain pairs of sites from having direct
routes to each other ("partial mesh").

In this document, we are particularly interested in the case where
the common backbone offers an IP service. We are primarily concerned
with the case in which an enterprise is outsourcing its backbone to a
service provider, or perhaps to a set of service providers, with
which it maintains contractual relationships. We are not focused on
providing VPNs over the public Internet.

In the rest of this introduction, we specify some properties which
VPNs should have. The remainder of this document outlines a VPN
model which has all these properties. The VPN Model of this document
appears to be an instance of the framework described in [4].

1.2. Edge Devices

We suppose that at each site, there are one or more Customer Edge
(CE) devices, each of which is attached via some sort of data link
(e.g., PPP, ATM, ethernet, Frame Relay, GRE tunnel, etc.) to one or
more Provider Edge (PE) routers.

If a particular site has a single host, that host may be the CE
device. If a particular site has a single subnet, that the CE device
may be a switch. In general, the CE device can be expected to be a
router, which we call the CE router.

We will say that a PE router is attached to a particular VPN if it is
attached to a CE device which is in that VPN. Similarly, we will say
that a PE router is attached to a particular site if it is attached
to a CE device which is in that site.

When the CE device is a router, it is a routing peer of the PE(s) to
which it is attached, but is not a routing peer of CE routers at

other sites. Routers at different sites do not directly exchange
routing information with each other; in fact, they do not even need
to know of each other at all (except in the case where this is
necessary for security purposes, see section 9). As a consequence,
very large VPNs (i.e., VPNs with a very large number of sites) are
easily supported, while the routing strategy for each individual site
is greatly simplified.

It is important to maintain clear administrative boundaries between
the SP and its customers (cf. [4]). The PE and P routers should be
administered solely by the SP, and the SP's customers should not have
any management access to it. The CE devices should be administered
solely by the customer (unless the customer has contracted the
management services out to the SP).

1.3. VPNs with Overlapping Address Spaces

We assume that any two non-intersecting VPNs (i.e., VPNs with no
sites in common) may have overlapping address spaces; the same
address may be reused, for different systems, in different VPNs. As
long as a given endsystem has an address which is unique within the
scope of the VPNs that it belongs to, the endsystem itself does not
need to know anything about VPNs.

In this model, the VPN owners do not have a backbone to administer,
not even a "virtual backbone". Nor do the SPs have to administer a
separate backbone or "virtual backbone" for each VPN. Site-to-site
routing in the backbone is optimal (within the constraints of the
policies used to form the VPNs), and is not constrained in any way by
an artificial "virtual topology" of tunnels.

1.4. VPNs with Different Routes to the Same System

Although a site may be in multiple VPNs, it is not necessarily the
case that the route to a given system at that site should be the same
in all the VPNs. Suppose, for example, we have an intranet
consisting of sites A, B, and C, and an extranet consisting of A, B,
C, and the "foreign" site D. Suppose that at site A there is a
server, and we want clients from B, C, or D to be able to use that
server. Suppose also that at site B there is a firewall. We want
all the traffic from site D to the server to pass through the
firewall, so that traffic from the extranet can be access controlled.
However, we don't want traffic from C to pass through the firewall on
the way to the server, since this is intranet traffic.

This means that it needs to be possible to set up two routes to the
server. One route, used by sites B and C, takes the traffic directly
to site A. The second route, used by site D, takes the traffic

instead to the firewall at site B. If the firewall allows the
traffic to pass, it then appears to be traffic coming from site B,
and follows the route to site A.

1.5. Multiple Forwarding Tables in PEs

Each PE router needs to maintain a number of separate forwarding
tables. Every site to which the PE is attached must be mapped to one
of those forwarding tables. When a packet is received from a
particular site, the forwarding table associated with that site is
consulted in order to determine how to route the packet. The
forwarding table associated with a particular site S is populated
only with routes that lead to other sites which have at least one VPN
in common with S. This prevents communication between sites which
have no VPN in common, and it allows two VPNs with no site in common
to use address spaces that overlap with each other.

1.6. SP Backbone Routers

The SP's backbone consists of the PE routers, as well as other
routers (P routers) which do not attach to CE devices.

If every router in an SP's backbone had to maintain routing
information for all the VPNs supported by the SP, this model would
have severe scalability problems; the number of sites that could be
supported would be limited by the amount of routing information that
could be held in a single router. It is important to require
therefore that the routing information about a particular VPN be
present ONLY in those PE routers which attach to that VPN. In
particular, the P routers should not need to have ANY per-VPN routing
information whatsoever.

VPNs may span multiple service providers. We assume though that when
the path between PE routers crosses a boundary between SP networks,
it does so via a private peering arrangement, at which there exists
mutual trust between the two providers. In particular, each provider
must trust the other to pass it only correct routing information, and
to pass it labeled (in the sense of MPLS [9]) packets only if those
packets have been labeled by trusted sources. We also assume that it
is possible for label switched paths to cross the boundary between
service providers.

1.7. Security

A VPN model should, even without the use of cryptographic security
measures, provide a level of security equivalent to that obtainable
when a level 2 backbone (e.g., Frame Relay) is used. That is, in the
absence of misconfiguration or deliberate interconnection of

different VPNs, it should not be possible for systems in one VPN to
gain access to systems in another VPN.

It should also be possible to deploy standard security procedures.

2. Sites and CEs

From the perspective of a particular backbone network, a set of IP
systems constitutes a site if those systems have mutual IP
interconnectivity, and communication between them occurs without use
of the backbone. In general, a site will consist of a set of systems
which are in geographic proximity. However, this is not universally
true; two geographic locations connected via a leased line, over
which OSPF is running, will constitute a single site, because
communication between the two locations does not involve the use of
the backbone.

A CE device is always regarded as being in a single site (though as
we shall see, a site may consist of multiple "virtual sites"). A
site, however, may belong to multiple VPNs.

A PE router may attach to CE devices in any number of different
sites, whether those CE devices are in the same or in different VPNs.
A CE device may, for robustness, attach to multiple PE routers, of
the same or of different service providers. If the CE device is a
router, the PE router and the CE router will appear as router
adjacencies to each other.

While the basic unit of interconnection is the site, the architecture
described herein allows a finer degree of granularity in the control
of interconnectivity. For example, certain systems at a site may be
members of an intranet as well as members of one or more extranets,
while other systems at the same site may be restricted to being
members of the intranet only.

3. Per-Site Forwarding Tables in the PEs

Each PE router maintains one or more "per-site forwarding tables".
Every site to which the PE router is attached is associated with one
of these tables. A particular packet's IP destination address is
looked up in a particular per-site forwarding table only if that
packet has arrived directly from a site which is associated with that
table.

How are the per-site forwarding tables populated?

As an example, let PE1, PE2, and PE3 be three PE routers, and let
CE1, CE2, and CE3 be three CE routers. Suppose that PE1 learns, from
CE1, the routes which are reachable at CE1's site. If PE2 and PE3
are attached respectively to CE2 and CE3, and there is some VPN V
containing CE1, CE2, and CE3, then PE1 uses BGP to distribute to PE2
and PE3 the routes which it has learned from CE1. PE2 and PE3 use
these routes to populate the forwarding tables which they associate
respectively with the sites of CE2 and CE3. Routes from sites which
are not in VPN V do not appear in these forwarding tables, which
means that packets from CE2 or CE3 cannot be sent to sites which are
not in VPN V.

If a site is in multiple VPNs, the forwarding table associated with
that site can contain routes from the full set of VPNs of which the
site is a member.

A PE generally maintains only one forwarding table per site, even if
it is multiply connected to that site. Also, different sites can
share the same forwarding table if they are meant to use exactly the
same set of routes.

Suppose a packet is received by a PE router from a particular
directly attached site, but the packet's destination address does not
match any entry in the forwarding table associated with that site.
If the SP is not providing Internet access for that site, then the
packet is discarded as undeliverable. If the SP is providing
Internet access for that site, then the PE's Internet forwarding
table will be consulted. This means that in general, only one
forwarding table per PE need ever contain routes from the Internet,
even if Internet access is provided.

To maintain proper isolation of one VPN from another, it is important
that no router in the backbone accept a labeled packet from any
adjacent non-backbone device unless (a) the label at the top of the
label stack was actually distributed by the backbone router to the
non-backbone device, and (b) the backbone router can determine that
use of that label will cause the packet to leave the backbone before
any labels lower in the stack will be inspected, and before the IP
header will be inspected. These restrictions are necessary in order
to prevent packets from entering a VPN where they do not belong.

The per-site forwarding tables in a PE are ONLY used for packets
which arrive from a site which is directly attached to the PE. They
are not used for routing packets which arrive from other routers that
belong to the SP backbone. As a result, there may be multiple
different routes to the same system, where the route followed by a
given packet is determined by the site from which the packet enters
the backbone. E.g., one may have one route to a given system for

packets from the extranet (where the route leads to a firewall), and
a different route to the same system for packets from the intranet
(including packets that have already passed through the firewall).

3.1. Virtual Sites

In some cases, a particular site may be divided by the customer into
several virtual sites, perhaps by the use of VLANs. Each virtual
site may be a member of a different set of VPNs. The PE then needs to
contain a separate forwarding table for each virtual site. For
example, if a CE supports VLANs, and wants each VLAN mapped to a
separate VPN, the packets sent between CE and PE could be contained
in the site's VLAN encapsulation, and this could be used by the PE,
along with the interface over which the packet is received, to assign
the packet to a particular virtual site.

Alternatively, one could divide the interface into multiple "sub-
interfaces" (particularly if the interface is Frame Relay or ATM),
and assign the packet to a VPN based on the sub-interface over which
it arrives. Or one could simply use a different interface for each
virtual site. In any case, only one CE router is ever needed per
site, even if there are multiple virtual sites. Of course, a
different CE router could be used for each virtual site, if that is
desired.

Note that in all these cases, the mechanisms, as well as the policy,
for controlling which traffic is in which VPN are in the hand of the
customer.

If it is desired to have a particular host be in multiple virtual
sites, then that host must determine, for each packet, which virtual
site the packet is associated with. It can do this, e.g., by sending
packets from different virtual sites on different VLANs, our out
different network interfaces.

These schemes do NOT require the CE to support MPLS. Section 8
contains a brief discussion of how the CE might support multiple
virtual sites if it does support MPLS.

4. VPN Route Distribution via BGP

PE routers use BGP to distribute VPN routes to each other (more
accurately, to cause VPN routes to be distributed to each other).

A BGP speaker can only install and distribute one route to a given
address prefix. Yet we allow each VPN to have its own address space,
which means that the same address can be used in any number of VPNs,
where in each VPN the address denotes a different system. It follows

that we need to allow BGP to install and distribute multiple routes
to a single IP address prefix. Further, we must ensure that POLICY
is used to determine which sites can be use which routes; given that
several such routes are installed by BGP, only one such must appear
in any particular per-site forwarding table.

We meet these goals by the use of a new address family, as specified
below.

4.1. The VPN-IPv4 Address Family

The BGP Multiprotocol Extensions [3] allow BGP to carry routes from
multiple "address families". We introduce the notion of the "VPN-
IPv4 address family". A VPN-IPv4 address is a 12-byte quantity,
beginning with an 8-byte "Route Distinguisher (RD)" and ending with a
4-byte IPv4 address. If two VPNs use the same IPv4 address prefix,
the PEs translate these into unique VPN-IPv4 address prefixes. This
ensures that if the same address is used in two different VPNs, it is
possible to install two completely different routes to that address,
one for each VPN.

The RD does not by itself impose any semantics; it contains no
information about the origin of the route or about the set of VPNs to
which the route is to be distributed. The purpose of the RD is
solely to allow one to create distinct routes to a common IPv4
address prefix. Other means are used to determine where to
redistribute the route (see section 4.2).

The RD can also be used to create multiple different routes to the
very same system. In section 3, we gave an example where the route
to a particular server had to be different for intranet traffic than
for extranet traffic. This can be achieved by creating two different
VPN-IPv4 routes that have the same IPv4 part, but different RDs.
This allows BGP to install multiple different routes to the same
system, and allows policy to be used (see section 4.2.3) to decide
which packets use which route.

The RDs are structured so that every service provider can administer
its own "numbering space" (i.e., can make its own assignments of
RDs), without conflicting with the RD assignments made by any other
service provider. An RD consists of a two-byte type field, an
administrator field, and an assigned number field. The value of the
type field determines the lengths of the other two fields, as well as
the semantics of the administrator field. The administrator field
identifies an assigned number authority, and the assigned number
field contains a number which has been assigned, by the identified
authority, for a particular purpose. For example, one could have an
RD whose administrator field contains an Autonomous System number

(ASN), and whose (4-byte) number field contains a number assigned by the SP to whom IANA has assigned that ASN. RDs are given this structure in order to ensure that an SP which provides VPN backbone service can always create a unique RD when it needs to do so. However, the structuring provides no semantics. When BGP compares two such address prefixes, it ignores the structure entirely.

If the Administrator subfield and the Assigned Number subfield of a VPN-IPv4 address are both set to all zeroes, the VPN-IPv4 address is considered to have exactly the same meaning as the corresponding globally unique IPv4 address. In particular, this VPN-IPv4 address and the corresponding globally unique IPv4 address will be considered comparable by BGP. In all other cases, a VPN-IPv4 address and its corresponding globally unique IPv4 address will be considered noncomparable by BGP.

A given per-site forwarding table will only have one VPN-IPv4 route for any given IPv4 address prefix. When a packet's destination address is matched against a VPN-IPv4 route, only the IPv4 part is actually matched.

A PE needs to be configured to associate routes which lead to particular CE with a particular RD. The PE may be configured to associate all routes leading to the same CE with the same RD, or it may be configured to associate different routes with different RDs, even if they lead to the same CE.

4.2. Controlling Route Distribution

In this section, we discuss the way in which the distribution of the VPN-IPv4 routes is controlled.

4.2.1. The Target VPN Attribute

Every per-site forwarding table is associated with one or more "Target VPN" attributes.

When a VPN-IPv4 route is created by a PE router, it is associated with one or more "Target VPN" attributes. These are carried in BGP as attributes of the route.

Any route associated with Target VPN T must be distributed to every PE router that has a forwarding table associated with Target VPN T. When such a route is received by a PE router, it is eligible to be installed in each of the PE's per-site forwarding tables that is associated with Target VPN T. (Whether it actually gets installed depends on the outcome of the BGP decision process.)

In essence, a Target VPN attribute identifies a set of sites.
Associating a particular Target VPN attribute with a route allows
that route to be placed in the per-site forwarding tables that are
used for routing traffic which is received from the corresponding
sites.

There is a set of Target VPNs that a PE router attaches to a route
received from site S. And there is a set of Target VPNs that a PE
router uses to determine whether a route received from another PE
router could be placed in the forwarding table associated with site
S. The two sets are distinct, and need not be the same.

The function performed by the Target VPN attribute is similar to that
performed by the BGP Communities Attribute. However, the format of
the latter is inadequate, since it allows only a two-byte numbering
space. It would be fairly straightforward to extend the BGP
Communities Attribute to provide a larger numbering space. It should
also be possible to structure the format, similar to what we have
described for RDs (see section 4.1), so that a type field defines the
length of an administrator field, and the remainder of the attribute
is a number from the specified administrator's numbering space.

When a BGP speaker has received two routes to the same VPN-IPv4
prefix, it chooses one, according to the BGP rules for route
preference.

Note that a route can only have one RD, but it can have multiple
Target VPNs. In BGP, scalability is improved if one has a single
route with multiple attributes, as opposed to multiple routes. One
could eliminate the Target VPN attribute by creating more routes
(i.e., using more RDs), but the scaling properties would be less
favorable.

How does a PE determine which Target VPN attributes to associate with
a given route? There are a number of different possible ways. The
PE might be configured to associate all routes that lead to a
particular site with a particular Target VPN. Or the PE might be
configured to associate certain routes leading to a particular site
with one Target VPN, and certain with another. Or the CE router,
when it distributes these routes to the PE (see section 6), might
specify one or more Target VPNs for each route. The latter method
shifts the control of the mechanisms used to implement the VPN
policies from the SP to the customer. If this method is used, it may
still be desirable to have the PE eliminate any Target VPNs that,
according to its own configuration, are not allowed, and/or to add in
some Target VPNs that according to its own configuration are
mandatory.

It might be more accurate, if less suggestive, to call this attribute the "Route Target" attribute instead of the "VPN Target" attribute. It really identifies only a set of sites which will be able to use the route, without prejudice to whether those sites constitute what might intuitively be called a VPN.

4.2.2. Route Distribution Among PEs by BGP

If two sites of a VPN attach to PEs which are in the same Autonomous System, the PEs can distribute VPN-IPv4 routes to each other by means of an IBGP connection between them. Alternatively, each can have an IBGP connection to a route reflector.

If two sites of VPN are in different Autonomous Systems (e.g., because they are connected to different SPs), then a PE router will need to use IBGP to redistribute VPN-IPv4 routes either to an Autonomous System Border Router (ASBR), or to a route reflector of which an ASBR is a client. The ASBR will then need to use EBGP to redistribute those routes to an ASBR in another AS. This allows one to connect different VPN sites to different Service Providers. However, VPN-IPv4 routes should only be accepted on EBGP connections at private peering points, as part of a trusted arrangement between SPs. VPN-IPv4 routes should neither be distributed to nor accepted from the public Internet.

If there are many VPNs having sites attached to different Autonomous Systems, there does not need to be a single ASBR between those two ASes which holds all the routes for all the VPNs; there can be multiple ASBRs, each of which holds only the routes for a particular subset of the VPNs.

When a PE router distributes a VPN-IPv4 route via BGP, it uses its own address as the "BGP next hop". It also assigns and distributes an MPLS label. (Essentially, PE routers distribute not VPN-IPv4 routes, but Labeled VPN-IPv4 routes. Cf. [8]) When the PE processes a received packet that has this label at the top of the stack, the PE will pop the stack, and send the packet directly to the site from to which the route leads. This will usually mean that it just sends the packet to the CE router from which it learned the route. The label may also determine the data link encapsulation.

In most cases, the label assigned by a PE will cause the packet to be sent directly to a CE, and the PE which receives the labeled packet will not look up the packet's destination address in any forwarding table. However, it is also possible for the PE to assign a label which implicitly identifies a particular forwarding table. In this case, the PE receiving a packet that label would look up the packet's destination address in one of its forwarding tables. While this can

be very useful in certain circumstances, we do not consider it
further in this paper.

Note that the MPLS label that is distributed in this way is only
usable if there is a label switched path between the router that
installs a route and the BGP next hop of that route. We do not make
any assumption about the procedure used to set up that label switched
path. It may be set up on a pre-established basis, or it may be set
up when a route which would need it is installed. It may be a "best
effort" route, or it may be a traffic engineered route. Between a
particular PE router and its BGP next hop for a particular route
there may be one LSP, or there may be several, perhaps with different
QoS characteristics. All that matters for the VPN architecture is
that some label switched path between the router and its BGP next hop
exists.

All the usual techniques for using route reflectors [2] to improve
scalability, e.g., route reflector hierarchies, are available. If
route reflectors are used, there is no need to have any one route
reflector know all the VPN-IPv4 routes for all the VPNs supported by
the backbone. One can have separate route reflectors, which do not
communicate with each other, each of which supports a subset of the
total set of VPNs.

If a given PE router is not attached to any of the Target VPNs of a
particular route, it should not receive that route; the other PE or
route reflector which is distributing routes to it should apply
outbound filtering to avoid sending it unnecessary routes. Of
course, if a PE router receives a route via BGP, and that PE is not
attached to any of the route's target VPNs, the PE should apply
inbound filtering to the route, neither installing nor redistributing
it.

A router which is not attached to any VPN, i.e., a P router, never
installs any VPN-IPv4 routes at all.

These distribution rules ensure that there is no one box which needs
to know all the VPN-IPv4 routes that are supported over the backbone.
As a result, the total number of such routes that can be supported
over the backbone is not bound by the capacity of any single device,
and therefore can increase virtually without bound.

4.2.3. The VPN of Origin Attribute

A VPN-IPv4 route may be optionally associated with a VPN of Origin
attribute. This attribute uniquely identifies a set of sites, and
identifies the corresponding route as having come from one of the
sites in that set. Typical uses of this attribute might be to

identify the enterprise which owns the site where the route leads, or
to identify the site's intranet. However, other uses are also
possible. This attribute could be encoded as an extended BGP
communities attribute.

In situations in which it is necessary to identify the source of a
route, it is this attribute, not the RD, which must be used. This
attribute may be used when "constructing" VPNs, as described below.

It might be more accurate, if less suggestive, to call this attribute
the "Route Origin" attribute instead of the "VPN of Origin"
attribute. It really identifies the route only has having come from
one of a particular set of sites, without prejudice as to whether
that particular set of sites really constitutes a VPN.

4.2.4. Building VPNs using Target and Origin Attributes

By setting up the Target VPN and VPN of Origin attributes properly,
one can construct different kinds of VPNs.

Suppose it is desired to create a Closed User Group (CUG) which
contains a particular set of sites. This can be done by creating a
particular Target VPN attribute value to represent the CUG. This
value then needs to be associated with the per-site forwarding tables
for each site in the CUG, and it needs to be associated with every
route learned from a site in the CUG. Any route which has this
Target VPN attribute will need to be redistributed so that it reaches
every PE router attached to one of the sites in the CUG.

Alternatively, suppose one desired, for whatever reason, to create a
"hub and spoke" kind of VPN. This could be done by the use of two
Target Attribute values, one meaning "Hub" and one meaning "Spoke".
Then routes from the spokes could be distributed to the hub, without
causing routes from the hub to be distributed to the spokes.

Suppose one has a number of sites which are in an intranet and an
extranet, as well as a number of sites which are in the intranet
only. Then there may be both intranet and extranet routes which have
a Target VPN identifying the entire set of sites. The sites which
are to have intranet routes only can filter out all routes with the
"wrong" VPN of Origin.

These two attributes allow great flexibility in allowing one to
control the distribution of routing information among various sets of
sites, which in turn provides great flexibility in constructing VPNs.

5. Forwarding Across the Backbone

   If the intermediate routes in the backbone do not have any
   information about the routes to the VPNs, how are packets forwarded
   from one VPN site to another?

   This is done by means of MPLS with a two-level label stack.

   PE routers (and ASBRs which redistribute VPN-IPv4 addresses) need to
   insert /32 address prefixes for themselves into the IGP routing
   tables of the backbone. This enables MPLS, at each node in the
   backbone network, to assign a label corresponding to the route to
   each PE router. (Certain procedures for setting up label switched
   paths in the backbone may not require the presence of the /32 address
   prefixes.)

   When a PE receives a packet from a CE device, it chooses a particular
   per-site forwarding table in which to look up the packet's
   destination address. Assume that a match is found.

   If the packet is destined for a CE device attached to this same PE,
   the packet is sent directly to that CE device.

   If the packet is not destined for a CE device attached to this same
   PE, the packet's "BGP Next Hop" is found, as well as the label which
   that BGP next hop assigned for the packet's destination address. This
   label is pushed onto the packet's label stack, and becomes the bottom
   label. Then the PE looks up the IGP route to the BGP Next Hop, and
   thus determines the IGP next hop, as well as the label assigned to
   the address of the BGP next hop by the IGP next hop. This label gets
   pushed on as the packet's top label, and the packet is then forwarded
   to the IGP next hop. (If the BGP next hop is the same as the IGP
   next hop, the second label may not need to be pushed on, however.)

   At this point, MPLS will carry the packet across the backbone and
   into the appropriate CE device. That is, all forwarding decisions by
   P routers and PE routers are now made by means of MPLS, and the
   packet's IP header is not looked at again until the packet reaches
   the CE device. The final PE router will pop the last label from the
   MPLS label stack before sending the packet to the CE device, thus the
   CE device will just see an ordinary IP packet. (Though see section 8
   for some discussion of the case where the CE desires to received
   labeled packets.)

   When a packet enters the backbone from a particular site via a
   particular PE router, the packet's route is determined by the
   contents of the forwarding table which that PE router associated with
   that site. The forwarding tables of the PE router where the packet

leaves the backbone are not relevant. As a result, one may have
multiple routes to the same system, where the particular route chosen
for a particular packet is based on the site from which the packet
enters the backbone.

Note that it is the two-level labeling that makes it possible to keep
all the VPN routes out of the P routers, and this in turn is crucial
to ensuring the scalability of the model. The backbone does not even
need to have routes to the CEs, only to the PEs.

6. How PEs Learn Routes from CEs

The PE routers which attach to a particular VPN need to know, for
each of that VPN's sites, which addresses in that VPN are at each
site.

In the case where the CE device is a host or a switch, this set of
addresses will generally be configured into the PE router attaching
to that device. In the case where the CE device is a router, there
are a number of possible ways that a PE router can obtain this set of
addresses.

The PE translates these addresses into VPN-IPv4 addresses, using a
configured RD. The PE then treats these VPN-IPv4 routes as input to
BGP. In no case will routes from a site ever be leaked into the
backbone's IGP.

Exactly which PE/CE route distribution techniques are possible
depends on whether a particular CE is in a "transit VPN" or not. A
"transit VPN" is one which contains a router that receives routes
from a "third party" (i.e., from a router which is not in the VPN,
but is not a PE router), and that redistributes those routes to a PE
router. A VPN which is not a transit VPN is a "stub VPN". The vast
majority of VPNs, including just about all corporate enterprise
networks, would be expected to be "stubs" in this sense.

The possible PE/CE distribution techniques are:

   1. Static routing (i.e., configuration) may be used. (This is
      likely to be useful only in stub VPNs.)

   2. PE and CE routers may be RIP peers, and the CE may use RIP to
      tell the PE router the set of address prefixes which are
      reachable at the CE router's site. When RIP is configured in
      the CE, care must be taken to ensure that address prefixes from
      other sites (i.e., address prefixes learned by the CE router
      from the PE router) are never advertised to the PE. More
      precisely: if a PE router, say PE1, receives a VPN-IPv4 route

R1, and as a result distributes an IPv4 route R2 to a CE, then
R2 must not be distributed back from that CE's site to a PE
router, say PE2, (where PE1 and PE2 may be the same router or
different routers), unless PE2 maps R2 to a VPN-IPv4 route
which is different than (i.e., contains a different RD than)
R1.

3. The PE and CE routers may be OSPF peers. In this case, the
   site should be a single OSPF area, the CE should be an ABR in
   that area, and the PE should be an ABR which is not in that
   area. Also, the PE should report no router links other than
   those to the CEs which are at the same site. (This technique
   should be used only in stub VPNs.)

4. The PE and CE routers may be BGP peers, and the CE router may
   use BGP (in particular, EBGP to tell the PE router the set of
   address prefixes which are at the CE router's site. (This
   technique can be used in stub VPNs or transit VPNs.)

   From a purely technical perspective, this is by far the best
   technique:

       a) Unlike the IGP alternatives, this does not require the
          PE to run multiple routing algorithm instances in order
          to talk to multiple CEs

       b) BGP is explicitly designed for just this function:
          passing routing information between systems run by
          different administrations

       c) If the site contains "BGP backdoors", i.e., routers
          with BGP connections to routers other than PE routers,
          this procedure will work correctly in all
          circumstances. The other procedures may or may not
          work, depending on the precise circumstances.

       d) Use of BGP makes it easy for the CE to pass attributes
          of the routes to the PE. For example, the CE may
          suggest a particular Target for each route, from among
          the Target attributes that the PE is authorized to
          attach to the route.

   On the other hand, using BGP is likely to be something new for
   the CE administrators, except in the case where the customer
   itself is already an Internet Service Provider (ISP).

If a site is not in a transit VPN, note that it need not have
a unique Autonomous System Number (ASN). Every CE whose site
which is not in a transit VPN can use the same ASN. This can
be chosen from the private ASN space, and it will be stripped
out by the PE. Routing loops are prevented by use of the Site
of Origin Attribute (see below).

If a set of sites constitute a transit VPN, it is convenient
to represent them as a BGP Confederation, so that the internal
structure of the VPN is hidden from any router which is not
within the VPN. In this case, each site in the VPN would need
two BGP connections to the backbone, one which is internal to
the confederation and one which is external to it. The usual
intra-confederation procedures would have to be slightly
modified in order to take account for the fact that the
backbone and the sites may have different policies. The
backbone is a member of the confederation on one of the
connections, but is not a member on the other. These
techniques may be useful if the customer for the VPN service
is an ISP. This technique allows a customer that is an ISP to
obtain VPN backbone service from one of its ISP peers.

(However, if a VPN customer is itself an ISP, and its CE
routers support MPLS, a much simpler technique can be used,
wherein the ISP is regarded as a stub VPN. See section 8.)

When we do not need to distinguish among the different ways in which
a PE can be informed of the address prefixes which exist at a given
site, we will simply say that the PE has "learned" the routes from
that site.

Before a PE can redistribute a VPN-IPv4 route learned from a site, it
must assign certain attributes to the route. There are three such
attributes:

- Site of Origin

  This attribute uniquely identifies the site from which the PE
  router learned the route. All routes learned from a particular
  site must be assigned the same Site of Origin attribute, even if
  a site is multiply connected to a single PE, or is connected to
  multiple PEs. Distinct Site of Origin attributes must be used
  for distinct sites. This attribute could be encoded as an
  extended BGP communities attribute (section 4.2.1).

- VPN of Origin

  See section 4.2.1.

        - Target VPN

        See section 4.2.1.

7. How CEs learn Routes from PEs

    In this section, we assume that the CE device is a router.

    In general, a PE may distribute to a CE any route which the PE has
    placed in the forwarding table which it uses to route packets from
    that CE. There is one exception: if a route's Site of Origin
    attribute identifies a particular site, that route must never be
    redistributed to any CE at that site.

    In most cases, however, it will be sufficient for the PE to simply
    distribute the default route to the CE. (In some cases, it may even
    be sufficient for the CE to be configured with a default route
    pointing to the PE.) This will generally work at any site which does
    not itself need to distribute the default route to other sites.
    (E.g., if one site in a corporate VPN has the corporation's access to
    the Internet, that site might need to have default distributed to the
    other site, but one could not distribute default to that site
    itself.)

    Whatever procedure is used to distribute routes from CE to PE will
    also be used to distribute routes from PE to CE.

8. What if the CE Supports MPLS?

    In the case where the CE supports MPLS, AND is willing to import the
    complete set of routes from its VPNs, the PE can distribute to it a
    label for each such route. When the PE receives a packet from the CE
    with such a label, it (a) replaces that label with the corresponding
    label that it learned via BGP, and (b) pushes on a label
    corresponding to the BGP next hop for the corresponding route.

8.1. Virtual Sites

    If the CE/PE route distribution is done via BGP, the CE can use MPLS
    to support multiple virtual sites. The CE may itself contain a
    separate forwarding table for each virtual site, which it populates
    as indicated by the VPN of Origin and Target VPN attributes of the
    routes it receives from the PE. If the CE receives the full set of
    routes from the PE, the PE will not need to do any address lookup at
    all on packets received from the CE. Alternatively, the PE may in
    some cases be able to distribute to the CE a single (labeled) default
    route for each VPN. Then when the PE receives a labeled packet from

the CE, it would know which forwarding table to look in; the label
placed on the packet by the CE would identify only the virtual site
from which the packet is coming.

8.2. Representing an ISP VPN as a Stub VPN

If a particular VPN is actually an ISP, but its CE routers support
MPLS, then the VPN can actually be treated as a stub VPN. The CE and
PE routers need only exchange routes which are internal to the VPN.
The PE router would distribute to the CE router a label for each of
these routes. Routers at different sites in the VPN can then become
BGP peers. When the CE router looks up a packet's destination
address, the routing lookup always resolves to an internal address,
usually the address of the packet's BGP next hop. The CE labels the
packet appropriately and sends the packet to the PE.

9. Security

Under the following conditions:

   a) labeled packets are not accepted by backbone routers from
      untrusted or unreliable sources, unless it is known that such
      packets will leave the backbone before the IP header or any
      labels lower in the stack will be inspected, and

   b) labeled VPN-IPv4 routes are not accepted from untrusted or
      unreliable sources,

the security provided by this architecture is virtually identical to
that provided to VPNs by Frame Relay or ATM backbones.

It is worth noting that the use of MPLS makes it much simpler to
provide this level of security than would be possible if one
attempted to use some form of IP-within-IP tunneling in place of
MPLS. It is a simple matter to refuse to accept a labeled packet
unless the first of the above conditions applies to it. It is rather
more difficult to configure the a router to refuse to accept an IP
packet if that packet is an IP-within-IP tunnelled packet which is
going to a "wrong" place.

The use of MPLS also allows a VPN to span multiple SPs without
depending in any way on the inter-domain distribution of IPv4 routing
information.

It is also possible for a VPN user to provide himself with enhanced
security by making use of Tunnel Mode IPSEC [5]. This is discussed
in the remainder of this section.

9.1. Point-to-Point Security Tunnels between CE Routers

A security-conscious VPN user might want to ensure that some or all
of the packets which traverse the backbone are authenticated and/or
encrypted. The standard way to obtain this functionality today would
be to create a "security tunnel" between every pair of CE routers in
a VPN, using IPSEC Tunnel Mode.

However, the procedures described so far do not enable the CE router
transmitting a packet to determine the identify of the next CE router
that the packet will traverse. Yet that information is required in
order to use Tunnel Mode IPSEC. So we must extend those procedures
to make this information available.

A way to do this is suggested in [6]. Every VPN-IPv4 route can have
an attribute which identifies the next CE router that will be
traversed if that route is followed. If this information is provided
to all the CE routers in the VPN, standard IPSEC Tunnel Mode can be
used.

If the CE and PE are BGP peers, it is natural to present this
information as a BGP attribute.

Each CE that is to use IPSEC should also be configured with a set of
address prefixes, such that it is prohibited from sending insecure
traffic to any of those addresses. This prevents the CE from sending
insecure traffic if, for some reason, it fails to obtain the
necessary information.

When MPLS is used to carry packets between the two endpoints of an
IPSEC tunnel, the IPSEC outer header does not really perform any
function. It might be beneficial to develop a form of IPSEC tunnel
mode which allows the outer header to be omitted when MPLS is used.

9.2. Multi-Party Security Associations

Instead of setting up a security tunnel between each pair of CE
routers, it may be advantageous to set up a single, multiparty
security association. In such a security association, all the CE
routers which are in a particular VPN would share the same security
parameters (.e.g., same secret, same algorithm, etc.). Then the
ingress CE wouldn't have to know which CE is the next one to receive
the data, it would only have to know which VPN the data is going to.
A CE which is in multiple VPNs could use different security
parameters for each one, thus protecting, e.g., intranet packets from
being exposed to the extranet.

With such a scheme, standard Tunnel Mode IPSEC could not be used, because there is no way to fill in the IP destination address field of the "outer header". However, when MPLS is used for forwarding, there is no real need for this outer header anyway; the PE router can use MPLS to get a packet to a tunnel endpoint without even knowing the IP address of that endpoint; it only needs to see the IP destination address of the "inner header".

A significant advantage of a scheme like this is that it makes routing changes (in particular, a change of egress CE for a particular address prefix) transparent to the security mechanism. This could be particularly important in the case of multi-provider VPNs, where the need to distribute information about such routing changes simply to support the security mechanisms could result in scalability issues.

Another advantage is that it eliminates the need for the outer IP header, since the MPLS encapsulation performs its role.

10. Quality of Service

Although not the focus of this paper, Quality of Service is a key component of any VPN service. In MPLS/BGP VPNs, existing L3 QoS capabilities can be applied to labeled packets through the use of the "experimental" bits in the shim header [10], or, where ATM is used as the backbone, through the use of ATM QoS capabilities. The traffic engineering work discussed in [1] is also directly applicable to MPLS/BGP VPNs. Traffic engineering could even be used to establish LSPs with particular QoS characteristics between particular pairs of sites, if that is desirable. Where an MPLS/BGP VPN spans multiple SPs, the architecture described in [7] may be useful. An SP may apply either intserv or diffserv capabilities to a particular VPN, as appropriate.

11. Scalability

We have discussed scalability issues throughout this paper. In this section, we briefly summarize the main characteristics of our model with respect to scalability.

The Service Provider backbone network consists of (a) PE routers, (b) BGP Route Reflectors, (c) P routers (which are neither PE routers nor Route Reflectors), and, in the case of multi-provider VPNs, (d) ASBRs.

P routers do not maintain any VPN routes. In order to properly
forward VPN traffic, the P routers need only maintain routes to the
PE routers and the ASBRs. The use of two levels of labeling is what
makes it possible to keep the VPN routes out of the P routers.

A PE router to maintains VPN routes, but only for those VPNs to which
it is directly attached.

Route reflectors and ASBRs can be partitioned among VPNs so that each
partition carries routes for only a subset of the VPNs provided by
the Service Provider. Thus no single Route Reflector or ASBR is
required to maintain routes for all the VPNs.

As a result, no single component within the Service Provider network
has to maintain all the routes for all the VPNs. So the total
capacity of the network to support increasing numbers of VPNs is not
limited by the capacity of any individual component.

12. Intellectual Property Considerations

Cisco Systems may seek patent or other intellectual property
protection for some of all of the technologies disclosed in this
document. If any standards arising from this document are or become
protected by one or more patents assigned to Cisco Systems, Cisco
intends to disclose those patents and license them on reasonable and
non-discriminatory terms.

13. Security Considerations

Security issues are discussed throughout this memo.

14. Acknowledgments

Significant contributions to this work have been made by Ravi
Chandra, Dan Tappan and Bob Thomas.

15. Authors' Addresses

Eric C. Rosen
Cisco Systems, Inc.
250 Apollo Drive
Chelmsford, MA, 01824

EMail: erosen@cisco.com

Yakov Rekhter
Cisco Systems, Inc.
170 Tasman Drive
San Jose, CA, 95134

EMail: yakov@cisco.com

16. References

[1] Awduche, Berger, Gan, Li, Swallow, and Srinavasan, "Extensions
    to RSVP for LSP Tunnels", Work in Progress.

[2] Bates, T. and R. Chandrasekaran, "BGP Route Reflection: An
    alternative to full mesh IBGP", RFC 1966, June 1996.

[3] Bates, T., Chandra, R., Katz, D. and Y. Rekhter, "Multiprotocol
    Extensions for BGP4", RFC 2283, February 1998.

[4] Gleeson, Heinanen, and Armitage, "A Framework for IP Based
    Virtual Private Networks", Work in Progress.

[5] Kent and Atkinson, "Security Architecture for the Internet
    Protocol", RFC 2401, November 1998.

[6] Li, "CPE based VPNs using MPLS", October 1998, Work in Progress.

[7] Li, T. and Y. Rekhter, "A Provider Architecture for
    Differentiated Services and Traffic Engineering (PASTE)", RFC
    2430, October 1998.

[8] Rekhter and Rosen, "Carrying Label Information in BGP4", Work in
    Progress.

[9] Rosen, Viswanathan, and Callon, "Multiprotocol Label Switching
    Architecture", Work in Progress.

[10] Rosen, Rekhter, Tappan, Farinacci, Fedorkow, Li, and Conta, "MPLS
     Label Stack Encoding", Work in Progress.

17. Full Copyright Statement

   Copyright (C) The Internet Society (1999). All Rights Reserved.

   This document and translations of it may be copied and furnished to
   others, and derivative works that comment on or otherwise explain it
   or assist in its implementation may be prepared, copied, published
   and distributed, in whole or in part, without restriction of any
   kind, provided that the above copyright notice and this paragraph are
   included on all such copies and derivative works. However, this
   document itself may not be modified in any way, such as by removing
   the copyright notice or references to the Internet Society or other
   Internet organizations, except as needed for the purpose of
   developing Internet standards in which case the procedures for
   copyrights defined in the Internet Standards process must be
   followed, or as required to translate it into languages other than
   English.

   The limited permissions granted above are perpetual and will not be
   revoked by the Internet Society or its successors or assigns.

   This document and the information contained herein is provided on an
   "AS IS" basis and THE INTERNET SOCIETY AND THE INTERNET ENGINEERING
   TASK FORCE DISCLAIMS ALL WARRANTIES, EXPRESS OR IMPLIED, INCLUDING
   BUT NOT LIMITED TO ANY WARRANTY THAT THE USE OF THE INFORMATION
   HEREIN WILL NOT INFRINGE ANY RIGHTS OR ANY IMPLIED WARRANTIES OF
   MERCHANTABILITY OR FITNESS FOR A PARTICULAR PURPOSE.

Network Working Group   D. Grossman
Request for Comments: 2684   Motorola, Inc.
Obsoletes: 1483   J. Heinanen
Category: Standards Track   Telia
                                                      September 1999

        Multiprotocol Encapsulation over ATM Adaptation Layer 5

Status of this Memo

Copyright Notice

Abstract

   This memo replaces RFC 1483. It describes two encapsulations methods
   for carrying network interconnect traffic over AAL type 5 over ATM.
   The first method allows multiplexing of multiple protocols over a
   single ATM virtual connection whereas the second method assumes that
   each protocol is carried over a separate ATM virtual connection.

Applicability

   This specification is intended to be used in implementations which
   use ATM networks to carry multiprotocol traffic among hosts, routers
   and bridges which are ATM end systems.

1. Introduction

   Asynchronous Transfer Mode (ATM) wide area, campus and local area
   networks are used to transport IP datagrams and other connectionless
   traffic between hosts, routers, bridges and other networking devices.
   This memo describes two methods for carrying connectionless routed
   and bridged Protocol Data Units (PDUs) over an ATM network. The "LLC
   Encapsulation" method allows multiplexing of multiple protocols over
   a single ATM virtual connection (VC). The protocol type of each PDU
   is identified by a prefixed IEEE 802.2 Logical Link Control (LLC)
   header. In the "VC Multiplexing" method, each ATM VC carries PDUs of
   exactly one protocol type. When multiple protocols need to be
   transported, there is a separate VC for each.

The unit of transport in ATM is a 53 octet fixed length PDU called a
cell. A cell consists of a 5 octet header and a 48 byte payload.
Variable length PDUs, including those addressed in this memo, must be
segmented by the transmitter to fit into the 48 octet ATM cell
payload, and reassembled by the receiver. This memo specifies the
use of the ATM Adaptation Layer type 5 (AAL5), as defined in ITU-T
Recommendation I.363.5 [2] for this purpose. Variable length PDUs are
carried in the Payload field of the AAL5 Common Part Convergence
Sublayer (CPCS) PDU.

This memo only describes how routed and bridged PDUs are carried
directly over the AAL5 CPCS, i.e., when the Service Specific
Convergence Sublayer (SSCS) of AAL5 is absent. If Frame Relay
Service Specific Convergence Sublayer (FR-SSCS), as defined in ITU-T
Recommendation I.365.1 [3], is used over the CPCS, then routed and
bridged PDUs are carried using the NLPID multiplexing method
described in RFC 2427 [4]. The RFC 2427 encapsulation MUST be used in
the special case that Frame Relay Network Interworking or transparent
mode Service Interworking [9] are used, but is NOT RECOMMENDED for
other applications. Appendix A (which is for information only) shows
the format of the FR-SSCS-PDU as well as how IP and CLNP PDUs are
encapsulated over FR-SSCS according to RFC 2427.

This memo also includes an optional encapsulation for use with
Virtual Private Networks that operate over an ATM subnet.

If it is desired to use the facilities which are designed for the
Point-to-Point Protocol (PPP), and there exists a point-to-point
relationship between peer systems, then RFC 2364, rather than this
memo, applies.

2. Conventions

The keywords MUST, MUST NOT, REQUIRED, SHALL, SHALL NOT, SHOULD,
SHOULD NOT, RECOMMENDED, NOT RECOMMENDED, MAY, and OPTIONAL, when
they appear in this document, are to be interpreted as described in
RFC 2119 [10].

3. Selection of the Multiplexing Method

The decision as to whether to use LLC encapsulation or VC-
multiplexing depends on implementation and system requirements. In
general, LLC encapsulation tends to require fewer VCs in a
multiprotocol environment. VC multiplexing tends to reduce
fragmentation overhead (e.g., an IPV4 datagram containing a TCP
control packet with neither IP nor TCP options exactly fits into a
single cell).

When two ATM end systems wish to exchange connectionless PDUs across
an ATM Permanent Virtual Connection (PVC), selection of the
multiplexing method is done by configuration. ATM connection control
signalling procedures are used to negotiate the encapsulation method
when ATM Switched Virtual Connections (SVCs) are to be used. [5] and
[8] specify how this negotiation is done.

4. AAL5 PDU Format

For both multiplexing methods, routed and bridged PDUs MUST be
encapsulated within the Payload field of an AAL5 CPCS-PDU.

ITU-T Recomendation I.363.5 [2] provides the complete definition of
the AAL5 PDU format and procedures at the sender and receiver. The
AAL5 message mode service, in the non-assured mode of operation MUST
be used. The corrupted delivery option MUST NOT be used. A
reassembly timer MAY be used. The following description is provided
for information.

The format of the AAL5 CPCS-PDU is shown below:

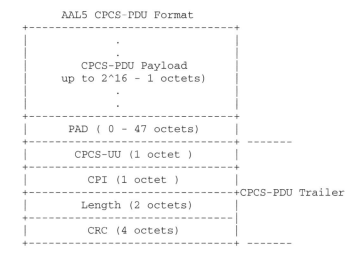

```
                    AAL5 CPCS-PDU Format
         +------------------------------+
         |              .               |
         |              .               |
         |      CPCS-PDU Payload        |
         |    up to 2^16 - 1 octets)    |
         |              .               |
         |              .               |
         +------------------------------+
         |     PAD ( 0 - 47 octets)     |
         +------------------------------+ -------
         |     CPCS-UU (1 octet )       |
         +------------------------------+
         |      CPI (1 octet )          |
         +------------------------------+CPCS-PDU Trailer
         |      Length (2 octets)       |
         +------------------------------|
         |       CRC (4 octets)         |
         +------------------------------+ -------
```

The Payload field contains user information up to 2^16 - 1 octets.

The PAD field pads the CPCS-PDU to fit exactly into the ATM cells
such that the last 48 octet cell payload created by the SAR sublayer
will have the CPCS-PDU Trailer right justified in the cell.

The CPCS-UU (User-to-User indication) field is used to transparently
transfer CPCS user to user information. The field is not used by the
multiprotocol ATM encapsulation described in this memo and MAY be set
to any value.

The CPI (Common Part Indicator) field aligns the CPCS-PDU trailer to
64 bits. This field MUST be coded as 0x00.

The Length field indicates the length, in octets, of the Payload
field. The maximum value for the Length field is 65535 octets. A
Length field coded as 0x00 is used for the abort function.

The CRC field is used to detect bit errors in the CPCS-PDU. A CRC-32
is used.

5.   LLC Encapsulation

LLC Encapsulation is needed when more than one protocol might be
carried over the same VC. In order to allow the receiver to properly
process the incoming AAL5 CPCS-PDU, the Payload Field contains
information necessary to identify the protocol of the routed or
bridged PDU. In LLC Encapsulation, this information MUST be encoded
in an LLC header placed in front of the carried PDU.

Although this memo only deals with protocols that operate over LLC
Type 1 (unacknowledged connectionless mode) service, the same
encapsulation principle also applies to protocols operating over LLC
Type 2 (connection-mode) service. In the latter case the format and
contents of the LLC header would be as described in IEEE 802.1 and
IEEE 802.2.

5.1. LLC Encapsulation for Routed Protocols

In LLC Encapsulation, the protocol type of routed PDUs MUST be
identified by prefixing an IEEE 802.2 LLC header to each PDU. In
some cases, the LLC header MUST be followed by an IEEE 802.1a
SubNetwork Attachment Point (SNAP) header. In LLC Type 1 operation,
the LLC header MUST consist of three one octet fields:

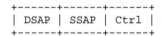
```
+------+------+------+
| DSAP | SSAP | Ctrl |
+------+------+------+
```

In LLC Encapsulation for routed protocols, the Control field MUST be
set to 0x03, specifying a Unnumbered Information (UI) Command PDU.

The LLC header value 0xFE-FE-03 MUST be used to identify a routed PDU in the ISO NLPID format (see [6] and Appendix B). For NLPID-formatted routed PDUs, the content of the AAL5 CPCS-PDU Payload field MUST be as follows:

Payload Format for Routed NLPID-formatted PDUs

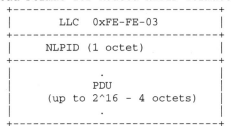

```
+------------------------------+
|      LLC  0xFE-FE-03         |
+------------------------------+
|      NLPID (1 octet)         |
+------------------------------+
|              .               |
|            PDU               |
|     (up to 2^16 - 4 octets)  |
|              .               |
+------------------------------+
```

The routed protocol MUST be identified by a one octet NLPID field that is part of Protocol Data. NLPID values are administered by ISO and ITU-T. They are defined in ISO/IEC TR 9577 [6] and some of the currently defined ones are listed in Appendix C.

An NLPID value of 0x00 is defined in ISO/IEC TR 9577 as the Null Network Layer or Inactive Set. Since it has no significance within the context of this encapsulation scheme, a NLPID value of 0x00 MUST NOT be used.

Although there is a NLPID value (0xCC) that indicates IP, the NLPID format MUST NOT be used for IP. Instead, IP datagrams MUST be identified by a SNAP header, as defined below.

The presence of am IEEE 802.1a SNAP header is indicated by the LLC header value 0xAA-AA-03. A SNAP header is of the form

```
+------+------+------+------+------+
|      OUI           |    PID     |
+------+------+------+------+------+
```

The SNAP header consists of a three octet Organizationally Unique Identifier (OUI) and a two octet Protocol Identifier (PID). The OUI is administered by IEEE and identifies an organization which administers the values which might be assigned to the PID. The SNAP header thus uniquely identifies a routed or bridged protocol. The OUI value 0x00-00-00 indicates that the PID is an EtherType.

The format of the AAL5 CPCS-PDU Payload field for routed non-NLPID
Formatted PDUs MUST be as follows:

```
      Payload Format for Routed non-NLPID formatted PDUs
      +-------------------------------+
      |      LLC   0xAA-AA-03         |
      +-------------------------------+
      |      OUI 0x00-00-00           |
      +-------------------------------+
      |    EtherType (2 octets)       |
      +-------------------------------+
      |                .              |
      |     Non-NLPID formatted PDU   |
      |      (up to 2^16 - 9 octets)  |
      |                .              |
      +-------------------------------+
```

In the particular case of an IPv4 PDU, the Ethertype value is 0x08-
00, and the payload format MUST be:

```
      Payload Format for Routed IPv4 PDUs
      +-------------------------------+
      |      LLC   0xAA-AA-03         |
      +-------------------------------+
      |      OUI 0x00-00-00           |
      +-------------------------------+
      |    EtherType 0x08-00          |
      +-------------------------------+
      |                .              |
      |         IPv4 PDU              |
      |      (up to 2^16 - 9 octets)  |
      |                .              |
      +-------------------------------+
```

This format is consistent with that defined in RFC 1042 [7].

5.2. LLC Encapsulation for Bridged Protocols

In LLC Encapsulation, bridged PDUs are encapsulated by identifying
the type of the bridged media in the SNAP header. The presence of
the SNAP header MUST be indicated by the LLC header value 0xAA-AA-03.
The OUI value in the SNAP header MUST be the 802.1 organization code
0x00-80-C2. The type of the bridged media MUST be specified by the
two octet PID. The PID MUST also indicate whether the original Frame
Check Sequence (FCS) is preserved within the bridged PDU. Appendix B
provides a list of media type (PID) values that can be used in ATM
encapsulation.

The AAL5 CPCS-PDU Payload field carrying a bridged PDU MUST have one
of the following formats. The necessary number of padding octets
MUST be added after the PID field in order to align the
Ethernet/802.3 LLC Data field, 802.4 Data Unit field, 802.5 Info
field, FDDI Info field or 802.6 Info field (respectively) of the
bridged PDU to begin at a four octet boundary. The bit ordering of
the MAC address MUST be the same as it would be on the LAN or MAN
(e.g., in canoncial form for bridged Ethernet/IEEE 802.3 PDUs, but in
802.5/FDDI format for bridged 802.5 PDUs).

Payload Format for Bridged Ethernet/802.3 PDUs

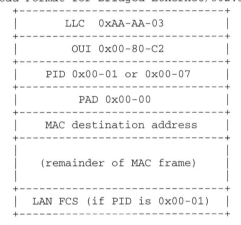

```
            +-------------------------------+
            |       LLC   0xAA-AA-03         |
            +-------------------------------+
            |        OUI 0x00-80-C2          |
            +-------------------------------+
            |    PID 0x00-01 or 0x00-07      |
            +-------------------------------+
            |        PAD 0x00-00             |
            +-------------------------------+
            |    MAC destination address    |
            +-------------------------------+
            |                               |
            |    (remainder of MAC frame)   |
            |                               |
            +-------------------------------+
            |  LAN FCS (if PID is 0x00-01)  |
            +-------------------------------+
```

The Ethernet/802.3 physical layer requires padding of frames to a
minimum size. A bridge that uses uses the Bridged Ethernet/802.3
encapsulation format with the preserved LAN FCS MUST include padding.
A bridge that uses the Bridged Ethernet/802.3 encapsulation format
without the preserved LAN FCS MAY either include padding, or omit it.
When a bridge receives a frame in this format without the LAN FCS, it
MUST be able to insert the necessary padding (if none is already
present) before forwarding to an Ethernet/802.3 subnetwork.

Payload Format for Bridged 802.4 PDUs
```
+-------------------------------+
|      LLC   0xAA-AA-03         |
+-------------------------------+
|       OUI 0x00-80-C2          |
+-------------------------------+
|   PID 0x00-02 or 0x00-08      |
+-------------------------------+
|      PAD 0x00-00-00           |
+-------------------------------+
|    Frame Control (1 octet)    |
+-------------------------------+
|   MAC destination address     |
+-------------------------------+
|                               |
|    (remainder of MAC frame)   |
|                               |
+-------------------------------+
|  LAN FCS (if PID is 0x00-02)  |
+-------------------------------+
```

Payload Format for Bridged 802.5 PDUs
```
+-------------------------------+
|      LLC   0xAA-AA-03         |
+-------------------------------+
|       OUI 0x00-80-C2          |
+-------------------------------+
|   PID 0x00-03 or 0x00-09      |
+-------------------------------+
|      PAD 0x00-00-XX           |
+-------------------------------+
|    Frame Control (1 octet)    |
+-------------------------------+
|   MAC destination address     |
+-------------------------------+
|                               |
|    (remainder of MAC frame)   |
|                               |
+-------------------------------+
|  LAN FCS (if PID is 0x00-03)  |
+-------------------------------+
```

Since the 802.5 Access Control (AC) field has no significance outside
the local 802.5 subnetwork, it is treated by this encapsulation as
the last octet of the three octet PAD field.   It MAY be set to any
value by the sending bridge and MUST be ignored by the receiving
bridge.

Payload Format for Bridged FDDI PDUs

```
+-------------------------------+
|      LLC   0xAA-AA-03         |
+-------------------------------+
|       OUI 0x00-80-C2          |
+-------------------------------+
|   PID 0x00-04 or 0x00-0A      |
+-------------------------------+
|       PAD 0x00-00-00          |
+-------------------------------+
|    Frame Control (1 octet)    |
+-------------------------------+
|    MAC destination address    |
+-------------------------------+
|                               |
|   (remainder of MAC frame)    |
|                               |
+-------------------------------+
|  LAN FCS (if PID is 0x00-04)  |
+-------------------------------+
```

Payload Format for Bridged 802.6 PDUs

```
+-------------------------------+
|      LLC   0xAA-AA-03         |
+-------------------------------+
|       OUI 0x00-80-C2          |
+-------------------------------+
|        PID 0x00-0B            |
+--------------+----------------+  ------
|   Reserved   |     BEtag      |  Common
+--------------+----------------+  PDU
|           BAsize              |  Header
+-------------------------------+  -------
|    MAC destination address    |
+-------------------------------+
|                               |
|   (remainder of MAC frame)    |
|                               |
+-------------------------------+
|                               |
|     Common PDU Trailer        |
|                               |
+-------------------------------+
```

In bridged 802.6 PDUs, the presence of a CRC-32 is indicated by the
CIB bit in the header of the MAC frame. Therefore, the same PID
value is used regardless of the presence or absence of the CRC-32 in
the PDU.

The Common Protocol Data Unit (PDU) Header and Trailer are conveyed
to allow pipelining at the egress bridge to an 802.6 subnetwork.
Specifically, the Common PDU Header contains the BAsize field, which
contains the length of the PDU. If this field is not available to
the egress 802.6 bridge, then that bridge cannot begin to transmit
the segmented PDU until it has received the entire PDU, calculated
the length, and inserted the length into the BAsize field. If the
field is available, the egress 802.6 bridge can extract the length
from the BAsize field of the Common PDU Header, insert it into the
corresponding field of the first segment, and immediately transmit
the segment onto the 802.6 subnetwork. Thus, the bridge can begin
transmitting the 802.6 PDU before it has received the complete PDU.

Note that the Common PDU Header and Trailer of the encapsulated frame
should not be simply copied to the outgoing 802.6 subnetwork because
the encapsulated BEtag value may conflict with the previous BEtag
value transmitted by that bridge.

An ingress 802.6 bridge can abort an AAL5 CPCS-PDU by setting its
Length field to zero. If the egress bridge has already begun
transmitting segments of the PDU to an 802.6 subnetwork and then
notices that the AAL5 CPCS-PDU has been aborted, it may immediately
generate an EOM cell that causes the 802.6 PDU to be rejected at the
receiving bridge. Such an EOM cell could, for example, contain an
invalid value in the Length field of the Common PDU Trailer.

```
                   Payload Format for BPDUs
         +-------------------------------+
         |     LLC   0xAA-AA-03          |
         +-------------------------------+
         |      OUI 0x00-80-C2           |
         +-------------------------------+
         |      PID 0x00-0E              |
         +-------------------------------+
         |                               |
         |    BPDU as defined by         |
         |    802.1(d) or 802.1(g)       |
         |                               |
         +-------------------------------+
```

6. VC Multiplexing

VC Multiplexing creates a binding between an ATM VC and the type of
the network protocol carried on that VC. Thus, there is no need for
protocol identification information to be carried in the payload of
each AAL5 CPCS-PDU. This reduces payload overhead and can reduce
per-packet processing. VC multiplexing can improve efficiency by
reducing the number of cells needed to carry PDUs of certain lengths.

For ATM PVCs, the type of the protocol to be carried over each PVC
MUST be determined by configuration. For ATM SVCs, the negotiations
specified in RFC 1755 [5] MUST be used.

6.1. VC Multiplexing of Routed Protocols

PDUs of routed protocols MUST be carried as the only content of the
Payload of the AAL5 CPCS-PDU. The format of the AAL5 CPCS-PDU
Payload field thus becomes:

Payload Format for Routed PDUs

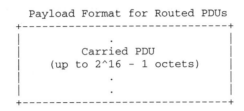

```
                     +------------------------------+
                     |               .              |
                     |         Carried PDU          |
                     |    (up to 2^16 - 1 octets)   |
                     |               .              |
                     |               .              |
                     +------------------------------+
```

6.2. VC Multiplexing of Bridged Protocols

PDUs of bridged protocols MUST be carried in the Payload of the AAL5
CPCS-PDU exactly as described in section 5.2, except that only the
fields after the PID field MUST be included. The AAL5 CPCS-PDU
Payload field carrying a bridged PDU MUST, therefore, have one of the
following formats.

Payload Format for Bridged Ethernet/802.3 PDUs

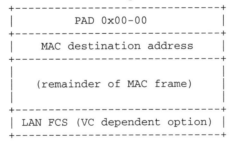

```
                   +------------------------------+
                   |         PAD 0x00-00          |
                   +------------------------------+
                   |    MAC destination address   |
                   +------------------------------+
                   |                              |
                   |    (remainder of MAC frame)  |
                   |                              |
                   +------------------------------+
                   | LAN FCS (VC dependent option)|
                   +------------------------------+
```

Payload Format for Bridged 802.4/802.5/FDDI PDUs

```
+------------------------------+
| PAD 0x00-00-00 or 0x00-00-XX |
+------------------------------+
|     Frame Control (1 octet)  |
+------------------------------+
|    MAC destination address   |
+------------------------------+
|                              |
|    (remainder of MAC frame)  |
|                              |
+------------------------------+
| LAN FCS (VC dependent option)|
+------------------------------+
```

Note that the 802.5 Access Control (AC) field has no significance
outside the local 802.5 subnetwork. It can thus be regarded as the
last octet of the three octet PAD field, which in case of 802.5 can
be set to any value (XX).

Payload Format for Bridged 802.6 PDUs

```
+---------------+---------------+  -------
|   Reserved    |     BEtag     |  Common
+---------------+---------------+  PDU
|             BAsize            |  Header
+------------------------------+  -------
|    MAC destination address   |
+------------------------------+
|                              |
|    (remainder of MAC frame)  |
|                              |
+------------------------------+
|                              |
|      Common PDU Trailer      |
|                              |
+------------------------------+
```

Payload Format for BPDUs

```
+------------------------------+
|                              |
|        BPDU as defined by    |
|        802.1(d) or 802.1(g)  |
|                              |
+------------------------------+
```

In case of Ethernet, 802.3, 802.4, 802.5, and FDDI PDUs the presense
or absence of the trailing LAN FCS shall be identified implicitly by
the VC, since the PID field is not included. PDUs with the LAN FCS
and PDUs without the LAN FCS are thus considered to belong to
different protocols even if the bridged media type would be the same.

7. Bridging in an ATM Network

    A bridge with an ATM interface that serves as a link to one or more
    other bridge MUST be able to flood, forward, and filter bridged PDUs.

    Flooding is performed by sending the PDU to all possible appropriate
    destinations. In the ATM environment this means sending the PDU
    through each relevant VC. This may be accomplished by explicitly
    copying it to each VC or by using a point-to-multipoint VC.

    To forward a PDU, a bridge MUST be able to associate a destination
    MAC address with a VC. It is unreasonable and perhaps impossible to
    require bridges to statically configure an association of every
    possible destination MAC address with a VC. Therefore, ATM bridges
    must provide enough information to allow an ATM interface to
    dynamically learn about foreign destinations beyond the set of ATM
    stations.

    To accomplish dynamic learning, a bridged PDU MUST conform to the
    encapsulation described in section 5. In this way, the receiving ATM
    interface will know to look into the bridged PDU and learn the
    association between foreign destination and an ATM station.

8. Virtual Private Network (VPN) identification

    The encapsulation defined in this section applies only to Virtual
    Private Networks (VPNs) that operate over an ATM subnet.

    A mechanism for globally unique identification of Virtual Private
    multiprotocol networks is defined in [11]. The 7-octet VPN-Id
    consists of a 3-octet VPN-related OUI (IEEE 802-1990 Organizationally
    Unique Identifier), followed by a 4-octet VPN index which is
    allocated by the owner of the VPN-related OUI. Typically, the VPN-
    related OUI value is assigned to a VPN service provider, which then
    allocates VPN index values for its customers.

8.1 VPN Encapsulation Header

The format of the VPN encapsulation header is as follows:

```
              VPN Encapsulation Header
       +-------------------------------+
       |      LLC  0xAA-AA-03          |
       +-------------------------------+
       |      OUI 0x00-00-5E           |
       +-------------------------------+
       |      PID 0x00-08              |
       +-------------------------------+
       |      PAD 0x00                 |
       +-------------------------------+
       |  VPN related OUI (3 octets)   |
       +-------------------------------+
       |  VPN Index (4 octets)         |
       +-------------------------------+
       |                               |
       |    (remainder of PDU)         |
       |                               |
       +-------------------------------+
```

When the encapsulation header is used, the remainder of the PDU MUST
be structured according to the appropiate format described in section
5 or 6 (i.e., the VPN encapsulation header is prepended to the PDU
within an AAL5 CPCS SDU).

8.2 LLC-encapsulated routed or bridged PDUs within a VPN

When a LLC-encapsulated routed or bridged PDU is sent within a VPN
using ATM over AAL5, a VPN encapsulation header MUST be prepended to
the appropriate routed or bridged PDU format defined in sections 5.1
and 5.2, respectively.

8.3 VC multiplexing of routed or bridged PDUs within a VPN

When a routed or bridged PDU is sent within a VPN using VC
multiplexing, the VPN identifier MAY either be specified a priori,
using ATM connection control signalling or adminstrative assignment
to an ATM interface, or it MAY be indicated using an encapsulation
header.

If the VPN is identified using ATM connection control signalling, all
PDUs carried by the ATM VC are associated with the same VPN. In this
case, the payload formats of routed and bridged PDUs MUST be as
defined in sections 6.1 and 6.2, respectively. If a PDU is received
containing a VPN encapsulation header when the VPN has been

identified using ATM signalling, the receiver MAY drop it and/or take
other actions which are implementation specific. Specification of
the mechanism in ATM connection control signalling for carrying VPN
identifiers is outside the scope of this Memo.

If a VPN identifier is administratively assigned to an ATM interface,
then all PDUs carried by any ATM VCs within that interface are
associated with that VPN. In this case, the payload formats of
routed and bridged PDUs MUST be as defined in sections 6.1 and 6.2,
respectively. If a PDU is received containing a VPN encapsulation
header when the VPN identifier has been administratively assigned,
the receiver MAY drop it and/or take other actions which are
implementation specific. Specification of mechanisms (such as MIBs)
for assigning VPN identifiers to ATM interfaces is outside the scope
of this memo.

If the VPN identifier is to be indicated using an encapsulation
header, then a VPN encapsulation header MUST be prepended to the
appropriate routed or bridged PDU format defined in sections 6.1 and
6.2, respectively.

9. Security Considerations

This memo defines mechanisms for multiprotocol encapsulation over
ATM. There is an element of trust in any encapsulation protocol: a
receiver must trust that the sender has correctly identified the
protocol being encapsulated. There is no way to ascertain that the
sender did use the proper protocol identification (nor would this be
desirable functionality). The encapsulation mechanisms described in
this memo are believed not to have any other properties that might be
exploited by an attacker. However, architectures and protocols
operating above the encapsulation layer may be subject to a variety
of attacks. In particular, the bridging architecture discussed in
section 7 has the same vulnerabilities as other bridging
architectures.

System security may be affected by the properties of the underlying
ATM network. The ATM Forum has published a security framework [12]
and a security specification [13] which may be relevant.

Acknowledgements

   This memo replaces RFC 1483, which was developed by the IP over ATM
   working group, and edited by Juha Heinanen (then at Telecom Finland,
   now at Telia). The update was developed in the IP-over-NBMA (ION)
   working group, and Dan Grossman (Motorola) was editor and also
   contributed to the work on RFC 1483.

   This material evolved from RFCs [1] and [4] from which much of the
   material has been adopted. Thanks to their authors Terry Bradley,
   Caralyn Brown, Andy Malis, Dave Piscitello, and C. Lawrence. Other
   key contributors to the work included Brian Carpenter (CERN), Rao
   Cherukuri (IBM), Joel Halpern (then at Network Systems), Bob Hinden
   (Sun Microsystems, presently at Nokia), and Gary Kessler (MAN
   Technology).

   The material concerning VPNs was developed by Barbara Fox (Lucent)
   and Bernhard Petri (Siemens).

References

   [1]   Piscitello, D. and C. Lawrence, "The Transmission of IP
         Datagrams over the SMDS Service", RFC 1209, March 1991.

   [2]   ITU-T Recommendation I.363.5, "B-ISDN ATM Adaptation Layer (AAL)
         Type 5 Specification", August 1996.

   [3]   ITU-T Recommendation I.365.1, "Frame Relaying Service Specific
         Convergence Sublayer (SSCS), November 1993.

   [4]   Brown, C. and A. Malis, "Multiprotocol Interconnect over Frame
         Relay", RFC 2427, September 1998.

   [5]   Perez M., Liaw, F., Mankin, E., Grossman, D. and A. Malis, "ATM
         Signalling Support for IP over ATM", RFC 1755, February 1995.

   [6]   Information technology - Telecommunications and Information
         Exchange Between Systems, "Protocol Identification in the
         Network Layer". ISO/IEC TR 9577, October 1990.

   [7]   Postel, J. and J. Reynolds, "A Standard for the Transmission of
         IP Datagrams over IEEE 802 Networks", STD 43, RFC 1042, February
         1988.

   [8]   Maher, M., "IP over ATM Signalling - SIG 4.0 Update", RFC 2331,
         April 1998.

[9]　ITU-T Recommendation I.555, "Frame Relay Bearer Service
　　　Interworking", September 1997.

[10] Bradner, S. "Key words for use in RFCs to Indicate Requirement
　　　Levels", BCP 14, RFC 2119, March 1997.

[11] Fox, B. and B. Gleeson, "Virtual Private Networks Identifier",
　　　RFC 2685, September 1999.

[12] The ATM Forum, "ATM Security Framework Version 1.0", af-sec-
　　　0096.000, February 1998.

[13] The ATM Forum, "ATM Security Specification v1.0", af-sec-
　　　0100.001, February 1999.

Appendix A. Multiprotocol Encapsulation over FR-SSCS

   ITU-T Recommendation I.365.1 defines a Frame Relaying Specific
   Convergence Sublayer (FR- SSCS) to be used on the top of the Common
   Part Convergence Sublayer CPCS) of the AAL type 5 for Frame Relay/ATM
   interworking. The service offered by FR-SSCS corresponds to the Core
   service for Frame Relaying as described in I.233.

   An FR-SSCS-PDU consists of Q.922 Address field followed by Q.922
   Information field. The Q.922 flags and the FCS are omitted, since
   the corresponding functions are provided by the AAL. The figure
   below shows an FR-SSCS-PDU embedded in the Payload of an AAL5 CPCS-
   PDU.

```
         FR-SSCS-PDU in Payload of AAL5 CPCS-PDU
       +-------------------------------+ -------
       |      Q.922 Address Field      | FR-SSCS-PDU Header
       |         (2-4 octets)          |
       +-------------------------------+ -------
       |                .              |
       |                .              |
       |     Q.922 Information field   | FR-SSCS-PDU Payload
       |                .              |
       |                .              |
       +-------------------------------+ -------
       |      AAL5 CPCS-PDU Trailer    |
       +-------------------------------+
```

   Routed and bridged PDUs are encapsulated inside the FR-SSCS-PDU as
   defined in RFC 2427. The Q.922 Information field starts with a Q.922
   Control field followed by an optional Pad octet that is used to align
   the remainder of the frame to a convenient boundary for the sender.
   The protocol of the carried PDU is then identified by prefixing the
   PDU by an ISO/IEC TR 9577 Network Layer Protocol ID (NLPID).

In the particular case of an IP PDU, the NLPID is 0xCC and the FR-
SSCS-PDU has the following format:

```
            FR-SSCS-PDU Format for Routed IP PDUs
        +-------------------------------+
        |         Q.922 Addr Field      |
        |         (2 or 4 octets)       |
        +-------------------------------+
        |      0x03 (Q.922 Control)     |
        +-------------------------------+
        |         NLPID  0xCC           |
        +-------------------------------+
        |                .              |
        |             IP PDU            |
        |     (up to 2^16 - 5 octets)   |
        |                .              |
        +-------------------------------+
```

Note that according to RFC 2427, the Q.922 Address field MUST be
either 2 or 4 octets, i.e., a 3 octet Address field MUST NOT be used.

In the particular case of a CLNP PDU, the NLPID is 0x81 and the FR-
SSCS-PDU has the following format:

```
           FR-SSCS-PDU Format for Routed CLNP PDUs
        +-------------------------------+
        |         Q.922 Addr Field      |
        |         (2 or 4 octets)       |
        +-------------------------------+
        |      0x03 (Q.922 Control)     |
        +-------------------------------+
        |         NLPID  0x81           |
        +-------------------------------+
        |                .              |
        |         Rest of CLNP PDU      |
        |     (up to 2^16 - 5 octets)   |
        |                .              |
        +-------------------------------+
```

Note that in case of ISO protocols the NLPID field forms the first
octet of the PDU itself and MUST not be repeated.

The above encapsulation applies only to those routed protocols that
have a unique NLPID assigned. For other routed protocols (and for
bridged protocols), it is necessary to provide another mechanism for
easy protocol identification. This can be achieved by using an NLPID
value 0x80 to indicate that an IEEE 802.1a SubNetwork Attachment
Point (SNAP) header follows.

See RFC 2427 for more details related to multiprotocol encapsulation over FRCS.

Appendix B.   List of Locally Assigned values of OUI 00-80-C2

with preserved FCS	w/o preserved FCS	Media
0x00-01	0x00-07	802.3/Ethernet
0x00-02	0x00-08	802.4
0x00-03	0x00-09	802.5
0x00-04	0x00-0A	FDDI
0x00-05	0x00-0B	802.6
	0x00-0D	Fragments
	0x00-0E	BPDUs

Appendix C.   Partial List of NLPIDs

0x00	Null Network Layer or Inactive Set (not used with ATM)
0x80	SNAP
0x81	ISO CLNP
0x82	ISO ESIS
0x83	ISO ISIS
0xCC	Internet IP

Appendix D. Applications of multiprotocol encapsulation

Mutiprotocol encapsulation is necessary, but generally not sufficient, for routing and bridging over the ATM networks.   Since the publication of RFC 1483 (the predecessor of this memo), several system specifications were developed by the IETF and the ATM Forum to address various aspects of, or scenarios for, bridged or routed protocols.   This appendix summarizes these applications.

1) Point-to-point connection between routers and bridges -- multiprotocol encapsulation over ATM PVCs has been used to provide a simple point-to-point link between bridges and routers across an ATM network.   Some amount of manual configuration (e.g., in lieu of INARP) was necessary in these scenarios.

2) Classical IP over ATM -- RFC 2225 (formerly RFC 1577) provides an environment where the ATM network serves as a logical IP subnet (LIS). ATM PVCs are supported, with address resolution provided by INARP.   For ATM SVCs, a new form of ARP, ATMARP, operates over the ATM network between a host (or router) and an ATMARP server. Where servers are replicated to provide higher availability or performance, a Server Synchronization Cache Protocol (SCSP) defined in RFC 2335 is used. Classical IP over ATM defaults to the LLC/SNAP encapsulation.

3) LAN Emulation -- The ATM Forum LAN Emulation specification
   provides an environment where the ATM network is enhanced by LAN
   Emulation Server(s) to behave as a bridged LAN. Stations obtain
   configuration information from, and register with, a LAN Emulation
   Configuration Server; they resolve MAC addresses to ATM addresses
   through the services of a LAN Emulation Server; they can send
   broadcast and multicast frames, and also send unicast frames for
   which they have no direct VC to a Broadcast and Unicast Server.
   LANE uses the VC multiplexing encapsulation foramts for Bridged
   Etherent/802.3 (without LAN FCS) or Bridged 802.5 (without LAN
   FCS) for the Data Direct, LE Multicast Send and Multicast Forward
   VCCS. However, the initial PAD field described in this memo is
   used as an LE header, and might not be set to all '0'.

4) Next Hop Resolution Protocol (NHRP) -- In some cases, the
   constraint that Classical IP over ATM serve a single LIS limits
   performance. NHRP, as defined in RFC 2332, extends Classical to
   allow 'shortcuts' over a an ATM network that supports several
   LISs.

5) Multiprotocol over ATM (MPOA) -- The ATM Forum Multiprotocol over
   ATM Specification integrates LANE and NHRP to provide a generic
   bridging/routing environment.

6) IP Multicast -- RFC 2022 extends Classical IP to support IP
   multicast. A multicast address resolution server (MARS) is used
   possibly in conjunction with a multicast server to provide IP
   multicast behavior over ATM point-to-multipoint and/or point to
   point virtual connections.

7) PPP over ATM -- RFC 2364 extends multiprotocol over ATM to the
   case where the encapsulated protocol is the Point-to-Point
   protocols. Both the VC based multiplexing and LLC/SNAP
   encapsulations are used. This approach is used when the ATM
   network is used as a point-to-point link and PPP functions are
   required.

Appendix E Differences from RFC 1483

This memo replaces RFC 1483. It was intended to remove anachronisms,
provide clarifications of ambiguities discovered by implementors or
created by changes to the base standards, and advance this work
through the IETF standards track process. A number of editorial
improvements were made, the RFC 2119 [10] conventions applied, and
the current RFC boilerplate added. The following substantive changes
were made. None of them is believed to obsolete implementations of
RFC 1483:

-- usage of NLPID encapsulation is clarified in terms of the RFC 2119 conventions

-- a pointer to RFC 2364 is added to cover the case of PPP over ATM

-- RFC 1755 and RFC 2331 are referenced to describe how encapsulations are negotiated, rather than a long-obsolete CCITT (now ITU-T) working document and references to work then in progress

-- usage of AAL5 is now a reference to ITU-T I.363.5. Options created in AAL5 since the publication of RFC 1483 are selected.

-- formatting of routed NLPID-formatted PDUs (which are called "routed ISO PDUs" in RFC 1483) is clarified

-- clarification is provided concerning the use of padding between the PID and MAC destination address in bridged PDUs and the bit ordering of the MAC address.

-- clarification is provided concerning the use of padding of Ethernet/802.3 frames

-- a new encapuslation for VPNs is added

-- substantive security considerations were added

-- a new appendix D provides a summary of applications of multiprotocol over ATM

Authors' Addresses

Dan Grossman
Motorola, Inc.
20 Cabot Blvd.
Mansfield, MA 02048

EMail: dan@dma.isg.mot.com

Juha Heinanen
Telia Finland
Myyrmaentie 2
01600 Vantaa, Finland

EMail: jh@telia.fi

Full Copyright Statement

Acknowledgement

Funding for the RFC Editor function is currently provided by the
Internet Society.

Network Working Group   D. Awduche
Request for Comments: 2702   J. Malcolm
Category: Informational   J. Agogbua
                                                            M. O'Dell
                                                            J. McManus
                                                    UUNET (MCI Worldcom)
                                                       September 1999

Requirements for Traffic Engineering Over MPLS

Status of this Memo

Copyright Notice

Abstract

   This document presents a set of requirements for Traffic Engineering
   over Multiprotocol Label Switching (MPLS). It identifies the
   functional capabilities required to implement policies that
   facilitate efficient and reliable network operations in an MPLS
   domain. These capabilities can be used to optimize the utilization of
   network resources and to enhance traffic oriented performance
   characteristics.

Table of Contents

1.0 Introduction

Multiprotocol Label Switching (MPLS) [1,2] integrates a label
swapping framework with network layer routing. The basic idea
involves assigning short fixed length labels to packets at the
ingress to an MPLS cloud (based on the concept of forwarding
equivalence classes [1,2]). Throughout the interior of the MPLS
domain, the labels attached to packets are used to make forwarding
decisions (usually without recourse to the original packet headers).

A set of powerful constructs to address many critical issues in the
emerging differentiated services Internet can be devised from this
relatively simple paradigm. One of the most significant initial
applications of MPLS will be in Traffic Engineering. The importance
of this application is already well-recognized (see [1,2,3]).

This manuscript is exclusively focused on the Traffic Engineering
applications of MPLS. Specifically, the goal of this document is to
highlight the issues and requirements for Traffic Engineering in a
large Internet backbone. The expectation is that the MPLS
specifications, or implementations derived therefrom, will address

the realization of these objectives. A description of the basic
capabilities and functionality required of an MPLS implementation to
accommodate the requirements is also presented.

It should be noted that even though the focus is on Internet
backbones, the capabilities described in this document are equally
applicable to Traffic Engineering in enterprise networks. In general,
the capabilities can be applied to any label switched network under
a single technical administration in which at least two paths exist
between two nodes.

Some recent manuscripts have focused on the considerations pertaining
to Traffic Engineering and Traffic management under MPLS, most
notably the works of Li and Rekhter [3], and others. In [3], an
architecture is proposed which employs MPLS and RSVP to provide
scalable differentiated services and Traffic Engineering in the
Internet. The present manuscript complements the aforementioned and
similar efforts. It reflects the authors' operational experience in
managing a large Internet backbone.

1.1 Terminology

The reader is assumed to be familiar with the MPLS terminology as
defined in [1].

The key words "MUST", "MUST NOT", "REQUIRED", "SHALL", "SHALL NOT",
"SHOULD", "SHOULD NOT", "RECOMMENDED", "MAY", and "OPTIONAL" in this
document are to be interpreted as described in RFC 2119 [11].

1.2 Document Organization

The remainder of this document is organized as follows: Section 2
discusses the basic functions of Traffic Engineering in the Internet.
Section 3, provides an overview of the traffic Engineering potentials
of MPLS. Sections 1 to 3 are essentially background material. Section
4 presents an overview of the fundamental requirements for Traffic
Engineering over MPLS. Section 5 describes the desirable attributes
and characteristics of traffic trunks which are pertinent to Traffic
Engineering. Section 6 presents a set of attributes which can be
associated with resources to constrain the routability of traffic
trunks and LSPs through them. Section 7 advocates the introduction of
a "constraint-based routing" framework in MPLS domains. Finally,
Section 8 contains concluding remarks.

2.0 Traffic Engineering

   This section describes the basic functions of Traffic Engineering in
   an Autonomous System in the contemporary Internet. The limitations of
   current IGPs with respect to traffic and resource control are
   highlighted. This section serves as motivation for the requirements
   on MPLS.

   Traffic Engineering (TE) is concerned with performance optimization
   of operational networks. In general, it encompasses the application
   of technology and scientific principles to the measurement, modeling,
   characterization, and control of Internet traffic, and the
   application of such knowledge and techniques to achieve specific
   performance objectives. The aspects of Traffic Engineering that are
   of interest concerning MPLS are measurement and control.

   A major goal of Internet Traffic Engineering is to facilitate
   efficient and reliable network operations while simultaneously
   optimizing network resource utilization and traffic performance.
   Traffic Engineering has become an indispensable function in many
   large Autonomous Systems because of the high cost of network assets
   and the commercial and competitive nature of the Internet. These
   factors emphasize the need for maximal operational efficiency.

2.1 Traffic Engineering Performance Objectives

   The key performance objectives associated with traffic engineering
   can be classified as being either:

   1. traffic oriented or

   2. resource oriented.

   Traffic oriented performance objectives include the aspects that
   enhance the QoS of traffic streams. In a single class, best effort
   Internet service model, the key traffic oriented performance
   objectives include: minimization of packet loss, minimization of
   delay, maximization of throughput, and enforcement of service level
   agreements. Under a single class best effort Internet service model,
   minimization of packet loss is one of the most important traffic
   oriented performance objectives. Statistically bounded traffic
   oriented performance objectives (such as peak to peak packet delay
   variation, loss ratio, and maximum packet transfer delay) might
   become useful in the forthcoming differentiated services Internet.

   Resource oriented performance objectives include the aspects
   pertaining to the optimization of resource utilization. Efficient
   management of network resources is the vehicle for the attainment of

resource oriented performance objectives. In particular, it is
generally desirable to ensure that subsets of network resources do
not become over utilized and congested while other subsets along
alternate feasible paths remain underutilized. Bandwidth is a crucial
resource in contemporary networks.   Therefore, a central function of
Traffic Engineering is to efficiently manage bandwidth resources.

Minimizing congestion is a primary traffic and resource oriented
performance objective.   The interest here is on congestion problems
that are prolonged rather than on transient congestion resulting from
instantaneous bursts.   Congestion typically manifests under two
scenarios:

1. When network resources are insufficient or inadequate to
   accommodate offered load.

2. When traffic streams are inefficiently mapped onto available
   resources; causing subsets of network resources to become
   over-utilized while others remain underutilized.

The first type of congestion problem can be addressed by either: (i)
expansion of capacity, or (ii) application of classical congestion
control techniques, or (iii) both. Classical congestion control
techniques attempt to regulate the demand so that the traffic fits
onto available resources. Classical techniques for congestion control
include: rate limiting, window flow control, router queue management,
schedule-based control, and others; (see [8] and the references
therein).

The second type of congestion problems, namely those resulting from
inefficient resource allocation, can usually be addressed through
Traffic Engineering.

In general, congestion resulting from inefficient resource allocation
can be reduced by adopting load balancing policies. The objective of
such strategies is to minimize maximum congestion or alternatively to
minimize maximum resource utilization, through efficient resource
allocation. When congestion is minimized through efficient resource
allocation, packet loss decreases, transit delay decreases, and
aggregate throughput increases. Thereby, the perception of network
service quality experienced by end users becomes significantly
enhanced.

Clearly, load balancing is an important network performance
optimization policy. Nevertheless, the capabilities provided for
Traffic Engineering should be flexible enough so that network
administrators can implement other policies which take into account
the prevailing cost structure and the utility or revenue model.

2.2 Traffic and Resource Control

   Performance optimization of operational networks is fundamentally a
   control problem. In the traffic engineering process model, the
   Traffic Engineer, or a suitable automaton, acts as the controller in
   an adaptive feedback control system. This system includes a set of
   interconnected network elements, a network performance monitoring
   system, and a set of network configuration management tools. The
   Traffic Engineer formulates a control policy, observes the state of
   the network through the monitoring system, characterizes the traffic,
   and applies control actions to drive the network to a desired state,
   in accordance with the control policy. This can be accomplished
   reactively by taking action in response to the current state of the
   network, or pro-actively by using forecasting techniques to
   anticipate future trends and applying action to obviate the predicted
   undesirable future states.

   Ideally, control actions should involve:

   1. Modification of traffic management parameters,

   2. Modification of parameters associated with routing, and

   3. Modification of attributes and constraints associated with
      resources.

   The level of manual intervention involved in the traffic engineering
   process should be minimized whenever possible. This can be
   accomplished by automating aspects of the control actions described
   above, in a distributed and scalable fashion.

2.3 Limitations of Current IGP Control Mechanisms

   This subsection reviews some of the well known limitations of current
   IGPs with regard to Traffic Engineering.

   The control capabilities offered by existing Internet interior
   gateway protocols are not adequate for Traffic Engineering. This
   makes it difficult to actualize effective policies to address network
   performance problems. Indeed, IGPs based on shortest path algorithms
   contribute significantly to congestion problems in Autonomous Systems
   within the Internet. SPF algorithms generally optimize based on a
   simple additive metric. These protocols are topology driven, so
   bandwidth availability and traffic characteristics are not factors
   considered in routing decisions. Consequently, congestion frequently
   occurs when:

1. the shortest paths of multiple traffic streams converge on
   specific links or router interfaces, or

2. a given traffic stream is routed through a link or router
   interface which does not have enough bandwidth to accommodate
   it.

These scenarios manifest even when feasible alternate paths with
excess capacity exist. It is this aspect of congestion problems (-- a
symptom of suboptimal resource allocation) that Traffic Engineering
aims to vigorously obviate. Equal cost path load sharing can be used
to address the second cause for congestion listed above with some
degree of success, however it is generally not helpful in alleviating
congestion due to the first cause listed above and particularly not
in large networks with dense topology.

A popular approach to circumvent the inadequacies of current IGPs is
through the use of an overlay model, such as IP over ATM or IP over
frame relay. The overlay model extends the design space by enabling
arbitrary virtual topologies to be provisioned atop the network's
physical topology. The virtual topology is constructed from virtual
circuits which appear as physical links to the IGP routing protocols.
The overlay model provides additional important services to support
traffic and resource control, including: (1) constraint-based routing
at the VC level, (2) support for administratively configurable
explicit VC paths, (3) path compression, (4) call admission control
functions, (5) traffic shaping and traffic policing functions, and
(6) survivability of VCs. These capabilities enable the actualization
of a variety of Traffic Engineering policies. For example, virtual
circuits can easily be rerouted to move traffic from over-utilized
resources onto relatively underutilized ones.

For Traffic Engineering in large dense networks, it is desirable to
equip MPLS with a level of functionality at least commensurate with
current overlay models. Fortunately, this can be done in a fairly
straight forward manner.

3.0 MPLS and Traffic Engineering

This section provides an overview of the applicability of MPLS to
Traffic Engineering. Subsequent sections discuss the set of
capabilities required to meet the Traffic Engineering requirements.

MPLS is strategically significant for Traffic Engineering because it
can potentially provide most of the functionality available from the
overlay model, in an integrated manner, and at a lower cost than the
currently competing alternatives. Equally importantly, MPLS offers

the possibility to automate aspects of the Traffic Engineering function. This last consideration requires further investigation and is beyond the scope of this manuscript.

A note on terminology: The concept of MPLS traffic trunks is used extensively in the remainder of this document. According to Li and Rekhter [3], a traffic trunk is an aggregation of traffic flows of the same class which are placed inside a Label Switched Path. Essentially, a traffic trunk is an abstract representation of traffic to which specific characteristics can be associated. It is useful to view traffic trunks as objects that can be routed; that is, the path through which a traffic trunk traverses can be changed. In this respect, traffic trunks are similar to virtual circuits in ATM and Frame Relay networks. It is important, however, to emphasize that there is a fundamental distinction between a traffic trunk and the path, and indeed the LSP, through which it traverses. An LSP is a specification of the label switched path through which the traffic traverses. In practice, the terms LSP and traffic trunk are often used synonymously. Additional characteristics of traffic trunks as used in this manuscript are summarized in section 5.0.

The attractiveness of MPLS for Traffic Engineering can be attributed to the following factors: (1) explicit label switched paths which are not constrained by the destination based forwarding paradigm can be easily created through manual administrative action or through automated action by the underlying protocols, (2) LSPs can potentially be efficiently maintained, (3) traffic trunks can be instantiated and mapped onto LSPs, (4) a set of attributes can be associated with traffic trunks which modulate their behavioral characteristics, (5) a set of attributes can be associated with resources which constrain the placement of LSPs and traffic trunks across them, (6) MPLS allows for both traffic aggregation and disaggregation whereas classical destination only based IP forwarding permits only aggregation, (7) it is relatively easy to integrate a "constraint-based routing" framework with MPLS, (8) a good implementation of MPLS can offer significantly lower overhead than competing alternatives for Traffic Engineering.

Additionally, through explicit label switched paths, MPLS permits a quasi circuit switching capability to be superimposed on the current Internet routing model. Many of the existing proposals for Traffic Engineering over MPLS focus only on the potential to create explicit LSPs. Although this capability is fundamental for Traffic Engineering, it is not really sufficient. Additional augmentations are required to foster the actualization of policies leading to performance optimization of large operational networks. Some of the necessary augmentations are described in this manuscript.

3.1 Induced MPLS Graph

This subsection introduces the concept of an "induced MPLS graph"
which is central to Traffic Engineering in MPLS domains. An induced
MPLS graph is analogous to a virtual topology in an overlay model. It
is logically mapped onto the physical network through the selection
of LSPs for traffic trunks.

An induced MPLS graph consists of a set of LSRs which comprise the
nodes of the graph and a set of LSPs which provide logical point to
point connectivity between the LSRs, and hence serve as the links of
the induced graph. it may be possible to construct hierarchical
induced MPLS graphs based on the concept of label stacks (see [1]).

Induced MPLS graphs are important because the basic problem of
bandwidth management in an MPLS domain is the issue of how to
efficiently map an induced MPLS graph onto the physical network
topology. The induced MPLS graph abstraction is formalized below.

Let G = (V, E, c) be a capacitated graph depicting the physical
topology of the network. Here, V is the set of nodes in the network
and E is the set of links; that is, for v and w in V, the object
(v,w) is in E if v and w are directly connected under G. The
parameter "c" is a set of capacity and other constraints associated
with E and V. We will refer to G as the "base" network topology.

Let H = (U, F, d) be the induced MPLS graph, where U is a subset of
V representing the set of LSRs in the network, or more precisely the
set of LSRs that are the endpoints of at least one LSP. Here, F is
the set of LSPs, so that for x and y in U, the object (x, y) is in F
if there is an LSP with x and y as endpoints. The parameter "d" is
the set of demands and restrictions associated with F. Evidently, H
is a directed graph. It can be seen that H depends on the
transitivity characteristics of G.

3.2 The Fundamental Problem of Traffic Engineering Over MPLS

There are basically three fundamental problems that relate to Traffic
Engineering over MPLS.

- The first problem concerns how to map packets onto forwarding
  equivalence classes.

- The second problem concerns how to map forwarding equivalence
  classes onto traffic trunks.

- The third problem concerns how to map traffic trunks onto the
  physical network topology through label switched paths.

This document is not focusing on the first two problems listed.
(even-though they are quite important). Instead, the remainder of
this manuscript will focus on the capabilities that permit the third
mapping function to be performed in a manner resulting in efficient
and reliable network operations. This is really the problem of
mapping an induced MPLS graph (H) onto the "base" network topology
(G).

4.0 Augmented Capabilities for Traffic Engineering Over MPLS

The previous sections reviewed the basic functions of Traffic
Engineering in the contemporary Internet. The applicability of MPLS
to that activity was also discussed. The remaining sections of this
manuscript describe the functional capabilities required to fully
support Traffic Engineering over MPLS in large networks.

The proposed capabilities consist of:

1. A set of attributes associated with traffic trunks which
   collectively specify their behavioral characteristics.

2. A set of attributes associated with resources which constrain
   the placement of traffic trunks through them. These can also be
   viewed as topology attribute constraints.

3. A "constraint-based routing" framework which is used to select
   paths for traffic trunks subject to constraints imposed by items
   1) and 2) above. The constraint-based routing framework does not
   have to be part of MPLS. However, the two need to be tightly
   integrated together.

The attributes associated with traffic trunks and resources, as well
as parameters associated with routing, collectively represent the
control variables which can be modified either through administrative
action or through automated agents to drive the network to a desired
state.

In an operational network, it is highly desirable that these
attributes can be dynamically modified online by an operator without
adversely disrupting network operations.

5.0 Traffic Trunk Attributes and Characteristics

This section describes the desirable attributes which can be
associated with traffic trunks to influence their behavioral
characteristics.

First, the basic properties of traffic trunks (as used in this
manuscript) are summarized below:

- A traffic trunk is an *aggregate* of traffic flows belonging
  to the same class. In some contexts, it may be desirable to
  relax this definition and allow traffic trunks to include
  multi-class traffic aggregates.

- In a single class service model, such as the current Internet,
  a traffic trunk could encapsulate all of the traffic between an
  ingress LSR and an egress LSR, or subsets thereof.

- Traffic trunks are routable objects (similar to ATM VCs).

- A traffic trunk is distinct from the LSP through which it
  traverses. In operational contexts, a traffic trunk can be
  moved from one path onto another.

- A traffic trunk is unidirectional.

In practice, a traffic trunk can be characterized by its ingress and
egress LSRs, the forwarding equivalence class which is mapped onto
it, and a set of attributes which determine its behavioral
characteristics.

Two basic issues are of particular significance: (1) parameterization
of traffic trunks and (2) path placement and maintenance rules for
traffic trunks.

5.1 Bidirectional Traffic Trunks

Although traffic trunks are conceptually unidirectional, in many
practical contexts, it is useful to simultaneously instantiate two
traffic trunks with the same endpoints, but which carry packets in
opposite directions. The two traffic trunks are logically coupled
together. One trunk, called the forward trunk, carries traffic from
an originating node to a destination node. The other trunk, called
the backward trunk, carries traffic from the destination node to the
originating node. We refer to the amalgamation of two such traffic
trunks as one bidirectional traffic trunk (BTT) if the following two
conditions hold:

- Both traffic trunks are instantiated through an atomic action at
  one LSR, called the originator node, or through an atomic action
  at a network management station.

- Neither of the composite traffic trunks can exist without the
  other. That is, both are instantiated and destroyed together.

The topological properties of BTTs should also be considered. A BTT can be topologically symmetric or topologically asymmetric. A BTT is said to be "topologically symmetric" if its constituent traffic trunks are routed through the same physical path, even though they operate in opposite directions. If, however, the component traffic trunks are routed through different physical paths, then the BTT is said to be "topologically asymmetric."

It should be noted that bidirectional traffic trunks are merely an administrative convenience. In practice, most traffic engineering functions can be implemented using only unidirectional traffic trunks.

5.2 Basic Operations on Traffic Trunks

The basic operations on traffic trunks significant to Traffic Engineering purposes are summarized below.

- Establish: To create an instance of a traffic trunk.

- Activate: To cause a traffic trunk to start passing traffic. The establishment and activation of a traffic trunk are logically separate events. They may, however, be implemented or invoked as one atomic action.

- Deactivate: To cause a traffic trunk to stop passing traffic.

- Modify Attributes: To cause the attributes of a traffic trunk to be modified.

- Reroute: To cause a traffic trunk to change its route. This can be done through administrative action or automatically by the underlying protocols.

- Destroy: To remove an instance of a traffic trunk from the network and reclaim all resources allocated to it. Such resources include label space and possibly available bandwidth.

The above are considered the basic operations on traffic trunks. Additional operations are also possible such as policing and traffic shaping.

5.3 Accounting and Performance Monitoring

Accounting and performance monitoring capabilities are very important to the billing and traffic characterization functions. Performance statistics obtained from accounting and performance monitoring

systems can be used for traffic characterization, performance
optimization, and capacity planning within the Traffic Engineering
realm..

The capability to obtain statistics at the traffic trunk level is so
important that it should be considered an essential requirement for
Traffic Engineering over MPLS.

5.4 Basic Traffic Engineering Attributes of Traffic Trunks

An attribute of a traffic trunk is a parameter assigned to it which
influences its behavioral characteristics.

Attributes can be explicitly assigned to traffic trunks through
administration action or they can be implicitly assigned by the
underlying protocols when packets are classified and mapped into
equivalence classes at the ingress to an MPLS domain. Regardless of
how the attributes were originally assigned, for Traffic Engineering
purposes, it should be possible to administratively modify such
attributes.

The basic attributes of traffic trunks particularly significant for
Traffic Engineering are itemized below.

- Traffic parameter attributes

- Generic Path selection and maintenance attributes

- Priority attribute

- Preemption attribute

- Resilience attribute

- Policing attribute

The combination of traffic parameters and policing attributes is
analogous to usage parameter control in ATM networks. Most of the
attributes listed above have analogs in well established
technologies. Consequently, it should be relatively straight forward
to map the traffic trunk attributes onto many existing switching and
routing architectures.

Priority and preemption can be regarded as relational attributes
because they express certain binary relations between traffic trunks.
Conceptually, these binary relations determine the manner in which
traffic trunks interact with each other as they compete for network
resources during path establishment and path maintenance.

5.5 Traffic parameter attributes

Traffic parameters can be used to capture the characteristics of the traffic streams (or more precisely the forwarding equivalence class) to be transported through the traffic trunk. Such characteristics may include peak rates, average rates, permissible burst size, etc. From a traffic engineering perspective, the traffic parameters are significant because they indicate the resource requirements of the traffic trunk. This is useful for resource allocation and congestion avoidance through anticipatory policies.

For the purpose of bandwidth allocation, a single canonical value of bandwidth requirements can be computed from a traffic trunk's traffic parameters. Techniques for performing these computations are well known. One example of this is the theory of effective bandwidth.

5.6 Generic Path Selection and Management Attributes

Generic path selection and management attributes define the rules for selecting the route taken by a traffic trunk as well as the rules for maintenance of paths that are already established.

Paths can be computed automatically by the underlying routing protocols or they can be defined administratively by a network operator. If there are no resource requirements or restrictions associated with a traffic trunk, then a topology driven protocol can be used to select its path. However, if resource requirements or policy restrictions exist, then a constraint-based routing scheme should be used for path selection.

In Section 7, a constraint-based routing framework which can automatically compute paths subject to a set of constraints is described. Issues pertaining to explicit paths instantiated through administrative action are discussed in Section 5.6.1 below.

Path management concerns all aspects pertaining to the maintenance of paths traversed by traffic trunks. In some operational contexts, it is desirable that an MPLS implementation can dynamically reconfigure itself, to adapt to some notion of change in "system state." Adaptivity and resilience are aspects of dynamic path management.

To guide the path selection and management process, a set of attributes are required. The basic attributes and behavioral characteristics associated with traffic trunk path selection and management are described in the remainder of this sub-section.

5.6.1 Administratively Specified Explicit Paths

An administratively specified explicit path for a traffic trunk is
one which is configured through operator action. An administratively
specified path can be completely specified or partially specified. A
path is completely specified if all of the required hops between the
endpoints are indicated. A path is partially specified if only a
subset of intermediate hops are indicated. In this case, the
underlying protocols are required to complete the path. Due to
operator errors, an administratively specified path can be
inconsistent or illogical. The underlying protocols should be able to
detect such inconsistencies and provide appropriate feedback.

A "path preference rule" attribute should be associated with
administratively specified explicit paths. A path preference rule
attribute is a binary variable which indicates whether the
administratively configured explicit path is "mandatory" or "non-
mandatory."

If an administratively specified explicit path is selected with a
"mandatory attribute, then that path (and only that path) must be
used. If a mandatory path is topological infeasible (e.g. the two
endpoints are topologically partitioned), or if the path cannot be
instantiated because the available resources are inadequate, then the
path setup process fails. In other words, if a path is specified as
mandatory, then an alternate path cannot be used regardless of
prevailing circumstance. A mandatory path which is successfully
instantiated is also implicitly pinned. Once the path is instantiated
it cannot be changed except through deletion and instantiation of a
new path.

However, if an administratively specified explicit path is selected
with a "non-mandatory" preference rule attribute value, then the path
should be used if feasible. Otherwise, an alternate path can be
chosen instead by the underlying protocols.

5.6.2 Hierarchy of Preference Rules For Multi-Paths

In some practical contexts, it can be useful to have the ability to
administratively specify a set of candidate explicit paths for a
given traffic trunk and define a hierarchy of preference relations on
the paths. During path establishment, the preference rules are
applied to select a suitable path from the candidate list. Also,
under failure scenarios the preference rules are applied to select an
alternate path from the candidate list.

5.6.3 Resource Class Affinity Attributes

Resource class affinity attributes associated with a traffic trunk
can be used to specify the class of resources (see Section 6) which
are to be explicitly included or excluded from the path of the
traffic trunk. These are policy attributes which can be used to
impose additional constraints on the path traversed by a given
traffic trunk. Resource class affinity attributes for a traffic can
be specified as a sequence of tuples:

  <resource-class, affinity>; <resource-class, affinity>; ..

The resource-class parameter identifies a resource class for which an
affinity relationship is defined with respect to the traffic trunk.
The affinity parameter indicates the affinity relationship; that is,
whether members of the resource class are to be included or excluded
from the path of the traffic trunk. Specifically, the affinity
parameter may be a binary variable which takes one of the following
values: (1) explicit inclusion, and (2) explicit exclusion.

If the affinity attribute is a binary variable, it may be possible to
use Boolean expressions to specify the resource class affinities
associated with a given traffic trunk.

If no resource class affinity attributes are specified, then a "don't
care" affinity relationship is assumed to hold between the traffic
trunk and all resources. That is, there is no requirement to
explicitly include or exclude any resources from the traffic trunk's
path. This should be the default in practice.

Resource class affinity attributes are very useful and powerful
constructs because they can be used to implement a variety of
policies. For example, they can be used to contain certain traffic
trunks within specific topological regions of the network.

A "constraint-based routing" framework (see section 7.0) can be used
to compute an explicit path for a traffic trunk subject to resource
class affinity constraints in the following manner:

1. For explicit inclusion, prune all resources not belonging
   to the specified classes prior to performing path computation.

2. For explicit exclusion, prune all resources belonging to the
   specified classes before performing path placement computations.

5.6.4 Adaptivity Attribute

Network characteristics and state change over time. For example, new resources become available, failed resources become reactivated, and allocated resources become deallocated. In general, sometimes more efficient paths become available. Therefore, from a Traffic Engineering perspective, it is necessary to have administrative control parameters that can be used to specify how traffic trunks respond to this dynamism. In some scenarios, it might be desirable to dynamically change the paths of certain traffic trunks in response to changes in network state. This process is called re-optimization. In other scenarios, re-optimization might be very undesirable.

An Adaptivity attribute is a part of the path maintenance parameters associated with traffic trunks. The adaptivity attribute associated with a traffic trunk indicates whether the trunk is subject to re-optimization. That is, an adaptivity attribute is a binary variable which takes one of the following values: (1) permit re-optimization and (2) disable re-optimization.

If re-optimization is enabled, then a traffic trunk can be rerouted through different paths by the underlying protocols in response to changes in network state (primarily changes in resource availability). Conversely, if re-optimization is disabled, then the traffic trunk is "pinned" to its established path and cannot be rerouted in response to changes in network state.

Stability is a major concern when re-optimization is permitted. To promote stability, an MPLS implementation should not be too reactive to the evolutionary dynamics of the network. At the same time, it must adapt fast enough so that optimal use can be made of network assets. This implies that the frequency of re-optimization should be administratively configurable to allow for tuning.

It is to be noted that re-optimization is distinct from resilience. A different attribute is used to specify the resilience characteristics of a traffic trunk (see section 5.9). In practice, it would seem reasonable to expect traffic trunks subject to re-optimization to be implicitly resilient to failures along their paths. However, a traffic trunk which is not subject to re-optimization and whose path is not administratively specified with a "mandatory" attribute can also be required to be resilient to link and node failures along its established path

Formally, it can be stated that adaptivity to state evolution through re-optimization implies resilience to failures, whereas resilience to failures does not imply general adaptivity through re-optimization to state changes.

5.6.5 Load Distribution Across Parallel Traffic Trunks

   Load distribution across multiple parallel traffic trunks between two
   nodes is an important consideration. In many practical contexts, the
   aggregate traffic between two nodes may be such that no single link
   (hence no single path) can carry the load. However, the aggregate
   flow might be less than the maximum permissible flow across a "min-
   cut" that partitions the two nodes. In this case, the only feasible
   solution is to appropriately divide the aggregate traffic into sub-
   streams and route the sub-streams through multiple paths between the
   two nodes.

   In an MPLS domain, this problem can be addressed by instantiating
   multiple traffic trunks between the two nodes, such that each traffic
   trunk carries a proportion of the aggregate traffic. Therefore, a
   flexible means of load assignment to multiple parallel traffic trunks
   carrying traffic between a pair of nodes is required.

   Specifically, from an operational perspective, in situations where
   parallel traffic trunks are warranted, it would be useful to have
   some attribute that can be used to indicate the relative proportion
   of traffic to be carried by each traffic trunk. The underlying
   protocols will then map the load onto the traffic trunks according to
   the specified proportions. It is also, generally desirable to
   maintain packet ordering between packets belong to the same microflow (same source address, destination address, and port number).

5.7 Priority attribute

   The priority attribute defines the relative importance of traffic
   trunks. If a constraint-based routing framework is used with MPLS,
   then priorities become very important because they can be used to
   determine the order in which path selection is done for traffic
   trunks at connection establishment and under fault scenarios.

   Priorities are also important in implementations permitting
   preemption because they can be used to impose a partial order on the
   set of traffic trunks according to which preemptive policies can be
   actualized.

5.8 Preemption attribute

   The preemption attribute determines whether a traffic trunk can
   preempt another traffic trunk from a given path, and whether another
   traffic trunk can preempt a specific traffic trunk. Preemption is
   useful for both traffic oriented and resource oriented performance

objectives. Preemption can used to assure that high priority traffic trunks can always be routed through relatively favorable paths within a differentiated services environment.

Preemption can also be used to implement various prioritized restoration policies following fault events.

The preemption attribute can be used to specify four preempt modes for a traffic trunk: (1) preemptor enabled, (2) non-preemptor, (3) preemptable, and (4) non-preemptable. A preemptor enabled traffic trunk can preempt lower priority traffic trunks designated as preemptable. A traffic specified as non-preemptable cannot be preempted by any other trunks, regardless of relative priorities. A traffic trunk designated as preemptable can be preempted by higher priority trunks which are preemptor enabled.

It is trivial to see that some of the preempt modes are mutually exclusive. Using the numbering scheme depicted above, the feasible preempt mode combinations for a given traffic trunk are as follows: (1, 3), (1, 4), (2, 3), and (2, 4). The (2, 4) combination should be the default.

A traffic trunk, say "A", can preempt another traffic trunk, say "B", only if *all* of the following five conditions hold: (i) "A" has a relatively higher priority than "B", (ii) "A" contends for a resource utilized by "B", (iii) the resource cannot concurrently accommodate "A" and "B" based on certain decision criteria, (iv) "A" is preemptor enabled, and (v) "B" is preemptable.

Preemption is not considered a mandatory attribute under the current best effort Internet service model although it is useful. However, in a differentiated services scenario, the need for preemption becomes more compelling. Moreover, in the emerging optical internetworking architectures, where some protection and restoration functions may be migrated from the optical layer to data network elements (such as gigabit and terabit label switching routers) to reduce costs, preemptive strategies can be used to reduce the restoration time for high priority traffic trunks under fault conditions.

5.9 Resilience Attribute

The resilience attribute determines the behavior of a traffic trunk under fault conditions. That is, when a fault occurs along the path through which the traffic trunk traverses. The following basic problems need to be addressed under such circumstances: (1) fault detection, (2) failure notification, (3) recovery and service restoration. Obviously, an MPLS implementation will have to incorporate mechanisms to address these issues.

Many recovery policies can be specified for traffic trunks whose
established paths are impacted by faults. The following are examples
of feasible schemes:

1. Do not reroute the traffic trunk. For example, a survivability
   scheme may already be in place, provisioned through an
   alternate mechanism, which guarantees service continuity
   under failure scenarios without the need to reroute traffic
   trunks. An example of such an alternate scheme (certainly
   many others exist), is a situation whereby multiple parallel
   label switched paths are provisioned between two nodes, and
   function in a manner such that failure of one LSP causes the
   traffic trunk placed on it to be mapped onto the remaining LSPs
   according to some well defined policy.

2. Reroute through a feasible path with enough resources. If none
   exists, then do not reroute.

3. Reroute through any available path regardless of resource
   constraints.

4. Many other schemes are possible including some which might be
   combinations of the above.

A "basic" resilience attribute indicates the recovery procedure to be
applied to traffic trunks whose paths are impacted by faults.
Specifically, a "basic" resilience attribute is a binary variable
which determines whether the target traffic trunk is to be rerouted
when segments of its path fail. "Extended" resilience attributes can
be used to specify detailed actions to be taken under fault
scenarios. For example, an extended resilience attribute might
specify a set of alternate paths to use under fault conditions, as
well as the rules that govern the relative preference of each
specified path.

Resilience attributes mandate close interaction between MPLS and
routing.

5.10 Policing attribute

The policing attribute determines the actions that should be taken by
the underlying protocols when a traffic trunk becomes non-compliant.
That is, when a traffic trunk exceeds its contract as specified in
the traffic parameters. Generally, policing attributes can indicate
whether a non-conformant traffic trunk is to be rate limited, tagged,
or simply forwarded without any policing action. If policing is
used, then adaptations of established algorithms such as the ATM
Forum's GCRA [11] can be used to perform this function.

Policing is necessary in many operational scenarios, but is quite undesirable in some others. In general, it is usually desirable to police at the ingress to a network (to enforce compliance with service level agreements) and to minimize policing within the core, except when capacity constraints dictate otherwise.

Therefore, from a Traffic Engineering perspective, it is necessary to be able to administratively enable or disable traffic policing for each traffic trunk.

6.0 Resource Attributes

Resource attributes are part of the topology state parameters, which are used to constrain the routing of traffic trunks through specific resources.

6.1 Maximum Allocation Multiplier

The maximum allocation multiplier (MAM) of a resource is an administratively configurable attribute which determines the proportion of the resource that is available for allocation to traffic trunks. This attribute is mostly applicable to link bandwidth. However, it can also be applied to buffer resources on LSRs. The concept of MAM is analogous to the concepts of subscription and booking factors in frame relay and ATM networks.

The values of the MAM can be chosen so that a resource can be under-allocated or over-allocated. A resource is said to be under-allocated if the aggregate demands of all traffic trunks (as expressed in the trunk traffic parameters) that can be allocated to it are always less than the capacity of the resource. A resource is said to be over-allocated if the aggregate demands of all traffic trunks allocated to it can exceed the capacity of the resource.

Under-allocation can be used to bound the utilization of resources. However,the situation under MPLS is more complex than in circuit switched schemes because under MPLS, some flows can be routed via conventional hop by hop protocols (also via explicit paths) without consideration for resource constraints.

Over-allocation can be used to take advantage of the statistical characteristics of traffic in order to implement more efficient resource allocation policies. In particular, over-allocation can be used in situations where the peak demands of traffic trunks do not coincide in time.

6.2 Resource Class Attribute

Resource class attributes are administratively assigned parameters which express some notion of "class" for resources. Resource class attributes can be viewed as "colors" assigned to resources such that the set of resources with the same "color" conceptually belong to the same class. Resource class attributes can be used to implement a variety of policies. The key resources of interest here are links. When applied to links, the resource class attribute effectively becomes an aspect of the "link state" parameters.

The concept of resource class attributes is a powerful abstraction. From a Traffic Engineering perspective, it can be used to implement many policies with regard to both traffic and resource oriented performance optimization. Specifically, resource class attributes can be used to:

1. Apply uniform policies to a set of resources that do not need to be in the same topological region.

2. Specify the relative preference of sets of resources for path placement of traffic trunks.

3. Explicitly restrict the placement of traffic trunks to specific subsets of resources.

4. Implement generalized inclusion / exclusion policies.

5. Enforce traffic locality containment policies. That is, policies   that seek to contain local traffic within specific topological regions of the network.

Additionally, resource class attributes can be used for identification purposes.

In general, a resource can be assigned more than one resource class attribute. For example, all of the OC-48 links in a given network may be assigned a distinguished resource class attribute. The subsets of OC-48 links which exist with a given abstraction domain of the network may be assigned additional resource class attributes in order to implement specific containment policies, or to architect the network in a certain manner.

7.0 Constraint-Based Routing

This section discusses the issues pertaining to constraint-based routing in MPLS domains. In contemporary terminology, constraint-based routing is often referred to as "QoS Routing" see [5,6,7,10].

This document uses the term "constraint-based routing" however, because it better captures the functionality envisioned, which generally encompasses QoS routing as a subset.

constraint-based routing enables a demand driven, resource reservation aware, routing paradigm to co-exist with current topology driven hop by hop Internet interior gateway protocols.

A constraint-based routing framework uses the following as input:

- The attributes associated with traffic trunks.

- The attributes associated with resources.

- Other topology state information.

Based on this information, a constraint-based routing process on each node automatically computes explicit routes for each traffic trunk originating from the node. In this case, an explicit route for each traffic trunk is a specification of a label switched path that satisfies the demand requirements expressed in the trunk's attributes, subject to constraints imposed by resource availability, administrative policy, and other topology state information.

A constraint-based routing framework can greatly reduce the level of manual configuration and intervention required to actualize Traffic Engineering policies.

In practice, the Traffic Engineer, an operator, or even an automaton will specify the endpoints of a traffic trunk and assign a set of attributes to the trunk which encapsulate the performance expectations and behavioral characteristics of the trunk. The constraint-based routing framework is then expected to find a feasible path to satisfy the expectations. If necessary, the Traffic Engineer or a traffic engineering support system can then use administratively configured explicit routes to perform fine grained optimization.

7.1 Basic Features of Constraint-Based Routing

A constraint-based routing framework should at least have the capability to automatically obtain a basic feasible solution to the traffic trunk path placement problem.

In general, the constraint-based routing problem is known to be intractable for most realistic constraints. However, in practice, a very simple well known heuristic (see e.g. [9]) can be used to find a feasible path if one exists:

  - First prune resources that do not satisfy the requirements of
    the traffic trunk attributes.

  - Next, run a shortest path algorithm on the residual graph.

  Clearly, if a feasible path exists for a single traffic trunk, then
  the above simple procedure will find it. Additional rules can be
  specified to break ties and perform further optimizations. In
  general, ties should be broken so that congestion is minimized. When
  multiple traffic trunks are to be routed, however, it can be shown
  that the above algorithm may not always find a mapping, even when a
  feasible mapping exists.

7.2 Implementation Considerations

  Many commercial implementations of frame relay and ATM switches
  already support some notion of constraint-based routing. For such
  devices or for the novel MPLS centric contraptions devised therefrom,
  it should be relatively easy to extend the current constraint-based
  routing implementations to accommodate the peculiar requirements of
  MPLS.

  For routers that use topology driven hop by hop IGPs, constraint-
  based routing can be incorporated in at least one of two ways:

  1. By extending the current IGP protocols such as OSPF and IS-IS to
     support constraint-based routing. Effort is already underway to
     provide such extensions to OSPF (see [5,7]).

  2. By adding a constraint-based routing process to each router which
     can co-exist with current IGPs. This scenario is depicted
     in Figure 1.

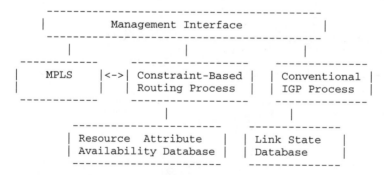

  Figure 1. Constraint-Based Routing Process on Layer 3 LSR

There are many important details associated with implementing
constraint-based routing on Layer 3 devices which we do not discuss
here. These include the following:

- Mechanisms for exchange of topology state information
  (resource availability information, link state information,
  resource attribute information) between constraint-based
  routing processes.

- Mechanisms for maintenance of topology state information.

- Interaction between constraint-based routing processes and
  conventional IGP processes.

- Mechanisms to accommodate the adaptivity requirements of
  traffic trunks.

- Mechanisms to accommodate the resilience and survivability
  requirements of traffic trunks.

In summary, constraint-based routing assists in performance
optimization of operational networks by automatically finding
feasible paths that satisfy a set of constraints for traffic trunks.
It can drastically reduce the amount of administrative explicit path
configuration and manual intervention required to achieve Traffic
Engineering objectives.

8.0 Conclusion

This manuscript presented a set of requirements for Traffic
Engineering over MPLS. Many capabilities were described aimed at
enhancing the applicability of MPLS to Traffic Engineering in the
Internet.

It should be noted that some of the issues described here can be
addressed by incorporating a minimal set of building blocks into
MPLS, and then using a network management superstructure to extend
the functionality in order to realize the requirements. Also, the
constraint-based routing framework does not have to be part of the
core MPLS specifications. However, MPLS does require some interaction
with a constraint-based routing framework in order to meet the
requirements.

9.0 Security Considerations

This document does not introduce new security issues beyond those inherent in MPLS and may use the same mechanisms proposed for this technology. It is, however, specifically important that manipulation of administratively configurable parameters be executed in a secure manner by authorized entities.

10.0 References

[1]   Rosen, E., Viswanathan, A. and R. Callon, "A Proposed Architecture for MPLS", Work in Progress.

[2]   Callon, R., Doolan, P., Feldman, N., Fredette, A., Swallow, G. and A. Viswanathan, "A Framework for Multiprotocol Label Switching", Work in Progress.

[3]   Li, T. and Y. Rekhter, "Provider Architecture for Differentiated Services and Traffic Engineering (PASTE)", RFC 2430, October 1998.

[4]   Rekhter, Y., Davie, B., Katz, D., Rosen, E. and G. Swallow, "Cisco Systems' Tag Switching Architecture - Overview", RFC 2105, February 1997.

[5]   Zhang, Z., Sanchez, C., Salkewicz, B. and E. Crawley "Quality of Service Extensions to OSPF", Work in Progress.

[6]   Crawley, E., Nair, F., Rajagopalan, B. and H. Sandick, "A Framework for QoS Based Routing in the Internet", RFC 2386, August 1998.

[7]   Guerin, R., Kamat, S., Orda, A., Przygienda, T. and D. Williams, "QoS Routing Mechanisms and OSPF Extensions", RFC 2676, August 1999.

[8]   C. Yang and A. Reddy, "A Taxonomy for Congestion Control Algorithms in Packet Switching Networks," IEEE Network Magazine, Volume 9, Number 5, July/August 1995.

[9]   W. Lee, M. Hluchyi, and P. Humblet, "Routing Subject to Quality of Service Constraints in Integrated Communication Networks," IEEE Network, July 1995, pp 46-55.

[10] ATM Forum, "Traffic Management Specification: Version 4.0" April 1996.

11.0 Acknowledgments

The authors would like to thank Yakov Rekhter for his review of an earlier draft of this document. The authors would also like to thank Louis Mamakos and Bill Barns for their helpful suggestions, and Curtis Villamizar for providing some useful feedback.

12.0 Authors' Addresses

    Daniel O. Awduche
    UUNET (MCI Worldcom)
    3060 Williams Drive
    Fairfax, VA 22031

    Phone: +1 703-208-5277
    EMail: awduche@uu.net

    Joe Malcolm
    UUNET (MCI Worldcom)
    3060 Williams Drive
    Fairfax, VA 22031

    Phone: +1 703-206-5895
    EMail: jmalcolm@uu.net

    Johnson Agogbua
    UUNET (MCI Worldcom)
    3060 Williams Drive
    Fairfax, VA 22031

    Phone: +1 703-206-5794
    EMail: ja@uu.net

    Mike O'Dell
    UUNET (MCI Worldcom)
    3060 Williams Drive
    Fairfax, VA 22031

    Phone: +1 703-206-5890
    EMail: mo@uu.net

    Jim McManus
    UUNET (MCI Worldcom)
    3060 Williams Drive
    Fairfax, VA 22031

    Phone: +1 703-206-5607
    EMail: jmcmanus@uu.net

13.0 Full Copyright Statement

Acknowledgement

Funding for the RFC Editor function is currently provided by the
Internet Society.

Network Working Group   B. Gleeson
Request for Comments: 2764   A. Lin
Category: Informational   Nortel Networks
                                                       J. Heinanen
                                                     Telia Finland
                                                       G. Armitage
                                                          A. Malis
                                               Lucent Technologies
                                                     February 2000

A Framework for IP Based Virtual Private Networks

Status of this Memo

Copyright Notice

IESG Note

   This document is not the product of an IETF Working Group. The IETF
   currently has no effort underway to standardize a specific VPN
   framework.

Abstract

   This document describes a framework for Virtual Private Networks
   (VPNs) running across IP backbones. It discusses the various
   different types of VPNs, their respective requirements, and proposes
   specific mechanisms that could be used to implement each type of VPN
   using existing or proposed specifications. The objective of this
   document is to serve as a framework for related protocol development
   in order to develop the full set of specifications required for
   widespread deployment of interoperable VPN solutions.

RFC 2764

Table of Contents

3

RFC 2764

1.0   Introduction

   This document describes a framework for Virtual Private Networks
   (VPNs) running across IP backbones. It discusses the various
   different types of VPNs, their respective requirements, and proposes
   specific mechanisms that could be used to implement each type of VPN
   using existing or proposed specifications. The objective of this
   document is to serve as a framework for related protocol development
   in order to develop the full set of specifications required for
   widespread deployment of interoperable VPN solutions.

   There is currently significant interest in the deployment of virtual
   private networks across IP backbone facilities. The widespread
   deployment of VPNs has been hampered, however, by the lack of
   interoperable implementations, which, in turn, derives from the lack
   of general agreement on the definition and scope of VPNs and
   confusion over the wide variety of solutions that are all described
   by the term VPN. In the context of this document, a VPN is simply
   defined as the 'emulation of a private Wide Area Network (WAN)
   facility using IP facilities' (including the public Internet, or
   private IP backbones). As such, there are as many types of VPNs as
   there are types of WANs, hence the confusion over what exactly
   constitutes a VPN.

   In this document a VPN is modeled as a connectivity object. Hosts
   may be attached to a VPN, and VPNs may be interconnected together, in
   the same manner as hosts today attach to physical networks, and
   physical networks are interconnected together (e.g., via bridges or
   routers). Many aspects of networking, such as addressing, forwarding
   mechanism, learning and advertising reachability, quality of service
   (QoS), security, and firewalling, have common solutions across both
   physical and virtual networks, and many issues that arise in the
   discussion of VPNs have direct analogues with those issues as
   implemented in physical networks. The introduction of VPNs does not
   create the need to reinvent networking, or to introduce entirely new
   paradigms that have no direct analogue with existing physical
   networks. Instead it is often useful to first examine how a
   particular issue is handled in a physical network environment, and
   then apply the same principle to an environment which contains

virtual as well as physical networks, and to develop appropriate
extensions and enhancements when necessary. Clearly having
mechanisms that are common across both physical and virtual networks
facilitates the introduction of VPNs into existing networks, and also
reduces the effort needed for both standards and product development,
since existing solutions can be leveraged.

This framework document proposes a taxonomy of a specific set of VPN
types, showing the specific applications of each, their specific
requirements, and the specific types of mechanisms that may be most
appropriate for their implementation. The intent of this document is
to serve as a framework to guide a coherent discussion of the
specific modifications that may be needed to existing IP mechanisms
in order to develop a full range of interoperable VPN solutions.

The document first discusses the likely expectations customers have
of any type of VPN, and the implications of these for the ways in
which VPNs can be implemented. It also discusses the distinctions
between Customer Premises Equipment (CPE) based solutions, and
network based solutions. Thereafter it presents a taxonomy of the
various VPN types and their respective requirements. It also
outlines suggested approaches to their implementation, hence also
pointing to areas for future standardization.

Note also that this document only discusses implementations of VPNs
across IP backbones, be they private IP networks, or the public
Internet. The models and mechanisms described here are intended to
apply to both IPV4 and IPV6 backbones. This document specifically
does not discuss means of constructing VPNs using native mappings
onto switched backbones - e.g., VPNs constructed using the LAN
Emulation over ATM (LANE) [1] or Multiprotocol over ATM (MPOA) [2]
protocols operating over ATM backbones. Where IP backbones are
constructed using such protocols, by interconnecting routers over the
switched backbone, the VPNs discussed operate on top of this IP
network, and hence do not directly utilize the native mechanisms of
the underlying backbone. Native VPNs are restricted to the scope of
the underlying backbone, whereas IP based VPNs can extend to the
extent of IP reachability. Native VPN protocols are clearly outside
the scope of the IETF, and may be tackled by such bodies as the ATM
Forum.

2.0 VPN Application and Implementation Requirements

2.1 General VPN Requirements

There is growing interest in the use of IP VPNs as a more cost
effective means of building and deploying private communication
networks for multi-site communication than with existing approaches.

Existing private networks can be generally categorized into two types - dedicated WANs that permanently connect together multiple sites, and dial networks, that allow on-demand connections through the Public Switched Telephone Network (PSTN) to one or more sites in the private network.

WANs are typically implemented using leased lines or dedicated circuits - for instance, Frame Relay or ATM connections - between the multiple sites. CPE routers or switches at the various sites connect these dedicated facilities together and allow for connectivity across the network. Given the cost and complexity of such dedicated facilities and the complexity of CPE device configuration, such networks are generally not fully meshed, but instead have some form of hierarchical topology. For example remote offices could be connected directly to the nearest regional office, with the regional offices connected together in some form of full or partial mesh.

Private dial networks are used to allow remote users to connect into an enterprise network using PSTN or Integrated Services Digital Network (ISDN) links. Typically, this is done through the deployment of Network Access Servers (NASs) at one or more central sites. Users dial into such NASs, which interact with Authentication, Authorization, and Accounting (AAA) servers to verify the identity of the user, and the set of services that the user is authorized to receive.

In recent times, as more businesses have found the need for high speed Internet connections to their private corporate networks, there has been significant interest in the deployment of CPE based VPNs running across the Internet. This has been driven typically by the ubiquity and distance insensitive pricing of current Internet services, that can result in significantly lower costs than typical dedicated or leased line services.

The notion of using the Internet for private communications is not new, and many techniques, such as controlled route leaking, have been used for this purpose [3]. Only in recent times, however, have the appropriate IP mechanisms needed to meet customer requirements for VPNs all come together. These requirements include the following:

2.1.1 Opaque Packet Transport:

The traffic carried within a VPN may have no relation to the traffic on the IP backbone, either because the traffic is multiprotocol, or because the customer's IP network may use IP addressing unrelated to that of the IP backbone on which the traffic is transported. In particular, the customer's IP network may use non-unique, private IP addressing [4].

2.1.2 Data Security

   In general customers using VPNs require some form of data security.
   There are different trust models applicable to the use of VPNs. One
   such model is where the customer does not trust the service provider
   to provide any form of security, and instead implements a VPN using
   CPE devices that implement firewall functionality and that are
   connected together using secure tunnels. In this case the service
   provider is used solely for IP packet transport.

   An alternative model is where the customer trusts the service
   provider to provide a secure managed VPN service. This is similar to
   the trust involved when a customer utilizes a public switched Frame
   Relay or ATM service, in that the customer trusts that packets will
   not be misdirected, injected into the network in an unauthorized
   manner, snooped on, modified in transit, or subjected to traffic
   analysis by unauthorized parties.

   With this model providing firewall functionality and secure packet
   transport services is the responsibility of the service provider.
   Different levels of security may be needed within the provider
   backbone, depending on the deployment scenario used. If the VPN
   traffic is contained within a single provider's IP backbone then
   strong security mechanisms, such as those provided by the IP Security
   protocol suite (IPSec) [5], may not be necessary for tunnels between
   backbone nodes. If the VPN traffic traverses networks or equipment
   owned by multiple administrations then strong security mechanisms may
   be appropriate. Also a strong level of security may be applied by a
   provider to customer traffic to address a customer perception that IP
   networks, and particularly the Internet, are insecure. Whether or
   not this perception is correct it is one that must be addressed by
   the VPN implementation.

2.1.3 Quality of Service Guarantees

   In addition to ensuring communication privacy, existing private
   networking techniques, building upon physical or link layer
   mechanisms, also offer various types of quality of service
   guarantees. In particular, leased and dial up lines offer both
   bandwidth and latency guarantees, while dedicated connection
   technologies like ATM and Frame Relay have extensive mechanisms for
   similar guarantees. As IP based VPNs become more widely deployed,
   there will be market demand for similar guarantees, in order to
   ensure end to end application transparency. While the ability of IP
   based VPNs to offer such guarantees will depend greatly upon the
   commensurate capabilities of the underlying IP backbones, a VPN
   framework must also address the means by which VPN systems can
   utilize such capabilities, as they evolve.

2.1.4 Tunneling Mechanism

   Together, the first two of the requirements listed above imply that
   VPNs must be implemented through some form of IP tunneling mechanism,
   where the packet formats and/or the addressing used within the VPN
   can be unrelated to that used to route the tunneled packets across
   the IP backbone. Such tunnels, depending upon their form, can
   provide some level of intrinsic data security, or this can also be
   enhanced using other mechanisms (e.g., IPSec).

   Furthermore, as discussed later, such tunneling mechanisms can also
   be mapped into evolving IP traffic management mechanisms. There are
   already defined a large number of IP tunneling mechanisms. Some of
   these are well suited to VPN applications, as discussed in section
   3.0.

2.2   CPE and Network Based VPNs

   Most current VPN implementations are based on CPE equipment. VPN
   capabilities are being integrated into a wide variety of CPE devices,
   ranging from firewalls to WAN edge routers and specialized VPN
   termination devices. Such equipment may be bought and deployed by
   customers, or may be deployed (and often remotely managed) by service
   providers in an outsourcing service.

   There is also significant interest in 'network based VPNs', where the
   operation of the VPN is outsourced to an Internet Service Provider
   (ISP), and is implemented on network as opposed to CPE equipment.
   There is significant interest in such solutions both by customers
   seeking to reduce support costs and by ISPs seeking new revenue
   sources. Supporting VPNs in the network allows the use of particular
   mechanisms which may lead to highly efficient and cost effective VPN
   solutions, with common equipment and operations support amortized
   across large numbers of customers.

   Most of the mechanisms discussed below can apply to either CPE based
   or network based VPNs. However particular mechanisms are likely to
   prove applicable only to the latter, since they leverage tools (e.g.,
   piggybacking on routing protocols) which are accessible only to ISPs
   and which are unlikely to be made available to any customer, or even
   hosted on ISP owned and operated CPE, due to the problems of
   coordinating joint management of the CPE gear by both the ISP and the
   customer. This document will indicate which techniques are likely to
   apply only to network based VPNs.

2.3 VPNs and Extranets

   The term 'extranet' is commonly used to refer to a scenario whereby
   two or more companies have networked access to a limited amount of
   each other's corporate data. For example a manufacturing company
   might use an extranet for its suppliers to allow it to query
   databases for the pricing and availability of components, and then to
   order and track the status of outstanding orders. Another example is
   joint software development, for instance, company A allows one
   development group within company B to access its operating system
   source code, and company B allows one development group in company A
   to access its security software. Note that the access policies can
   get arbitrarily complex. For example company B may internally
   restrict access to its security software to groups in certain
   geographic locations to comply with export control laws, for example.

   A key feature of an extranet is thus the control of who can access
   what data, and this is essentially a policy decision. Policy
   decisions are typically enforced today at the interconnection points
   between different domains, for example between a private network and
   the Internet, or between a software test lab and the rest of the
   company network. The enforcement may be done via a firewall, router
   with access list functionality, application gateway, or any similar
   device capable of applying policy to transit traffic. Policy
   controls may be implemented within a corporate network, in addition
   to between corporate networks. Also the interconnections between
   networks could be a set of bilateral links, or could be a separate
   network, perhaps maintained by an industry consortium. This separate
   network could itself be a VPN or a physical network.

   Introducing VPNs into a network does not require any change to this
   model. Policy can be enforced between two VPNs, or between a VPN and
   the Internet, in exactly the same manner as is done today without
   VPNs. For example two VPNs could be interconnected, which each
   administration locally imposing its own policy controls, via a
   firewall, on all traffic that enters its VPN from the outside,
   whether from another VPN or from the Internet.

   This model of a VPN provides for a separation of policy from the
   underlying mode of packet transport used. For example, a router may
   direct voice traffic to ATM Virtual Channel Connections (VCCs) for
   guaranteed QoS, non-local internal company traffic to secure tunnels,
   and other traffic to a link to the Internet. In the past the secure
   tunnels may have been frame relay circuits, now they may also be
   secure IP tunnels or MPLS Label Switched Paths (LSPs)

Other models of a VPN are also possible. For example there is a
model whereby a set of application flows is mapped into a VPN. As
the policy rules imposed by a network administrator can get quite
complex, the number of distinct sets of application flows that are
used in the policy rulebase, and hence the number of VPNs, can thus
grow quite large, and there can be multiple overlapping VPNs.
However there is little to be gained by introducing such new
complexity into a network. Instead a VPN should be viewed as a
direct analogue to a physical network, as this allows the leveraging
of existing protocols and procedures, and the current expertise and
skill sets of network administrators and customers.

3.0 VPN Tunneling

As noted above in section 2.1, VPNs must be implemented using some
form of tunneling mechanism. This section looks at the generic
requirements for such VPN tunneling mechanisms. A number of
characteristics and aspects common to any link layer protocol are
taken and compared with the features offered by existing tunneling
protocols. This provides a basis for comparing different protocols
and is also useful to highlight areas where existing tunneling
protocols could benefit from extensions to better support their
operation in a VPN environment.

An IP tunnel connecting two VPN endpoints is a basic building block
from which a variety of different VPN services can be constructed.
An IP tunnel operates as an overlay across the IP backbone, and the
traffic sent through the tunnel is opaque to the underlying IP
backbone. In effect the IP backbone is being used as a link layer
technology, and the tunnel forms a point-to-point link.

A VPN device may terminate multiple IP tunnels and forward packets
between these tunnels and other network interfaces in different ways.
In the discussion of different types of VPNs, in later sections of
this document, the primary distinguishing characteristic of these
different types is the manner in which packets are forwarded between
interfaces (e.g., bridged or routed). There is a direct analogy with
how existing networking devices are characterized today. A two-port
repeater just forwards packets between its ports, and does not
examine the contents of the packet. A bridge forwards packets using
Media Access Control (MAC) layer information contained in the packet,
while a router forwards packets using layer 3 addressing information
contained in the packet. Each of these three scenarios has a direct
VPN analogue, as discussed later. Note that an IP tunnel is viewed
as just another sort of link, which can be concatenated with another
link, bound to a bridge forwarding table, or bound to an IP
forwarding table, depending on the type of VPN.

The following sections look at the requirements for a generic IP
tunneling protocol that can be used as a basic building block to
construct different types of VPNs.

3.1 Tunneling Protocol Requirements for VPNs

There are numerous IP tunneling mechanisms, including IP/IP [6],
Generic Routing Encapsulation (GRE) tunnels [7], Layer 2 Tunneling
Protocol (L2TP) [8], IPSec [5], and Multiprotocol Label Switching
(MPLS) [9]. Note that while some of these protocols are not often
thought of as tunneling protocols, they do each allow for opaque
transport of frames as packet payload across an IP network, with
forwarding disjoint from the address fields of the encapsulated
packets.

Note, however, that there is one significant distinction between each
of the IP tunneling protocols mentioned above, and MPLS. MPLS can be
viewed as a specific link layer for IP, insofar as MPLS specific
mechanisms apply only within the scope of an MPLS network, whereas IP
based mechanisms extend to the extent of IP reachability. As such,
VPN mechanisms built directly upon MPLS tunneling mechanisms cannot,
by definition, extend outside the scope of MPLS networks, any more so
than, for instance, ATM based mechanisms such as LANE can extend
outside of ATM networks. Note however, that an MPLS network can span
many different link layer technologies, and so, like an IP network,
its scope is not limited by the specific link layers used. A number
of proposals for defining a set of mechanisms to allow for
interoperable VPNs specifically over MPLS networks have also been
produced ([10] [11] [12] [13], [14] and [15]).

There are a number of desirable requirements for a VPN tunneling
mechanism, however, that are not all met by the existing tunneling
mechanisms. These requirements include:

3.1.1 Multiplexing

There are cases where multiple VPN tunnels may be needed between the
same two IP endpoints. This may be needed, for instance, in cases
where the VPNs are network based, and each end point supports
multiple customers. Traffic for different customers travels over
separate tunnels between the same two physical devices. A
multiplexing field is needed to distinguish which packets belong to
which tunnel. Sharing a tunnel in this manner may also reduce the
latency and processing burden of tunnel set up. Of the existing IP
tunneling mechanisms, L2TP (via the tunnel-id and session-id fields),
MPLS (via the label) and IPSec (via the Security Parameter Index
(SPI) field) have a multiplexing mechanism. Strictly speaking GRE
does not have a multiplexing field. However the key field, which was

intended to be used for authenticating the source of a packet, has sometimes been used as a multiplexing field. IP/IP does not have a multiplexing field.

The IETF [16] and the ATM Forum [17] have standardized on a single format for a globally unique identifier used to identify a VPN (a VPN-ID). A VPN-ID can be used in the control plane, to bind a tunnel to a VPN at tunnel establishment time, or in the data plane, to identify the VPN associated with a packet, on a per-packet basis. In the data plane a VPN encapsulation header can be used by MPLS, MPOA and other tunneling mechanisms to aggregate packets for different VPNs over a single tunnel. In this case an explicit indication of VPN-ID is included with every packet, and no use is made of any tunnel specific multiplexing field. In the control plane a VPN-ID field can be included in any tunnel establishment signalling protocol to allow for the association of a tunnel (e.g., as identified by the SPI field) with a VPN. In this case there is no need for a VPN-ID to be included with every data packet. This is discussed further in section 5.3.1.

3.1.2 Signalling Protocol

There is some configuration information that must be known by an end point in advance of tunnel establishment, such as the IP address of the remote end point, and any relevant tunnel attributes required, such as the level of security needed. Once this information is available, the actual tunnel establishment can be completed in one of two ways - via a management operation, or via a signalling protocol that allows tunnels to be established dynamically.

An example of a management operation would be to use an SNMP Management Information Base (MIB) to configure various tunneling parameters, e.g., MPLS labels, source addresses to use for IP/IP or GRE tunnels, L2TP tunnel-ids and session-ids, or security association parameters for IPSec.

Using a signalling protocol can significantly reduce the management burden however, and as such, is essential in many deployment scenarios. It reduces the amount of configuration needed, and also reduces the management co-ordination needed if a VPN spans multiple administrative domains. For example, the value of the multiplexing field, described above, is local to the node assigning the value, and can be kept local if distributed via a signalling protocol, rather than being first configured into a management station and then distributed to the relevant nodes. A signalling protocol also allows nodes that are mobile or are only intermittently connected to establish tunnels on demand.

When used in a VPN environment a signalling protocol should allow for
the transport of a VPN-ID to allow the resulting tunnel to be
associated with a particular VPN. It should also allow tunnel
attributes to be exchanged or negotiated, for example the use of
frame sequencing or the use of multiprotocol transport. Note that
the role of the signalling protocol need only be to negotiate tunnel
attributes, not to carry information about how the tunnel is used,
for example whether the frames carried in the tunnel are to be
forwarded at layer 2 or layer 3. (This is similar to Q.2931 ATM
signalling - the same signalling protocol is used to set up Classical
IP logical subnetworks as well as for LANE emulated LANs.

Of the various IP tunneling protocols, the following ones support a
signalling protocol that could be adapted for this purpose: L2TP (the
L2TP control protocol), IPSec (the Internet Key Exchange (IKE)
protocol [18]), and GRE (as used with mobile-ip tunneling [19]). Also
there are two MPLS signalling protocols that can be used to establish
LSP tunnels. One uses extensions to the MPLS Label Distribution
Protocol (LDP) protocol [20], called Constraint-Based Routing LDP
(CR-LDP) [21], and the other uses extensions to the Resource
Reservation Protocol (RSVP) for LSP tunnels [22].

3.1.3 Data Security

A VPN tunneling protocol must support mechanisms to allow for
whatever level of security may be desired by customers, including
authentication and/or encryption of various strengths. None of the
tunneling mechanisms discussed, other than IPSec, have intrinsic
security mechanisms, but rely upon the security characteristics of
the underlying IP backbone. In particular, MPLS relies upon the
explicit labeling of label switched paths to ensure that packets
cannot be misdirected, while the other tunneling mechanisms can all
be secured through the use of IPSec. For VPNs implemented over non-
IP backbones (e.g., MPOA, Frame Relay or ATM virtual circuits), data
security is implicitly provided by the layer two switch
infrastructure.

Overall VPN security is not just a capability of the tunnels alone,
but has to be viewed in the broader context of how packets are
forwarded onto those tunnels. For example with VPRNs implemented
with virtual routers, the use of separate routing and forwarding
table instances ensures the isolation of traffic between VPNs.
Packets on one VPN cannot be misrouted to a tunnel on a second VPN
since those tunnels are not visible to the forwarding table of the
first VPN.

If some form of signalling mechanism is used by one VPN end point to
dynamically establish a tunnel with another endpoint, then there is a
requirement to be able to authenticate the party attempting the
tunnel establishment. IPSec has an array of schemes for this
purpose, allowing, for example, authentication to be based on preshared keys, or to use digital signatures and certificates. Other
tunneling schemes have weaker forms of authentication. In some cases
no authentication may be needed, for example if the tunnels are
provisioned, rather than dynamically established, or if the trust
model in use does not require it.

Currently the IPSec Encapsulating Security Payload (ESP) protocol
[23] can be used to establish SAs that support either encryption or
authentication or both. However the protocol specification precludes
the use of an SA where neither encryption or authentication is used.
In a VPN environment this "null/null" option is useful, since other
aspects of the protocol (e.g., that it supports tunneling and
multiplexing) may be all that is required. In effect the "null/null"
option can be viewed as just another level of data security.

3.1.4 Multiprotocol Transport

In many applications of VPNs, the VPN may carry opaque, multiprotocol
traffic. As such, the tunneling protocol used must also support
multiprotocol transport. L2TP is designed to transport Point-to-
Point Protocol (PPP) [24] packets, and thus can be used to carry
multiprotocol traffic since PPP itself is multiprotocol. GRE also
provides for the identification of the protocol being tunneled.
IP/IP and IPSec tunnels have no such protocol identification field,
since the traffic being tunneled is assumed to be IP.

It is possible to extend the IPSec protocol suite to allow for the
transport of multiprotocol packets. This can be achieved, for
example, by extending the signalling component of IPSec - IKE, to
indicate the protocol type of the traffic being tunneled, or to carry
a packet multiplexing header (e.g., an LLC/SNAP header or GRE header)
with each tunneled packet. This approach is similar to that used for
the same purpose in ATM networks, where signalling is used to
indicate the encapsulation used on the VCC, and where packets sent on
the VCC can use either an LLC/SNAP header or be placed directly into
the AAL5 payload, the latter being known as VC-multiplexing (see
[25]).

3.1.5 Frame Sequencing

One quality of service attribute required by customers of a VPN may
be frame sequencing, matching the equivalent characteristic of
physical leased lines or dedicated connections. Sequencing may be

required for the efficient operation of particular end to end
protocols or applications. In order to implement frame sequencing,
the tunneling mechanism must support a sequencing field. Both L2TP
and GRE have such a field. IPSec has a sequence number field, but it
is used by a receiver to perform an anti-replay check, not to
guarantee in-order delivery of packets.

It is possible to extend IPSec to allow the use of the existing
sequence field to guarantee in-order delivery of packets. This can
be achieved, for example, by using IKE to negotiate whether or not
sequencing is to be used, and to define an end point behaviour which
preserves packet sequencing.

3.1.6 Tunnel Maintenance

The VPN end points must monitor the operation of the VPN tunnels to
ensure that connectivity has not been lost, and to take appropriate
action (such as route recalculation) if there has been a failure.

There are two approaches possible. One is for the tunneling protocol
itself to periodically check in-band for loss of connectivity, and to
provide an explicit indication of failure. For example L2TP has an
optional keep-alive mechanism to detect non-operational tunnels.

The other approach does not require the tunneling protocol itself to
perform this function, but relies on the operation of some out-of-
band mechanism to determine loss of connectivity. For example if a
routing protocol such as Routing Information Protocol (RIP) [26] or
Open Shortest Path First (OSPF) [27] is run over a tunnel mesh, a
failure to hear from a neighbor within a certain period of time will
result in the routing protocol declaring the tunnel to be down.
Another out-of-band approach is to perform regular ICMP pings with a
peer. This is generally sufficient assurance that the tunnel is
operational, due to the fact the tunnel also runs across the same IP
backbone.

When tunnels are established dynamically a distinction needs to be
drawn between the static and dynamic tunnel information needed.
Before a tunnel can be established some static information is needed
by a node, such as the identify of the remote end point and the
attributes of the tunnel to propose and accept. This is typically
put in place as a result of a configuration operation. As a result
of the signalling exchange to establish a tunnel, some dynamic state
is established in each end point, such as the value of the
multiplexing field or keys to be used. For example with IPSec, the
establishment of a Security Association (SA) puts in place the keys
to be used for the lifetime of that SA.

Different policies may be used as to when to trigger the
establishment of a dynamic tunnel. One approach is to use a data-
driven approach and to trigger tunnel establishment whenever there is
data to be transferred, and to timeout the tunnel due to inactivity.
This approach is particularly useful if resources for the tunnel are
being allocated in the network for QoS purposes. Another approach is
to trigger tunnel establishment whenever the static tunnel
configuration information is installed, and to attempt to keep the
tunnel up all the time.

3.1.7 Large MTUs

An IP tunnel has an associated Maximum Transmission Unit (MTU), just
like a regular link. It is conceivable that this MTU may be larger
than the MTU of one or more individual hops along the path between
tunnel endpoints. If so, some form of frame fragmentation will be
required within the tunnel.

If the frame to be transferred is mapped into one IP datagram, normal
IP fragmentation will occur when the IP datagram reaches a hop with
an MTU smaller than the IP tunnel's MTU. This can have undesirable
performance implications at the router performing such mid-tunnel
fragmentation.

An alternative approach is for the tunneling protocol itself to
incorporate a segmentation and reassembly capability that operates at
the tunnel level, perhaps using the tunnel sequence number and an
end-of-message marker of some sort. (Note that multilink PPP uses a
mechanism similar to this to fragment packets). This avoids IP level
fragmentation within the tunnel itself. None of the existing
tunneling protocols support such a mechanism.

3.1.8 Minimization of Tunnel Overhead

There is clearly benefit in minimizing the overhead of any tunneling
mechanisms. This is particularly important for the transport of
jitter and latency sensitive traffic such as packetized voice and
video. On the other hand, the use of security mechanisms, such as
IPSec, do impose their own overhead, hence the objective should be to
minimize overhead over and above that needed for security, and to not
burden those tunnels in which security is not mandatory with
unnecessary overhead.

One area where the amount of overhead may be significant is when
voluntary tunneling is used for dial-up remote clients connecting to
a VPN, due to the typically low bandwidth of dial-up links. This is
discussed further in section 6.3.

3.1.9 Flow and congestion control

   During the development of the L2TP protocol procedures were developed
   for flow and congestion control. These were necessitated primarily
   because of the need to provide adequate performance over lossy
   networks when PPP compression is used, which, unlike IP Payload
   Compression Protocol (IPComp) [28], is stateful across packets.
   Another motivation was to accommodate devices with very little
   buffering, used for example to terminate low speed dial-up lines.
   However the flow and congestion control mechanisms defined in the
   final version of the L2TP specification are used only for the control
   channels, and not for data traffic.

   In general the interactions between multiple layers of flow and
   congestion control schemes can be very complex. Given the
   predominance of TCP traffic in today's networks and the fact that TCP
   has its own end-to-end flow and congestion control mechanisms, it is
   not clear that there is much benefit to implementing similar
   mechanisms within tunneling protocols. Good flow and congestion
   control schemes, that can adapt to a wide variety of network
   conditions and deployment scenarios are complex to develop and test,
   both in themselves and in understanding the interaction with other
   schemes that may be running in parallel. There may be some benefit,
   however, in having the capability whereby a sender can shape traffic
   to the capacity of a receiver in some manner, and in providing the
   protocol mechanisms to allow a receiver to signal its capabilities to
   a sender. This is an area that may benefit from further study.

   Note also the work of the Performance Implications of Link
   Characteristics (PILC) working group of the IETF, which is examining
   how the properties of different network links can have an impact on
   the performance of Internet protocols operating over those links.

3.1.10 QoS / Traffic Management

   As noted above, customers may require that VPNs yield similar
   behaviour to physical leased lines or dedicated connections with
   respect to such QoS parameters as loss rates, jitter, latency and
   bandwidth guarantees. How such guarantees could be delivered will,
   in general, be a function of the traffic management characteristics
   of the VPN nodes themselves, and the access and backbone networks
   across which they are connected.

   A full discussion of QoS and VPNs is outside the scope of this
   document, however by modeling a VPN tunnel as just another type of
   link layer, many of the existing mechanisms developed for ensuring
   QoS over physical links can also be applied. For example at a VPN
   node, the mechanisms of policing, marking, queuing, shaping and

scheduling can all be applied to VPN traffic with VPN-specific parameters, queues and interfaces, just as for non-VPN traffic. The techniques developed for Diffserv, Intserv and for traffic engineering in MPLS are also applicable. See also [29] for a discussion of QoS and VPNs.

It should be noted, however, that this model of tunnel operation is not necessarily consistent with the way in which specific tunneling protocols are currently modeled. While a model is an aid to comprehension, and not part of a protocol specification, having differing models can complicate discussions, particularly if a model is misinterpreted as being part of a protocol specification or as constraining choice of implementation method. For example, IPSec tunnel processing can be modeled both as an interface and as an attribute of a particular packet flow.

3.2 Recommendations

IPSec is needed whenever there is a requirement for strong encryption or strong authentication. It also supports multiplexing and a signalling protocol - IKE. However extending the IPSec protocol suite to also cover the following areas would be beneficial, in order to better support the tunneling requirements of a VPN environment.

- the transport of a VPN-ID when establishing an SA (3.1.2)

- a null encryption and null authentication option (3.1.3)

- multiprotocol operation (3.1.4)

- frame sequencing (3.1.5)

L2TP provides no data security by itself, and any PPP security mechanisms used do not apply to the L2TP protocol itself, so that in order for strong security to be provided L2TP must run over IPSec. Defining specific modes of operation for IPSec when it is used to support L2TP traffic will aid interoperability. This is currently a work item for the proposed L2TP working group.

4.0 VPN Types: Virtual Leased Lines

The simplest form of a VPN is a 'Virtual Leased Line' (VLL) service. In this case a point-to-point link is provided to a customer, connecting two CPE devices, as illustrated below. The link layer type used to connect the CPE devices to the ISP nodes can be any link layer type, for example an ATM VCC or a Frame Relay circuit. The CPE devices can be either routers bridges or hosts.

The two ISP nodes are both connected to an IP network, and an IP
tunnel is set up between them. Each ISP node is configured to bind
the stub link and the IP tunnel together at layer 2 (e.g., an ATM VCC
and the IP tunnel). Frames are relayed between the two links. For
example the ATM Adaptation Layer 5 (AAL5) payload is taken and
encapsulated in an IPSec tunnel, and vice versa. The contents of the
AAL5 payload are opaque to the ISP node, and are not examined there.

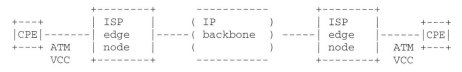

```
            +--------+      ----------        +--------+
+---+       | ISP    |    ( IP       )        | ISP    |       +---+
|CPE|-------| edge   |-----( backbone ) -----| edge   |------|CPE|
+---+ ATM   | node   |    (           )       | node   |  ATM +---+
     VCC    +--------+      ----------        +--------+  VCC

           <--------- IP Tunnel -------->

10.1.1.5              subnet = 10.1.1.4/30              10.1.1.6
         Addressing used by customer (transparent to provider)
```

Figure 4.1: VLL Example

To a customer it looks the same as if a single ATM VCC or Frame Relay
circuit were used to interconnect the CPE devices, and the customer
could be unaware that part of the circuit was in fact implemented
over an IP backbone. This may be useful, for example, if a provider
wishes to provide a LAN interconnect service using ATM as the network
interface, but does not have an ATM network that directly
interconnects all possible customer sites.

It is not necessary that the two links used to connect the CPE
devices to the ISP nodes be of the same media type, but in this case
the ISP nodes cannot treat the traffic in an opaque manner, as
described above. Instead the ISP nodes must perform the functions of
an interworking device between the two media types (e.g., ATM and
Frame Relay), and perform functions such as LLC/SNAP to NLPID
conversion, mapping between ARP protocol variants and performing any
media specific processing that may be expected by the CPE devices
(e.g., ATM OAM cell handling or Frame Relay XID exchanges).

The IP tunneling protocol used must support multiprotocol operation
and may need to support sequencing, if that characteristic is
important to the customer traffic. If the tunnels are established
using a signalling protocol, they may be set up in a data driven
manner, when a frame is received from a customer link and no tunnel
exists, or the tunnels may be established at provisioning time and
kept up permanently.

Note that the use of the term 'VLL' in this document is different to
that used in the definition of the Diffserv Expedited Forwarding Per
Hop Behaviour (EF-PHB) [30]. In that document a VLL is used to mean
a low latency, low jitter, assured bandwidth path, which can be
provided using the described PHB. Thus the focus there is primarily
on link characteristics that are temporal in nature. In this document
the term VLL does not imply the use of any specific QoS mechanism,
Diffserv or otherwise. Instead the focus is primarily on link
characteristics that are more topological in nature, (e.g., such as
constructing a link which includes an IP tunnel as one segment of the
link). For a truly complete emulation of a link layer both the
temporal and topological aspects need to be taken into account.

5.0 VPN Types: Virtual Private Routed Networks

5.1 VPRN Characteristics

A Virtual Private Routed Network (VPRN) is defined to be the
emulation of a multi-site wide area routed network using IP
facilities. This section looks at how a network-based VPRN service
can be provided. CPE-based VPRNs are also possible, but are not
specifically discussed here. With network-based VPRNs many of the
issues that need to be addressed are concerned with configuration and
operational issues, which must take into account the split in
administrative responsibility between the service provider and the
service user.

The distinguishing characteristic of a VPRN, in comparison to other
types of VPNs, is that packet forwarding is carried out at the
network layer. A VPRN consists of a mesh of IP tunnels between ISP
routers, together with the routing capabilities needed to forward
traffic received at each VPRN node to the appropriate destination
site. Attached to the ISP routers are CPE routers connected via one
or more links, termed 'stub' links. There is a VPRN specific
forwarding table at each ISP router to which members of the VPRN are
connected. Traffic is forwarded between ISP routers, and between ISP
routers and customer sites, using these forwarding tables, which
contain network layer reachability information (in contrast to a
Virtual Private LAN Segment type of VPN (VPLS) where the forwarding
tables contain MAC layer reachability information - see section 7.0).

An example VPRN is illustrated in the following diagram, which shows
3 ISP edge routers connected via a full mesh of IP tunnels, used to
interconnect 4 CPE routers. One of the CPE routers is multihomed to
the ISP network. In the multihomed case, all stub links may be
active, or, as shown, there may be one primary and one or more backup
links to be used in case of failure of the primary. The term '
backdoor' link is used to refer to a link between two customer sites

that does not traverse the ISP network.

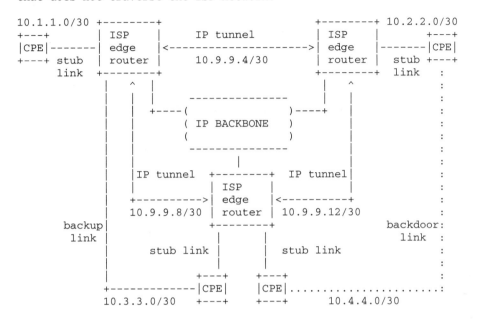

Figure 5.1: VPRN Example

The principal benefit of a VPRN is that the complexity and the
configuration of the CPE routers is minimized. To a CPE router, the
ISP edge router appears as a neighbor router in the customer's
network, to which it sends all traffic, using a default route. The
tunnel mesh that is set up to transfer traffic extends between the
ISP edge routers, not the CPE routers. In effect the burden of
tunnel establishment and maintenance and routing configuration is
outsourced to the ISP. In addition other services needed for the
operation of a VPN such as the provision of a firewall and QoS
processing can be handled by a small number of ISP edge routers,
rather than a large number of potentially heterogeneous CPE devices.
The introduction and management of new services can also be more
easily handled, as this can be achieved without the need to upgrade
any CPE equipment. This latter benefit is particularly important
when there may be large numbers of residential subscribers using VPN
services to access private corporate networks. In this respect the
model is somewhat akin to that used for telephony services, whereby
new services (e.g., call waiting) can be introduced with no change in
subscriber equipment.

The VPRN type of VPN is in contrast to one where the tunnel mesh extends to the CPE routers, and where the ISP network provides layer 2 connectivity alone. The latter case can be implemented either as a set of VLLs between CPE routers (see section 4.0), in which case the ISP network provides a set of layer 2 point-to-point links, or as a VPLS (see section 7.0), in which case the ISP network is used to emulate a multiaccess LAN segment. With these scenarios a customer may have more flexibility (e.g., any IGP or any protocol can be run across all customer sites) but this usually comes at the expense of a more complex configuration for the customer. Thus, depending on customer requirements, a VPRN or a VPLS may be the more appropriate solution.

Because a VPRN carries out forwarding at the network layer, a single VPRN only directly supports a single network layer protocol. For multiprotocol support, a separate VPRN for each network layer protocol could be used, or one protocol could be tunneled over another (e.g., non-IP protocols tunneled over an IP VPRN) or alternatively the ISP network could be used to provide layer 2 connectivity only, such as with a VPLS as mentioned above.

The issues to be addressed for VPRNs include initial configuration, determination by an ISP edge router of the set of links that are in each VPRN, the set of other routers that have members in the VPRN, and the set of IP address prefixes reachable via each stub link, determination by a CPE router of the set of IP address prefixes to be forwarded to an ISP edge router, the mechanism used to disseminate stub reachability information to the correct set of ISP routers, and the establishment and use of the tunnels used to carry the data traffic. Note also that, although discussed first for VPRNs, many of these issues also apply to the VPLS scenario described later, with the network layer addresses being replaced by link layer addresses.

Note that VPRN operation is decoupled from the mechanisms used by the customer sites to access the Internet. A typical scenario would be for the ISP edge router to be used to provide both VPRN and Internet connectivity to a customer site. In this case the CPE router just has a default route pointing to the ISP edge router, with the latter being responsible for steering private traffic to the VPRN and other traffic to the Internet, and providing firewall functionality between the two domains. Alternatively a customer site could have Internet connectivity via an ISP router not involved in the VPRN, or even via a different ISP. In this case the CPE device is responsible for splitting the traffic into the two domains and providing firewall functionality.

5.1.1 Topology

   The topology of a VPRN may consist of a full mesh of tunnels between
   each VPRN node, or may be an arbitrary topology, such as a set of
   remote offices connected to the nearest regional site, with these
   regional sites connected together via a full or partial mesh. With
   VPRNs using IP tunnels there is much less cost assumed with full
   meshing than in cases where physical resources (e.g., a leased line)
   must be allocated for each connected pair of sites, or where the
   tunneling method requires resources to be allocated in the devices
   used to interconnect the edge routers (e.g., Frame Relay DLCIs). A
   full mesh topology yields optimal routing, since it precludes the
   need for traffic between two sites to traverse a third. Another
   attraction of a full mesh is that there is no need to configure
   topology information for the VPRN. Instead, given the member routers
   of a VPRN, the topology is implicit. If the number of ISP edge
   routers in a VPRN is very large, however, a full mesh topology may
   not be appropriate, due to the scaling issues involved, for example,
   the growth in the number of tunnels needed between sites, (which for
   n sites is $n(n-1)/2$), or the number of routing peers per router.
   Network policy may also lead to non full mesh topologies, for example
   an administrator may wish to set up the topology so that traffic
   between two remote sites passes through a central site, rather than
   go directly between the remote sites. It is also necessary to deal
   with the scenario where there is only partial connectivity across the
   IP backbone under certain error conditions (e.g. A can reach B, and B
   can reach C, but A cannot reach C directly), which can occur if
   policy routing is being used.

   For a network-based VPRN, it is assumed that each customer site CPE
   router connects to an ISP edge router through one or more point-to-
   point stub links (e.g. leased lines, ATM or Frame Relay connections).
   The ISP routers are responsible for learning and disseminating
   reachability information amongst themselves. The CPE routers must
   learn the set of destinations reachable via each stub link, though
   this may be as simple as a default route.

   The stub links may either be dedicated links, set up via
   provisioning, or may be dynamic links set up on demand, for example
   using PPP, voluntary tunneling (see section 6.3), or ATM signalling.
   With dynamic links it is necessary to authenticate the subscriber,
   and determine the authorized resources that the subscriber can access
   (e.g. which VPRNs the subscriber may join). Other than the way the
   subscriber is initially bound to the VPRN, (and this process may
   involve extra considerations such as dynamic IP address assignment),
   the subsequent VPRN mechanisms and services can be used for both
   types of subscribers in the same way.

5.1.2 Addressing

   The addressing used within a VPRN may have no relation to the
   addressing used on the IP backbone over which the VPRN is
   instantiated. In particular non-unique private IP addressing may be
   used [4]. Multiple VPRNs may be instantiated over the same set of
   physical devices, and they may use the same or overlapping address
   spaces.

5.1.3 Forwarding

   For a VPRN the tunnel mesh forms an overlay network operating over an
   IP backbone. Within each of the ISP edge routers there must be VPN
   specific forwarding state to forward packets received from stub links
   ('ingress traffic') to the appropriate next hop router, and to
   forward packets received from the core ('egress traffic') to the
   appropriate stub link. For cases where an ISP edge router supports
   multiple stub links belonging to the same VPRN, the tunnels can, as a
   local matter, either terminate on the edge router, or on a stub link.
   In the former case a VPN specific forwarding table is needed for
   egress traffic, in the latter case it is not. A VPN specific
   forwarding table is generally needed in the ingress direction, in
   order to direct traffic received on a stub link onto the correct IP
   tunnel towards the core.

   Also since a VPRN operates at the internetwork layer, the IP packets
   sent over a tunnel will have their Time to Live (TTL) field
   decremented in the normal manner, preventing packets circulating
   indefinitely in the event of a routing loop within the VPRN.

5.1.4 Multiple concurrent VPRN connectivity

   Note also that a single customer site may belong concurrently to
   multiple VPRNs and may want to transmit traffic both onto one or more
   VPRNs and to the default Internet, over the same stub link. There
   are a number of possible approaches to this problem, but these are
   outside the scope of this document.

5.2 VPRN Related Work

   VPRN requirements and mechanisms have been discussed previously in a
   number of different documents. One of the first was [10], which
   showed how the same VPN functionality can be implemented over both
   MPLS and non-MPLS networks. Some others are briefly discussed below.

   There are two main variants as regards the mechanisms used to provide
   VPRN membership and reachability functionality, - overlay and
   piggybacking. These are discussed in greater detail in sections

5.3.2, 5.3.3 and 5.3.4 below. An example of the overlay model is described in [14], which discusses the provision of VPRN functionality by means of a separate per-VPN routing protocol instance and route and forwarding table instantiation, otherwise known as virtual routing. Each VPN routing instance is isolated from any other VPN routing instance, and from the routing used across the backbone. As a result any routing protocol (e.g. OSPF, RIP2, IS-IS) can be run with any VPRN, independently of the routing protocols used in other VPRNs, or in the backbone itself. The VPN model described in [12] is also an overlay VPRN model using virtual routing. That document is specifically geared towards the provision of VPRN functionality over MPLS backbones, and it describes how VPRN membership dissemination can be automated over an MPLS backbone, by performing VPN neighbor discovery over the base MPLS tunnel mesh. [31] extends the virtual routing model to include VPN areas, and VPN border routers which route between VPN areas. VPN areas may be defined for administrative or technical reasons, such as different underlying network infrastructures (e.g. ATM, MPLS, IP).

In contrast [15] describes the provision of VPN functionality using a piggybacking approach for membership and reachability dissemination, with this information being piggybacked in Border Gateway Protocol 4 (BGP) [32] packets. VPNs are constructed using BGP policies, which are used to control which sites can communicate with each other. [13] also uses BGP for piggybacking membership information, and piggybacks reachability information on the protocol used to establish MPLS LSPs (CR-LDP or extended RSVP). Unlike the other proposals, however, this proposal requires the participation on the CPE router to implement the VPN functionality.

5.3 VPRN Generic Requirements

There are a number of common requirements which any network-based VPRN solution must address, and there are a number of different mechanisms that can be used to meet these requirements. These generic issues are

1) The use of a globally unique VPN identifier in order to be able to refer to a particular VPN.

2) VPRN membership determination. An edge router must learn of the local stub links that are in each VPRN, and must learn of the set of other routers that have members in that VPRN.

3) Stub link reachability information. An edge router must learn the set of addresses and address prefixes reachable via each stub link.

4) Intra-VPRN reachability information. Once an edge router has
   determined the set of address prefixes associated with each of its
   stub links, then this information must be disseminated to each
   other edge router in the VPRN.

5) Tunneling mechanism. An edge router must construct the necessary
   tunnels to other routers that have members in the VPRN, and must
   perform the encapsulation and decapsulation necessary to send and
   receive packets over the tunnels.

5.3.1 VPN Identifier

The IETF [16] and the ATM Forum [17] have standardized on a single
format for a globally unique identifier used to identify a VPN - a
VPN-ID. Only the format of the VPN-ID has been defined, not its
semantics or usage. The aim is to allow its use for a wide variety
of purposes, and to allow the same identifier to used with different
technologies and mechanisms. For example a VPN-ID can be included in
a MIB to identify a VPN for management purposes. A VPN-ID can be
used in a control plane protocol, for example to bind a tunnel to a
VPN at tunnel establishment time. All packets that traverse the
tunnel are then implicitly associated with the identified VPN. A
VPN-ID can be used in a data plane encapsulation, to allow for an
explicit per-packet identification of the VPN associated with the
packet. If a VPN is implemented using different technologies (e.g.,
IP and ATM) in a network, the same identifier can be used to identify
the VPN across the different technologies. Also if a VPN spans
multiple administrative domains the same identifier can be used
everywhere.

Most of the VPN schemes developed (e.g. [11], [12], [13], [14])
require the use of a VPN-ID that is carried in control and/or data
packets, which is used to associate the packet with a particular VPN.
Although the use of a VPN-ID in this manner is very common, it is not
universal. [15] describes a scheme where there is no protocol field
used to identify a VPN in this manner. In this scheme the VPNs as
understood by a user, are administrative constructs, built using BGP
policies. There are a number of attributes associated with VPN
routes, such as a route distinguisher, and origin and target "VPN",
that are used by the underlying protocol mechanisms for
disambiguation and scoping, and these are also used by the BGP policy
mechanism in the construction of VPNs, but there is nothing
corresponding with the VPN-ID as used in the other documents.

Note also that [33] defines a multiprotocol encapsulation for use
over ATM AAL5 that uses the standard VPN-ID format.

5.3.2 VPN Membership Information Configuration and Dissemination

In order to establish a VPRN, or to insert new customer sites into an
established VPRN, an ISP edge router must determine which stub links
are associated with which VPRN. For static links (e.g. an ATM VCC)
this information must be configured into the edge router, since the
edge router cannot infer such bindings by itself. An SNMP MIB
allowing for bindings between local stub links and VPN identities is
one solution.

For subscribers that attach to the network dynamically (e.g. using
PPP or voluntary tunneling) it is possible to make the association
between stub link and VPRN as part of the end user authentication
processing that must occur with such dynamic links. For example the
VPRN to which a user is to be bound may be derived from the domain
name the used as part of PPP authentication. If the user is
successfully authenticated (e.g. using a Radius server), then the
newly created dynamic link can be bound to the correct VPRN. Note
that static configuration information is still needed, for example to
maintain the list of authorized subscribers for each VPRN, but the
location of this static information could be an external
authentication server rather than on an ISP edge router. Whether the
link was statically or dynamically created, a VPN-ID can be
associated with that link to signify to which VPRN it is bound.

After learning which stub links are bound to which VPRN, each edge
router must learn either the identity of, or, at least, the route to,
each other edge router supporting other stub links in that particular
VPRN. Implicit in the latter is the notion that there exists some
mechanism by which the configured edge routers can then use this edge
router and/or stub link identity information to subsequently set up
the appropriate tunnels between them. The problem of VPRN member
dissemination between participating edge routers, can be solved in a
variety of ways, discussed below.

5.3.2.1 Directory Lookup

The members of a particular VPRN, that is, the identity of the edge
routers supporting stub links in the VPRN, and the set of static stub
links bound to the VPRN per edge router, could be configured into a
directory, which edge routers could query, using some defined
mechanism (e.g. Lightweight Directory Access Protocol (LDAP) [34]),
upon startup.

Using a directory allows either a full mesh topology or an arbitrary
topology to be configured. For a full mesh, the full list of member
routers in a VPRN is distributed everywhere. For an arbitrary
topology, different routers may receive different member lists.

Using a directory allows for authorization checking prior to
disseminating VPRN membership information, which may be desirable
where VPRNs span multiple administrative domains. In such a case,
directory to directory protocol mechanisms could also be used to
propagate authorized VPRN membership information between the
directory systems of the multiple administrative domains.

There also needs to be some form of database synchronization
mechanism (e.g. triggered or regular polling of the directory by edge
routers, or active pushing of update information to the edge routers
by the directory) in order for all edge routers to learn the identity
of newly configured sites inserted into an active VPRN, and also to
learn of sites removed from a VPRN.

5.3.2.2 Explicit Management Configuration

A VPRN MIB could be defined which would allow a central management
system to configure each edge router with the identities of each
other participating edge router and the identity of each of the
static stub links bound to the VPRN. Like the use of a directory,
this mechanism allows both full mesh and arbitrary topologies to be
configured. Another mechanism using a centralized management system
is to use a policy server and use the Common Open Policy Service
(COPS) protocol [35] to distribute VPRN membership and policy
information, such as the tunnel attributes to use when establishing a
tunnel, as described in [36].

Note that this mechanism allows the management station to impose
strict authorization control; on the other hand, it may be more
difficult to configure edge routers outside the scope of the
management system. The management configuration model can also be
considered a subset of the directory method, in that the management
directories could use MIBs to push VPRN membership information to the
participating edge routers, either subsequent to, or as part of, the
local stub link configuration process.

5.3.2.3 Piggybacking in Routing Protocols

VPRN membership information could be piggybacked into the routing
protocols run by each edge router across the IP backbone, since this
is an efficient means of automatically propagating information
throughout the network to other participating edge routers.
Specifically, each route advertisement by each edge router could
include, at a minimum, the set of VPN identifiers associated with
each edge router, and adequate information to allow other edge
routers to determine the identity of, and/or, the route to, the
particular edge router. Other edge routers would examine received
route advertisements to determine if any contained information was

relevant to a supported (i.e., configured) VPRN; this determination
could be done by looking for a VPN identifier matching a locally
configured VPN. The nature of the piggybacked information, and
related issues, such as scoping, and the means by which the nodes
advertising particular VPN memberships will be identified, will
generally be a function both of the routing protocol and of the
nature of the underlying transport.

Using this method all the routers in the network will have the same
view of the VPRN membership information, and so a full mesh topology
is easily supported. Supporting an arbitrary topology is more
difficult, however, since some form of pruning would seem to be
needed.

The advantage of the piggybacking scheme is that it allows for
efficient information dissemination, but it does require that all
nodes in the path, and not just the participating edge routers, be
able to accept such modified route advertisements. A disadvantage is
that significant administrative complexity may be required to
configure scoping mechanisms so as to both permit and constrain the
dissemination of the piggybacked advertisements, and in itself this
may be quite a configuration burden, particularly if the VPRN spans
multiple routing domains (e.g. different autonomous systems / ISPs).

Furthermore, unless some security mechanism is used for routing
updates so as to permit only all relevant edge routers to read the
piggybacked advertisements, this scheme generally implies a trust
model where all routers in the path must perforce be authorized to
know this information. Depending upon the nature of the routing
protocol, piggybacking may also require intermediate routers,
particularly autonomous system (AS) border routers, to cache such
advertisements and potentially also re-distribute them between
multiple routing protocols.

Each of the schemes described above have merit in particular
situations. Note that, in practice, there will almost always be some
centralized directory or management system which will maintain VPRN
membership information, such as the set of edge routers that are
allowed to support a certain VPRN, the bindings of static stub links
to VPRNs, or authentication and authorization information for users
that access the network via dynamics links. This information needs
to be configured and stored in some form of database, so that the
additional steps needed to facilitate the configuration of such
information into edge routers, and/or, facilitate edge router access
to such information, may not be excessively onerous.

5.3.3 Stub Link Reachability Information

There are two aspects to stub site reachability - the means by which
VPRN edge routers determine the set of VPRN addresses and address
prefixes reachable at each stub site, and the means by which the CPE
routers learn the destinations reachable via each stub link. A
number of common scenarios are outlined below. In each case the
information needed by the ISP edge router is the same - the set of
VPRN addresses reachable at the customer site, but the information
needed by the CPE router differs.

5.3.3.1 Stub Link Connectivity Scenarios

5.3.3.1.1 Dual VPRN and Internet Connectivity

The CPE router is connected via one link to an ISP edge router, which
provides both VPRN and Internet connectivity.

This is the simplest case for the CPE router, as it just needs a
default route pointing to the ISP edge router.

5.3.3.1.2 VPRN Connectivity Only

The CPE router is connected via one link to an ISP edge router, which
provides VPRN, but not Internet, connectivity.

The CPE router must know the set of non-local VPRN destinations
reachable via that link. This may be a single prefix, or may be a
number of disjoint prefixes. The CPE router may be either statically
configured with this information, or may learn it dynamically by
running an instance of an Interior Gateway Protocol (IGP). For
simplicity it is assumed that the IGP used for this purpose is RIP,
though it could be any IGP. The ISP edge router will inject into
this instance of RIP the VRPN routes which it learns by means of one
of the intra-VPRN reachability mechanisms described in section 5.3.4.
Note that the instance of RIP run to the CPE, and any instance of a
routing protocol used to learn intra-VPRN reachability (even if also
RIP) are separate, with the ISP edge router redistributing the routes
from one instance to another.

5.3.3.1.3 Multihomed Connectivity

The CPE router is multihomed to the ISP network, which provides VPRN connectivity.

In this case all the ISP edge routers could advertise the same VPRN routes to the CPE router, which then sees all VPRN prefixes equally reachable via all links. More specific route redistribution is also possible, whereby each ISP edge router advertises a different set of prefixes to the CPE router.

5.3.3.1.4 Backdoor Links

The CPE router is connected to the ISP network, which provides VPRN connectivity, but also has a backdoor link to another customer site

In this case the ISP edge router will advertise VPRN routes as in case 2 to the CPE device. However now the same destination is reachable via both the ISP edge router and via the backdoor link. If the CPE routers connected to the backdoor link are running the customer's IGP, then the backdoor link may always be the favored link as it will appear an an 'internal' path, whereas the destination as injected via the ISP edge router will appear as an 'external' path (to the customer's IGP). To avoid this problem, assuming that the customer wants the traffic to traverse the ISP network, then a separate instance of RIP should be run between the CPE routers at both ends of the backdoor link, in the same manner as an instance of RIP is run on a stub or backup link between a CPE router and an ISP edge router. This will then also make the backdoor link appear as an external path, and by adjusting the link costs appropriately, the ISP path can always be favored, unless it goes down, when the backdoor link is then used.

The description of the above scenarios covers what reachability information is needed by the ISP edge routers and the CPE routers, and discusses some of the mechanisms used to convey this information. The sections below look at these mechanisms in more detail.

5.3.3.1 Routing Protocol Instance

A routing protocol can be run between the CPE edge router and the ISP edge router to exchange reachability information. This allows an ISP edge router to learn the VPRN prefixes reachable at a customer site, and also allows a CPE router to learn the destinations reachable via the provider network.

The extent of the routing domain for this protocol instance is
generally just the ISP edge router and the CPE router although if the
customer site is also running the same protocol as its IGP, then the
domain may extend into customer site. If the customer site is
running a different routing protocol then the CPE router
redistributes the routes between the instance running to the ISP edge
router, and the instance running into the customer site.

Given the typically restricted scope of this routing instance, a
simple protocol will generally suffice. RIP is likely to be the most
common protocol used, though any routing protocol, such as OSPF, or
BGP run in internal mode (IBGP), could also be used.

Note that the instance of the stub link routing protocol is different
from any instance of a routing protocol used for intra-VPRN
reachability. For example, if the ISP edge router uses routing
protocol piggybacking to disseminate VPRN membership and reachability
information across the core, then it may redistribute suitably
labeled routes from the CPE routing instance to the core routing
instance. The routing protocols used for each instance are
decoupled, and any suitable protocol can be used in each case. There
is no requirement that the same protocol, or even the same stub link
reachability information gathering mechanism, be run between each CPE
router and associated ISP edge router in a particular VPRN, since
this is a purely local matter.

This decoupling allows ISPs to deploy a common (across all VPRNs)
intra-VPRN reachability mechanism, and a common stub link
reachability mechanism, with these mechanisms isolated both from each
other, and from the particular IGP used in a customer network. In
the first case, due to the IGP-IGP boundary implemented on the ISP
edge router, the ISP can insulate the intra-VPRN reachability
mechanism from misbehaving stub link protocol instances. In the
second case the ISP is not required to be aware of the particular IGP
running in a customer site. Other scenarios are possible, where the
ISP edge routers are running a routing protocol in the same instance
as the customer's IGP, but are unlikely to be practical, since it
defeats the purpose of a VPRN simplifying CPE router configuration.
In cases where a customer wishes to run an IGP across multiple sites,
a VPLS solution is more suitable.

Note that if a particular customer site concurrently belongs to
multiple VPRNs (or wishes to concurrently communicate with both a
VPRN and the Internet), then the ISP edge router must have some means
of unambiguously mapping stub link address prefixes to particular
VPRNs. A simple way is to have multiple stub links, one per VPRN.
It is also possible to run multiple VPRNs over one stub link. This
could be done either by ensuring (and appropriately configuring the

ISP edge router to know) that particular disjoint address prefixes
are mapped into separate VPRNs, or by tagging the routing
advertisements from the CPE router with the appropriate VPN
identifier. For example if MPLS was being used to convey stub link
reachability information, different MPLS labels would be used to
differentiate the disjoint prefixes assigned to particular VPRNs. In
any case, some administrative procedure would be required for this
coordination.

5.3.3.2 Configuration

The reachability information across each stub link could be manually
configured, which may be appropriate if the set of addresses or
prefixes is small and static.

5.3.3.3 ISP Administered Addresses

The set of addresses used by each stub site could be administered and
allocated via the VPRN edge router, which may be appropriate for
small customer sites, typically containing either a single host, or a
single subnet. Address allocation can be carried out using protocols
such as PPP or DHCP [37], with, for example, the edge router acting
as a Radius client and retrieving the customer's IP address to use
from a Radius server, or acting as a DHCP relay and examining the
DHCP reply message as it is relayed to the customer site. In this
manner the edge router can build up a table of stub link reachability
information. Although these address assignment mechanisms are
typically used to assign an address to a single host, some vendors
have added extensions whereby an address prefix can be assigned,
with, in some cases, the CPE device acting as a "mini-DHCP" server
and assigning addresses for the hosts in the customer site.

Note that with these schemes it is the responsibility of the address
allocation server to ensure that each site in the VPN received a
disjoint address space. Note also that an ISP would typically only
use this mechanism for small stub sites, which are unlikely to have
backdoor links.

5.3.3.4 MPLS Label Distribution Protocol

In cases where the CPE router runs MPLS, LDP can be used to convey
the set of prefixes at a stub site to a VPRN edge router. Using the
downstream unsolicited mode of label distribution the CPE router can
distribute a label for each route in the stub site. Note however
that the processing carried out by the edge router in this case is
more than just the normal LDP processing, since it is learning new
routes via LDP, rather than the usual case of learning labels for
existing routes that it has learned via standard routing mechanisms.

5.3.4   Intra-VPN Reachability Information

Once an edge router has determined the set of prefixes associated
with each of its stub links, then this information must be
disseminated to each other edge router in the VPRN. Note also that
there is an implicit requirement that the set of reachable addresses
within the VPRN be locally unique that is, each VPRN stub link (not
performing load sharing) maintain an address space disjoint from any
other, so as to permit unambiguous routing. In practical terms, it
is also generally desirable, though not required, that this address
space be well partitioned i.e., specific, disjoint address prefixes
per edge router, so as to preclude the need to maintain and
disseminate large numbers of host routes.

The problem of intra-VPN reachability information dissemination can
be solved in a number of ways, some of which include the following:

5.3.4.1   Directory Lookup

Along with VPRN membership information, a central directory could
maintain a listing of the address prefixes associated with each
customer site. Such information could be obtained by the server
through protocol interactions with each edge router. Note that the
same directory synchronization issues discussed above in section
5.3.2 also apply in this case.

5.3.4.2   Explicit Configuration

The address spaces associated with each edge router could be
explicitly configured into each other router. This is clearly a
non-scalable solution, particularly when arbitrary topologies are
used, and also raises the question of how the management system
learns such information in the first place.

5.3.4.3   Local Intra-VPRN Routing Instantiations

In this approach, each edge router runs an instance of a routing
protocol (a 'virtual router') per VPRN, running across the VPRN
tunnels to each peer edge router, to disseminate intra-VPRN
reachability information. Both full-mesh and arbitrary VPRN
topologies can be easily supported, since the routing protocol itself
can run over any topology. The intra-VPRN routing advertisements
could be distinguished from normal tunnel data packets either by
being addressed directly to the peer edge router, or by a tunnel
specific mechanism.

Note that this intra-VPRN routing protocol need have no relationship either with the IGP of any customer site or with the routing protocols operated by the ISPs in the IP backbone. Depending on the size and scale of the VPRNs to be supported either a simple protocol like RIP or a more sophisticated protocol like OSPF could be used. Because the intra-VPRN routing protocol operates as an overlay over the IP backbone it is wholly transparent to any intermediate routers, and to any edge routers not within the VPRN. This also implies that such routing information can remain opaque to such routers, which may be a necessary security requirements in some cases. Also note that if the routing protocol runs directly over the same tunnels as the data traffic, then it will inherit the same level of security as that afforded the data traffic, for example strong encryption and authentication.

If the tunnels over which an intra-VPRN routing protocol runs are dedicated to a specific VPN (e.g. a different multiplexing field is used for each VPN) then no changes are needed to the routing protocol itself. On the other hand if shared tunnels are used, then it is necessary to extend the routing protocol to allow a VPN-ID field to be included in routing update packets, to allow sets of prefixes to be associated with a particular VPN.

5.3.4.4 Link Reachability Protocol

By link reachability protocol is meant a protocol that allows two nodes, connected via a point-to-point link, to exchange reachability information. Given a full mesh topology, each edge router could run a link reachability protocol, for instance some variation of MPLS CR-LDP, across the tunnel to each peer edge router in the VPRN, carrying the VPN-ID and the reachability information of each VPRN running across the tunnel between the two edge routers. If VPRN membership information has already been distributed to an edge router, then the neighbor discovery aspects of a traditional routing protocol are not needed, as the set of neighbors is already known. TCP connections can be used to interconnect the neighbors, to provide reliability. This approach may reduce the processing burden of running routing protocol instances per VPRN, and may be of particular benefit where a shared tunnel mechanism is used to connect a set of edge routers supporting multiple VPRNs.

Another approach to developing a link reachability protocol would be to base it on IBGP. The problem that needs to be solved by a link reachability protocol is very similar to that solved by IBGP - conveying address prefixes reliably between edge routers.

Using a link reachability protocol it is straightforward to support a full mesh topology - each edge router conveys its own local reachability information to all other routers, but does not redistribute information received from any other router. However once an arbitrary topology needs to be supported, the link reachability protocol needs to develop into a full routing protocol, due to the need to implement mechanisms to avoid loops, and there would seem little benefit in reinventing another routing protocol to deal with this. Some reasons why partially connected meshes may be needed even in a tunneled environment are discussed in section 5.1.1.

5.3.4.5 Piggybacking in IP Backbone Routing Protocols

As with VPRN membership, the set of address prefixes associated with each stub interface could also be piggybacked into the routing advertisements from each edge router and propagated through the network. Other edge routers extract this information from received route advertisements in the same way as they obtain the VPRN membership information (which, in this case, is implicit in the identification of the source of each route advertisement). Note that this scheme may require, depending upon the nature of the routing protocols involved, that intermediate routers, e.g. border routers, cache intra-VPRN routing information in order to propagate it further. This also has implications for the trust model, and for the level of security possible for intra-VPRN routing information.

Note that in any of the cases discussed above, an edge router has the option of disseminating its stub link prefixes in a manner so as to permit tunneling from remote edge routers directly to the egress stub links. Alternatively, it could disseminate the information so as to associate all such prefixes with the edge router, rather than with specific stub links. In this case, the edge router would need to implement a VPN specific forwarding mechanism for egress traffic, to determine the correct egress stub link. The advantage of this is that it may significantly reduce the number of distinct tunnels or tunnel label information which need to be constructed and maintained. Note that this choice is purely a local manner and is not visible to remote edge routers.

5.3.5 Tunneling Mechanisms

Once VPRN membership information has been disseminated, the tunnels comprising the VPRN core can be constructed.

One approach to setting up the tunnel mesh is to use point-to-point IP tunnels, and the requirements and issues for such tunnels have been discussed in section 3.0. For example while tunnel establishment can be done through manual configuration, this is

clearly not likely to be a scalable solution, given the O(n^2)
problem of meshed links. As such, tunnel set up should use some form
of signalling protocol to allow two nodes to construct a tunnel to
each other knowing only each other's identity.

Another approach is to use the multipoint to point 'tunnels' provided
by MPLS. As noted in [38], MPLS can be considered to be a form of IP
tunneling, since the labels of MPLS packets allow for routing
decisions to be decoupled from the addressing information of the
packets themselves. MPLS label distribution mechanisms can be used
to associate specific sets of MPLS labels with particular VPRN
address prefixes supported on particular egress points (i.e., stub
links of edge routers) and hence allow other edge routers to
explicitly label and route traffic to particular VPRN stub links.

One attraction of MPLS as a tunneling mechanism is that it may
require less processing within each edge router than alternative
tunneling mechanisms. This is a function of the fact that data
security within a MPLS network is implicit in the explicit label
binding, much as with a connection oriented network, such as Frame
Relay. This may hence lessen customer concerns about data security
and hence require less processor intensive security mechanisms (e.g.,
IPSec). However there are other potential security concerns with
MPLS. There is no direct support for security features such as
authentication, confidentiality, and non-repudiation and the trust
model for MPLS means that intermediate routers, (which may belong to
different administrative domains), through which membership and
prefix reachability information is conveyed, must be trusted, not
just the edge routers themselves.

5.4 Multihomed Stub Routers

The discussion thus far has implicitly assumed that stub routers are
connected to one and only one VPRN edge router. In general, this
restriction should be capable of being relaxed without any change to
VPRN operation, given general market interest in multihoming for
reliability and other reasons. In particular, in cases where the
stub router supports multiple redundant links, with only one
operational at any given time, with the links connected either to the
same VPRN edge router, or to two or more different VPRN edge routers,
then the stub link reachability mechanisms will both discover the
loss of an active link, and the activation of a backup link. In the
former situation, the previously connected VPRN edge router will
cease advertising reachability to the stub node, while the VPRN edge
router with the now active link will begin advertising reachability,
hence restoring connectivity.

An alternative scenario is where the stub node supports multiple active links, using some form of load sharing algorithm. In such a case, multiple VPRN edge routers may have active paths to the stub node, and may so advertise across the VPRN. This scenario should not cause any problem with reachability across the VPRN providing that the intra-VPRN reachability mechanism can accommodate multiple paths to the same prefix, and has the appropriate mechanisms to preclude looping - for instance, distance vector metrics associated with each advertised prefix.

5.5 Multicast Support

Multicast and broadcast traffic can be supported across VPRNs either by edge replication or by native multicast support in the backbone. These two cases are discussed below.

5.5.1 Edge Replication

This is where each VPRN edge router replicates multicast traffic for transmission across each link in the VPRN. Note that this is the same operation that would be performed by CPE routers terminating actual physical links or dedicated connections. As with CPE routers, multicast routing protocols could also be run on each VPRN edge router to determine the distribution tree for multicast traffic and hence reduce unnecessary flood traffic. This could be done by running instances of standard multicast routing protocols, e.g. Protocol Independent Multicast (PIM) [39] or Distance Vector Multicast Routing Protocol (DVMRP) [40], on and between each VPRN edge router, through the VPRN tunnels, in the same way that unicast routing protocols might be run at each VPRN edge router to determine intra-VPN unicast reachability, as discussed in section 5.3.4. Alternatively, if a link reachability protocol was run across the VPRN tunnels for intra-VPRN reachability, then this could also be augmented to allow VPRN edge routers to indicate both the particular multicast groups requested for reception at each edge node, and also the multicast sources at each edge site.

In either case, there would need to be some mechanism to allow for the VPRN edge routers to determine which particular multicast groups were requested at each site and which sources were present at each site. How this could be done would, in general, be a function of the capabilities of the CPE stub routers at each site. If these run multicast routing protocols, then they can interact directly with the equivalent protocols at each VPRN edge router. If the CPE device does not run a multicast routing protocol, then in the absence of Internet Group Management Protocol (IGMP) proxying [41] the customer site would be limited to a single subnet connected to the VPRN edge router via a bridging device, as the scope of an IGMP message is

limited to a single subnet. However using IGMP-proxying the CPE
router can engage in multicast forwarding without running a multicast
routing protocol, in constrained topologies. On its interfaces into
the customer site the CPE router performs the router functions of
IGMP, and on its interface to the VPRN edge router it performs the
host functions of IGMP.

5.5.2 Native Multicast Support

This is where VPRN edge routers map intra-VPRN multicast traffic onto
a native IP multicast distribution mechanism across the backbone.
Note that intra-VPRN multicast has the same requirements for
isolation from general backbone traffic as intra-VPRN unicast
traffic. Currently the only IP tunneling mechanism that has native
support for multicast is MPLS. On the other hand, while MPLS
supports native transport of IP multicast packets, additional
mechanisms would be needed to leverage these mechanisms for the
support of intra-VPRN multicast.

For instance, each VPRN router could prefix multicast group addresses
within each VPRN with the VPN-ID of that VPRN and then redistribute
these, essentially treating this VPN-ID/intra-VPRN multicast address
tuple as a normal multicast address, within the backbone multicast
routing protocols, as with the case of unicast reachability, as
discussed previously. The MPLS multicast label distribution
mechanisms could then be used to set up the appropriate multicast
LSPs to interconnect those sites within each VPRN supporting
particular multicast group addresses. Note, however, that this would
require each of the intermediate LSRs to not only be aware of each
intra-VPRN multicast group, but also to have the capability of
interpreting these modified advertisements. Alternatively,
mechanisms could be defined to map intra-VPRN multicast groups into
backbone multicast groups.

Other IP tunneling mechanisms do not have native multicast support.
It may prove feasible to extend such tunneling mechanisms by
allocating IP multicast group addresses to the VPRN as a whole and
hence distributing intra-VPRN multicast traffic encapsulated within
backbone multicast packets. Edge VPRN routers could filter out
unwanted multicast groups. Alternatively, mechanisms could also be
defined to allow for allocation of backbone multicast group addresses
for particular intra-VPRN multicast groups, and to then utilize
these, through backbone multicast protocols, as discussed above, to
limit forwarding of intra-VPRN multicast traffic only to those nodes
within the group.

A particular issue with the use of native multicast support is the
provision of security for such multicast traffic. Unlike the case of
edge replication, which inherits the security characteristics of the
underlying tunnel, native multicast mechanisms will need to use some
form of secure multicast mechanism. The development of architectures
and solutions for secure multicast is an active research area, for
example see [42] and [43]. The Secure Multicast Group (SMuG) of the
IRTF has been set up to develop prototype solutions, which would then
be passed to the IETF IPSec working group for standardization.

However considerably more development is needed before scalable
secure native multicast mechanisms can be generally deployed.

5.6 Recommendations

The various proposals that have been developed to support some form
of VPRN functionality can be broadly classified into two groups -
those that utilize the router piggybacking approach for distributing
VPN membership and/or reachability information ([13],[15]) and those
that use the virtual routing approach ([12],[14]). In some cases the
mechanisms described rely on the characteristics of a particular
infrastructure (e.g. MPLS) rather than just IP.

Within the context of the virtual routing approach it may be useful
to develop a membership distribution protocol based on a directory or
MIB. When combined with the protocol extensions for IP tunneling
protocols outlined in section 3.2, this would then provide the basis
for a complete set of protocols and mechanisms that support
interoperable VPRNs that span multiple administrations over an IP
backbone. Note that the other major pieces of functionality needed -
the learning and distribution of customer reachability information,
can be performed by instances of standard routing protocols, without
the need for any protocol extensions.

Also for the constrained case of a full mesh topology, the usefulness
of developing a link reachability protocol could be examined, however
the limitations and scalability issues associated with this topology
may not make it worthwhile to develop something specific for this
case, as standard routing will just work.

Extending routing protocols to allow a VPN-ID to carried in routing
update packets could also be examined, but is not necessary if VPN
specific tunnels are used.

6.0 VPN Types: Virtual Private Dial Networks

A Virtual Private Dial Network (VPDN) allows for a remote user to connect on demand through an ad hoc tunnel into another site. The user is connected to a public IP network via a dial-up PSTN or ISDN link, and user packets are tunneled across the public network to the desired site, giving the impression to the user of being 'directly' connected into that site. A key characteristic of such ad hoc connections is the need for user authentication as a prime requirement, since anyone could potentially attempt to gain access to such a site using a switched dial network.

Today many corporate networks allow access to remote users through dial connections made through the PSTN, with users setting up PPP connections across an access network to a network access server, at which point the PPP sessions are authenticated using AAA systems running such standard protocols as Radius [44]. Given the pervasive deployment of such systems, any VPDN system must in practice allow for the near transparent re-use of such existing systems.

The IETF have developed the Layer 2 Tunneling Protocol (L2TP) [8] which allows for the extension of of user PPP sessions from an L2TP Access Concentrator (LAC) to a remote L2TP Network Server (LNS). The L2TP protocol itself was based on two earlier protocols, the Layer 2 Forwarding protocol (L2F) [45], and the Point-to-Point Tunneling Protocol (PPTP) [46], and this is reflected in the two quite different scenarios for which L2TP can be used - compulsory tunneling and voluntary tunneling, discussed further below in sections 6.2 and 6.3.

This document focuses on the use of L2TP over an IP network (using UDP), but L2TP may also be run directly over other protocols such as ATM or Frame Relay. Issues specifically related to running L2TP over non-IP networks, such as how to secure such tunnels, are not addressed here.

6.1 L2TP protocol characteristics

This section looks at the characteristics of the L2TP tunneling protocol using the categories outlined in section 3.0.

6.1.1 Multiplexing

L2TP has inherent support for the multiplexing of multiple calls from different users over a single link. Between the same two IP endpoints, there can be multiple L2TP tunnels, as identified by a tunnel-id, and multiple sessions within a tunnel, as identified by a session-id.

6.1.2 Signalling

This is supported via the inbuilt control connection protocol, allowing both tunnels and sessions to be established dynamically.

6.1.3 Data Security

By allowing for the transparent extension of PPP from the user, through the LAC to the LNS, L2TP allows for the use of whatever security mechanisms, with respect to both connection set up, and data transfer, may be used with normal PPP connections. However this does not provide security for the L2TP control protocol itself. In this case L2TP could be further secured by running it in combination with IPSec through IP backbones [47], [48], or related mechanisms on non-IP backbones [49].

The interaction of L2TP with AAA systems for user authentication and authorization is a function of the specific means by which L2TP is used, and the nature of the devices supporting the LAC and the LNS. These issues are discussed in depth in [50].

The means by which the host determines the correct LAC to connect to, and the means by which the LAC determines which users to further tunnel, and the LNS parameters associated with each user, are outside the scope of the operation of a VPDN, but may be addressed, for instance, by evolving Internet roaming specifications [51].

6.1.4 Multiprotocol Transport

L2TP transports PPP packets (and only PPP packets) and thus can be used to carry multiprotocol traffic since PPP itself is multiprotocol.

6.1.5 Sequencing

L2TP supports sequenced delivery of packets. This is a capability that can be negotiated at session establishment, and that can be turned on and off by an LNS during a session. The sequence number field in L2TP can also be used to provide an indication of dropped packets, which is needed by various PPP compression algorithms to operate correctly. If no compression is in use, and the LNS determines that the protocols in use (as evidenced by the PPP NCP negotiations) can deal with out of sequence packets (e.g. IP), then it may disable the use of sequencing.

6.1.6 Tunnel Maintenance

   A keepalive protocol is used by L2TP in order to allow it to
   distinguish between a tunnel outage and prolonged periods of tunnel
   inactivity.

6.1.7 Large MTUs

   L2TP itself has no inbuilt support for a segmentation and reassembly
   capability, but when run over UDP/IP IP fragmentation will take place
   if necessary. Note that a LAC or LNS may adjust the Maximum Receive
   Unit (MRU) negotiated via PPP in order to preclude fragmentation, if
   it has knowledge of the MTU used on the path between LAC and LNS. To
   this end, there is a proposal to allow the use of MTU discovery for
   cases where the L2TP tunnel transports IP frames [52].

6.1.8 Tunnel Overhead

   L2TP as used over IP networks runs over UDP and must be used to carry
   PPP traffic. This results in a significant amount of overhead, both
   in the data plane with UDP, L2TP and PPP headers, and also in the
   control plane, with the L2TP and PPP control protocols. This is
   discussed further in section 6.3

6.1.9 Flow and Congestion Control

   L2TP supports flow and congestion control mechanisms for the control
   protocol, but not for data traffic. See section 3.1.9 for more
   details.

6.1.10 QoS / Traffic Management

   An L2TP header contains a 1-bit priority field, which can be set for
   packets that may need preferential treatment (e.g. keepalives) during
   local queuing and transmission. Also by transparently extending PPP,
   L2TP has inherent support for such PPP mechanisms as multi-link PPP
   [53] and its associated control protocols [54], which allow for
   bandwidth on demand to meet user requirements.

   In addition L2TP calls can be mapped into whatever underlying traffic
   management mechanisms may exist in the network, and there are
   proposals to allow for requests through L2TP signalling for specific
   differentiated services behaviors [55].

6.1.11 Miscellaneous

Since L2TP is designed to transparently extend PPP, it does not
attempt to supplant the normal address assignment mechanisms
associated with PPP. Hence, in general terms the host initiating the
PPP session will be assigned an address by the LNS using PPP
procedures. This addressing may have no relation to the addressing
used for communication between the LAC and LNS. The LNS will also
need to support whatever forwarding mechanisms are needed to route
traffic to and from the remote host.

6.2 Compulsory Tunneling

Compulsory tunneling refers to the scenario in which a network node -
a dial or network access server, for instance - acting as a LAC,
extends a PPP session across a backbone using L2TP to a remote LNS,
as illustrated below. This operation is transparent to the user
initiating the PPP session to the LAC. This allows for the
decoupling of the location and/or ownership of the modem pools used
to terminate dial calls, from the site to which users are provided
access. Support for this scenario was the original intent of the L2F
specification, upon which the L2TP specification was based.

There are a number of different deployment scenarios possible. One
example, shown in the diagram below, is where a subscriber host dials
into a NAS acting as a LAC, and is tunneled across an IP network
(e.g. the Internet) to a gateway acting as an LNS. The gateway
provides access to a corporate network, and could either be a device
in the corporate network itself, or could be an ISP edge router, in
the case where a customer has outsourced the maintenance of LNS
functionality to an ISP. Another scenario is where an ISP uses L2TP
to provide a subscriber with access to the Internet. The subscriber
host dials into a NAS acting as a LAC, and is tunneled across an
access network to an ISP edge router acting as an LNS. This ISP edge
router then feeds the subscriber traffic into the Internet. Yet
other scenarios are where an ISP uses L2TP to provide a subscriber
with access to a VPRN, or with concurrent access to both a VPRN and
the Internet.

A VPDN, whether using compulsory or voluntary tunneling, can be
viewed as just another type of access method for subscriber traffic,
and as such can be used to provide connectivity to different types of
networks, e.g. a corporate network, the Internet, or a VPRN. The last
scenario is also an example of how a VPN service as provided to a
customer may be implemented using a combination of different types of
VPN.

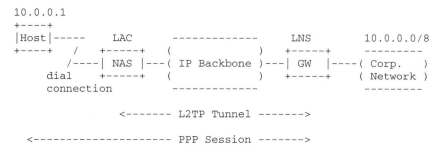

```
     10.0.0.1
     +----+
     |Host|-----     LAC          -------------     LNS          10.0.0.0/8
     +----+    /   +-----+   (                 )   +-----+      ---------
             /----| NAS |---( IP Backbone )---| GW  |----( Corp.   )
         dial     +-----+   (                 )   +-----+      ( Network )
         connection        -------------                      ---------

                      <------- L2TP Tunnel ------->

         <-------------------- PPP Session ------->
```

Figure 6.1: Compulsory Tunneling Example

Compulsory tunneling was originally intended for deployment on
network access servers supporting wholesale dial services, allowing
for remote dial access through common facilities to an enterprise
site, while precluding the need for the enterprise to deploy its own
dial servers. Another example of this is where an ISP outsources its
own dial connectivity to an access network provider (such as a Local
Exchange Carrier (LEC) in the USA) removing the need for an ISP to
maintain its own dial servers and allowing the LEC to serve multiple
ISPs. More recently, compulsory tunneling mechanisms have also been
proposed for evolving Digital Subscriber Line (DSL) services [56],
[57], which also seek to leverage the existing AAA infrastructure.

Call routing for compulsory tunnels requires that some aspect of the
initial PPP call set up can be used to allow the LAC to determine the
identity of the LNS. As noted in [50], these aspects can include the
user identity, as determined through some aspect of the access
network, including calling party number, or some attribute of the
called party, such as the Fully Qualified Domain Name (FQDN) of the
identity claimed during PPP authentication.

It is also possible to chain two L2TP tunnels together, whereby a LAC
initiates a tunnel to an intermediate relay device, which acts as an
LNS to this first LAC, and acts as a LAC to the final LNS. This may
be needed in some cases due to administrative, organizational or
regulatory issues pertaining to the split between access network
provider, IP backbone provider and enterprise customer.

6.3 Voluntary Tunnels

   Voluntary tunneling refers to the case where an individual host
   connects to a remote site using a tunnel originating on the host,
   with no involvement from intermediate network nodes, as illustrated
   below.   The PPTP specification, parts of which have been incorporated
   into L2TP, was based upon a voluntary tunneling model.

   As with compulsory tunneling there are different deployment scenarios
   possible. The diagram below shows a subscriber host accessing a
   corporate network with either L2TP or IPSec being used as the
   voluntary tunneling mechanism. Another scenario is where voluntary
   tunneling is used to provide a subscriber with access to a VPRN.

6.3.1 Issues with Use of L2TP for Voluntary Tunnels

   The L2TP specification has support for voluntary tunneling, insofar
   as the LAC can be located on a host, not only on a network node.
   Note that such a host has two IP addresses - one for the LAC-LNS IP
   tunnel, and another, typically allocated via PPP, for the network to
   which the host is connecting. The benefits of using L2TP for
   voluntary tunneling are that the existing authentication and address
   assignment mechanisms used by PPP can be reused without modification.
   For example an LNS could also include a Radius client, and
   communicate with a Radius server to authenticate a PPP PAP or CHAP
   exchange, and to retrieve configuration information for the host such
   as its IP address and a list of DNS servers to use. This information
   can then be passed to the host via the PPP IPCP protocol.

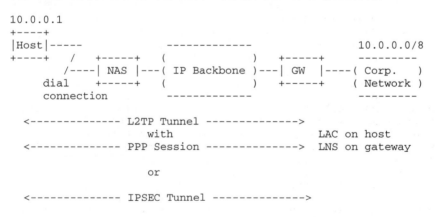

```
   10.0.0.1
   +----+
   |Host|-----                 -------------                  10.0.0.0/8
   +----+   /    +-----+      (             )  +-----+        ---------
           /----| NAS |---( IP Backbone )---| GW  |----( Corp.   )
        dial    +-----+      (             )  +-----+      ( Network )
        connection          -------------                  ---------


      <-------------- L2TP Tunnel -------------->
                         with                      LAC on host
      <-------------- PPP Session -------------->  LNS on gateway


                      or

      <-------------- IPSEC Tunnel -------------->
```

                 Figure 6.2: Voluntary Tunneling Example

The above procedure is not without its costs, however. There is considerable overhead with such a protocol stack, particularly when IPSec is also needed for security purposes, and given that the host may be connected via a low-bandwidth dial up link. The overhead consists of both extra headers in the data plane and extra control protocols needed in the control plane. Using L2TP for voluntary tunneling, secured with IPSec, means a web application, for example, would run over the following stack

   HTTP/TCP/IP/PPP/L2TP/UDP/ESP/IP/PPP/AHDLC

It is proposed in [58] that IPSec alone be used for voluntary tunnels reducing overhead, using the following stack.

   HTTP/TCP/IP/ESP/IP/PPP/AHDLC

In this case IPSec is used in tunnel mode, with the tunnel terminating either on an IPSec edge device at the enterprise site, or on the provider edge router connected to the enterprise site. There are two possibilities for the IP addressing of the host. Two IP addresses could be used, in a similar manner to the L2TP case. Alternatively the host can use a single public IP address as the source IP address in both inner and outer IP headers, with the gateway performing Network Address Translation (NAT) before forwarding the traffic to the enterprise network. To other hosts in the enterprise network the host appears to have an 'internal' IP address. Using NAT has some limitations and restrictions, also pointed out in [58].

Another area of potential problems with PPP is due to the fact that the characteristics of a link layer implemented via an L2TP tunnel over an IP backbone are quite different to a link layer run over a serial line, as discussed in the L2TP specification itself. For example, poorly chosen PPP parameters may lead to frequent resets and timeouts, particularly if compression is in use. This is because an L2TP tunnel may misorder packets, and may silently drop packets, neither of which normally occurs on serial lines. The general packet loss rate could also be significantly higher due to network congestion. Using the sequence number field in an L2TP header addresses the misordering issue, and for cases where the LAC and LNS are coincident with the PPP endpoints, as in voluntary tunneling, the sequence number field can also be used to detect a dropped packet, and to pass a suitable indication to any compression entity in use, which typically requires such knowledge in order to keep the compression histories in synchronization at both ends. (In fact this is more of an issue with compulsory tunneling since the LAC may have to deliberately issue a corrupted frame to the PPP host, to give an indication of packet loss, and some hardware may not allow this).

6.3.2   Issues with Use of IPSec for Voluntary Tunnels

If IPSec is used for voluntary tunneling, the functions of user
authentication and host configuration, achieved by means of PPP when
using L2TP, still need to be carried out. A distinction needs to be
drawn here between machine authentication and user authentication. '
Two factor' authentication is carried out on the basis of both
something the user has, such as a machine or smartcard with a digital
certificate, and something the user knows, such as a password.
(Another example is getting money from an bank ATM machine - you need
a card and a PIN number). Many of the existing legacy schemes
currently in use to perform user authentication are asymmetric in
nature, and are not supported by IKE. For remote access the most
common existing user authentication mechanism is to use PPP between
the user and access server, and Radius between the access server and
authentication server. The authentication exchanges that occur in
this case, e.g. a PAP or CHAP exchange, are asymmetric. Also CHAP
supports the ability for the network to reauthenticate the user at
any time after the initial session has been established, to ensure
that the current user is the same person that initiated the session.

While IKE provides strong support for machine authentication, it has
only limited support for any form of user authentication and has no
support for asymmetric user authentication. While a user password
can be used to derive a key used as a preshared key, this cannot be
used with IKE Main Mode in a remote access environment, as the user
will not have a fixed IP address, and while Aggressive Mode can be
used instead, this affords no identity protection. To this end there
have been a number of proposals to allow for support of legacy
asymmetric user level authentication schemes with IPSec. [59]
defines a new IKE message exchange - the transaction exchange - which
allows for both Request/Reply and Set/Acknowledge message sequences,
and it also defines attributes that can be used for client IP stack
configuration. [60] and [61] describe mechanisms that use the
transaction message exchange, or a series of such exchanges, carried
out between the IKE Phase 1 and Phase 2 exchanges, to perform user
authentication. A different approach, that does not extend the IKE
protocol itself, is described in [62]. With this approach a user
establishes a Phase 1 SA with a security gateway and then sets up a
Phase 2 SA to the gateway, over which an existing authentication
protocol is run. The gateway acts as a proxy and relays the protocol
messages to an authentication server.

In addition there have also been proposals to allow the remote host
to be configured with an IP address and other configuration
information over IPSec. For example [63] describes a method whereby
a remote host first establishes a Phase 1 SA with a security gateway
and then sets up a Phase 2 SA to the gateway, over which the DHCP

protocol is run. The gateway acts as a proxy and relays the protocol
messages to the DHCP server. Again, like [62], this proposal does
not involve extensions to the IKE protocol itself.

Another aspect of PPP functionality that may need to supported is
multiprotocol operation, as there may be a need to carry network
layer protocols other than IP, and even to carry link layer protocols
(e.g. ethernet) as would be needed to support bridging over IPSec.
This is discussed in section 3.1.4.

The methods of supporting legacy user authentication and host
configuration capabilities in a remote access environment are
currently being discussed in the IPSec working group.

6.4 Networked Host Support

The current PPP based dial model assumes a host directly connected to
a connection oriented dial access network. Recent work on new access
technologies such as DSL have attempted to replicate this model [57],
so as to allow for the re-use of existing AAA systems. The
proliferation of personal computers, printers and other network
appliances in homes and small businesses, and the ever lowering costs
of networks, however, are increasingly challenging the directly
connected host model. Increasingly, most hosts will access the
Internet through small, typically Ethernet, local area networks.

There is hence interest in means of accommodating the existing AAA
infrastructure within service providers, whilst also supporting
multiple networked hosts at each customer site. The principal
complication with this scenario is the need to support the login
dialogue, through which the appropriate AAA information is exchanged.
A number of proposals have been made to address this scenario:

6.4.1 Extension of PPP to Hosts Through L2TP

A number of proposals (e.g. [56]) have been made to extend L2TP over
Ethernet so that PPP sessions can run from networked hosts out to the
network, in much the same manner as a directly attached host.

6.4.2 Extension of PPP Directly to Hosts:

There is also a specification for mapping PPP directly onto Ethernet
(PPPOE) [64] which uses a broadcast mechanism to allow hosts to find
appropriate access servers with which to connect. Such servers could
then further tunnel, if needed, the PPP sessions using L2TP or a
similar mechanism.

6.4.3 Use of IPSec

The IPSec based voluntary tunneling mechanisms discussed above can be used either with networked or directly connected hosts.

Note that all of these methods require additional host software to be used, which implements either LAC, PPPOE client or IPSec client functionality.

6.5 Recommendations

The L2TP specification has been finalized and will be widely used for compulsory tunneling. As discussed in section 3.2, defining specific modes of operation for IPSec when used to secure L2TP would be beneficial.

Also, for voluntary tunneling using IPSec, completing the work needed to provide support for the following areas would be useful

- asymmetric / legacy user authentication (6.3)

- host address assignment and configuration (6.3)

along with any other issues specifically related to the support of remote hosts. Currently as there are many different non-interoperable proprietary solutions in this area.

7.0 VPN Types: Virtual Private LAN Segment

A Virtual Private LAN Segment (VPLS) is the emulation of a LAN segment using Internet facilities. A VPLS can be used to provide what is sometimes known also as a Transparent LAN Service (TLS), which can be used to interconnect multiple stub CPE nodes, either bridges or routers, in a protocol transparent manner. A VPLS emulates a LAN segment over IP, in the same way as protocols such as LANE emulate a LAN segment over ATM. The primary benefits of a VPLS are complete protocol transparency, which may be important both for multiprotocol transport and for regulatory reasons in particular service provider contexts.

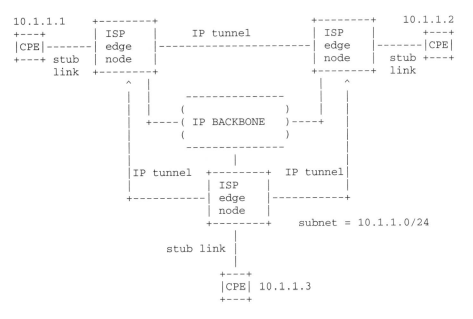

Figure 7.1: VPLS Example

7.1 VPLS Requirements

Topologically and operationally a VPLS can be most easily modeled as being essentially equivalent to a VPRN, except that each VPLS edge node implements link layer bridging rather than network layer forwarding. As such, most of the VPRN tunneling and configuration mechanisms discussed previously can also be used for a VPLS, with the appropriate changes to accommodate link layer, rather than network layer, packets and addressing information. The following sections discuss the primary changes needed in VPRN operation to support VPLSs.

7.1.1 Tunneling Protocols

The tunneling protocols employed within a VPLS can be exactly the same as those used within a VPRN, if the tunneling protocol permits the transport of multiprotocol traffic, and this is assumed below.

7.1.2 Multicast and Broadcast Support

A VPLS needs to have a broadcast capability. This is needed both for broadcast frames, and for link layer packet flooding, where a unicast frame is flooded because the path to the destination link layer address is unknown. The address resolution protocols that run over a bridged network typically use broadcast frames (e.g. ARP). The same set of possible multicast tunneling mechanisms discussed earlier for VPRNs apply also to a VPLS, though the generally more frequent use of broadcast in VPLSs may increase the pressure for native multicast support that reduces, for instance, the burden of replication on VPLS edge nodes.

7.1.3 VPLS Membership Configuration and Topology

The configuration of VPLS membership is analogous to that of VPRNs since this generally requires only knowledge of the local VPN link assignments at any given VPLS edge node, and the identity of, or route to, the other edge nodes in the VPLS; in particular, such configuration is independent of the nature of the forwarding at each VPN edge node. As such, any of the mechanisms for VPN member configuration and dissemination discussed for VPRN configuration can also be applied to VPLS configuration. Also as with VPRNs, the topology of the VPLS could be easily manipulated by controlling the configuration of peer nodes at each VPLS edge node, assuming that the membership dissemination mechanism was such as to permit this. It is likely that typical VPLSs will be fully meshed, however, in order to preclude the need for traffic between two VPLS nodes to transit through another VPLS node, which would then require the use of the Spanning Tree protocol [65] for loop prevention.

7.1.4 CPE Stub Node Types

A VPLS can support either bridges or routers as a CPE device.

CPE routers would peer transparently across a VPLS with each other without requiring any router peering with any nodes within the VPLS. The same scalability issues that apply to a full mesh topology for VPRNs, apply also in this case, only that now the number of peering routers is potentially greater, since the ISP edge device is no longer acting as an aggregation point.

With CPE bridge devices the broadcast domain encompasses all the CPE sites as well as the VPLS itself. There are significant scalability constraints in this case, due to the need for packet flooding, and

the fact that any topology change in the bridged domain is not
localized, but is visible throughout the domain. As such this
scenario is generally only suited for support of non-routable
protocols.

The nature of the CPE impacts the nature of the encapsulation,
addressing, forwarding and reachability protocols within the VPLS,
and are discussed separately below.

7.1.5 Stub Link Packet Encapsulation

7.1.5.1 Bridge CPE

In this case, packets sent to and from the VPLS across stub links are
link layer frames, with a suitable access link encapsulation. The
most common case is likely to be ethernet frames, using an
encapsulation appropriate to the particular access technology, such
as ATM, connecting the CPE bridges to the VPLS edge nodes. Such
frames are then forwarded at layer 2 onto a tunnel used in the VPLS.
As noted previously, this does mandate the use of an IP tunneling
protocol which can transport such link layer frames. Note that this
does not necessarily mandate, however, the use of a protocol
identification field in each tunnel packet, since the nature of the
encapsulated traffic (e.g. ethernet frames) could be indicated at
tunnel setup.

7.1.5.2 Router CPE

In this case, typically, CPE routers send link layer packets to and
from the VPLS across stub links, destined to the link layer addresses
of their peer CPE routers. Other types of encapsulations may also
prove feasible in such a case, however, since the relatively
constrained addressing space needed for a VPLS to which only router
CPE are connected, could allow for alternative encapsulations, as
discussed further below.

7.1.6 CPE Addressing and Address Resolution

7.1.6.1 Bridge CPE

Since a VPLS operates at the link layer, all hosts within all stub
sites, in the case of bridge CPE, will typically be in the same
network layer subnet. (Multinetting, whereby multiple subnets
operate over the same LAN segment, is possible, but much less
common). Frames are forwarded across and within the VPLS based upon
the link layer addresses - e.g. IEEE MAC addresses - associated with
the individual hosts. The VPLS needs to support broadcast traffic,
such as that typically used for the address resolution mechanism used

to map the host network addresses to their respective link addresses. The VPLS forwarding and reachability algorithms also need to be able to accommodate flooded traffic.

7.1.6.2 Router CPE

A single network layer subnet is generally used to interconnect router CPE devices, across a VPLS. Behind each CPE router are hosts in different network layer subnets. CPE routers transfer packets across the VPLS by mapping next hop network layer addresses to the link layer addresses of a router peer. A link layer encapsulation is used, most commonly ethernet, as for the bridge case.

As noted above, however, in cases where all of the CPE nodes connected to the VPLS are routers, then it may be possible, due to the constrained addressing space of the VPLS, to use encapsulations that use a different address space than normal MAC addressing. See, for instance, [11], for a proposed mechanism for VPLSs over MPLS networks, leveraging earlier work on VPRN support over MPLS [38], which proposes MPLS as the tunneling mechanism, and locally assigned MPLS labels as the link layer addressing scheme to identify the CPE LSR routers connected to the VPLS.

7.1.7 VPLS Edge Node Forwarding and Reachability Mechanisms

7.1.7.1 Bridge CPE

The only practical VPLS edge node forwarding mechanism in this case is likely to be standard link layer packet flooding and MAC address learning, as per [65]. As such, no explicit intra-VPLS reachability protocol will be needed, though there will be a need for broadcast mechanisms to flood traffic, as discussed above. In general, it may not prove necessary to also implement the Spanning Tree protocol between VPLS edge nodes, if the VPLS topology is such that no VPLS edge node is used for transit traffic between any other VPLS edge nodes - in other words, where there is both full mesh connectivity and transit is explicitly precluded. On the other hand, the CPE bridges may well implement the spanning tree protocol in order to safeguard against 'backdoor' paths that bypass connectivity through the VPLS.

7.1.7.2 Router CPE

Standard bridging techniques can also be used in this case. In addition, the smaller link layer address space of such a VPLS may also permit other techniques, with explicit link layer routes between CPE routers. [11], for instance, proposes that MPLS LSPs be set up, at the insertion of any new CPE router into the VPLS, between all CPE

LSRs. This then precludes the need for packet flooding. In the more
general case, if stub link reachability mechanisms were used to
configure VPLS edge nodes with the link layer addresses of the CPE
routers connected to them, then modifications of any of the intra-VPN
reachability mechanisms discussed for VPRNs could be used to
propagate this information to each other VPLS edge node. This would
then allow for packet forwarding across the VPLS without flooding.

Mechanisms could also be developed to further propagate the link
layer addresses of peer CPE routers and their corresponding network
layer addresses across the stub links to the CPE routers, where such
information could be inserted into the CPE router's address
resolution tables. This would then also preclude the need for
broadcast address resolution protocols across the VPLS.

Clearly there would be no need for the support of spanning tree
protocols if explicit link layer routes were determined across the
VPLS. If normal flooding mechanisms were used then spanning tree
would only be required if full mesh connectivity was not available
and hence VPLS nodes had to carry transit traffic.

7.2 Recommendations

There is significant commonality between VPRNs and VPLSs, and, where
possible, this similarity should be exploited in order to reduce
development and configuration complexity. In particular, VPLSs
should utilize the same tunneling and membership configuration
mechanisms, with changes only to reflect the specific characteristics
of VPLSs.

8.0 Summary of Recommendations

In this document different types of VPNs have been discussed
individually, but there are many common requirements and mechanisms
that apply to all types of VPNs, and many networks will contain a mix
of different types of VPNs. It is useful to have as much commonality
as possible across these different VPN types. In particular, by
standardizing a relatively small number of mechanisms, it is possible
to allow a wide variety of VPNs to be implemented.

The benefits of adding support for the following mechanisms should be
carefully examined.

For IKE/IPSec:

- the transport of a VPN-ID when establishing an SA (3.1.2)

- a null encryption and null authentication option (3.1.3)

- multiprotocol operation (3.1.4)

- frame sequencing (3.1.5)

- asymmetric / legacy user authentication (6.3)

- host address assignment and configuration (6.3)

For L2TP:

- defining modes of operation of IPSec when used to support L2TP
  (3.2)

For VPNs generally:

- defining a VPN membership information configuration and
  dissemination mechanism, that uses some form of directory or MIB
  (5.3.2)

- ensure that solutions developed, as far as possible, are
  applicable to different types of VPNs, rather than being specific
  to a single type of VPN.

9.0 Security Considerations

Security considerations are an integral part of any VPN mechanisms,
and these are discussed in the sections describing those mechanisms.

10.0 Acknowledgements

Thanks to Anthony Alles, of Nortel Networks, for his invaluable
assistance with the generation of this document, and who developed
much of the material on which early versions of this document were
based. Thanks also to Joel Halpern for his helpful review comments.

11.0 References

[1] ATM Forum. "LAN Emulation over ATM 1.0", af-lane-0021.000,
     January 1995.

[2] ATM Forum. "Multi-Protocol Over ATM Specification v1.0", af-
     mpoa-0087.000, June 1997.

[3] Ferguson, P. and Huston, G. "What is a VPN?", Revision 1, April
     1 1998; http://www.employees.org/~ferguson/vpn.pdf.

[4] Rekhter, Y., Moskowitz, B., Karrenberg, D., de Groot, G. and E.
     Lear, "Address Allocation for Private Internets", BCP 5, RFC
     1918, February 1996.

[5] Kent, S. and R. Atkinson, "Security Architecture for the
     Internet Protocol", RFC 2401, November 1998.

[6] Perkins, C., "IP Encapsulation within IP", RFC 2003, October
     1996.

[7] Hanks, S., Li, T., Farinacci, D. and P. Traina, "Generic Routing
     Encapsulation (GRE)", RFC 1701, October 1994.

[8] Townsley, W., Valencia, A., Rubens, A., Pall, G., Zorn, G. and
     B. Palter, "Layer Two Tunneling Protocol "L2TP"", RFC 2661,
     August 1999.

[9] Rosen, E., et al., "Multiprotocol Label Switching Architecture",
     Work in Progress.

[10] Heinanen, J., et al., "MPLS Mappings of Generic VPN Mechanisms",
     Work in Progress.

[11] Jamieson, D., et al., "MPLS VPN Architecture", Work in Progress.

[12] Casey, L., et al., "IP VPN Realization using MPLS Tunnels", Work
     in Progress.

[13] Li, T. "CPE based VPNs using MPLS", Work in Progress.

[14] Muthukrishnan, K. and A. Malis, "Core MPLS IP VPN Architecture",
     Work in Progress.

[15] Rosen, E. and Y. Rekhter, "BGP/MPLS VPNs", RFC 2547, March 1999.

[16] Fox, B. and B. Gleeson, "Virtual Private Networks Identifier",
     RFC 2685, September 1999.

[17] Petri, B. (editor) "MPOA v1.1 Addendum on VPN support", ATM
     Forum, af-mpoa-0129.000.

[18] Harkins, D. and C. Carrel, "The Internet Key Exchange (IKE)",
     RFC 2409, November 1998.

[19] Calhoun, P., et al., "Tunnel Establishment Protocol", Work in
     Progress.

[20] Andersson, L., et al., "LDP Specification", Work in Progress.

[21] Jamoussi, B., et al., "Constraint-Based LSP Setup using LDP"
     Work in Progress.

[22] Awduche, D., et al., "Extensions to RSVP for LSP Tunnels", Work
     in Progress.

[23] Kent, S. and R. Atkinson, "IP Encapsulating Security Protocol
     (ESP)", RFC 2406, November 1998.

[24] Simpson, W., Editor, "The Point-to-Point Protocol (PPP)", STD
     51, RFC 1661, July 1994.

[25] Perez, M., Liaw, F., Mankin, A., Hoffman, E., Grossman, D. and
     A. Malis, "ATM Signalling Support for IP over ATM", RFC 1755,
     February 1995.

[26] Malkin, G. "RIP Version 2 Carrying Additional Information",
     RFC 1723, November 1994.

[27] Moy, J., "OSPF Version 2", STD 54, RFC 2328, April 1998.

[28] Shacham, A., Monsour, R., Pereira, R. and M. Thomas, "IP Payload
     Compression Protocol (IPComp)", RFC 2393, December 1998.

[29] Duffield N., et al., "A Performance Oriented Service Interface
     for Virtual Private Networks", Work in Progress.

[30] Jacobson, V., Nichols, K. and B. Poduri, "An Expedited
     Forwarding PHB", RFC 2598, June 1999.

[31] Casey, L., "An extended IP VPN Architecture", Work in Progress.

[32] Rekhter, Y., and T. Li, "A Border Gateway Protocol 4 (BGP-4),"
     RFC 1771, March 1995.

[33] Grossman, D. and J. Heinanen, "Multiprotocol Encapsulation over
     ATM Adaptation Layer 5", RFC 2684, September 1999.

[34] Wahl, M., Howes, T. and S. Kille, "Lightweight Directory Access
     Protocol (v3)", RFC 2251, December 1997.

[35] Boyle, J., et al., "The COPS (Common Open Policy Service)
     Protocol", RFC 2748, January 2000.

[36] MacRae, M. and S. Ayandeh, "Using COPS for VPN Connectivity"
     Work in Progress.

[37] Droms, R., "Dynamic Host Configuration Protocol", RFC 2131,
     March 1997.

[38] Heinanen, J. and E. Rosen, "VPN Support with MPLS", Work in
     Progress.

[39] Estrin, D., Farinacci, D., Helmy, A., Thaler, D., Deering, S.,
     Handley, M., Jacobson, V., Liu, C., Sharma, P. and L. Wei,
     "Protocol Independent Multicast-Sparse Mode (PIM-SM): Protocol
     Specification", RFC 2362, June 1998.

[40] Waitzman, D., Partridge, C., and S. Deering, "Distance Vector
     Multicast Routing Protocol", RFC 1075, November 1988.

[41] Fenner, W., "IGMP-based Multicast Forwarding (IGMP Proxying)",
     Work in Progress.

[42] Wallner, D., Harder, E. and R. Agee, "Key Management for
     Multicast: Issues and Architectures", RFC 2627, June 1999.

[43] Hardjono, T., et al., "Secure IP Multicast: Problem areas,
     Framework, and Building Blocks", Work in Progress.

[44] Rigney, C., Rubens, A., Simpson, W. and S. Willens, "Remote
     Authentication Dial In User Service (RADIUS)", RFC 2138, April
     1997.

[45] Valencia, A., Littlewood, M. and T. Kolar, "Cisco Layer Two
     Forwarding (Protocol) "L2F"", RFC 2341, May 1998.

[46] Hamzeh, K., Pall, G., Verthein, W., Taarud, J., Little, W. and
     G. Zorn, "Point-to-Point Tunneling Protocol (PPTP)", RFC 2637,
     July 1999.

[47] Patel, B., et al., "Securing L2TP using IPSEC", Work in
     Progress.

[48] Srisuresh, P., "Secure Remote Access with L2TP", Work in
     Progress.

[49] Calhoun, P., et al., "Layer Two Tunneling Protocol "L2TP"
     Security Extensions for Non-IP networks", Work in Progress.

[50] Aboba, B. and Zorn, G. "Implementation of PPTP/L2TP Compulsory
     Tunneling via RADIUS", Work in progress.

[51] Aboba, B. and G. Zorn, "Criteria for Evaluating Roaming
     Protocols", RFC 2477, January 1999.

[52] Shea, R., "L2TP-over-IP Path MTU Discovery (L2TPMTU)", Work in
     Progress.

[53] Sklower, K., Lloyd, B., McGregor, G., Carr, D. and T.
     Coradetti, "The PPP Multilink Protocol (MP)", RFC 1990, August
     1996.

[54] Richards, C. and K. Smith, "The PPP Bandwidth Allocation
     Protocol (BAP) The PPP Bandwidth Allocation Control Protocol
     (BACP)", RFC 2125, March 1997.

[55] Calhoun, P. and K. Peirce, "Layer Two Tunneling Protocol "L2TP"
     IP Differential Services Extension", Work in Progress.

[56] ADSL Forum. "An Interoperable End-to-end Broadband Service
     Architecture over ADSL Systems (Version 3.0)", ADSL Forum 97-
     215.

[57] ADSL Forum. "Core Network Architectures for ADSL Access Systems
     (Version 1.01)", ADSL Forum 98-017.

[58] Gupta, V., "Secure, Remote Access over the Internet using
     IPSec", Work in Progress.

[59] Pereira, R., et al., "The ISAKMP Configuration Method", Work in
     Progress.

[60] Pereira, R. and S. Beaulieu, "Extended Authentication Within
     ISAKMP/Oakley", Work in Progress.

[61] Litvin, M., et al., "A Hybrid Authentication Mode for IKE", Work
     in Progress.

[62] Kelly, S., et al., "User-level Authentication Mechanisms for
     IPsec", Work in Progress.

[63] Patel, B., et al., "DHCP Configuration of IPSEC Tunnel Mode",
     Work in Progress.

[64] Mamakos, L., Lidl, K., Evarts, J., Carrel, D., Simone, D. and R.
     Wheeler, "A Method for Transmitting PPP Over Ethernet (PPPoE)",
     RFC 2516, February 1999.

[65] ANSI/IEEE - 10038: 1993 (ISO/IEC) Information technology -
     Telecommunications and information exchange between systems -
     Local area networks - Media access control (MAC) bridges,
     ANSI/IEEE Std 802.1D, 1993 Edition.

RFC 2764

60

12.0 Author Information

Bryan Gleeson
Nortel Networks
4500 Great America Parkway
Santa Clara CA 95054
USA

Phone: +1 (408) 548 3711
EMail: bgleeson@shastanets.com

Juha Heinanen
Telia Finland, Inc.
Myyrmaentie 2
01600 VANTAA
Finland

Phone: +358 303 944 808
EMail: jh@telia.fi

Arthur Lin
Nortel Networks
4500 Great America Parkway
Santa Clara CA 95054
USA

Phone: +1 (408) 548 3788
EMail: alin@shastanets.com

Grenville Armitage
Bell Labs Research Silicon Valley
Lucent Technologies
3180 Porter Drive,
Palo Alto, CA 94304
USA

EMail: gja@lucent.com

Andrew G. Malis
Lucent Technologies
1 Robbins Road
Westford, MA 01886
USA

Phone: +1 978 952 7414
EMail: amalis@lucent.com

13.0   Full Copyright Statement

Acknowledgement

Funding for the RFC Editor function is currently provided by the
Internet Society.

RFC 2764

62

Network Working Group   S. Brim
Request for Comments: 2836   B. Carpenter
Category: Standards Track   F. Le Faucheur
                                                              May 2000

                   Per Hop Behavior Identification Codes

Status of this Memo

Copyright Notice

Table of Contents:

1. Introduction

   Differentiated Services [RFC 2474, RFC 2475] introduces the notion of
   Per Hop Behaviors (PHBs) that define how traffic belonging to a
   particular behavior aggregate is treated at an individual network
   node. In IP packet headers, PHBs are not indicated as such; instead
   Differentiated Services Codepoint (DSCP) values are used. There are
   only 64 possible DSCP values, but there is no such limit on the
   number of PHBs. In a given network domain, there is a locally defined
   mapping between DSCP values and PHBs. Standardized PHBs recommend a
   DSCP mapping, but network operators may choose alternative mappings.

In some cases it is necessary or desirable to identify a particular
PHB in a protocol message, such as a message negotiating bandwidth
management or path selection, especially when such messages pass
between management domains. Examples where work is in progress
include communication between bandwidth brokers, and MPLS support of
diffserv.

In certain cases, what needs to be identified is not an individual
PHB, but a set of PHBs. One example is a set of PHBs that must follow
the same physical path to prevent re-ordering. An instance of this
is the set of three PHBs belonging to a single Assured Forwarding
class, such as the PHBs AF11, AF12 and AF13 [RFC 2597].

This document defines a binary encoding to uniquely identify PHBs
and/or sets of PHBs in protocol messages. This encoding MUST be used
when such identification is required.

The key words "MUST", "MUST NOT", "REQUIRED", "SHALL", "SHALL NOT",
"SHOULD", "SHOULD NOT", "RECOMMENDED", "MAY", and "OPTIONAL" in this
document are to be interpreted as described in [RFC2119].

1.1. Usage Scenarios

Diffserv services are expected to be supported over various
underlying technologies which we broadly refer to as "link layers"
for the purpose of this discussion. For the transport of IP packets,
some of these link layers make use of connections or logical
connections where the forwarding behavior supported by each link
layer device is a property of the connection. In particular, within
the link layer domain, each link layer node will schedule traffic
depending on which connection the traffic is transported in. Examples
of such "link layers" include ATM and MPLS.

For efficient support of diffserv over these link layers, one model
is for different Behavior Aggregates (BAs) (or sets of Behavior
Aggregates) to be transported over different connections so that they
are granted different (and appropriate) forwarding behaviors inside
the link layer cloud. When those connections are dynamically
established for the transport of diffserv traffic, it is very useful
to communicate at connection establishment time what forwarding
behavior(s) is(are) to be granted to each connection by the link
layer device so that the BAs transported experience consistent
forwarding behavior inside the link layer cloud. This can be achieved
by including in the connection establishment signaling messages the
encoding of the corresponding PHB, or set of PHBs, as defined in this
document. Details on proposed usage of PHB encodings by some MPLS
label distribution protocols (RSVP and LDP) for support of Diff-Serv
over MPLS, can be found in [MPLS-DS].

RFC 2836

In another approach, the ATM Forum has a requirement to indicate
desired IP QOS treatments in ATM signaling, so that ATM switches can
be just as supportive of the desired service as are IP forwarders.
To do so the Forum is defining a new VC call setup information
element is which will carry PHB identification codes (although will
be generalized to do more if needed).

2. Encoding

   PHBs and sets of PHBs are encoded in an unsigned 16 bit binary field.

   The 16 bit field is arranged as follows:

   Case 1: PHBs defined by standards action, as per [RFC 2474].

   The encoding for a single PHB is the recommended DSCP value for that
   PHB, left-justified in the 16 bit field, with bits 6 through 15 set
   to zero. Note that the recommended DSCP value MUST be used, even if
   the network in question has chosen a different mapping.

   The encoding for a set of PHBs is the numerically smallest of the set
   of encodings for the various PHBs in the set, with bit 14 set to 1.
   (Thus for the AF1x PHBs, the encoding is that of the AF11 PHB, with
   bit 14 set to 1.)

```
    0   1   2   3   4   5   6   7   8   9  10  11  12  13  14  15
  +---+---+---+---+---+---+---+---+---+---+---+---+---+---+---+---+
  |         DSCP          | 0   0   0   0   0   0   0   0   X   0 |
  +---+---+---+---+---+---+---+---+---+---+---+---+---+---+---+---+
```

   Case 2: PHBs not defined by standards action, i.e. experimental or
   local use PHBs as allowed by [RFC 2474]. In this case an arbitrary 12
   bit PHB identification code, assigned by the IANA, is placed left-
   justified in the 16 bit field. Bit 15 is set to 1, and bit 14 is zero
   for a single PHB or 1 for a set of PHBs. Bits 12 and 13 are zero.

```
    0   1   2   3   4   5   6   7   8   9  10  11  12  13  14  15
  +---+---+---+---+---+---+---+---+---+---+---+---+---+---+---+---+
  |                  PHB id code              | 0   0   X   1 |
  +---+---+---+---+---+---+---+---+---+---+---+---+---+---+---+---+
```

   Bits 12 and 13 are reserved either for expansion of the PHB
   identification code, or for other use, at some point in the future.

3. IANA Considerations

   IANA is requested to create a new assignment registry for "Per-Hop
   Behavior Identification Codes", initially allowing values in the
   range 0 to 4095 decimal.

   Assignment of values in this field require:

      -the identity of the assignee
      -a brief description of the new PHB, with enough detail to
       distinguish it from existing standardized and non-standardized
       PHBs. In the case of a set of PHBs, this description should cover
       all PHBs in the set.
      -a reference to a stable document describing the PHB in detail.

   During the first year of existence of this registry, IANA is
   requested to refer all requests to the IETF diffserv WG for review.
   Subsequently, requests should be reviewed by the IETF Transport Area
   Directors or by an expert that they designate.

   If the number of assignments begins to approach 4096, the Transport
   Area Directors should be alerted.

4. Security Considerations

   This encoding in itself raises no security issues. However, users of
   this encoding should consider that modifying a PHB identification
   code may constitute theft or denial of service, so protocols using
   this encoding must be adequately protected.

References

   [RFC 2119] Bradner, S., "Key words for use in RFCs to Indicate
              Requirement Levels", BCP 14, RFC 2119, March 1997.

   [RFC 2474] Nichols, K., Blake, S., Baker, F. and D. Black,
              "Definition of the Differentiated Services Field (DS
              Field) in the IPv4 and IPv6 Headers", RFC 2474, December
              1998.

   [RFC 2475] Blake, S., Black, D., Carlson, M., Davies, E., Wang, Z.
              and W. Weiss, "An Architecture for Differentiated
              Services", RFC 2475, December 1998.

   [RFC 2597] Heinanen, J., Baker, F., Weiss, W. and J. Wroclawski,
              "Assured Forwarding PHB Group", RFC 2597, June 1999.

    [MPLS-DS]   MPLS Support of Differentiated Services, Francois Le
                Faucheur, Liwen Wu, Bruce Davie, Shahram Davari, Pasi
                Vaananen, Ram Krishnan, Pierrick Cheval, Juha Heinanen,
                Work in Progress.

Authors' Addresses

    Scott W. Brim
    146 Honness Lane
    Ithaca, NY 14850
    USA

    EMail: sbrim@cisco.com

    Brian E. Carpenter
    IBM
    c/o iCAIR
    Suite 150
    1890 Maple Avenue
    Evanston, IL 60201
    USA

    EMail: brian@icair.org

    Francois Le Faucheur
    Cisco Systems
    Petra B - Les Lucioles
    291, rue Albert Caquot
    06560 Valbonne
    France

    EMail: flefauch@cisco.com

Intellectual Property

The IETF takes no position regarding the validity or scope of any
intellectual property or other rights that might be claimed to
pertain to the implementation or use of the technology described in
this document or the extent to which any license under such rights
might or might not be available; neither does it represent that it
has made any effort to identify any such rights. Information on the
IETF's procedures with respect to rights in standards-track and
standards-related documentation can be found in BCP-11. Copies of
claims of rights made available for publication and any assurances of
licenses to be made available, or the result of an attempt made to
obtain a general license or permission for the use of such
proprietary rights by implementors or users of this specification can
be obtained from the IETF Secretariat.

The IETF invites any interested party to bring to its attention any
copyrights, patents or patent applications, or other proprietary
rights which may cover technology that may be required to practice
this standard. Please address the information to the IETF Executive
Director.

RFC 2836

6

Full Copyright Statement

Acknowledgement

   Funding for the RFC Editor function is currently provided by the
   Internet Society.

Network Working Group   K. Muthukrishnan
Request for Comments: 2917   Lucent Technologies
Category: Informational   A. Malis
                                              Vivace Networks, Inc.
                                                    September 2000

                    A Core MPLS IP VPN Architecture

Status of this Memo

Copyright Notice

Abstract

   This memo presents an approach for building core Virtual Private
   Network (VPN) services in a service provider's MPLS backbone. This
   approach uses Multiprotocol Label Switching (MPLS) running in the
   backbone to provide premium services in addition to best effort
   services. The central vision is for the service provider to provide a
   virtual router service to their customers. The keystones of this
   architecture are ease of configuration, user security, network
   security, dynamic neighbor discovery, scaling and the use of existing
   routing protocols as they exist today without any modifications.

1. Acronyms

        ARP   Address Resolution Protocol
        CE   Customer Edge router
        LSP   Label Switched Path
        PNA   Private Network Administrator
        SLA   Service Level Agreement
        SP   Service Provider
        SPED   Service Provider Edge Device
        SPNA   SP Network Administrator
        VMA   VPN Multicast Address
        VPNID   VPN Identifier
        VR   Virtual Router
        VRC   Virtual Router Console

2. Introduction

   This memo describes an approach for building IP VPN services out of
   the backbone of the SP's network. Broadly speaking, two possible
   approaches present themselves: the overlay model and the virtual
   router approach. The overlay model is based on overloading some
   semantic(s) of existing routing protocols to carry reachability
   information. In this document, we focus on the virtual router
   service.

   The approach presented here does not depend on any modifications of
   any existing routing protocols. Neighbor discovery is aided by the
   use of an emulated LAN and is achieved by the use of ARP. This memo
   makes a concerted effort to draw the line between the SP and the PNA:
   the SP owns and manages layer 1 and layer 2 services while layer 3
   services belong to and are manageable by the PNA. By the provisioning
   of fully logically independent routing domains, the PNA has been
   given the flexibility to use private and unregistered addresses. Due
   to the use of private LSPs and the use of VPNID encapsulation using
   label stacks over shared LSPs, data security is not an issue.

   The approach espoused in this memo differs from that described in RFC
   2547 [Rosen1] in that no specific routing protocol has been
   overloaded to carry VPN routes. RFC 2547 specifies a way to modify
   BGP to carry VPN unicast routes across the SP's backbone. To carry
   multicast routes, further architectural work will be necessary.

3. Virtual Routers

   A virtual router is a collection of threads, either static or
   dynamic, in a routing device, that provides routing and forwarding
   services much like physical routers. A virtual router need not be a
   separate operating system process (although it could be); it simply
   has to provide the illusion that a dedicated router is available to
   satisfy the needs of the network(s) to which it is connected. A
   virtual router, like its physical counterpart, is an element in a
   routing domain. The other routers in this domain could be physical or
   virtual routers themselves. Given that the virtual router connects to
   a specific (logically discrete) routing domain and that a physical
   router can support multiple virtual routers, it follows that a
   physical router supports multiple (logically discreet) routing
   domains.

   From the user (VPN customer) standpoint, it is imperative that the
   virtual router be as equivalent to a physical router as possible. In
   other words, with very minor and very few exceptions, the virtual
   router should appear for all purposes (configuration, management,
   monitoring and troubleshooting) like a dedicated physical router. The

main motivation behind this requirement is to avoid upgrading or re-
configuring the large installed base of routers and to avoid
retraining of network administrators.

The aspects of a router that a virtual router needs to emulate are:

1. Configuration of any combination of routing protocols

2. Monitoring of the network

3. Troubleshooting.

Every VPN has a logically independent routing domain. This enhances
the SP's ability to offer a fully flexible virtual router service
that can fully serve the SP's customer without requiring physical
per-VPN routers. This means that the SP's "hardware" investments,
namely routers and links between them, can be re-used by multiple
customers.

4. Objectives

   1. Easy, scalable configuration of VPN endpoints in the service
      provider network. At most, one piece of configuration should be
      necessary when a CE is added.

   2. No use of SP resources that are globally unique and hard to get
      such as IP addresses and subnets.

   3. Dynamic discovery of VRs (Virtual Routers) in the SP's cloud. This
      is an optional, but extremely valuable "keep it simple" goal.

   4. Virtual Routers should be fully configurable and monitorable by
      the VPN network administrator. This provides the PNA with the
      flexibility to either configure the VPN themselves or outsource
      configuration tasks to the SP.

   5. Quality of data forwarding should be configurable on a VPN-by-VPN
      basis. This should translate to continuous (but perhaps discrete)
      grades of service. Some examples include best effort, dedicated
      bandwidth, QOS, and policy based forwarding services.

   6. Differentiated services should be configurable on a VPN-by-VPN
      basis, perhaps based on LSPs set up for exclusive use for
      forwarding data traffic in the VPN.

7. Security of internet routers extended to virtual routers. This
   means that the virtual router's data forwarding and routing
   functions should be as secure as a dedicated, private physical
   router. There should be no unintended leak of information (user
   data and reachability information) from one routing domain to
   another.

8. Specific routing protocols should not be mandated between virtual
   routers. This is critical to ensuring the VPN customer can setup
   the network and policies as the customer sees fit. For example,
   some protocols are strong in filtering, while others are strong in
   traffic engineering. The VPN customer might want to exploit both
   to achieve "best of breed" network quality.

9. No special extensions to existing routing protocols such as BGP,
   RIP, OSPF, ISIS etc. This is critical to allowing the future
   addition of other services such as NHRP and multicast. In
   addition, as advances and addenda are made to existing protocols
   (such as traffic engineering extensions to ISIS and OSPF), they
   can be easily incorporated into the VPN implementation.

5. Architectural Requirements

   The service provider network must run some form of multicast routing
   to all nodes that will have VPN connections and to nodes that must
   forward multicast datagrams for virtual router discovery. A specific
   multicast routing protocol is not mandated. An SP may run MOSPF or
   DVMRP or any other protocol.

6. Architectural Outline

   1. Every VPN is assigned a VPNID which is unique within the SP's
       network. This identifier unambiguously identifies the VPN with
       which a packet or connection is associated. The VPNID of zero is
       reserved; it is associated with and represents the public
       internet. It is recommended, but not required that these VPN
       identifiers will be compliant with RFC 2685 [Fox].

   2. The VPN service is offered in the form of a Virtual Router
       service. These VRs reside in the SPED and are as such confined
       to the edge of the SP's cloud. The VRs will use the SP's network
       for data and control packet forwarding but are otherwise
       invisible outside the SPEDs.

   3. The "size" of the VR contracted to the VPN in a given SPED is
       expressed by the quantity of IP resources such as routing
       interfaces, route filters, routing entries etc. This is entirely
       under the control of the SP and provides the fine granularity

that the SP requires to offer virtually infinite grades of VR
service on a per-SPED level. [Example: one SPED may be the
aggregating point (say headquarters of the corporation) for a
given VPN and a number of other SPEDs may be access points
(branch offices). In this case, the SPED connected to the
headquarters may be contracted to provide a large VR while the
SPEDs connected to the branch offices may house small, perhaps
stub VRs]. This provision also allows the SP to design the
network with an end goal of distributing the load among the
routers in the network.

4. One indicator of the VPN size is the number of SPEDs in the SP's
    network that have connections to CPE routers in that VPN. In
    this respect, a VPN with many sites that need to be connected is
    a "large" VPN whereas one with a few sites is a "small" VPN.
    Also, it is conceivable that a VPN grows or shrinks in size over
    time. VPNs may even merge due to corporate mergers, acquisitions
    and partnering agreements. These changes are easy to accommodate
    in this architecture, as globally unique IP resources do not have
    to be dedicated or assigned to VPNs. The number of SPEDs is not
    limited by any artificial configuration limits.

5. The SP owns and manages Layer 1 and Layer 2 entities. To be
    specific, the SP controls physical switches or routers, physical
    links, logical layer 2 connections (such as DLCI in Frame Relay
    and VPI/VCI in ATM) and LSPs (and their assignment to specific
    VPNs). In the context of VPNs, it is the SP's responsibility to
    contract and assign layer 2 entities to specific VPNs.

6. Layer 3 entities belong to and are manageable by the PNA.
    Examples of these entities include IP interfaces, choice of
    dynamic routing protocols or static routes, and routing
    interfaces. Note that although Layer 3 configuration logically
    falls under the PNA's area of responsibility, it is not necessary
    for the PNA to execute it. It is quite viable for the PNA to
    outsource the IP administration of the virtual routers to the
    Service Provider. Regardless of who assumes responsibility for
    configuration and monitoring, this approach provides a full
    routing domain view to the PNA and empowers the PNA to design the
    network to achieve intranet, extranet and traffic engineering
    goals.

7. The VPNs can be managed as if physical routers rather than VRs
    were deployed. Therefore, management may be performed using SNMP
    or other similar methods or directly at the VR console (VRC).

8. Industry-standard troubleshooting tools such as 'ping,'
    'traceroute,' in a routing domain domain comprised exclusively of
    dedicated physical routers. Therefore, monitoring and .bp
    troubleshooting may be performed using SNMP or similar methods,
    but may also include the use of these standard tools. Again, the
    VRC may be used for these purposes just like any physical router.

9. Since the VRC is visible to the user, router specific security
    checks need to be put in place to make sure the VPN user is
    allowed access to Layer 3 resources in that VPN only and is
    disallowed from accessing physical resources in the router. Most
    routers achieve this through the use of database views.

10. The VRC is available to the SP as well. If configuration and
    monitoring has been outsourced to the SP, the SP may use the VRC
    to accomplish these tasks as if it were the PNA.

11. The VRs in the SPEDs form the VPN in the SP's network. Together,
    they represent a virtual routing domain. They dynamically
    discover each other by utilizing an emulated LAN resident in the
    SP's network.

Each VPN in the SP's network is assigned one and only one multicast
address. This address is chosen from the administratively scoped
range (239.192/14) [Meyer] and the only requirement is that the
multicast address can be uniquely mapped to a specific VPN. This is
easily automated by routers by the use of a simple function to
unambiguously map a VPNid to the multicast address. Subscription to
this multicast address allows a VR to discover and be discovered by
other VRs. It is important to note that the multicast address does
not have to be configured.

12. Data forwarding may be done in one of several ways:

    1. An LSP with best-effort characteristics that all VPNS can use.

    2. An LSP dedicated to a VPN and traffic engineered by the VPN
       customer.

    3. A private LSP with differentiated characteristics.

    4. Policy based forwarding on a dedicated L2 Virtual Circuit

The choice of the preferred method is negotiable between the SP and
the VPN customer, perhaps constituting part of the SLA between them.
This allows the SP to offer different grades of service to different
VPN customers.

Of course, hop-by-hop forwarding is also available to forward routing
packets and to forward user data packets during periods of LSP
establishment and failure.

13. This approach does not mandate that separate operating system
    tasks for each of the routing protocols be run for each VR that
    the SPED houses. Specific implementations may be tailored to the
    particular SPED in use. Maintaining separate routing databases
    and forwarding tables, one per VR, is one way to get the highest
    performance for a given SPED.

7. Scalable Configuration

   A typical VPN is expected to have 100s to 1000s of endpoints within
   the SP cloud. Therefore, configuration should scale (at most)
   linearly with the number of end points. To be specific, the
   administrator should have to add a couple of configuration items when
   a new customer site joins the set of VRs constituting a specific VPN.
   Anything worse will make this task too daunting for the service
   provider. In this architecture, all that the service provider needs
   to allocate and configure is the ingress/egress physical link (e.g.
   Frame Relay DLCI or ATM VPI/VCI) and the virtual connection between
   the VR and the emulated LAN.

8. Dynamic Neighbor Discovery

   The VRs in a given VPN reside in a number of SPEDs in the network.
   These VRs need to learn about each other and be connected.

   One way to do this is to require the manual configuration of
   neighbors. As an example, when a new site is added to a VPN, this
   would require the configuration of all the other VRs as neighbors.
   This is obviously not scalable from a configuration and network
   resource standpoint.

   The need then arises to allow these VRs to dynamically discover each
   other. Neighbor discovery is facilitated by providing each VPN with
   a limited emulated LAN. This emulated LAN is used in several ways:

   1. Address resolution uses this LAN to resolve next-hop (private) IP
      addresses associated with the other VRs.

   2. Routing protocols such as RIP and OSPF use this limited emulated
      LAN for neighbor discovery and to send routing updates.

   The per-VPN LAN is emulated using an IP multicast address. In the
   interest of conserving public address space and because this
   multicast address needs to be visible only in the SP network space,

we would use an address from the Organizationally scoped multicast
addresses (239.192/14) as described in [Meyer]. Each VPN is allocated
an address from this range. To completely eliminate configuration in
this regard, this address is computed from the VPNID.

9. VPN IP Domain Configuration

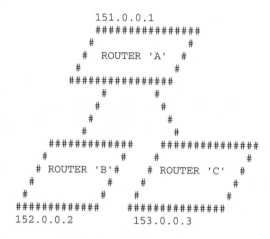

Figure 1 'Physical Routing Domain'

The physical domain in the SP's network is shown in the above figure.
In this network, physical routers A, B and C are connected together.
Each of the routers has a 'public' IP address assigned to it. These
addresses uniquely identify each of the routers in the SP's network.

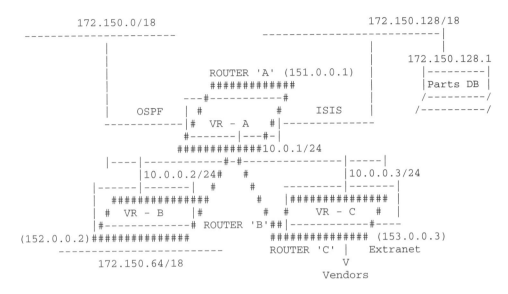

Figure 2 'Virtual Routing Domain'

Each Virtual Router is configurable by the PNA as though it were a
private physical router. Of course, the SP limits the resources that
this Virtual Router may consume on a SPED-by-SPED basis. Each VPN has
a number of physical connections (to CPE routers) and a number of
logical connections (to the emulated LAN). Each connection is IP-
capable and can be configured to utilize any combination of the
standard routing protocols and routing policies to achieve specific
corporate network goals.

To illustrate, in Figure 1, 3 VRs reside on 3 SPEDs in VPN 1. Router
'A' houses VR-A, router 'B' houses VR-B and router 'C' houses VR-C.
VR-C and VR-B have a physical connection to CPE equipment, while VR-A
has 2 physical connections. Each of the VRs has a fully IP-capable
logical connection to the emulated LAN. VR-A has the (physical)
connections to the headquarters of the company and runs OSPF over
those connections. Therefore, it can route packets to 172.150.0/18
and 172.150.128/18. VR-B runs RIP in the branch office (over the
physical connection) and uses RIP (over the logical connection) to
export 172.150.64/18 to VR-A. VR-A advertises a default route to VR-B
over the logical connection. Vendors use VR-C as the extranet
connection to connect to the parts database at 172.150.128.1. Hence,
VR-C advertises a default route to VR-A over the logical connection.
VR-A exports only 175.150.128.1 to VR-C. This keeps the rest of the
corporate network from a security problem.

The network administrator will configure the following:

1. OSPF connections to the 172.150.0/18 and 172.150.128/18 network in VR-A.

2. RIP connections to VR-B and VR-C on VR-A.

3. Route policies on VR-A to advertise only the default route to VR-B.

4. Route policies on VR-A to advertise only 172.159.128.1 to VR-C.

5. RIP on VR-B to VR-A.

6. RIP on VR-C to advertise a default route to VR-A.

10. Neighbor Discovery Example

In Figure #1, the SPED that houses VR-A (SPED-A) uses a public address of 150.0.0.1/24, SPED-B uses 150.0.0.2/24 and SPED-C uses 150.0.0.3/24. As noted, the connection between the VRs is via an emulated LAN. For interface addresses on the emulated LAN connection, VR-A uses 10.0.0.1/24, VR-B uses 10.0.0.2/24 and VR-C uses 10.0.0.3/24.

Let's take the case of VR-A sending a packet to VR-B. To get VR-B's address (SPED-B's address), VR-A sends an ARP request packet with the address of VR-B (10.0.0.2) as the logical address. The source logical address is 10.0.0.1 and the hardware address is 151.0.0.1. This ARP request is encapsulated in this VPN's multicast address and sent out. SPED B and SPED-C receive a copy of the packet. SPED-B recognizes 10.0.0.2 in the context of VPN 1 and responds with 152.0.0.2 as the "hardware" address. This response is sent to the VPN multicast address to promote the use of promiscuous ARP and the resulting decrease in network traffic.

Manual configuration would be necessary if neighbor discovery were not used. In this example, VR-A would be configured with a static ARP entry for VR-B's logical address (10.0.0.1) with the "hardware" address set to 152.0.0.2.

11. Forwarding

As mentioned in the architectural outline, data forwarding may be done in one of several ways. In all techniques except the Hop-by-Hop technique for forwarding routing/control packets, the actual method

is configurable. At the high end, policy based forwarding for quick
service and at the other end best effort forwarding using public LSP
is used. The order of forwarding preference is as follows:

1. Policy based forwarding.

2. Optionally configured private LSP.

3. Best-effort public LSP.

11.1 Private LSP

This LSP is optionally configured on a per-VPN basis. This LSP is
usually associated with non-zero bandwidth reservation and/or a
specific differentiated service or QOS class. If this LSP is
available, it is used for user data and for VPN private control data
forwarding.

11.2 Best Effort Public LSP

VPN data packets are forwarded using this LSP if a private LSP with
specified bandwidth and/or QOS characteristics is either not
configured or not presently available. The LSP used is the one
destined for the egress router in VPN 0. The VPNID in the shim header
is used to de-multiplex data packets from various VPNs at the egress
router.

12. Differentiated Services

Configuring private LSPs for VPNs allows the SP to offer
differentiated services to paying customers. These private LSPs could
be associated with any available L2 QOS class or Diff-Serv
codepoints. In a VPN, multiple private LSPs with different service
classes could be configured with flow profiles for sorting the
packets among the LSPs. This feature, together with the ability to
size the virtual routers, allows the SP to offer truly differentiated
services to the VPN customer.

13. Security Considerations

13.1 Routing Security

The use of standard routing protocols such as OSPF and BGP in their
unmodified form means that all the encryption and security methods
(such as MD5 authentication of neighbors) are fully available in VRs.
Making sure that routes are not accidentally leaked from one VPN to
another is an implementation issue. One way to achieve this is to
maintain separate routing and forwarding databases.

13.2 Data Security

   This allows the SP to assure the VPN customer that data packets in
   one VPN never have the opportunity to wander into another. From a
   routing standpoint, this could be achieved by maintaining separate
   routing databases for each virtual router. From a data forwarding
   standpoint, the use of label stacks in the case of shared LSPs
   [Rosen2] [Callon] or the use of private LSPs guarantees data privacy.
   Packet filters may also be configured to help ease the problem.

13.3 Configuration Security

   Virtual routers appear as physical routers to the PNA. This means
   that they may be configured by the PNA to achieve connectivity
   between offices of a corporation. Obviously, the SP has to guarantee
   that the PNA and the PNA's designees are the only ones who have
   access to the VRs on the SPEDs the private network has connections
   to. Since the virtual router console is functionally equivalent to a
   physical router, all of the authentication methods available on a
   physical console such as password, RADIUS, etc. are available to the
   PNA.

13.4 Physical Network Security

   When a PNA logs in to a SPED to configure or monitor the VPN, the PNA
   is logged into the VR for the VPN. The PNA has only layer 3
   configuration and monitoring privileges for the VR. Specifically, the
   PNA has no configuration privileges for the physical network. This
   provides the guarantee to the SP that a VPN administrator will not be
   able to inadvertently or otherwise adversely affect the SP's network.

14. Virtual Router Monitoring

   All of the router monitoring features available on a physical router
   are available on the virtual router. This includes utilities such as
   "ping" and "traceroute". In addition, the ability to display private
   routing tables, link state databases, etc. are available.

15. Performance Considerations

   For the purposes of discussing performance and scaling issues,
   today's routers can be split into two planes: the routing (control)
   plane and the forwarding plane.

   In looking at the routing plane, most modern-day routing protocols
   use some form of optimized calculation methodologies to calculate the
   shortest path(s) to end stations. For instance, OSPF and ISIS use the
   Djikstra algorithm while BGP uses the "Decision Process". These

algorithms are based on parsing the routing database and computing
the best paths to end stations. The performance characteristics of
any of these algorithms is based on either topological
characteristics (ISIS and OSPF) or the number of ASs in the path to
the destinations (BGP). But it is important to note that the overhead
in setting up and beginning these calculations is very little for
most any modern day router. This is because, although we refer to
routing calculation input as "databases", these are memory resident
data structures.

Therefore, the following conclusions can be drawn:

1. Beginning a routing calculation for a routing domain is nothing
   more than setting up some registers to point to the right database
   objects.

2. Based on 1, the performance of a given algorithm is not
   significantly worsened by the overhead required to set it up.

3. Based on 2, it follows that, when a number of routing calculations
   for a number of virtual routers has to be performed by a physical
   router, the complexity of the resulting routing calculation is
   nothing more than the sum of the complexities of the routing
   calculations of the individual virtual routers.

4. Based on 3, it follows that whether an overlay model is used or a
   virtual routing model is employed, the performance characteristics
   of a router are dependent purely on its hardware capabilities and
   the choice of data structures and algorithms.

To illustrate, let's say a physical router houses N VPNs, all running
some routing protocol say RP. Let's also suppose that the average
performance of RP's routing calculation algorithm is f(X,Y) where x
and y are parameters that determine performance of the algorithm for
that routing protocol. As an example, for Djikstra algorithm users
such as OSPF, X could be the number of nodes in the area while Y
could be the number of links. The performance of an arbitrary VPN n
is f (Xn, Yn). The performance of the (physical) router is the sum of
f(Xi, Yi) for all values of i in 0 <= i <= N. This conclusion is
independent of the chosen VPN approach (virtual router or overlay
model).

In the usual case, the forwarding plane has two inputs: the
forwarding table and the packet header. The main performance
parameter is the lookup algorithm. The very best performance one can
get for a IP routing table lookup is by organizing the table as some
form of a tree and use binary search methods to do the actual lookup.
The performance of this algorithm is O(log n).

Hence, as long as the virtual routers' routing tables are distinct from each other, the lookup cost is constant for finding the routing table and O(log n) to find the entry. This is no worse or different from any router and no different from a router that employs overlay techniques to deliver VPN services. However, when the overlay router utilizes integration of multiple VPNs' routing tables, the performance is O(log m*n) where 'm' is the number of VPNs that the routing table holds routes for.

16. Acknowledgements

The authors wish to thank Dave Ryan, Lucent Technologies for his invaluable in-depth review of this version of this memo.

17. References

[Callon] Callon R., et al., "A Framework for Multiprotocol Label
          Switching", Work in Progress.

[Fox]   Fox, B. and B. Gleeson, "Virtual Private Networks
          Identifier", RFC 2685, September 1999.

[Meyer]   Meyer, D., "Administratively Scoped IP Multicast", RFC 2365,
          July 1998.

[Rosen1] Rosen, E. and Y. Rekhter, "BGP/MPLS VPNs", RFC 2547, March
          1999.

[Rosen2] Rosen E., Viswanathan, A. and R. Callon, "Multiprotocol
          Label Switching Architecture", Work in Progress.

18. Authors' Addresses

Karthik Muthukrishnan
Lucent Technologies
1 Robbins Road
Westford, MA 01886

Phone: (978) 952-1368
EMail: mkarthik@lucent.com

Andrew Malis
Vivace Networks, Inc.
2730 Orchard Parkway
San Jose, CA 95134

Phone: (408) 383-7223
EMail: Andy.Malis@vivacenetworks.com

19. Full Copyright Statement

Acknowledgement

   Funding for the RFC Editor function is currently provided by the
   Internet Society.

Index